D0871203

Houghton Mifflin Company Editorial Adviser in Education

HEROLD C. HUNT

Charles William Eliot Professor of Education

Harvard University

Educating Exceptional Children

SAMUEL A. KIRK *Director, Institute for Research on Exceptional Children, University of Illinois*

HOUGHTON MIFFLIN COMPANY · BOSTON

To the memory of

RAY GRAHAM,

humanitarian and friend,
whose dynamic and effective leadership
in Illinois and in the nation
has left a lasting imprint on all
who labor to make life more meaningful
to children who are in some way "different."

. . . Of a good leader
who talks little
When his work is done,
his aim fulfilled,
They will say,
"We did this ourselves."
Lao-tzu

Contents

List of Figures

List of Tables

Preface

There probably is no such thing as a perfect textbook. Undoubtedly, this book is no exception. But ever since 1935, when I taught my first course in exceptional children, I have felt the need for a more integrated and unified text in this field. At that time I had been asked to teach two consecutive courses in exceptional children. The first was entitled "The Psychology of Exceptional Children," and it was followed by a course in "The Education of Exceptional Children." I soon found from the available literature that the title of the psychology course was a misnomer, since the content included biology, physiology, and sociology, as well as psychology. To describe the characteristics of the children it was necessary to describe them in physical, psychological, and social terms. Similarly, the course in the education of exceptional children could not be taught in a vacuum. It was necessary to review the characteristics of the children for whom educational modifications were to be made. Subdividing the subject matter on exceptional children into the various academic disciplines of a university may simplify the writing of books, but it does not provide a unified approach to the necessary learnings of a student.

The field of exceptional children is so extensive that it is difficult for one person to be sufficiently versed in all areas to write a comprehensive text; and I attempt this task with some temerity. The tendency has been to prepare such a text through multiple authorship, which of course, has the advantage of utilizing experts in each field. Having prepared and edited *The Education of Exceptional Children* (the Forty-ninth Yearbook of the National Society for the Study of Education), I am also aware of the difficulties involved in working with a number of authors, who have different styles and different philosophies, and who are inclined to present overlapping content.

This book is intended to be the basis for an introductory course in exceptional children. Customarily, students enrolled in such a course will have had introductory courses in psychology or educational psychology and in education. An attempt is made here to avoid content which would overlap with that of other courses and to include only information specific to this field.

In attempting to provide an integrated and unified book on exceptional children, I have relied on some concepts from child development. I have been especially influenced by the comprehensive records of growth patterns of children reported over the years by Dr. Willard Olson of the University of Michigan. The concept of split growth, or discrepancies in growth, seemed particularly applicable to exceptional children. I have found that this approach clarifies and unifies the concept of exceptionality, and by following it throughout the book I have tried to supply an integrating element which will give meaning to both the characteristics of the children and the resulting suitable modifications of educational practice. Instead of entitling the first chapter "Introduction," I have called it "Discrepancies in Growth and Development." This application of the concept of discrepancies I consider to be the main contribution of the book.

The preparation of this text required professional advice and assistance from many sources. My colleagues have been most gracious in reviewing and criticizing many of the chapters. Professors Alice Streng, William Desmond Phillips, and Kenneth Mangan have reviewed and evaluated the material on auditory handicaps. Professor James J. Gallagher was most generous of his time in critically reviewing the chapters dealing with the gifted and with behavior deviations. Professor Bernard Farber likewise contributed suggestions to the latter chapter. Professor Severina Nelson contributed materially to the organization and content of the chapter dealing with speech-handicapped children. In addition to these colleagues, I am grateful to my graduate assistant, Barbara Bateman, who reviewed literature and made valuable contributions to many of the chapters. My wife, Winifred D. Kirk, assisted in technical and professional areas and in the final editing of the book and deserves more credit than this acknowledgment provides.

I also wish to express appreciation for the patience, tolerance, and technical ability of those who were able to transform my handwriting into a readable and accurate manuscript for the printer. Those responsible for its production were Mrs. Marjorie DeFries, Mrs. Barbara Schulman, and Mrs. Lavena George.

SAMUEL A. KIRK

Educating

Exceptional

Children

I

Discrepancies in
Growth and Development

Education in any society tends to reflect the political philosophy of that society. Under Hitler, for example, the Nazi political philosophy asserted that man exists for the welfare of the state. Nazi education was therefore geared to making the individual useful to the state. Under such a philosophy it was felt that the severely handicapped were not worth educating — or even keeping alive. Under a democracy as practiced in the United States, where the state is believed to exist for the welfare of the individual, education must be organized primarily to achieve this end.

"All men are created equal" has become trite, but it still has important meaning for education in a democratic society. Although it was used by the founding fathers to denote equality before the law, it has also been interpreted to mean equality of opportunity. This implies educational opportunity for *all* children — the right of each child to receive help in learning to the limits of his capacity, whether that capacity be small or great.

It is consistent with a democratic philosophy that all children be given the opportunity to learn, whether they are average, bright, dull, retarded, blind, deaf, crippled, delinquent, emotionally disturbed, or otherwise limited or deviant in their capacities to learn. Our schools have evolved, therefore, numerous modifications of regular school programs to adapt

3

instruction to children who deviate from the average and who cannot profit substantially from the regular program. These modified programs have been designated as programs for exceptional children.

The programs for exceptional children in school systems have been found to benefit not only the deviant child but also other children. Handicapped or gifted children in a regular classroom sometimes require individual attention. It is inevitable that if a regular classroom teacher devotes adequate time to a deviant child he must curtail the attention which he ordinarily gives the other children. But when special services are offered the deviant child, the normal pupils benefit by having more of the regular teacher's time.

A second contribution which has been made to all children has come indirectly from studies of handicapped and gifted children. Today, for example, mental and educational tests are used throughout school systems as guidance aids for all children. The development of individual psychological testing began when the French government assigned Binet the task of devising an objective means of identifying mentally retarded children. The Binet-Simon intelligence test, with various modifications, is still being used extensively all over the world with all types of children.

Similar contributions have been made in instruction and curriculums. Programs for exceptional children have served as laboratories for developing methods and procedures which in some cases have a universal application. Just as we learn about the normal from the abnormal, so we can learn about teaching in general from programs of teaching exceptional children.

Who Is the Exceptional Child?

The term "exceptional" means different things to different people. Some use it when referring to the particularly bright child or the child with unusual talent. Others use it when they refer to any atypical or deviant child. The term "exceptional child" has been generally accepted, however, to mean either the handicapped or the gifted child: (1) the child who has a physical handicap, such as a crippling condition, deafness, or blindness; (2) the child who deviates mentally, whether he is very bright or very dull or mentally retarded; and (3) the child who is maladjusted or emotionally disturbed.

There have been various attempts to define an exceptional child. Any definition includes a brief description of characteristics, and needs considerable elaboration before it is understood. For present purposes the exceptional child is defined as *that child who deviates from the average or normal child in mental, physical, or social characteristics to such an extent that he requires a modification of school practices, or special educational services, in order to develop to his maximum capacity.*

But this is a very general definition and raises many questions. "What is average or normal?" "How extensive must the deviation be to require special education?" "What is special education?"

To complicate the picture further, the exceptional or deviating child has been studied by various disciplines — psychology, sociology, physiology, medicine, and education — and thus from varying points of view. If we define an exceptional child as one who deviates from the norm of his group, then we have many kinds of exceptionalities. A redheaded child in a class becomes an exceptional child because he differs from the norm of his group. A child with a defective or missing thumb becomes exceptional. Actually, such deviations, although of possible importance to physicians, psychologists, geneticists, or others, are of little concern to the teacher. A redheaded child is not an exceptional child, educationally speaking, because the educational program of the class does not have to be modified to serve his needs. A child is considered educationally exceptional only when it is necessary to alter the educational program to meet his needs. Hence, the use of "exceptional children" in education may differ from its use in biology, psychology, or other disciplines and professions. A child is *educationally exceptional* if his deviation is of such kind and degree that it interferes with his development under ordinary classroom procedures and necessitates special education, either in conjunction with the regular class or in a special class or school, for his maximum development.

History and Philosophy of the Education of Exceptional Children

As we look back into history we find that the entire concept of educating each child to the height of his ability is relatively new. The current use of the term "exceptional" is itself a reflection of radical changes in society's view of those who deviate. We have come a long way from the Spartans' practice of killing the deviant or malformed infant, but the journey was by slow stages.[1] Exploitation of the handicapped in the role of court jester several hundred years ago can still be found in today's circus side shows. But certainly, on the whole, tremendous changes have taken place in society's attitude toward the exceptional person. And this change is still going on; for example, the mentally gifted have

[1] J. E. Wallace Wallin, *The Education of Handicapped Children* (Boston: Houghton Mifflin Company, 1924), p. 3.

recently moved upward in the American value system as a result of Russia's Sputnik.

Historically, three stages in the development of attitudes toward the handicapped child can be recognized.[2] First, during the pre-Christian era the handicapped were persecuted, neglected, and mistreated. Second, during the spread of Christianity they were protected and pitied. Third, in very recent years there has been a movement toward accepting the handicapped and integrating them into society to the fullest extent possible. In education, *integration* denotes a trend toward educating the exceptional child with his normal peers to whatever extent is compatible with his fullest potential development.

The three stages in the development of attitudes toward the deviant can be seen in the educational history of our own country. Prior to the 1800's there were no educational provisions for the handicapped child. The mentally subnormal individual was generally relegated to an attic or to the role of village idiot. In the first decades of the nineteenth century such leaders as Horace Mann, Samuel Gridley Howe, and Dorothea Dix gave impetus to the movement for establishing residential schools for the blind, deaf, retarded, epileptic, orphaned, and others, as was being done in Europe. These schools offered training, but equally important was the protective environment, often covering the life span of the individual.

Interestingly, however, as early as 1871 Samuel Gridley Howe, according to Irwin,[3] was able to predict future educational provisions for the exceptional child. He was speaking particularly of the blind, but his interests and insights extended to other areas of special education. He felt that a sure trend in the education of exceptional children would be toward integrating them into the "common" schools with "common" classmates in all areas possible. He also saw a decrease in the extent to which residential schools would be utilized with some forms of exceptionality.

The public school movement began slowly in the early 1900's. Since then it has spread in various forms until now almost all types and degrees of exceptionality can be found in public school programs.

The student, noting the several million children classed as exceptional today and the proliferation of programs and provisions for them, may well ask why these deviations were not a source of concern much earlier. The notion of free and compulsory education for all who are educable is slightly more than 100 years old. The changing economy of our coun-

---

[2] Merle E. Frampton and Elena D. Gall, eds., *Special Education for the Exceptional* (Boston: Porter Sargent, 1955) I, 2–8.

[3] Robert Irwin, *As I Saw It* (New York: American Foundation for the Blind, 1955), p. 128.

try has affected the role, function, and scope of education for all our citizens, the exceptional included. The area of individual differences has been of scientific concern for less than 100 years. It is well known that Wundt, who is considered the father of modern psychology, established the first laboratory for psychological studies in Leipzig in 1879, but it is perhaps not so well known that he ruled out individual differences as a legitimate field of interest for psychologists. He felt that psychology ought to be concerned with the "generalized human mind." Thus children, psychotics, and animals were excluded from psychology, as was the study of individual differences. Only with the advent of the mental testing movement in the early 1900's did refined techniques for assessing individual differences in areas other than the physical begin to be developed. With these diagnostic methods came ideas and concepts which made the modern programs of education for exceptional children possible.

Individual Differences

Education has long recognized that grouping children in grades according to chronological age does not assure homogeneity of grouping in other characteristics. Within every grade in every school, children differ from one another to some extent. Two boys of the same age and height may differ in weight; two children of the same age and mental level may differ in their reading or spelling ability. Every classroom teacher must organize his instructional methods and assignments to meet the needs of children who vary one to three grades above or below the grade in which they are placed.

The concept of individual differences (meaning that in some respects Johnny is different from — more advanced or less advanced than — Billy in the same grade) is only one of the factors to be taken into account in considering the characteristics of the exceptional child. He does differ from the average child in class. He may be intellectually superior or inferior, he may not see or hear as well, he may not have the mobility of the average child, he may not have the degree of language or speech of the average child, or he may be a deviant in interpersonal relations.[4]

There is another characteristic of exceptionality in children which must

[4] "Interpersonal relations" refers not only to *how well* a person relates to or "gets along" with others but also to the *way or manner* in which he approaches them. The field which includes a study of the effect of physical deviation on interpersonal relations is known as somatopsychology. The interested reader will find this discussed in Beatrice A. Wright's *Physical Disability — A Psychological Approach* (New York: Harper & Brothers, 1960).

7

be taken into consideration in planning an educational program. This is the difference in development within the child himself. The exceptional child has what is known as *discrepancies in growth*. This has led many to say that the exceptional child is a normal child who has exceptionalities or deviations only in some characteristics. In other words, they feel that the similarities in characteristics between the exceptional child and the average child far exceed the differences.

To illustrate (1) how the exceptional child differs from the average and (2) how the exceptional child grows unevenly, the following pages will present the major types of exceptional children in the form of profiles as well as descriptive material. In subsequent chapters each of these characteristics of exceptional children will be discussed in greater detail, not only with specific profiles of development, but also with suggested educational programs adapted to the discrepancies in growth. This chapter gives a very brief overview of discrepancies in each area of deviation.

Mental Deviates — the Intellectually Gifted and the Mentally Retarded

Intellectually gifted and mentally retarded children represent the upper and lower groups on the intelligence scale. In Figure 1, which represents the distribution of IQ's as found by Terman, the lower left-hand part of the curve shows that children with an IQ below 70 constitute 2.63 per cent of the population studied and represents the group Terman has labeled mentally retarded or mentally deficient. The right-hand or upper portion of the curve shows children with IQ's above 140 and represents 1.33 per cent of the population. These are labeled very superior or gifted. Similarly, another 5.6 per cent of the population are borderline deficient and 14.5 per cent are low average, according to Terman. The 46.5 per cent of the population at the center of the curve are considered average or normal. Above this, Terman has designated IQ's between 110 and 120 (18.1 per cent) as high average and IQ's between 120 and 140 (11.3 per cent) as superior.

It is with the two extreme groups, the intellectually gifted and the mentally retarded, that we are at present concerned. Their unique characteristics and educational programs will be discussed in later chapters. Here it is well to take a look at a picture of the development of these two kinds of exceptional children to see how they deviate in growth from the normal and how they differ in growth within themselves.

Figure 2 shows the discrepancies in growth of an *intellectually gifted child* and of a *mentally retarded child*. Both children are 10 years of

FIGURE 1

Distribution of Composite IQ's (Form L-M)

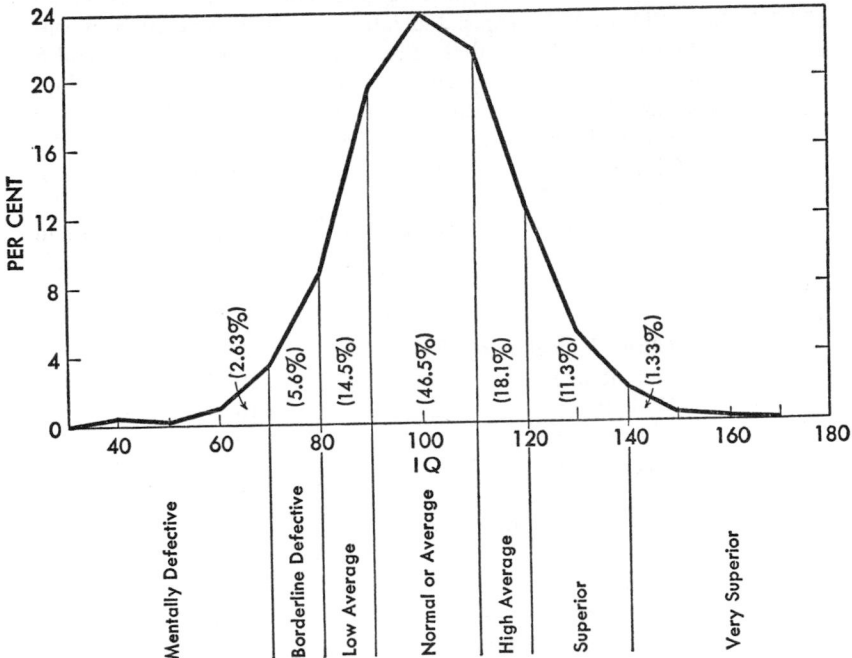

Source: Adapted from Lewis M. Terman and Maud A. Merrill, *Stanford-Binet Intelligence Scale, Manual for the Third Revision Form L-M* (Boston: Houghton Mifflin Company, 1960), p. 18.

age; both are in a fifth-grade class; both have normal hearing and vision. But the similarities stop here. They differ markedly from the average child in many characteristics and, in addition, vary in growth within themselves. The history and status of these two children, typical of their types of exceptionality, can best be illustrated by a description of their characteristics and development and by a profile as shown in Figure 2.

John, the gifted child, was the older of two children. His father was employed as a teacher in the local high school. John's developmental history showed that he learned to talk at an earlier age than most children and that he walked at the age of 10 months. He became interested in books, and at the age of 5½ was reading some books and simple picture stories.

Upon entering school at the age of 6, he quickly learned to read and by the end of the year he was a fluent reader in third-grade material. He was not allowed to advance in school beyond his age group and by the age of 10 he was in the fifth grade. At this time a series of examinations was administered to him.

Test results are given in various forms. For example, John had an IQ of 140 and a mental age of 14 years. His height was 4 feet, 6½ inches (54.5 inches). This can be translated into a height age of 10–8, meaning that his height is similar to that of an average boy of 10 years and 8 months, even though John is only 10 years of age (10–0). On a reading test his score was Grade 7–7, meaning that his reading level was similar to the average of children in the seventh month of the seventh grade, even though John was in the fifth grade. His reading age, when translated in this fashion, was 12 years, 7 months (12–7).

On the various tests given to John the scores were translated into age norms so that they could be readily compared. His scores were as follows:

Chronological age	10–0
Height age	10–8
Weight age	10–8
Motor coordination age	10–11
Mental age	14–0
Social age	11–6
Speech development age	12–8
Language age	13–10
Reading age	12–7
Arithmetic reasoning age	12–2
Arithmetic computation age	11–4
Spelling age	12–4
General information age	13–2

There are other characteristics of an individual that cannot be stated in terms of age. For example, vision and hearing are either normal or defective. John's vision and hearing were normal. Interpersonal relations do not necessarily increase with age; hence, there are no age norms. In the profile these characteristics will be represented on a five-point scale: (1) very superior, (2) above average, (3) average, (4) below average, and (5) very defective.

Figure 2 shows John's growth patterns at the life age of 10. Note that there are some points on the profile showing John to be like other children of his age. In vision and hearing he is like other children with normal sense organs, neither superior nor inferior. His height, weight, and motor coordination are slightly superior to those of most children, but not abnormally so. His mental age, however, deviates very markedly from the average of other 10-year-olds and is four years beyond his age and grade placement. His social-maturity age is not as advanced as his mental age, being only a year and one-half accelerated. His achievements

FIGURE 2

Profiles of a Gifted and a Retarded Child

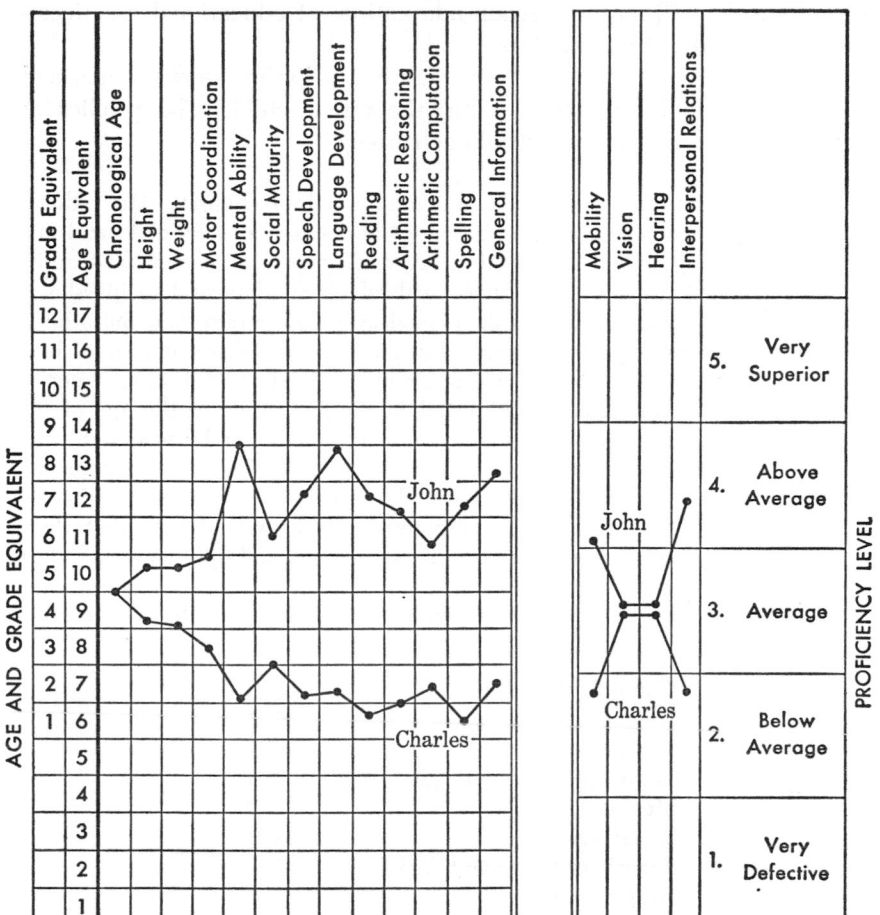

in school vary but in general are more accelerated than the physical factors, though not as far as is the mental-age level. Note that general information, language, speech, and reading are more advanced than arithmetic computation. This is a quite common finding among intellectually advanced children.

On the scaled portion of the profile, John shows above average mobility, average hearing and vision, and above average interpersonal relations. He presents a developmental picture different from that of a child who is average in all respects. In Figure 2, such a child would be evenly developed at the age of 10 in all of his characteristics.

11

Not only does John differ from the average child in many characteristics, but he also varies within himself in some of his characteristics. In this respect he is said to have *discrepancies in growth*. Because of these deviations, he will require certain adaptations of educational practices — to be described in later chapters.

The mentally retarded child in Figure 2, Charles, shows a markedly different profile from that of John, the gifted child. The profiles are very nearly mirror counterparts of each other.

Charles was the second child in a family of four children. His father worked as a machinist. During infancy Charles was a sickly child and at the age of 1 year had a very high fever, diagnosed as encephalitis and later assumed to have had neurological effects fundamental to his slow mental development. Charles developed at a slower rate than the other children. He walked at 16 months but did not talk in sentences until he was 3 years of age. (On the average, children begin to talk in sentences at 2 years of age.) He was admitted to the first grade at the age of 6 and in spite of his inability to learn was promoted year by year until at the age of 10 he, like John, was in the fifth grade. The school system in which he was enrolled believed that children should be neither held back in school nor accelerated. The philosophy of the school held that the teacher should adapt her instruction to wide individual differences among children.

In the fifth grade Charles was given a series of examinations. He obtained the following ratings:

Chronological age	10–0
Height age	9–2
Weight age	9–1
Motor coordination age	8–5
Mental age	7–2
Social age	8–0
Speech development age	7–3
Language age	7–4
Reading age	6–8
Arithmetic reasoning age	7–0
Arithmetic computation age	7–5
Spelling age	6–6
General information age	7–6
Mobility	below average
Vision	average
Hearing	average
Interpersonal relations	below average

When these age scores and ratings are plotted in Figure 2 we find that Charles, with an IQ of 72, presents a reversal of the picture represented by John. Although both boys are 10 years old and have normal hearing and vision, their growth patterns in other characteristics are very different.

As with most mentally retarded children, Charles' profile indicates that he can be considered normal or near normal in height, weight, mobility, motor coordination, and in vision and hearing. But he is exceptional in other areas of development. He differs from the average child in social, mental, and educational growth, and he differs from his own physical levels in these developmental characteristics. Although, like John, Charles is 10 years old, his mental age is 7–2. In the academic subjects of reading, spelling, and arithmetic, he tests at educational ages of 6–8, 6–6, 7–0, and 7–5; that is, after four years in school his educational accomplishments are at the first- and beginning second-grade level. His deviation from the majority of children in the fifth grade in mental, social, and academic abilities, in spite of his similarity to the other children in physical characteristics, again requires a special adaptation of school practices, which will be discussed in later chapters.

The Auditorily Handicapped Child

Figure 3 shows the developmental pattern of Tony, a 10-year-old deaf child. Auditorily handicapped children may be totally deaf or only hard of hearing. They may have been born deaf or they may have acquired deafness after learning language and speech. Tony was born deaf. He does not have sufficient hearing even with the use of a hearing aid to develop language and speech through the sense of hearing.

Tony's profile shows that he is average in height, weight, and vision. He is slightly below other 10-year-olds in mobility, motor coordination, and mental age but is considered within the average range in these characteristics. The lowest point is, of course, his hearing, which is rated as very defective. In Tony's case this defect is irremediable. He will have to live with it all his life. The question here is how deafness affects his other traits. First of all, we notice that it affects speech development most. Even with special instruction his speech is no better than that of a 2-year-old child. His next lowest points are in language, reading, and spelling. Although he is average in mental development, his achievement in language, reading, and spelling is similar to that of a first-grade child. The hearing defect has interfered with his development in these areas. Furthermore, his difficulty with communication skills has created problems in interpersonal relations and prevented normal social maturity.

Thus Tony, who is normal in many ways, differs from the average

FIGURE 3

Profile of an Auditorily Handicapped Child

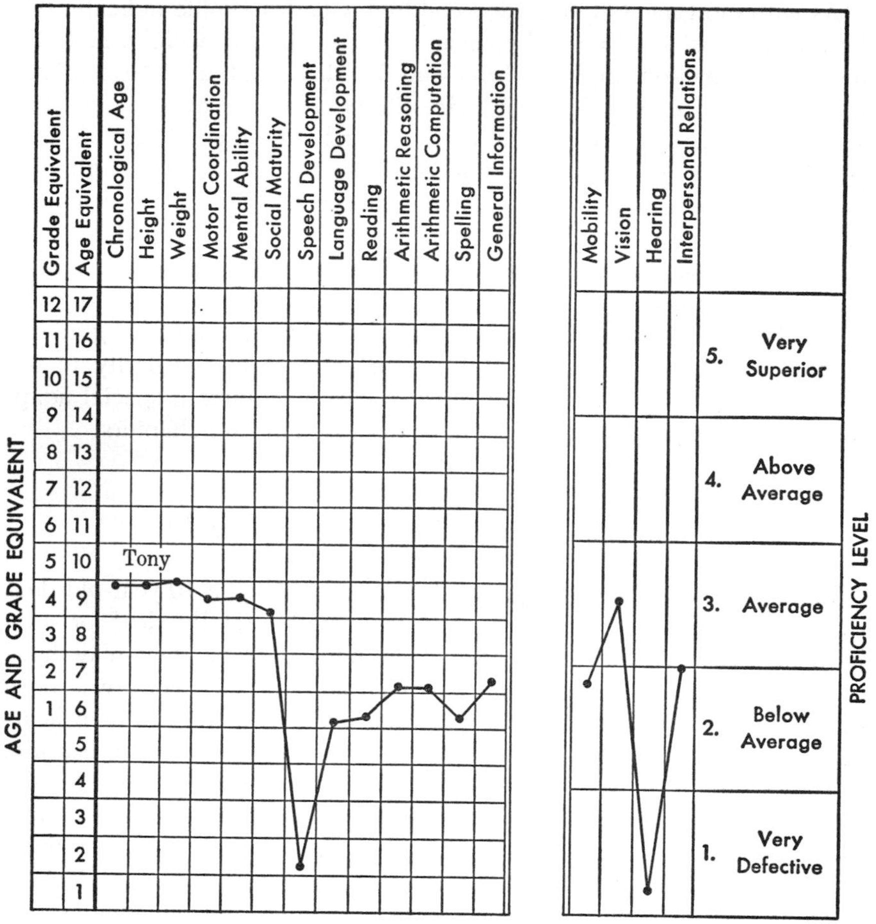

child in his response to the usual school program. He has greater discrepancies in growth; he differs within himself in many characteristics. An educational program must take into consideration his deviations from the average and the deviations within himself. It must organize instruction so as to circumvent the irremediable deafness. For Tony's adequate development, special education must use channels of communication other than hearing.

The hard-of-hearing child is not as retarded as the deaf child in speech, language, and school subjects. The less the disability, the less special education is needed. But whether he is mildly or severely hard of hearing, his retardation below average children and below his other abilities is considerably less. In most instances he remains in the regular classroom but receives special instruction in speech and auditory training to assist him in coping with the regular school curriculum. While the deaf child requires a great deal of teaching in a special class and by a skilled teacher, the hard-of-hearing child requires only extra consideration and some specialized education. How much of the latter he needs is dependent upon the discrepancies in his growth. This total program will be discussed in greater detail in Chapters 6 and 7.

The Visually Handicapped Child

Children with visual handicaps fall into several categories for educational purposes. In the first group are those whose visual defects can be corrected through medical treatment or optical aids. Such children are not regarded as exceptional but with correction are considered normal and can be educated without modification of school practices.

In the second group are children whose vision is quite defective even after correction. They have difficulty in the regular grades and need instructional compensations for their defects. They utilize their eyes in learning, but to a lesser degree than does the average child. They are referred to as "partially seeing children." Since they can use some vision in learning, they are not considered blind.

In the third group are the blind. These children, like the deaf, require instruction through other senses.

Figure 4 shows the developmental pattern of Sarah, a blind 10-year-old. Since she has no vision, this is her lowest point on the profile. Associated with blindness are retarded mobility, restricted interpersonal relations, and lowered school achievement. Because Sarah cannot see to learn to read, she learns reading through the tactile sense by means of braille. The process is generally more time-consuming than learning to read through the use of the eyes and for this reason Sarah is retarded educationally.

Another profile could show the growth patterns of a partially seeing child. In general, the educational retardation would not be as great. The differences between the average child and the partially seeing child are fewer. The discrepancies in growth within the child are also fewer. Hence, the modifications of school practice and the adaptations of instructional material are not as radical or as great as they are for the blind child. The methods of instruction are consequently less "special."

FIGURE 4

Profile of a Blind Child

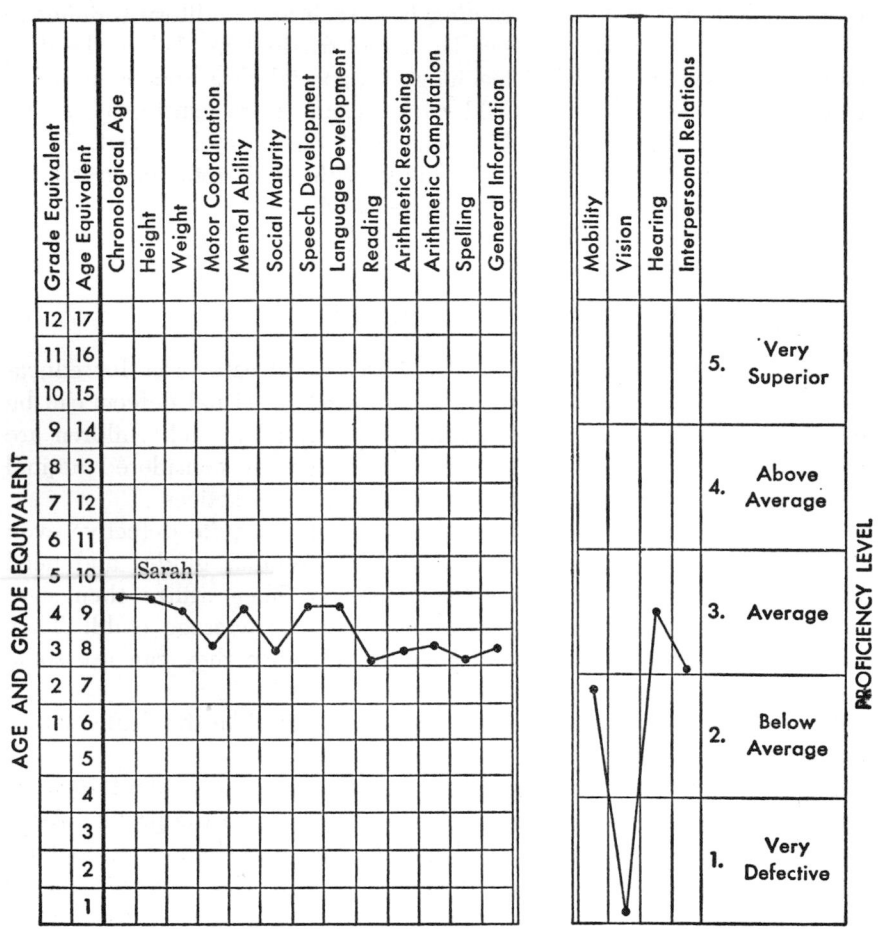

The Speech Defective

Speech is one of the major characteristics differentiating man from the lower animals. Much communication among people is dependent upon their ability to speak and to understand the spoken word. Any defect in one's speaking ability is likely to interfere with his interpersonal relations.

There are many forms of speech disorders, ranging from complete inability to speak to minor articulatory defects. There are also many causes for speech difficulties. This problem is sometimes associated with other handicapping conditions, such as deafness, mental retardation, or cerebral palsy, as will be discussed in subsequent chapters.

Figure 5 shows the developmental pattern of a speech-defective child of 10 years. Betty's profile differs markedly from that of the gifted or mentally retarded or deaf child. She is, for educational purposes, normal except that speech and, to a lesser extent, language development are below average. No very extensive educational adaptations have to be made for her in the regular grades. Special classes are not usually organized

FIGURE 5

Profile of a Speech-Defective Child

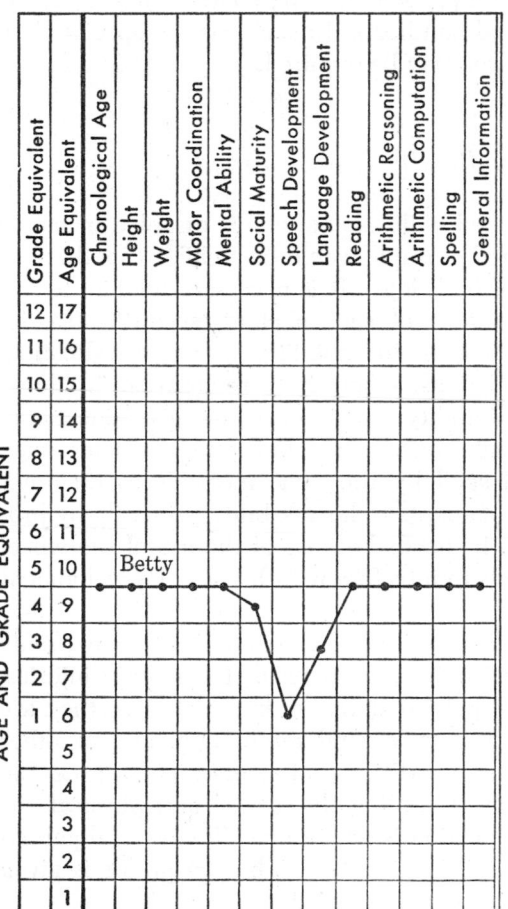
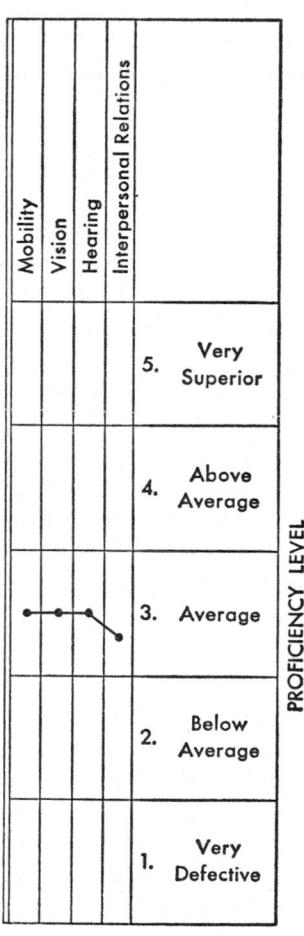

for this type of handicapped child, who is usually left in the regular grades and progresses in school with other children. An itinerant speech teacher gives Betty corrective lessons several times a week. With this help and that of the regular classroom teacher Betty's difficulties can probably be removed.

Thus, the speech-defective child with an otherwise average developmental pattern does not differ from the normal, nor does he differ within himself except for the one specific difficulty, speech. He does not have widely varying discrepancies in growth. His educational program is like that of the other children. Special education is provided for him on a part-time basis by an itinerant speech correctionist while he is being educated in the regular grades.

As will be discussed in Chapter 12, speech-handicapped children often have other handicaps. A cerebral-palsied child may have a motor handicap, speech handicap, and visual handicap. In such cases a special class instead of only an itinerant teacher may be required.

The Orthopedically Handicapped

The orthopedically handicapped child is one who is disabled in motor abilities. A simple, uncomplicated example would be a child who, through an accident, had lost the use of both legs. It is necessary for him to use a wheel chair. The growth pattern of such a child, according to the profile of Mark, shows deficiencies in mobility, motor coordination, social age, and interpersonal relations. There is no retardation in educational subjects. The motor disability does not affect his educational achievements in school although consequent emotional problems may. He learns to read, write, and spell by the same methods as do other children in the class. The school adapts to his disability primarily by providing physical facilities which he needs because of the use of the wheel chair. His lack of mobility tends to interfere with his social development and his interpersonal relations.

Not all orthopedically handicapped children show the same profile as Mark's in Figure 6. Motor handicaps can result from brain injuries, such as those found in cerebral-palsied children, in which case they are often associated with speech defects, mental retardation, and/or other handicapping conditions. These conditions, of course, complicate the educational picture, for the more disabling the mental and physical circumstance, the more special education is necessary. The cerebral-palsied child is discussed in greater detail in Chapter 10, but no profile is given here because the individual patterns are so varied.

FIGURE 6

Profile of an Orthopedically Handicapped Child

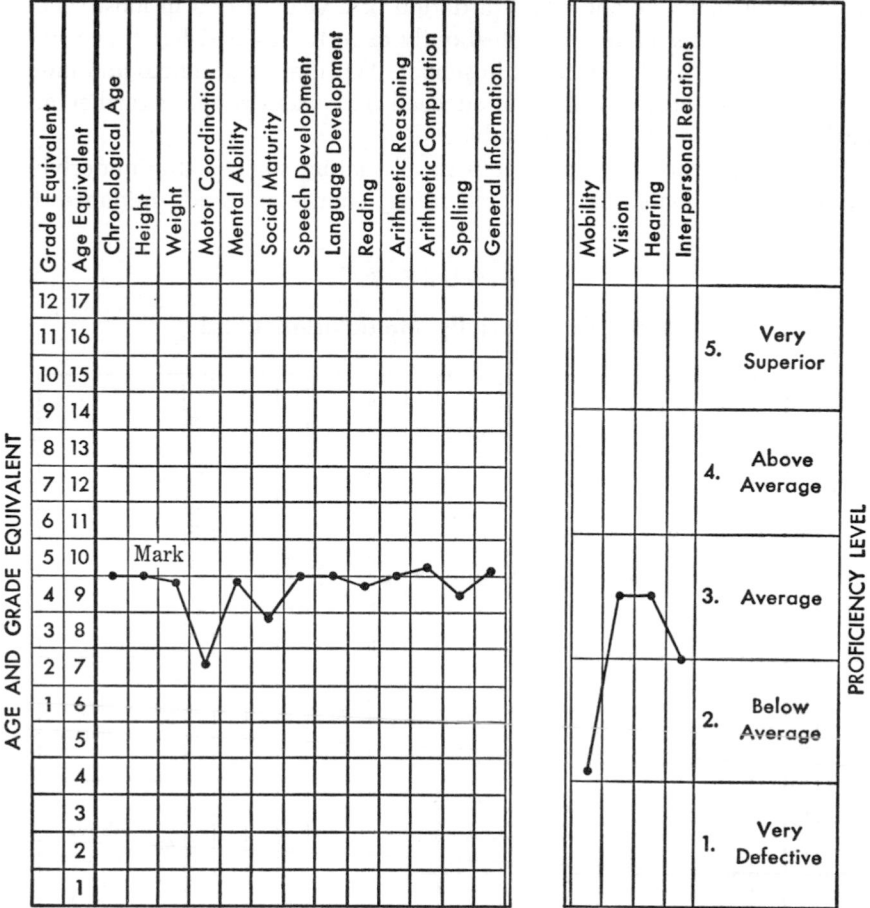

The Child with Behavior Deviations

Behavior deviations may take a variety of forms and stem from a variety of causes. There may be hostility and aggression or withdrawal and restraint. There may be a high or low IQ. There may or may not be physical concomitants. There may be academic success but more often failure in at least some school subjects. The category of those with behavior deviations may include psychotic and neurotic children, children with lesser emotional difficulties, and delinquent children.

The child represented in Figure 7 was a rebellious truant 10 years old. As can be seen by reading his profile, Steve was normal mentally and physically but, in addition to his low scores in interpersonal relations and social adjustment, he showed retardation of a year or two in most school subjects. A series of unfortunate family experiences had left Steve with hostile attitudes and no interest in school. With many absences and much failure he had no motivation to succeed and was dropping farther and farther behind in his academic subjects.

Such a child needs specific help in alleviating some of the underlying causes of his maladjustment, including counseling and guidance by

FIGURE 7

Profile of a Socially Maladjusted Child

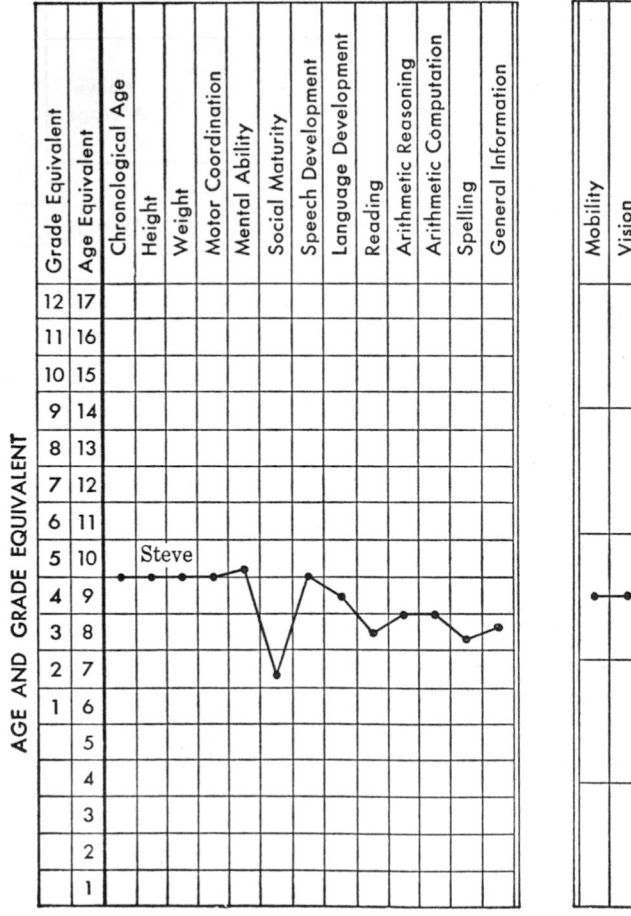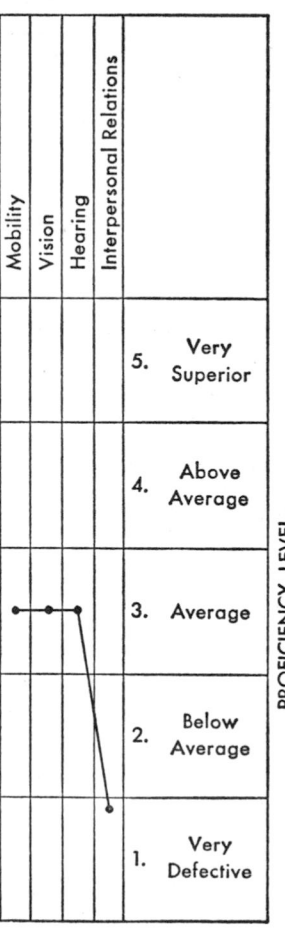

professional workers at home and at school. In addition, there will have to be some adaptation of the school program. Steve, for example, may need some individual tutoring and certainly modified materials since he is educationally unable to function at a fourth-grade level. Only for extreme cases, and in a few communities, are there special classes or special schools. If Steve's problems bring him into too great a conflict with society, he may even require institutionalization.

Other Handicapping Conditions

There are other types of handicapping conditions which make modification of school practices necessary. Most of these are health problems. A tuberculous child, for example, needs an opportunity for rest during the school day. Children with cardiac disabilities may find the regular class too strenuous. For many of these children, however, the educational program is not altered. Only the physical arrangements are varied from those for the average child.

In many instances we find multiple handicaps or other combinations of divergences from the normal. A crippled child can be gifted. A deaf child can be blind. A cerebral-palsied child can have many deviations; he may be partially seeing, hard of hearing, mentally retarded (or gifted), and defective in speech. Sometimes two handicaps are so severe that the child cannot adapt to a special class for either one. In such cases other arrangements must be made, using itinerant teachers, homebound education, or more specifically adapted special classes. In other cases the child can be placed in a class designed to take into account his major disability.

The preceding profiles representing discrepancies in growth of different kinds of exceptional children were specific to the conditions discussed. For any particular child, such discrepancies may be less or greater than was represented. In all of these cases, however, educational adaptations are needed for the maximum development of the child. The differences in growth and development will be discussed in greater detail in the subsequent chapters which deal separately with each kind of exceptional child.

Prevalence of Exceptional Children

Various attempts have been made to determine the prevalence of handicapped and gifted children in the population. These attempts have yielded such diverse results that investigators hesitate to give a definite figure for each type of exceptional child. Much of this difficulty stems from the fact that the line of demarcation between a normal and an exceptional child is not agreed upon. For example, some define a gifted child as one having an IQ of 120 and above on an individual intelligence test. Others use a criterion of 135 IQ and above, or 140 and above. Still others use an achievement criterion in addition to an intelligence test, such as 130 IQ and an acceleration in school achievement of two or more years. It is obvious that with these different criteria there will be different percentage figures. In the field of speech correction the estimates vary from 2 per cent to 20 per cent, depending on what is meant by a speech defect. In addition to differences in criteria, communities themselves differ. For example, a national figure of 2 per cent mentally retarded does not apply to all communities. Some areas may have 3 or 4 per cent, others less than 2 per cent, even though they all use the same criterion.

Despite these difficulties in determining the incidence of exceptional children in school, various writers have been able to hazard guesses based on different studies. The U.S. Office of Education has from time to time issued estimates of the frequency of exceptional children in the school population. In 1944 it estimated that 12.4 per cent of all school children (or 4,000,000) required special services.[5]

In a later report (1954) from the U.S. Office of Education, Mackie and Dunn[6] estimated that the percentage of exceptional children in the schools of the United States stood at 12.7, distributed as shown in Table I.

The authors believe that these rough estimates are minimal and give some indication of the extent of the problem. Another indication is the number of children enrolled in special schools and classes in the United States, as reported by the Office of Education, which has surveyed enrollment in special schools and classes approximately every five years since 1922. The figures given in Table II are not complete, since the information was obtained from questionnaires to local systems and not all questionnaires were returned. The figures are subject, too, to changing definitions and changing conditions. The statistics do not include exceptional children in residential institutions, even though the majority of deaf children and many blind children are educated in residential schools for the deaf and the blind. Furthermore, some differences in manner of reporting and categorizing occurred between 1940 and 1948.

In spite of the above qualifications, however, the statistics in Table II do reflect the trend in public school provisions for the various categories

---

[5] Elise H. Martens, *Needs of Exceptional Children*, U.S. Office of Education, Leaflet No. 74 (Washington: Government Printing Office, 1944).

[6] Romaine P. Mackie and Lloyd M. Dunn, *College and University Programs for the Preparation of Teachers of Exceptional Children*, U.S. Office of Education, Bulletin No. 13 (Washington: Goverment Printing Office, 1954), p. 12.

TABLE I
Estimate of Incidence of Exceptional Children of School Age

Areas of Exceptionality	Per Cent of Incidence	Estimated Number of School-Aged Children
Visually handicapped	0.20	
Blind		10,000
Partially seeing		58,000
Crippled	1.50	510,000
Special health problems	1.50	510,000
Deaf and hard of hearing	1.50	510,000
Speech-handicapped	2.00	680,000
Socially maladjusted	2.00	680,000
Mentally retarded	2.00	680,000
Gifted	2.00	680,000
Total	12.70	4,318,000

Source: Romaine P. Mackie and Lloyd M. Dunn, *College and University Programs for the Preparation of Teachers of Exceptional Children,* U.S. Office of Education Bulletin No. 13 (Washington: Government Printing Office, 1954).

TABLE II
Enrollments in Public Special Schools and Classes, 1922–1958

	1922[a]	1932[a]	1940[a]	1948[b]	1952[c]	1958[c]
Mentally retarded	23,252	75,099	98,416	87,030	113,565	213,402
Speech-defective	no data	22,735	126,146	182,308	306,747	474,643
Crippled	no data	16,166	25,784	14,510	17,813	28,355
Deaf and hard of hearing	2,911	4,434	13,478	13,959	15,867	19,199
Blind and partially seeing	no data	5,308	8,875	8,185	8,853	11,008
Special health problems	no data	24,020	27,291	19,579	11,455	21,714
Gifted	no data	1,834	3,255	20,712	22,916	52,005
Socially maladjusted	no data	14,354	10,477	15,340	no data	27,447

[a] *Statistics of Special Schools and Classes for Exceptional Children,* Biennial Survey of Education in the United States, 1946–48 (Washington: Federal Security Agency, Office of Education, 1948), p. 10.
[b] *Statistics of Special Education for Exceptional Children,* Biennial Survey of Education in the United States, 1952–54 (Washington: U.S. Department of Health, Education and Welfare, Office of Education, 1954), p. 15.
[c] Romaine P. Mackie and Patricia P. Robbins, "Exceptional Children in Local Public Schools," *School Life,* 43 (November, 1960), 15.

of exceptional children. The following comments and interpretations of the statistics on enrollment are in order:

1. It should be noted that the greatest increase in enrollment has been in the areas of mental retardation and speech correction.

2. The period 1940–1948 showed little increase in enrollment and even decreases for some of the groups of exceptional children. This reflects a possible lack of emphasis on the education of exceptional children, as well as a shortage of teachers, facilities, and funds during World War II.

3. Of interest is the relative constancy of enrollment in classes for crippled children and those with special health problems. This phenomenon is probably due to advances in medical science. For example, epileptic children formerly placed in special schools or classes are now being enrolled in regular grades since epileptic seizures can now be better controlled through medication. Tubercular children are now being cured by the use of antibiotics. The Salk vaccine may also have assisted in decreasing the number of crippled children enrolled in classes in 1958. These decreases may have been offset by greater enrollment of cerebral-palsied children in special classes.

4. The proportionate increase in enrollment of deaf and hard-of-hearing children since 1940 has not been as great as in some fields. There has been a substantial increase in the number of deaf children in the public schools, the enrollment jumping from 3514 in 1948 to 6162 in 1958, but the hard of hearing have increased only slightly perhaps because of greater use of hearing aids by hard-of-hearing children in the regular classes.

5. There has been a substantial increase in special provisions for gifted children in public schools. These figures, however, do not necessarily adequately reflect the status of education for the gifted. Often enrichment in the regular grades and acceleration of children are not reported as special provisions. The figures reflect only enrollment in special classes and special schools, a practice not always approved by educators. In spite of these qualifications, the statistics reveal several interesting trends. It will be noted that there was a marked increase in enrollment in classes for the gifted during World War II, from 3255 in 1940 to 20,712 in 1948. This may be due to a rising awareness of the need for high-level leadership and technology during a war period. The same situation obtained between 1952 (when the enrollment was 22,916) and 1958 (when it jumped to 52,005). This increase may be attributed to a greater interest in special provisions for the gifted in response to the Soviet advances in technical and scientific education and the launching of Sputnik.

6. Enrollment in classes for the blind and partially seeing remained

relatively constant between 1932 and 1952, taking into consideration the increases in population and more adequate diagnostic procedures. The apparent rise in 1958 over 1952 can in large part be explained by (a) the occurrence of a new disease causing blindness (retrolental fibroplasia, which will be discussed in Chapter 9) and (b) increased interest in educating blind children in public schools rather than only in residential schools.

7. Since 1940 the largest number of exceptional children served has been in the area of speech correction. These children are generally being educated in the regular grades, receiving speech correction two or three times a week for short periods. A speech correctionist can carry a case load of up to 100 children. This area of special education differs from most of the other areas in that the latter require special classrooms and a teacher for every five to fifteen children.

8. The most phenomenal rise in numbers enrolled in special classes has been in the area of mental retardation. This reflects greater public awareness of the problem of mental retardation in our society, resulting partly from the organization of state and national parents' groups, which have vigorously brought the problem to the attention of the general public, school administrators, and legislators.

9. In an analysis of the 1958 survey Mackie stated, "These figures [for 1958] represent a rate of growth three times that of local public elementary and secondary school enrollments during the same period."[7]

10. As a general over-all statement Mackie continues, "It may be that, all together, as many as 1¼ million children and young people are receiving special education. (This statement referred to both the known enrollments in public day schools and an estimate of the enrollments in private day and residential schools.) Specialists in the field believe, however, that these 1¼ million children represent only one-fourth of those who need special education."[8]

How Exceptional Children Are Educated

The large majority of exceptional children are educated in public school systems. Some exceptional children are educated in residential schools. To provide for these children and their different disabilities and abilities, various kinds of organizations have evolved to meet their unique needs.

---

[7] Romaine P. Mackie and Patricia P. Robbins, "Exceptional Children in Local Public Schools," *School Life*, 43 (November, 1960), 14.
[8] *Ibid.*

Itinerant Personnel

Speech correctionists, social workers, school psychologists, remedial reading teachers, and other special education personnel may deal with exceptional children on an itinerant basis. They may serve several schools and travel over a considerable area, visiting the exceptional child and his teacher at regular intervals or whenever necessary. Thus, the youngster spends the major part of his time in the regular classroom and is taken out of the room only for short periods. A speech correctionist, for example, may work with the speech-defective child several times a week for short periods, while an itinerant teacher for the partially sighted child might visit only once a month to bring sight-saving materials and to confer with the regular teacher. In both cases the primary responsibility for the general education of the exceptional child rests with the regular classroom teacher.

If a child is homebound, an itinerant teacher may work with him in his own home, sometimes for an hour or more a day if the youngster's condition permits. The case load of a home teacher varies with the type of disability involved and the academic load carried by each child.

The school social worker and psychologist may interview and confer with a child, his parents, and his teacher and generally assist in the adjustment of the socially or emotionally disturbed child in the home and school. They may counsel a child consistently over an extended period of time or only occasionally.

The itinerant special-teacher type of program is particularly valuable in rural areas where the exceptional children are few and scattered over a wide area. Thus one teacher may serve several schools. This program is also well suited to certain types of exceptionality such as defective speech or partial vision which require limited services or materials. Often one of the itinerant teacher's primary roles will be that of a consultant or resource person for the classroom teacher.

Special Class and Resource Room

Classrooms for mentally retarded, gifted, deaf, blind, partially seeing, auditorily handicapped, or crippled children may be organized within a school system. If the exceptional child is enrolled in such a class with a specially trained teacher, and spends most of the day there, it is usually referred to as a *special class*. If, on the other hand, the exceptional child is enrolled in the regular classroom and goes to the special room only for specialized instruction, it is usually called a *resource room*. There may be many gradations of these two programs, the difference in terminology usually being dependent upon the amount of time spent in the special room. Deaf children, for example, usually are assigned to a special class of six to eight youngsters and spend the entire day in it. A program for the gifted, however, may be organized so that the gifted child spends a half-day in the regular room and the other half-day in a special room. A mentally handicapped child may spend nearly half of the time with normal children in physical education, art, music, home-making, and so forth, and yet be a member of the special class. Often a blind child goes to the resource room only for brief periods of braille instruction, sometimes spending the entire day in the regular classroom. We may think of these two types of organization as being roughly at opposite ends of a continuum with various degrees of activity in the special rooms.

The special class teacher or resource teacher is trained in methods not used by the regular teacher. She also has access to special equipment not available in a regular classroom.

Advantages of the special class or resource room over residential schools or special day schools include the fact that the youngster remains in his own community and in close association with normal children and yet has the benefits of individualized and specialized training.

Disadvantages often pointed out include the possibility of a youngster's having to travel a considerable distance to the school which houses the special class. This may separate him from his neighborhood friends. It is also possible that, although a special class is physically integrated in a school system, it may simultaneously be socially isolated and so unduly emphasize the exceptional child's deviation.

Special Schools

Some school systems have organized special schools for different kinds of exceptional children, especially the socially maladjusted, crippled, and multiply handicapped. Particularly in large cities, schools for the socially maladjusted have been organized, where professional personnel in addition to teachers help in the adjustment of disturbed, truant, or delinquent children. Some schools with special provisions for crippled children also enroll normal children. In general, there is a trend toward organizing special class programs within neighborhood schools and a decrease in special school organization, at least for certain types of handicapping conditions. Physically handicapped and mentally handicapped children, for example, can make a certain modicum of adjustment with normal children. Likewise, it is felt that contact with normal children provides the gifted with a better preparation for future life. There are still, however, many special schools, especially for the emotionally and socially maladjusted.

Residential Schools

All the states of the union have residential schools or institutions for various types of handicapped children, including the mentally retarded, delinquent, blind, deaf, crippled, and emotionally disturbed. These institutions are sometimes privately administered but usually administered by a state agency other than that of education. Historically, residential schools are the oldest educational provision for exceptional children. They tended to be built away from population centers and to become too often segregated, sheltered asylums with little community contact. In recent years this fault has been recognized and to an extent remedied. Disadvantages of a residential school include removal of the child from home and neighborhood, emphasis on the handicap, and rigidity of institutional life. This is not to say, however, that such a program no longer meets the needs of some exceptional children, for it does indeed. In a sparsely populated area no other provision may be feasible, especially for a condition, like deafness, which requires extensive equipment and special training on the part of the teacher. In some cases the defect itself demands professional attention for more than a few hours a day. Often with young deaf-blind children specialized treatment, stimulation, and education are carried out in the dormitory or cottage of the residential school on a twenty-four-hour-a-day basis. There may be situations within the child's home which require that for the welfare of the family and the child he must be placed in a residential school, at least for a time.

There is no reason to believe that any of the types of programs discussed will disappear in the immediate future; they will continue to supplement each other. A changing role may, however, be seen for many residential schools. As public school special education programs expand and enroll more of the most able exceptional children, the residential schools may emphasize programs for the severely and multiply handicapped children.

Hospital Schools

Sometimes physically handicapped children are confined to a hospital for long periods of time for serious disabilities. To avoid educational retardation during their convalescence, hospital schools have been established. Generally the local school system assigns teachers to the hospital to educate these children on an individual basis. This program not only continues their education but also contributes to the mental health of these children, who in most instances must remain physically inactive during their hospital confinement.

Special Education — its Meaning and Philosophy

The term "special education" has been used to denote those aspects of education which are applied to handicapped and gifted children but not usually used with the majority of average children. "Special" is defined by Webster as "distinguished by some unusual quality; uncommon; noteworthy; extraordinary; additional to the regular; extra; utilized or employed for a certain purpose in addition to the ordinary." These definitions are certainly applicable to special education, which consists of the modifications of, or additions to, school practices intended for the ordinary child — practices that are unique, uncommon, of unusual quality, and in particular are in addition to the organization and instructional procedures used with the majority of children.

It should be pointed out that special education is not a total program which is entirely different from the education of the ordinary child. It refers only to those aspects of education which are unique and/or in addition to the regular program for all children. For example, the general educational program for a child with a speech defect is carried out in all phases by his regular classroom teacher. The *special* part of his education is the correction of his speech defect by a speech correctionist. This may be carried on for only two hours a week out of a possible thirty hours in the regular classroom. The ordinary child does not receive this additional help, which we call special education, because he does not need it. On the other hand, a deaf child is usually assigned to a special class for the deaf for the whole day. His teacher for the regular portions of his education is the same teacher who ministers to his special needs, which in the case of the deaf are lip reading, speech development, special techniques of language training, and so forth. What the deaf child receives as special education is, of course, a great deal more *special* than that received by a child with a minor speech handicap.

The amount and kind of special education which is needed by an exceptional child depends upon many factors, among them the degree of discrepancy between his development and the development of the ordinary child (the greater the degree of discrepancy, the greater the extent to which special education is needed); the discrepancies in development within the child himself; the effects of the disability on other areas of achievement. Various areas of special education will be described in subsequent chapters. It suffices at this point to say that special education, its quality, kind, and amount, is dependent upon the growth pattern of the child in relation to his peers and the discrepancies in growth within himself.

The need for special education can be recognized in the problem faced by a regular teacher. In many schools a teacher has a class of thirty-five children, one of whom is gifted and one of whom is mentally retarded. She also has one child who stutters and one who is a behavior problem. Asked to organize an educational program for a fifth-grade class, she must adapt instruction for the mentally retarded child who reads barely at the second-grade level, for the gifted child, who reads at nearly the eighth-grade level, for the speech defective, for the problem child, and for the other thirty-one children in her class, who also deviate, but not to the extent of those mentioned. Because of the difficulty of this task, special education programs have evolved in a large number of school systems. They are designed not only to help the exceptional child but also to help the regular class teacher with her responsibility, so that she can devote most of the class time to a more homogeneous group of children. The organization of special education, then, benefits the average child in the regular grade as well as the exceptional child.

Education often begins where medicine stops. For example, fitting a partially seeing child with glasses or a hard-of-hearing youngster with a hearing aid is a medical concern. But teaching the child to use what vision and hearing he has most effectively and aiding him in using his other senses compensatorily is a special education function.

If a hearing loss, for example, can be corrected, this problem is solely a medical, not an educational, concern. If it cannot be corrected, it must be ameliorated to whatever extent is possible by decreasing its effects. Hearing aids, auditory training, and lip reading are directly geared to strengthening the ability to function auditorily and are considered amelioration, not cure.

In the case of total blindness for which medicine offers no remedy or improvement, the problem becomes solely an educational concern. Instruction in braille, provision of special braille materials, travel training, and counseling are but a few of the aspects of a special education program.

One of the general aims of special education is first to ameliorate the deficit by medicine, training, or whatever means are feasible, and then to compensate for the residual deficit by strengthening other abilities and providing specially adapted materials.

The emphasis on the exceptional child in the public schools has had its advocates and also its opponents. Some feel that the support of programs for exceptional children is detracting from the major purpose of the public school — the education of the normal or average child. This point of view has been presented in the following verse:

> Johnny Jones has lost a leg,
> Fanny's deaf and dumb,

Marie has epileptic fits,
Tom's eyes are on the bum.
Sadie stutters when she talks,
Mabel has T.B.,
Morris is a splendid case
Of imbecility.
Billy Brown's a truant,
And Harold is a thief,
Teddy's parents gave him dope
And so he came to grief.
Gwendolin's a millionaire,
Gerald is a fool;
So every one of these darned kids
Goes to a special school.
They've specially nice teachers,
And special things to wear,
And special time to play in,
And a special kind of air.
They've special lunches right in school,
While I — it makes me wild! —
I haven't any specialties;
I'm just a normal child.[9]

Summary

Inherent in the philosophy of a democracy is the right of all children to develop to their maximum. This philosophy has led to the organization of programs for exceptional children within the public schools. We have considered the following concepts:

1. Exceptional children have been defined as those children who deviate from average children in mental, physical, and/or social characteristics to such an extent that they require a modification of school practices or services in order to develop to their maximum. This definition includes both the gifted and the handicapped.

2. Individual differences in the field of exceptional children involve two dimensions: (a) the difference between the exceptional child and the majority of children in ability or disability and (b) the differences in development within the child as represented by discrepancies in growth. Discrepancies in physical, social, intellectual, and educational achievement have been presented in the form of profiles. The profiles showed typical assets and deficits in growth which necessitate different educational methods and programs for various types of deviant children: the gifted, mentally retarded, auditorily handicapped, visually handi-

[9] From the *School Board Journal,* quoted by N. V. Scheideman, *The Psychology of Exceptional Children* (Boston: Houghton Mifflin Company, 1931), p. 2.

capped, speech handicapped, crippled, socially maladjusted, and multiply handicapped.

3. Special education has been defined as that additional educational service over and above the regular school program, which is provided for an exceptional child to assist in the development of his potentialities and/or in the amelioration of his disabilities.

4. The educational facilities developed for exceptional children include itinerant personnel, special classes and resource rooms, special schools, residential schools, and hospital schools.

5. The prevalence of exceptional children has been estimated conservatively as about 12.5 per cent of the school population. Approximately one and one-quarter million children are being offered special education in public and private schools and residential institutions. It has also been estimated that approximately one out of four exceptional children in the United States is being offered special educational opportunities.

DISCUSSION QUESTIONS

1. Which one of the following boys should be considered exceptional, and why? (a) John, age 10, IQ 75, achievement level Second Grade, placed in a Fourth Grade where the average IQ is 90 and the average educational achievement about Third Grade; (b) Billy, age 10, IQ 75, achievement level Second Grade, placed in a Fourth Grade where the average IQ is 120, and the average achievement Fifth-Grade level.

2. What terms other than "exceptional" can be used to describe the handicapped? What other terms can be used for both the handicapped and the gifted? Which term do you prefer to be used, and why?

3. Draw profiles for John and Charles (Figure 2) as they would be at fourteen years of age if their growth and development proceed at the present rate.

4. What do the high points in a child's profile mean? What do the low points mean? How do you utilize the high and low points in adapting the educational program?

5. How can you tell from a child's profile whether he needs a special class or special help in a particular area in the regular class? (See Figures 3 and 5.)

6. Shangri-La is a city of 2,000,000 population. About 20% of this population consists of school-age children. Utilizing the statistics on prevalence in Table I and the enrollment statistics in Table II, outline the number of children, number of classes, and types of services that would be found in Shangri-La if there were a comprehensive program of special education.

7. Outline the most comprehensive arguments you can for special education programs based on the benefits which accrue to the regular teachers and children from such special education facilities.

8. Give examples of what is meant by the text's statement that "special education begins where medicine stops."

9. Table II gives enrollments in special education programs in 1958. Assuming a constant increase in population, extrapolate the enrollment figures to 1968. Which areas do you expect to decrease, drop out, or increase, and why?

10. How do you differentiate between special education facilities as discussed in this chapter and the many special services offered children in a school system, such as psychological or social services, driver training, and special instruction in art, music, and other special subjects?

SELECTED READINGS

Baker, Harry J. *Introduction to Exceptional Children.* New York: The Macmillan Company, 3rd ed., 1959.

Barker, Roger G., Beatrice Wright, Lee Meyerson, and Mollie Gornick. *Adjustment to Physical Handicap and Illness: A Survey of the Social Psychology of Physique and Disability.* New York: Social Science Research Council, 1953.

Brotemarkle, Robert A., ed. *Clinical Psychology; Studies in Honor of Lightner Witmer.* Philadelphia: University of Pennsylvania Press, 1931.

Cruickshank, W. M., ed. *Psychology of Exceptional Children and Youth.* Englewood Cliffs, N.J.: Prentice-Hall, Inc., 1955.

Cruickshank, W. M., and G. O. Johnson, eds. *Education of Exceptional Children and Youth.* Englewood Cliffs, N.J.: Prentice-Hall, Inc., 1959.

"The Education of Exceptional Children," *Review of Educational Research,* Vol. 14, No. 3, June, 1944; Vol. 23, No. 5, December, 1953; Vol. 29, No. 5, December, 1959. Washington: American Educational Research Association, National Education Association.

"The Education of Handicapped and Gifted Pupils in the Secondary School," *Bulletin of the National Association of Secondary School Principals,* Vol. 39, No. 207. Washington: The Association, January, 1955.

Frampton, Merle E., and Elena D. Gall, eds. *Special Education for the Exceptional.* 3 vols. Boston: Porter Sargent, 1955.

Garrison, Karl C., and Dewey G. Force, Jr. *The Psychology of Exceptional Children.* New York: Ronald Press Company, 3rd ed., 1959.

Goodenough, Florence L. *Exceptional Children.* New York: Appleton-Century-Crofts, Inc., 1956.

Heck, A. O. *The Education of Exceptional Children: Its Challenge to Teachers, Parents, and Laymen.* New York: McGraw-Hill Book Company, 2nd ed., 1953.

Horn, J. L. *The Education of Exceptional Children: A Consideration of Public School Problems and Policies in the Field of Differentiated Education.* New York: The Century Company, 1924.

Jenks, William F. *The Atypical Child.* Washington: Catholic University of America Press, 1954.

Kirk, Samuel A., Chairman. *The Education of Exceptional Children, Forty-ninth Yearbook of the National Society for the Study of Education,* Part II. Chicago: University of Chicago Press, 1950.

Louttit, C. M. *Clinical Psychology of Exceptional Children.* New York: Harper & Brothers, 3rd ed., 1957.

Magary, James F., and John R. Eichorn. *The Exceptional Child: A Book of Readings.* New York: Holt, Rinehart and Winston, Inc., 1960.

Magnifico, L. X. *Education for the Exceptional Child.* New York: Longmans, Green and Company, 1st ed., 1958.

Pintner, R., J. Eisenson, and Mildred Stanton. *The Psychology of the Physically Handicapped.* New York: Appleton-Century-Crofts, Inc., 1941.

Scheideman, N. V. *The Psychology of Exceptional Children.* 2 vols. Boston: Houghton Mifflin Company, 1931.

Taylor, Wallace W., and Isabelle W. Taylor. *Special Education of Physically Handicapped Children in Western Europe.* New York: International Society for the Rehabilitation of the Disabled, 1960.

Van Sickle, James H., Lightner Witmer, and Leonard P. Ayres. *Provision for Exceptional Children in Public Schools.* U.S. Bureau of Education, Bulletin No. 14. Washington: Government Printing Office, 1911.

Wallin, J. E. W. *Children with Mental and Physical Handicaps.* New York: Prentice-Hall, Inc., 1949.

Wallin, J. E. W. *The Education of Handicapped Children.* Boston: Houghton Mifflin Company, 1924.

White House Conference on Child Health and Protection. *Special Education: The Handicapped and the Gifted.* New York: The Century Company, 1931.

White House Conference on Child Health and Protection. *Organization for the Care of Handicapped Children: National, State and Local.* New York: The Century Company, 1932.

White House Conference on Child Health and Protection. *The Handicapped Child.* New York: Appleton-Century Company, 1933.

2

The Intellectually Gifted Child

During the 1950's interest in the education of gifted children in the United States intensified. This interest, of course, is not new; throughout the centuries various cultures have attempted to develop those individuals who were of superior intelligence. Concern for the gifted, like that for many other exceptional children, arises from the needs and social and political philosophy of the society and the times.

In ancient Greece, over 2000 years ago, Plato advocated that children with superior intellect be selected at an early age and offered a specialized form of instruction in science, philosophy, and metaphysics. The most intelligent and knowledgeable would then become the leaders of the state. Plato felt that the survival of Greek democracy was contingent upon its ability to educate the superior citizens for leadership positions in that society.

In the sixteenth century, Suleiman the Magnificent made special efforts to identify the gifted Christian youth throughout the Turkish Empire and provide them with education in the Moslem faith and in war, art, science, and philosophy.[1] His talent scouts, who surveyed the population at regular intervals, were able to select and educate a large group of superior individuals. Thus, within a generation after this system of education

[1] Merle R. Sumption and Evelyn M. Luecking, *Education of the Gifted* (New York: Ronald Press Company, 1960), p. 23.

began, the Ottoman Empire became a great power in art, science, culture, and war, and even attempted to conquer the whole of Europe.

During the nineteenth and twentieth centuries little organized effort was made in Europe to select gifted children or to offer them special education. This was not felt to be necessary since secondary schools and universities were in general keyed to the education of those in the higher social strata, from which it was believed the more intelligent leadership would come. Even today the masses attend common schools and learn a trade. In many countries in Europe a small proportion of the population of children (usually those coming from influential families) is separated at the fourth or sixth grade and assigned to academic secondary schools, while the masses continue in the common schools; the percentage of children who attend secondary schools or universities is much smaller than the percentage who attend such schools in the United States.

In the United States the concentration of effort in public education has been on the education of "all of the children of all of the people," generally by mass education procedures. With a few exceptions, opportunities for education under public auspices have been offered all children without differentiation. There has been an implicit faith that "all men are created equal" and that education is the avenue through which this equality could express itself. A noted behaviorist psychologist, John B. Watson, bolstered this point of view when he stated that he could take any well-formed, healthy baby and make of it what he pleased — "rich man, poor man, beggar man, thief."

In spite of the efforts of some individuals who advocated special provisions (over and above the regular school programs) and even of some school systems which initiated special classes or special programs for the gifted, these programs did not receive wide public support. The rationale of those who opposed special education of the gifted was that we were already offering diversified curriculums in the secondary schools — commercial courses, vocational and trades courses, and others of a less academic nature, as well as college preparatory curriculums. This multiple-track plan was believed to be the most suitable for enriching the programs for brighter children. Furthermore, colleges and universities were originally organized for the superior students; hence it may be argued that the public has been providing extended education for those of superior intellect.

The argument that American society has supplied colleges and universities for the most able did not take into consideration that not all superior students were economically able to attend college. In a study during the depression years of 1930 to 1940, Goetsch presented an alarming picture of the waste of human resources resulting from economic factors. Ninety per cent of the superior high school graduates who came from families in the higher-income groups were able to attend college, but less than 20 per cent of superior high school graduates from the lower-income groups attended college.[2] According to this study, American society was providing higher education only for superior students who were economically able to attend college.

One of the effects of World War II was the creation of the G.I. Bill, which offered stipends to veterans for higher education. This bill, to some extent and for a limited time, tended to offset the implications of the Goetsch study, since it provided the opportunity for many young men and women who otherwise could not have afforded it to go to college. In addition, the number of scholarships and fellowships now offered to college students, and particularly to graduate students, is decreasing the economic deterrents.

The recent public interest in the special education of the gifted child in the United States (not only at the college level but at the elementary and secondary levels as well) stems from a number of national and international situations. Gallagher has given some of the major reasons for this acceleration of interest:

> . . . This sharp conflict of ideology between world powers has given a new sense of urgency to the complaints about the role of the gifted child in the American educational system. A casual reading of the literature will reveal that the same complaints — low standards for gifted children, unimaginative teaching and planning, and inadequate stimulation of their mental potential — that have been given such wide publicity today were being made in the 1920's and 1930's by educators and psychologists such as Hollingworth, Terman, and Pressey. Apparently the culture was not yet ready at that time to respond to their challenge.
>
> A direct conflict between two great world powers has undeniable dramatic implications. There is reason to believe, however, that there are other changes taking place in the world culture which may, in the long run, cause more attention to be directed to the educational opportunities for intellectually superior children. There has been much talk of the 'Population Explosion' in recent years. Not much has been said about the 'Knowledge Explosion.' . . . Only a half-century ago, many fields and professions that are important to our lives were non-existent. Entire areas of inquiry and work such as economics, sociology, group dynamics, atomic physics, radiology, electronics, servomechanisms, jet propulsion, and many others were either unthought of or in their infancy. In some of these fields today books sometimes become outdated before they come off the presses.[3]

[2] Helen B. Goetsch, *Parental Income and College Opportunities,* Teachers College Contributions to Education, No. 795 (New York: Teachers College, Columbia University, 1940).

[3] James J. Gallagher, *Analysis of Research on the Education of Gifted Children* (Springfield, Ill.: Office of the Superintendent of Public Instruction, 1960), p. 1–2.

Who Are the Gifted?

There are many kinds of talented and gifted children, and no real agreement as to who is a gifted child. The major reason for disagreement is that among the many kinds of talents there are various degrees of talents. Guilford, in analyzing the structure of intellect, postulates as many as 120 different intellectual abilities.[4] Thus if a person is facile in one set of abilities, he may be talented along one line; if facile in a different set of abilities, he may show quite different talents. Some authorities use the term "gifted" to refer only to those highly capable in a wide variety of abilities, whereas others use it to mean anyone highly competent in any one area. Some think of giftedness only in terms of a high IQ or a high degree of abstract and symbolic learning ability; others include facility in music, art, or mechanics.

One definition of giftedness is presented in a recent yearbook: "A talented or gifted child is one who shows consistently remarkable performance in any worth-while line of endeavor. Thus, we shall include not only the intellectually gifted but also those who show promise in music, the graphic arts, creative writing, dramatics, mechanical skills, and social leadership."[5]

This definition not only allows a very narrow ability to qualify for giftedness but relies solely on performance rather than potentiality for development. It does not include the underachieving gifted child or the child who has not made use of his abilities in socially acceptable channels. A child with an IQ of 150 who does not perform in school or along socially acceptable lines would not be considered gifted. A potentially gifted child with an underprivileged or foreign background might easily be overlooked because he does not appear to perform well.

Sumption and Luecking define the gifted as "Those who possess a superior central nervous system characterized by the potential to perform tasks requiring a comparatively high degree of intellectual abstraction or creative imagination or both."[6] Fliegler and Bish use the following definition: ". . . the term *gifted* encompasses those children who possess a superior intellectual potential and functional ability to achieve academically in the top 15 to 20 per cent of the school population; and/or talent of a high order in such special areas as mathematics, mechanics,

---

[4] J. P. Guilford, "Three Faces of Intellect," *American Psychologist,* 14 (August, 1959), 469–479.

[5] *Education for the Gifted, Fifty-seventh Yearbook of the National Society for the Study of Education,* Part II (Chicago: University of Chicago Press, 1958), p. 19.

[6] Sumption and Luecking, *op. cit.,* p. 6.

science, expressive arts, creative writing, music, and social leadership; and a unique creative ability to deal with their environment."[7]

In defining giftedness there is a current effort to avoid depending too heavily on the IQ, but when it comes to identifying or selecting gifted children most schools and research workers rely on a standardized intelligence test, partly because there are few other measuring devices. Perhaps some of the current attempts to measure creativity as another facet of intelligence may bear fruit. It has been found[8] that highly creative (but not highest IQ) children achieve the same academically as high IQ (but not highly creative) children.

Another reason the IQ has been depended upon is that it does tap a wide variety of abilities. In order to obtain a high IQ a child has to show either considerable ability in many areas or tremendous ability in more limited areas. It is possible, however, that present measures of intelligence leave some areas untapped.

When the IQ has been used to define intelligence, there has been a wide divergence in determining the cutoff point above which a child is considered gifted. Various authorities for various purposes have used anywhere from 115 IQ to 180 IQ as the dividing line.

DeHaan and Havighurst have divided the intellectually gifted into two groups for educational purposes.[9] The highest 1 per cent they call "first-order" or extremely gifted and the remaining upper 10 per cent "second-order" gifted. The extremely gifted are very rare and may require a different kind of education from that given the second-order gifted.

With giftedness showing itself in so many different ways perhaps we can think of it in more general terms for practical purposes as *superior ability to deal with facts, ideas, or relationships*, whether this ability comes from a high IQ or a less well-defined creativity. We can then refer to those with special aptitudes in more specific fields as talented, such as:

> the socially talented
> the mechanically talented
> the artistically talented
> the musically talented
> the physically talented
> the linguistically talented
> the academically talented

[7] Louis A. Fliegler and Charles E. Bish, "Summary of Research on the Academically Talented Student," *Review of Educational Research*, 29 (December, 1959), 409.

[8] J. W. Getzels and P. W. Jackson, "The Study of Giftedness: A Multidimensional Approach," *The Gifted Student*, Cooperative Research Monograph No. 2 (Washington: U.S. Department of Health, Education and Welfare, 1960), pp. 1–18.

[9] Robert F. DeHaan and Robert J. Havighurst, *Educating Gifted Children* (Chicago: University of Chicago Press, 1957), p. 1.

Obviously there is much overlapping. The intellectually gifted may also be socially talented; the musically talented may also be intellectually and mathematically gifted. The academically talented are usually intellectually gifted, although not all intellectually gifted are academically talented. Usually a high degree of talent in one or more areas is accompanied by intellectual giftedness. DeHaan and Havighurst, in trying to identify the top 10 per cent in each of several areas of talent, found so much overlapping that in the end they found that these groups constituted only 15 per cent of the high school population.[10] This gives support to the use of general intelligence measures as criteria for defining giftedness.

To be highly endowed in an intellectual field requires a gifted intellect, but the direction which that intellect follows is dependent on many other factors such as experience, motivation, interest, emotional stability, hero worship, parental urgings, and even chance. Many an intellectually gifted individual might also have been successful in another area had his interests and training been in that direction.

Usually the very talented are also intellectually gifted but there are cases of special talents of a nonintellectual nature or abilities narrow in range in which the individual is not able to handle ideas and relationships outside a very limited field.

Admitting that superior intelligence is only one factor in determining success, achievement, or contribution to society, it still remains a basic ingredient of what we call giftedness. Other qualities are necessary for successful accomplishment, but our major concern here is with cognitive reasoning abilities. By trying to include in a definition of giftedness those other factors which are commendable (such as social leadership, performance, worth-whileness) we are confusing the concept of giftedness with our goals for gifted children. We do have so-called gifted children who are not performing because of emotional, motivational, or circumstantial factors; we do have so-called gifted children who are not outstanding in creativity; we do have so-called gifted children who are using their talents in socially unacceptable ways. But the common denominator is intellectual superiority.

How Many Gifted Children Are There?

The question of prevalence of gifted children in a particular school population depends to a large extent on two factors: (1) the criterion for identifying them and (2) the type of community being studied.

If the criterion used is an IQ, the number of gifted in a given com-

[10] *Ibid.*

munity depends on the IQ cutoff point. Leta Hollingworth, for example, studied children with IQ's above 180.[11] With this high a criterion of giftedness probably only one child in a million would be considered gifted. If we used an IQ of 115 and above on the Stanford-Binet test as the criterion, we would find 15 to 20 per cent of most school populations in this category. Using varying cutoff points, we could divide the group of high-IQ children according to degree of ability into (1) superior children, with IQ's of 116 to 132; (2) very superior children, with IQ's of 132 to 148; and (3) gifted children, with IQ's above 148. Programs of education for these children would probably differ somewhat according to the intellectual level of the children in the group as well as to other factors.

The intellectual and cultural level of a community also influences the number of gifted children found. Communities composed largely of professional people show a higher percentage of gifted children than do communities of a lower socioeconomic status.

The early experiences of the children from higher socioeconomic and educational levels are probably much more conducive to the development of reasoning ability, seeing relationships, understanding abstract concepts, and other abilities usually considered indicative of intellectual capacity. If so, society could do much more than it now does to develop and cultivate giftedness. Pressey calls attention to the greater frequency of certain types of genius during particular periods of history when emphasis was placed on them. Pointing up the importance of early training and stimulation, he postulates that ". . . a practicing genius is produced by giving a precocious able youngster early encouragement, intensive instruction, continuing opportunity as he advances, a congruent stimulating social life, and cumulative success experiences."[12]

The greater frequency with which gifted children are found in communities of a higher cultural and socioeconomic level suggests that had children from other communities had the same experiences we would have more high-level manpower. This is the group which should receive extra attention in trying to locate the potentially gifted, the more so since their true ability is less likely to be spotted by our predominantly verbal and abstract intelligence tests.

Gallagher has formulated an estimate of gifted children in various IQ categories and in two different socioeconomic groups, as presented in Table III; there may be less than 1 per 100 school children (taking the IQ of 140 and above in an average community) to over 45 in 100 (taking the lowest IQ of 115 in a superior socioeconomic community.) Actually,

[11] Leta Hollingworth, *Children Above 180 IQ* (Yonkers-on-Hudson, N.Y.: World Book Company, 1942).
[12] S. L. Pressey, "Concerning the Nature and Nurture of Genius," *Educating the Gifted,* Joseph L. French, ed. (New York: Henry Holt and Company, 1960), p. 14.

TABLE III

Approximate Proportions of School Populations at Various Intellectual Levels

Stanford-Binet Intellectual Levels	Per Cent of School Population		Educational Expectations
	Average Community	Superior Socioeconomic Community	
IQ above 140	.5 to 1%	2 to 3%	Graduate college
IQ above 130	2 to 4	6 to 12	(medicine, law,
IQ above 125	5 to 7	15 to 20	Ph.D. programs in physical and social sciences)
IQ above 120	10 to 12	30 to 40	Undergraduate
IQ above 115	16 to 20	45 to 60	college

Source: James J. Gallagher, *The Gifted Child in the Elementary School* (*What Research Says to the Teacher,* No. 17, 1st ed.) (Washington: American Educational Research Association, N.E.A., Department of Classroom Teachers, 1959), p. 5. Reproduced with the permission of James J. Gallagher.

the only way to find out in a particular place is to examine the whole school population, and then the percentage will be relatively accurate for only that community.

Finding Gifted Children

Salvaging our wasted high-level manpower is more than a problem of establishing classes or other measures for developing gifted children. Before these children can be helped they must be found — and not just the obvious ones who have already achieved but also those who are "hiding their light under a bushel." In every generation many gifted children pass through school unidentified and uncultivated. Children from low socioeconomic or foreign cultures whose lack of verbal ability conceals their merit, those who have to drop out of school for economic reasons, those from minority groups, and those with emotional problems are often not detected as potentially gifted.

The man on the street expects that of course the teacher will spot these children and do something for them, but various studies have shown that teachers do not do a very good job of recognizing the gifted child; in fact they fail to identify from 10 to 50 per cent of their gifted. Pegnato and Birch, for example, in evaluating various methods of identifying gifted children, found that teachers were not able to select such children at all accurately.[13] They picked many children (31.4 per cent of their choices) who were not gifted and missed more than half of the really gifted children in their classes. Children who are successful academically, who have a high degree of social leadership, who have a cultivated ability in dramatics or the arts, or who have successful achievement in some other line of endeavor are readily identified as probably gifted. But the child who is not achieving in school, or who is inhibited and lacking in outgoing personality traits, or who is nonconforming in habits and attitudes may have potentialities which are easily overlooked.

However, if given some guidance in making observations, teachers can provide much significant information. In fact, their observations probably provide the greatest single resource (other than objective tests) in identifying gifted children. Kough and DeHaan have developed a *Teacher's Guidance Handbook* providing observational methods for discovering special abilities and disabilities.[14] (It can be used for maladjusted and handicapped children as well as the gifted.) It provides a list of identifying characteristics in the areas of intellectual ability, scientific abilities, talents in the fine arts, social leadership ability, mechanical skills, and physical skills. For example, the following distinguishing characteristics are to be checked in the area of intellectual ability:

1. Learns rapidly and easily.
2. Uses a lot of common sense and practical knowledge.
3. Reasons things out, thinks clearly, recognizes relationships, comprehends meanings.
4. Retains what he has heard or read without much rote drill.
5. Knows about many things of which other children are unaware.
6. Uses a large number of words easily and accurately.
7. Can read books that are one to two years in advance of the rest of the class.
8. Performs difficult mental tasks.
9. Asks many questions. Is interested in a wide range of things.
10. Does some academic work one to two years in advance of the class.
11. Is original, uses good but unusual methods or ideas.
12. Is alert, keenly observant, responds quickly.[15]

Children's opinions of other children are also helpful in expanding information about potentially gifted children. Their opinions are of particular value since they know each other both in school and out. The

[13] Carl W. Pegnato and Jack W. Birch, "Locating Gifted Children in Junior High School," *Exceptional Children*, 25 (March, 1959), 300–304.
[14] Jack Kough and Robert F. DeHaan, *Teacher's Guidance Handbook. I, Identifying Children Who Need Help* (Chicago: Science Research Associates, 1955).
[15] *Ibid.,* p. 44.

"Who Are They?" Test[16] has been used to get children to identify their peers who seem to have social leadership qualities. The children are asked to identify which child fits certain brief word pictures describing a particular behavior.

Intellectually gifted children can sometimes be identified by their parents or family friends before entering school. Their accelerated development in the areas of language and understanding relationships often ᶜhows up quite early. Witty has summarized these areas as follows:

1. The early use of a large and accurately employed vocabulary.
2. Language proficiency — the use of entire sentences, and ability to tell or reproduce a story at an early age.
3. Keen observation and retention of information about things observed.
4. Interest in and liking for books — later enjoyment of atlases, dictionaries, and encyclopedia.
5. Early interest in calendars, in telling time, and in clocks.
6. The ability to attend or concentrate for a longer period than is usual for children.
7. Demonstrations of proficiency in drawing, music, or other art forms.
8. Interest in exploration and discovery of cause-and-effect relationships.
9. The early development of ability to read.[17]

Subjective evaluation, such as teacher or parent referral, needs to be checked by more objective measures of ability such as standardizd tests. Any program for identifying the gifted children in a school system should include both subjective and objective methods of evaluation. Some types of behavior are best observed informally, some by a more controlled method. Classroom behavior, for example, may point up a child's ability in organizing and utilizing material and interpreting it to other people better than a test can, whereas a class situation seldom taxes an accelerated child to the limit of his ability, as can be done in a test situation. Many aspects of creativity and verbal fluency are also best observed in a classroom or in informal experiences.

Most schools have some test scores available from group intelligence tests or group achievement tests. Although these are not sufficient in and of themselves they serve as a starting point in selecting candidates for a special program. Certain pitfalls are widely recognized in utilizing this material: (1) group intelligence tests are not as reliable as individual tests; (2) they seldom differentiate abilities at the upper limits; (3) some children do not function adequately in a timed test situation. Group

---

[16] Paul H. Bowman *et al.*, *Studying Children and Training Counselors in a Community Program*, Supplementary Educational Monograph No. 78 (Chicago: University of Chicago Press, 1953), pp. 32–33.

[17] Paul Witty, "Gifted Children — Our Greatest Resource," *Nursing Outlook* Vol. 3 (September, 1955), p. 499.

intelligence tests, however, are practical for screening purposes, since it is financially prohibitive to expect all children to be given individual examinations. Those children who are near the cutoff point or for whom it is felt the group test is not representative are usually given individual tests.

Achievement tests are even less discriminating; the same criticisms hold, and in addition they detect only children who are achieving academically. Emotional disturbance, family problems, peer-group standards of mediocrity, poor study habits, a foreign-language background, and many other factors may affect a child's ability to perform academically. In the opposite direction, there are some children who because of family pressures, good study habits, or intense motivation achieve at a higher educational level than is consistent with their other abilities or their apparent mental level.

Gallagher has summarized the limitations of various techniques of identifying gifted children:

SUMMARY OF METHODS OF IDENTIFYING GIFTED CHILDREN[18]

Method	Limitations
Individual intelligence test	The best method, but expensive in use of professional time and service. Not practical as general screening tool in schools with limited psychological services.
Group intelligence test	Generally good for screening. May not identify those with reading difficulties and emotional or motivational problems.
Achievement test batteries	Will not identify underachieving gifted children. In addition, same limitations as group intelligence test.
Teacher observation	May miss underachievers, motivational problems, emotional problems, and children with belligerent or apathetic attitude toward the school program. Definitely needs supplementing with standardized tests of intelligence and achievement (see above).

Case Studies of the Intellectually Gifted

To illustrate the achievements of individuals who are considered intellectually gifted, two types of illustrations follow: (1) life sketches of

[18] James J. Gallagher, *The Gifted Child in the Elementary School* (Washington: American Educational Research Association, National Education Association, 1959), p. 9.

a few great men, and (2) profiles of gifted children in the elementary school.

Histories of Great Men

The term "genius" has been applied to outstanding individuals who have attained eminence in some field of intellectual or creative endeavor. Sometimes the individual is recognized as a child prodigy at a young age; sometimes he is not recognized as "great" until he has become known for a unique contribution at a later stage of his life or in some instances after his death.

John Stuart Mill (1806–1873). John Stuart Mill is considered one of the greatest philosophers of the nineteenth century. He was the son of an English author and philosopher who had himself been self-educated. His life history and education have been reported by Cox[19] and in his own writings. According to Mill's own report, "My father's scheme of education could not have been accomplished if he had not carefully kept me from having any great amount of intercourse with other boys."[20] His father kept him out of school and away from other children to avoid the "contagion of vulgar modes of thought and feeling." He educated John Stuart at home until the boy was 14 years of age. John Stuart began the study of Greek at the age of 3, and geometry and algebra at the age of 8. When he was 12 he began to study philosophy and logic. It is reported that he wrote a history of Rome at the age of 6½. His productive professional career began at age 17. Cox estimated his IQ to be between 190 and 200.

The reactions of John Stuart Mill to his education by the tutorial system of his father (out of school and with little influence of a society of his peers) can best be expressed by direct quotations from his own writings. "I consequently remained long, and in a less degree have always remained, inexpert in anything requiring manual dexterity. . . . The education which my father gave me, was in itself much more fitted for training me to *know* than to *do*."[21]

The history and accomplishments of John Stuart Mill raise a number of questions. First, is it necessary to exclude very superior children from their childhood peers in order to educate them for a scholarly career? Second, can such an education be accomplished in a school situation? And third, is such achievement the result of a tutorial system which can

---

[19] Catherine M. Cox, *Genetic Studies of Genius, The Early Mental Traits of Three Hundred Geniuses* (Stanford, Calif.: Stanford University Press, 1926), Vol. II.

[20] John Stuart Mill, *Autobiography* (New York: Columbia University Press, 1924), p. 24.

[21] *Ibid.*, pp. 25–26.

begin at an early age, uncontaminated by a school curriculum and grade placement?

Norbert Wiener (1894–).[22] Norbert Wiener is one of the great men of our present age, known for his theories of cybernetics from which have been developed the "electronic brains" of various forms, including the high-speed digital computers.

Wiener's father was a German intellectual who migrated to the United States. He, like Mill's father, devoted a great deal of time to tutoring his son at home but, unlike Mill, allowed the boy to attend school. Thus Norbert obtained a combination of home tutoring and a somewhat erratic school career.

Norbert Wiener began to read at the age of 3½ and read *Alice in Wonderland* and *The Arabian Nights* when he was 4. Refused admission to school because he was not yet 6, he attended a one-room country school for a time. At the age of 7 he entered a city school and was placed in the third grade. Soon he was accelerated to the fourth grade but was then taken out of school until the age of 9, when he was admitted to a high school. He graduated from high school at the age of 11 and entered Harvard College the next year. He obtained his Ph.D. in mathematics at age 18. Wiener states that his father tutored him at home, but at times he was tutored in certain subjects by others. His father was a perfectionist and a "task master" and in a sense reproduced a similar educational program for Norbert as was given to John Stuart Mill, with the exception of additional school and college attendance. Wiener's adjustment to college at such a young age was not made without great difficulty.

In view of Wiener's distinction in theoretical mathematics, it is interesting to note that in school he counted on his fingers long after this method was acceptable. In spite of the fact that he had great difficulty in learning by rote the addition combinations and the multiplication tables, he had an understanding of complicated operations in mathematics at an early age. He stated: "My understanding of the subject was too fast for my manipulation, and on the other hand, my demands in the nature of the fundamentals went too far for the explanations of a book devoted to manipulation."[23]

Wiener's achievements and educational career also raise numerous questions. We can state that his early educational acceleration was not the result of the program of the schools he attended. Was it the result of inherent mental abilities that would have led to inevitable achieve-

[22] Norbert Wiener, *Ex-Prodigy: My Childhood and Youth* (New York: Simon and Schuster, 1953).
[23] *Ibid.,* p. 46.

ment, or was it the result of home tutoring by a parent who insisted on perfect learning, thinking, and achieving at a high theoretical level?

Albert Einstein (1879–1955). The education and early history of Albert Einstein differ markedly from the early education of Mill or Wiener. Reiser[24] reported that Einstein was retiring in personality and slow in learning to talk, and that his parents believed him retarded in development. The father was a merchant conducting an electrical business in Munich, Germany. He was without theoretical training but had abilities in technical matters. Einstein's school experiences were not happy ones nor did they necessarily contribute to his basic interest in physics and mathematics. Actually he attended the Luifold Gymnasium in Munich, where the basic studies were in the humanities — Latin, Greek, and ancient history. He was bored with school and recalls only one instructor who inspired him in the classical world.

Einstein's interest in mathematics was aroused by his uncle, his father's partner in the factory. After he had learned the essentials of algebra and heard about the Pythagorean theorem, he studied mathematics on his own and outside of school. At the age of 14 he had mastered the essentials of higher mathematics, which his school did not teach. He continued to be mediocre in school as a language student.

At the age of 15 he left school to go to his parents, who had moved to Milan. Later he failed the entrance examination of the Polytechnic Academy at Zurich. He returned to the secondary school and later was admitted to the Zurich Technical Academy. He became interested in physics, but even here school was not inspiring. He missed classes to read in a wide range of fields, including physics. He completed his work at the University of Zurich, then obtained positions, once as teacher and once in a patent office. In 1909 he procured a professorship at Zurich. He later held professorships in Austria and finally became Director of the Kaiser Wilhelm Institute for Theoretical Physics in Berlin. Einstein's theory of relativity became famous after World War I when its implications began to be understood by the scientists of the world. His life after 1933 was spent at Princeton University in the Institute of Advanced Study.

Einstein was never conceited and never requested from society more than a meager livelihood. Although by nature a pacifist, he wrote to President Roosevelt in 1939 suggesting the possibilities of developing an atomic bomb. In spite of his greatness, he retained a kind, humble nature. It should be recalled that Mill was kept away from children and school so that he would not develop conceit because of his superiority,

---

[24] Anton Reiser, *Albert Einstein* (New York: Albert and Charles Boni, Inc., 1930).

and Wiener's father was careful not to allow Norbert to recognize his superiority.

The story of Einstein indicates that he did not show precocity at an early age, that he did not come from a family of high educational attainments, and that his early school years did not contribute materially to his later accomplishments in physics and mathematics.

Wernher Von Braun (1912–   ). Von Braun is known for his invention of the German V-2 rocket during World War II and his leading role in America's present missile and space program.

Von Braun was the middle son of Baron Magnus Von Braun, a local state administrator in eastern Germany. His mother was an enthusiastic amateur astronomer, who pointed out to her son the planets and constellations. About this experience Wernher stated, "For my confirmation I didn't get a watch and my first pair of long pants, like most Lutheran boys. I got a telescope. My mother thought it would make the best gift."[25]

Aside from his mother's interest in astronomy, Wernher did not receive extraordinary tutoring during his childhood. He attended the regular schools in Germany and received his Ph.D. at the age of 22. In his early teens he obtained a book on interplanetary rockets and found that it contained considerable mathematics, which he disliked and in which he had done poorly in school. This motivated him to learn mathematics and physics, which he later taught to his classmates.

Beginning at the age of 20, he was the top civilian specialist for the German army rocket program. He continued to be recognized as such until he was captured by the American army in 1944 and brought to the United States. He elected to remain in the United States after the war and to work for the American government on missile and space programs.

The experiences of Von Braun indicate that accomplishment is possible without the tutorial systems used with Mill and Wiener. It should be pointed out, however, that his interest and accomplishments in rocketry were initiated by him and acquired without a specialized course in this area. He had the combination of intelligence, interest, motivation, and availability of basic scientific information.

Thomas A. Edison (1847–1931).[26] Thomas Edison is considered one of the great inventors of the nineteenth and twentieth centuries because of his inventions of the phonograph (1877), the incandescent electric

[25] *Time*, February 17, 1958, pp. 21–25.
[26] Frank Lewis Dyer and Thomas C. Martin, *Edison: His Life and Inventions* (New York: Harper & Brothers, 1929), Vols. I and II.

lamp (1879), the motion-picture camera (1891), the magnetic ore separator (1908), and many other mechanical devices.

Edison was raised in an average American midwestern family of his time, his father having been engaged in small business enterprises. His mother, who educated Thomas later, was a former schoolteacher. Throughout his career, he attended public school for only three months. During this time, at the age of 7, he was always at the foot of his class. Furthermore, his teacher reported to the local school inspector in Port Huron, Michigan, that the boy was "addled" and should be kept out of school. His mother became incensed at this recommendation, withdrew the boy from school, and taught him at home, never again admitting him to school.

By the age of 12 he had covered such books as Gibbon's *Decline and Fall of the Roman Empire* and Hume's *History of England*. He was, however, unable to master mathematics. At the age of 15 he became editor of his own paper, called "The Weekly Herald."

The history of Edison shows a creative mind in the development of mechanical and electrical devices. Although he did not contribute greatly to theoretical knowledge, he is considered creative in a practical sense. It is of note, however, that his education was acquired on a tutorial basis, and his achievements were accomplished without the stimulus of formal schooling.

Profiles of Intellectually Gifted Children

To understand the special educational needs of a gifted child it is necessary to make an individual study of that child. One of education's difficulties is that educational programs are organized on the basis of averages derived from studies of groups. The application of averages of populations to an individual is sometimes deceptive, since it does not always follow that what is relevant to a group is relevant to a particular individual. There are, for example, marked differences among children all of whom have been classified as intellectually gifted.

The profiles of George and Ignatius are presented in Figure 8. A series of examinations given to these boys at the age of 10, when they were in the fifth grade, yields the results shown on page 51.

The test results on George and Ignatius and the corresponding profiles in Figure 8 show two boys who can be classified as intellectually gifted but whose growth patterns are markedly different. George's IQ on the Stanford-Binet Scale is 135; Ignatius' IQ is 132. Both boys are in the fifth grade. George's age is 10–4, and Ignatius' is 10–5. Physically, George is accelerated, since his height, weight, motor coordination, and mobility are similar to those of 11-year-old boys in the sixth grade. He

	George	Ignatius
Chronological age	10–4	10–5
Height age	11–9	9–6
Weight age	11–7	9–3
Motor coordination age	12–1	9–4
Mental age	13–11	13–9
Social maturity age	11–5	9–8
Speech development age	13–0	12–0
Language development age	12–7	12–2
Reading age	12–8	12–7
Arithmetic reasoning age	12–1	11–7
Arithmetic computation age	11–5	11–6
Spelling age	11–6	12–0
General information age	11–10	11–6
Mobility	above average	average
Vision	normal	normal
Hearing	normal	normal
Interpersonal relations	above average	average

is likewise accelerated in social maturity, in interpersonal relations, and in school achievement. Actually, with the exception of the accident of birth 10 years and 4 months previous to the examination, George is more like 11- and 12-year-old children. The discrepancies between his physical, social, mental, and achievement levels are really not very great. He is above his chronological age group in all areas of development. He does not have wide discrepancies within himself. Educationally, this child could be accelerated to the sixth or seventh grade, since he is more similar to that group than to the 10-year-olds with whom he is placed under the school's policy of year-by-year promotion.

Ignatius scores about as high as George in mental ability and in educational achievement. But Ignatius has wide discrepancies in growth between his physical, social, mental, and educational abilities. He is not large for his age of 10–5. As a matter of fact, he is more like 9-year-old children in height, weight, and motor coordination. He is also like 9-year-old children in social maturity. His mobility and interpersonal relations are not superior to those of other children in his grade. His only areas of acceleration are his mental ability and his achievement in speech, language, and academic areas. From an educational point of view, this child should not be accelerated to be with older children. The marked unevenness in his physical, social, and mental development presents different educational problems from those presented by George.

These two cases demonstrate why some educators are opposed to acceleration of gifted children while others are in favor of it. Usually those

FIGURE 8

Profiles of Two Intellectually Gifted Children

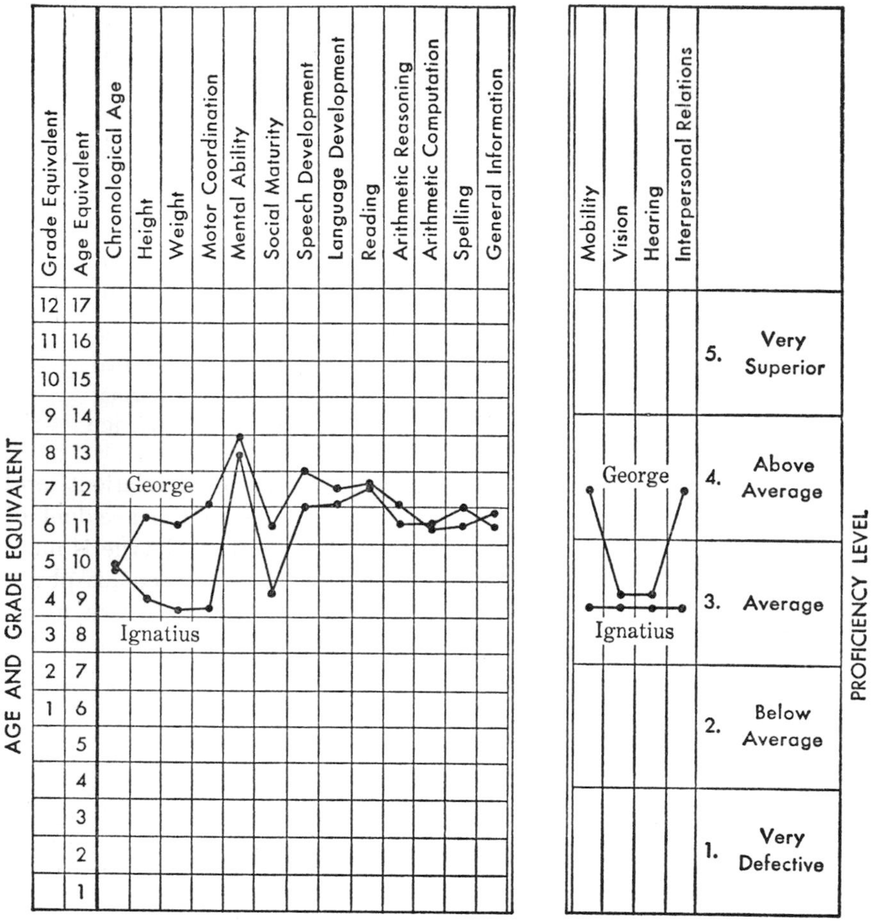

in favor of acceleration are thinking of boys like George, while those opposed to it have in mind boys like Ignatius. That is one reason why easy solutions to the education of this heterogeneous group of the gifted are not readily available.

The cases of George and Ignatius illustrate differences among children of the same age and IQ. There are countless other combinations. Allen, for example, scores higher on intelligence tests than did George or Ignatius. Yet he shows a very different profile. He is an underachieving gifted child who, from his performance, would not be classified as gifted.

Below are his test scores in the fifth grade, which are also represented by a profile in Figure 9.

Chronological age	10–6
Height age	10–2
Weight age	9–10
Motor coordination age	10–0
Mental age	14–7 (IQ 140)
Social maturity age	10–5
Speech development age	12–2
Language age	13–4
Reading age	10–1
Arithmetic reasoning age	10–3
Arithmetic computation age	9–4
Spelling age	9–4
General information	11–2
Mobility	average for age
Vision	normal
Hearing	normal
Interpersonal relations	below average

The scores on examinations as represented in Figure 9 show a boy of high abstract intelligence, accelerated language and speech development, but average physical, social, and educational characteristics for his age. His basic disability is in the area of personality as represented in his below average interpersonal relations. He does not seem to get along well with the other children, is not accepted by them, and resents authority and assignments by teachers. He utilizes his intelligence with his peer group by using vocabulary they do not understand and by arguing with them on various issues. He devotes much of his time to being a nonconformist at home and in school. This boy is considered an underachieving gifted child whose personality problems, anxieties, and attitudes are retarding his performance. His educational program will necessarily be different from the educational programs of George and Ignatius if he is to attain achievement more in harmony with his potentiality.

Characteristics of Intellectually Gifted Children

Gifted children have been the object of interest of numerous investigators. Many of the studies on the characteristics of gifted children, however, are short-term ones and tend to confirm the results of a longitudinal

FIGURE 9

Profile of an Underachieving Gifted Child

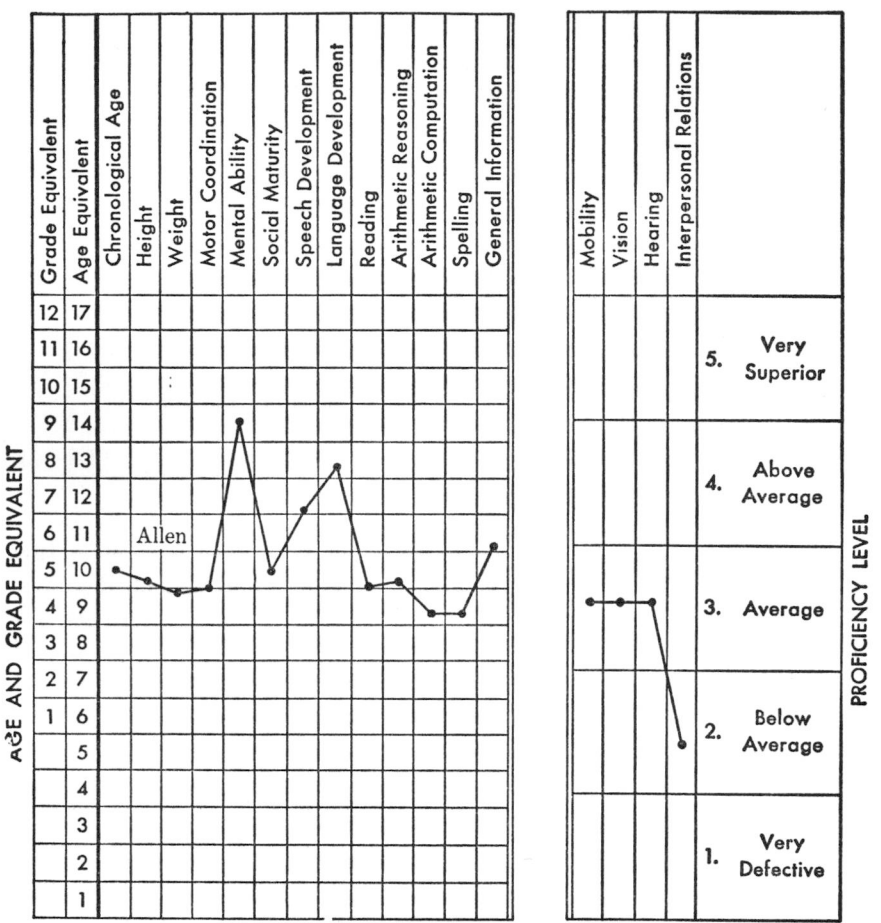

study over a period of a third of a century by Lewis Terman. Since Terman's research is considered the *magnum opus* of all studies of the gifted it is reviewed first.

The Terman Studies

Following his revision and publication of the Binet-Simon tests of intelligence in 1916, Lewis A. Terman, a distinguished professor of psychology at Stanford University, became interested in gifted children. He devoted the rest of his life to the study of 1528 gifted children whom he had identified in 1920, following this group for thirty-five years, until his death in 1956. During this period he was instrumental in writing a series of five books entitled *Genetic Studies of Genius.*[27]

Terman's search for gifted children was conducted in the public schools of California. Teacher nominations and group intelligence tests were used as screening procedures. The final selection of most subjects was based on an IQ of 140 and above on the 1916 Stanford-Binet Individual Intelligence Scale. Terman estimated that this method identified 90 per cent of the eligible students. The average IQ for the more than a thousand children selected by the Binet test was 151. The remainder, who were selected on the basis of the Terman Group Test of Mental Abilities, had an average group IQ score of 142.6. For the total group of 1528 gifted children, the ratio of boys to girls was 116 to 100. Terman believed that this difference was due to a greater variability in intelligence in males.

Among the subjects there were 100 per cent more Jewish children than in the general population, 25 per cent more children of native-born parents, and a slight excess of Scottish children. On the other hand, there were fewer Italian, Portuguese, Mexican, and Negro children than in the general population.

These gifted children came from homes which were notably in the higher socioeconomic levels. Their parents averaged four to five years' more schooling than the average for the United States, and the median family income was more than twice the California average. There was a low incidence of broken homes. It may be that some of the differences Terman found between the gifted group and the control group were due to their superior homes as much as to their high intelligence.

Physical Characteristics. In physique and general health the high-IQ children surpassed the best standards for general American children. At birth they averaged three quarters of a pound heavier than average. Height and strength were also superior. They learned to walk a month earlier than average and talked three and a half months earlier. As children they slept significantly more than the controls. Each child was given a complete medical examination, and the doctors' reports showed that the incidence of sensory defects, dental caries, poor posture, malnutrition, and so forth, was below that usually reported by school doctors in the best medical surveys of school populations in the United States. This physical superiority of the gifted has been maintained throughout the years. At the average age of 44 their mortality rate was four-fifths that of the general population.

Intellectual and Educational Characteristics. The intellectual supe-

[27] Lewis M. Terman, ed., *Genetic Studies of Genius* (Stanford, Calif.: Stanford University Press, 1925–1959), Vols. I–V.

riority of Terman's subjects was established when they were children. In 1940 they were retested on a difficult adult intelligence test to determine whether superiority of intelligence had been maintained. At this time no subject had regressed to the intelligence level of the average adult and no more than 10 per cent were below the 85 percentile rank. Terman concluded that the group as a whole remained intellectually superior, although some bright children did not maintain their degree of superiority. As a rule, he says, the bright child remains bright.

While the gifted children entered school at the usual age (6¼ years) nearly one-half learned to read before the age of 6. Concerning their academic advancement during their school years, Terman stated, "It is a conservative estimate that more than half . . . had already mastered the school curriculum to a point two full grades beyond the one in which they were enrolled, and some of them as much as three or four grades beyond."[28] These children tended to be advanced in all areas of schoolwork, showing no more variation among subjects than unselected children.

The rates of college attendance (90 per cent for men and 86 per cent for women) and graduation (70 per cent for men and 67 per cent for women) were eight times those of the general population in California. Although they were graduated a year younger than the average, they participated in extracurricular activities to a greater than average extent. Surprisingly, 8 per cent of the men and 2 per cent of the women "flunked" out of college (although half of these re-entered and graduated).

Interests and Preoccupations. In scholastic areas the gifted children were more interested than the controls in abstract subjects such as literature, debate, and ancient history, and less interested in "practical" subjects such as penmanship and manual training. Gifted and controls were equally interested in games and sports.

The gifted appear less "sociable" in their interests. They show a stronger liking for playing with just *one* other person than do controls. On a scale of sociability of play interest, almost half of the gifted fall in the lowest quartile of control-group scores.

Character Tests and Trait Ratings. A battery of seven character tests showed gifted children above average on every rating. They were less prone to make overstatements and to cheat. Their book and character preferences were judged more wholesome and mature, and they scored above average on an emotional stability test. On all seven tests taken together, 86 per cent of the gifted boys and 84 per cent of the girls scored above the mean for the control groups.

[28] Lewis M. Terman and Melita H. Oden, eds., *The Gifted Child Grows Up*, Genetic Studies of Genius, Vol. IV (Stanford, Calif.: Stanford University Press, 1947), p. 28,

Two facts stand out in the study of character tests and trait ratings for gifted children: (1) Desirable traits tend to be positively correlated with each other, and (2) the upward deviation is not the same in all traits, that is, gifted children are more outstanding in some traits than in others.

Mental Health and General Adjustment. In 1945, more than twenty years after the study began, the subjects were followed up. One of the areas investigated was mental health and adjustment. At this time approximately 80 per cent showed "satisfactory adjustment," about 15 per cent had "some maladjustment," and 5 per cent had "serious maladjustment." This rate is slightly lower than the national expectancy for serious maladjustment. The delinquency rate was far below that of the general population. Alcoholism was found in 1.5 per cent of the men and .9 per cent of the women. Terman concluded that the superior emotional adjustment seen in childhood was maintained in adulthood.

Marriage, Divorce, Fertility. The marriage rate for the gifted group as adults is about the same as that for the general population (84 per cent) and higher than is found for college graduates. The divorce rate to 1955 is somewhat less than that for the general population.

A total of 1525 offspring of the gifted group have been tested. The mean IQ is 132.7. About one-third test above 140 and only 2 per cent below 100.

In general, the gifted group tends slightly toward more and happier marriages, fewer divorces, and fewer offspring. However, it is still too soon for these trends to be definite.

Vocational and Occupational Status. The occupational status of the gifted men reported in 1955 shows about eight times as many men in the professions as is true for the general population. About 80 per cent of gifted men are in the two highest occupational groups — Group I, the professional, and Group II, semiprofessional and higher business. In the entire population only 14 per cent are found in these two groups. The incomes for the gifted group are considerably higher than the national average. The most successful gifted men were compared with the least successful gifted and many striking differences were found. Terman states, "Everything considered, there is nothing in which the A [most successful] and C [least successful] groups present a greater contrast than in drive to achieve and in all-round social adjustment."[29] Success for the gifted was associated with well-balanced temperament and freedom from excessive frustration.

[29] Lewis M. Terman and Melita Oden, "The Stanford Studies of the Gifted," *The Gifted Child*, Paul Witty, ed., American Association for Gifted Children (Boston: D. C. Heath and Company, 1951), p. 37.

The Stanford *Genetic Studies of Genius,* under the direction of Lewis Madison Terman, stand out as one of the monolithic investigations of one kind of exceptional children, thus far unsurpassed by any other study in the field. They will remain as a monument to their brilliant author, who has contributed so much to our knowledge of intelligence.

Other Research on Characteristics of Gifted Children

Racial and Ethnic Differences. Intellectual giftedness is no respecter of color, race, or creed. It is found in every class and culture. The fact that some groups seem to have a higher proportion of gifted individuals than do others may well be the result of the kinds of intelligence tests and other means of identification used. And again, though according to some studies[30] there are proportionately fewer gifted identified among Negroes than among Caucasians, this finding may be due to limited or subnormal educational and cultural environments. The same thing is probably true of other minority groups. A notable exception is to be observed in the very high rate of giftedness found among Jews. Strodtbeck suggests a possible relationship between the upward mobility or high achievement of Jewish groups and a belief that man can master and control his environment.[31] The Italian families, in contrast to the Jewish families, were more inclined to feel themselves under the domination of fate or destiny. We may conclude that some racial and ethnic groups do tend to produce disproportionate numbers of gifted children, but quite probably because of cultural and value-system differences rather than because of any inherent differences in intelligence level.

Peer Acceptance of Gifted Children. The myth that many or most gifted children are social misfits and rejected by their classmates has been thoroughly disproved. Yet it persists because people tend to note and then remember the occasional maladjusted bright person they have known. Terman has shown the superior social and emotional traits of the gifted,[32] as discussed earlier. Miller found that gifted children were significantly more popular than average or retarded pupils.[33] Kerstetter studied a group of highly gifted children (IQ 160 and above) in special

[30] W. B. Barbe, "A Study of the Family Background of the Gifted," *Journal of Educational Psychology,* No. 47 (May, 1956), pp. 302–309. Terman and Oden, *The Gifted Child Grows Up.*

[31] F. L. Strodtbeck, "Family Interaction, Values, and Achievement," *Talent and Society; New Perspectives in the Identification of Talent,* David C. McClelland, ed. (Princeton, N.J.: D. Van Nostrand Company, 1958).

[32] Terman and Oden, *The Gifted Child Grows Up.*

[33] Robert V. Miller, "Social Status and Socio-empathic Differences Among Mentally Superior, Mentally Typical, and Mentally Retarded Children," *Exceptional Children,* 23 (December, 1956), 114–119.

classes and found them, on the whole, socially well adjusted.[34] She saw no relationship between level of intelligence and poor social adjustment.

Gallagher[35] and Martyn[36] both found that the gifted rated as high as or higher than the average in popularity. Gallagher[37] concluded that gifted children were better able than average children to predict who would choose them for friends. This social perceptiveness or socioempathy might account for the above average popularity of the gifted group.

The evidence is clear that the gifted are accepted by their classmates, but several questions are as yet unanswered. The degree of acceptance may vary with the community (many of the studies were done in communities of a high educational level such as Palo Alto, California, and Champaign-Urbana, Illinois). The level of giftedness may also affect popularity, as the suggestion is often made that the very highly gifted (IQ above 165 or 170) may have more social adjustment problems than the less gifted, who numerically constitute the majority of subjects in the studies. The type of program — for example, special class versus enrichment — may have a bearing on popularity with peers. Grade level may prove important, as there are some reasons to believe that elementary children are more warmly disposed toward the gifted than are high school students. Even though these factors and others do influence the social status of the gifted, we may be sure that the gifted are socially accepted by their peers.

Creativity and Productive Thinking. An aspect of giftedness which is receiving more and more attention and will continue to do so is that of creativity and productive thinking. Getzels and Jackson[38] have utilized tests based on Guilford's[39] theory of the structure of intellect. These tests assess such characteristics as intellectual fluency and flexibility, originality, and foresight. Previous intelligence tests have not measured these kinds of traits. A group of secondary level children were identified as being "high creative" but not "high IQ." When "high IQ" and "high creative" children were compared it was found that both

[34] Leona Kerstetter, "A Sociometric Study of the Classroom Roles of a Group of Highly Gifted Children," unpublished doctoral dissertation, New York University, 1952.

[35] James J. Gallagher, "Peer Acceptance of Highly Gifted Children in Elementary School," *Elementary School Journal,* 58 (May, 1958), 465–470.

[36] Kenneth A. Martyn, "The Social Acceptance of Gifted Students," unpublished doctoral dissertation, Stanford University, 1957.

[37] James J. Gallagher, "Social Status of Children Related to Intelligence, Propinquity, and Social Perception," *Elementary School Journal,* 58 (January, 1958), 225–231.

[38] Getzels and Jackson, *op. cit.*

[39] J. P. Guilford, "The Structure of Intellect," *Psychological Bulletin,* 53 (July, 1956), 267–293.

groups achieved equally well in school. This study has also been done at the elementary level by Torrence[40] with the same findings. Teachers prefer to have the high-IQ student in class rather than the high-creative, as the latter are often very nonconforming. The high-creative children are not as well rated sociometrically, since they may seem "peculiar." Evidence submitted by Smith[41] and Lucito[42] suggests that gifted children in general are more independent and less conforming in behavior than average. It remains to be shown whether this trait is related to degree or type of intelligence.

Many differences between gifted and nongifted children have been pointed out in this and the preceeding section. Are the favorable personality, social, and emotional traits which tend to occur with giftedness a direct result of high intelligence? Bonsall and Stefflre compared gifted and average children on thoughtfulness, general activity, restraint, emotional stability, and other traits and found the usual superiority of the gifted.[43] However, when socioeconomic level was controlled and gifted children were compared only with average children from the same level, these differences disappeared. The implication is strong that many of the differences which have been presented and discussed are actually a result of socioeconomic rather than intellectual factors.

Three Approaches to Educating Gifted Children

Adapting education to gifted children is not an easy task in a system of mass education. The number of such children is small and the group is heterogeneous so that it has been difficult to find a single system to apply to the group as a whole. Some authorities advocate special classes, others recommend acceleration, and still others favor enrichment in the regular grades. Combinations of these are also suggested. Thus controversies concerning the education of the gifted persist from generation to generation.

Acceleration

Acceleration of gifted pupils has been practiced in various forms for

[40] E. P. Torrance, *Explorations in Creative Thinking in the Early School Years, VI, Highly Intelligent and Highly Creative Children in a Laboratory School* (Minneapolis: Bureau of Educational Research, University of Minnesota, 1959).

[41] D. C. Smith, "Inter- and Intra-personal Adjustment of Adolescents Testing at the Superior and Average Levels of Intelligence," unpublished doctoral dissertation, Syracuse University, 1959.

[42] L. J. Lucito, "A Comparison of the Independence-Conformity Behavior of Intellectually Bright and Dull Children," unpublished doctoral dissertation, University of Illinois, 1959.

[43] Marcella Bonsall and B. Stefflre, "The Temperament of Gifted Children," *California Journal of Educational Research*, 6 (1955), 162–165.

many years. It refers to (1) admitting gifted children to kindergarten or first grade according to mental age rather than chronological age, (2) skipping grades, (3) telescoping grades, (4) early admission to secondary schools or colleges, and (5) other methods such as passing courses in high school and college by examination. All of these administrative procedures are designed to cut down the time a person must remain in school.

Early School Admission. Admission to kindergarten or first grade is a matter of law in most states. The age is generally set at 5 years for kindergarten and 6 years for first grade, with a few months leeway for each. In some states the child's sixth birthday must come by December 1 if he is to be eligible for enrollment in the first grade in the preceding September. A child born December 2 would thus have to wait until the following September before he could be admitted; he would be 6 years and 9 months old when he entered Grade 1.

Research indicates that early admission to kindergarten or first grade for children who are advanced intellectually has not been detrimental as was frequently believed. Hobson reported a follow-up of pupils admitted to kindergarten on the basis of mental age.[44] He found that the younger children (the brightest) made the best records in school through the eighth grade and after. They were superior in academic achievement to their older classmates and were also superior in honors received in extracurricular activities and in their success in being admitted to college. Worcester summarized a series of studies of children who were admitted early to kindergarten.[45] He stated that although these children averaged eight months younger than the others, there was no difference in physical development and they did as well or better than their older classmates in academic achievement, in social and emotional adjustment, and in acceptance by their peers. Birch also found that gifted children admitted to first grade before the age of 6 were superior later as rated by teachers and administration.[46]

Skipping Grades. This form of acceleration refers to completely eliminating one grade or one semester in school. Contrary to current belief, and as evidenced by the Terman study and others already cited,

[44] James R. Hobson, "Mental Age as a Workable Criterion for School Admission," *Elementary School Journal,* 48 (February, 1948), 312–321; James R. Hobson, "Scholastic Standing and Activity Participation of Underage High School Pupils Originally Admitted to Kindergarten on the Basis of Physical and Psychological Examinations," *Newsletter,* American Psychological Association, Division of School Psychologists, September, 1956.

[45] D. A. Worcester, *The Education of Children of Above-Average Mentality* (Lincoln: University of Nebraska Press, 1956).

[46] Jack W. Birch, "Early School Admission for Mentally Advanced Children," *Exceptional Children,* 21 (December, 1954), 84–87.

children who have skipped grades have shown social, educational, and vocational adjustment superior or comparable to that of equally intelligent non-accelerates.

Telescoping Grades. Since skipping a grade sometimes leaves a gap in a child's experiences, some school systems have established programs which enable a child to cover the same material as is offered in the regular curriculum but in a shorter period. The ungraded primary program is a good example. In this program children may progress through the first three grades as rapidly as they are able. Some may finish in two years, some take four, and a few even finish three grades in one year. Occasionally seventh and eighth grades are combined in order to accelerate a group of capable students at that level.

Another type of telescoping is sometimes done on an individual basis in high school. By carrying extra courses each term certain students go through high school in three years instead of four.

Early College Admission. By early admission to first grade, skipping grades, or telescoping grade levels, some children are ready to enter college younger. In summarizing the studies on this topic Pressey pointed out[47] that since 1888, when President Eliot of Harvard called for early admission to college, statistics have shown that those who enter college at a younger age (presumably the gifted) are generally superior to the others both in studies and in conduct. "The evidence was practically unanimous that younger entrants were most likely to graduate, had the best academic records, won the most honors, and presented the fewest disciplinary difficulties. The evidence is also that the younger entrants are highest in ability."[48] Pressey also remarked that "Academic programs appear to be paced for the average student, with the consequence that their superiors can readily and often desirably move faster. However, educational convention puts a premium on the educational lock step. Greater flexibility of programs and better guidance should then save time for both students and instructors, with even less handicap for the abler younger persons."[49]

Terman and Oden divided their group of gifted children into accelerates (those graduating from high school before the age of 16 years, 6 months) and non-accelerates (those graduating after age 16 years, 6 months).[50] The accelerates were graduated on the average at age 15.9, while the non-accelerates had a mean age of 17.4 at the time of gradua-

[47] S. L. Pressey, *Educational Acceleration; Appraisal and Basic Problems,* Educational Research Monographs, No. 31 (Columbus: Bureau of Educational Research, Ohio State University, 1949).

[48] *Ibid.*, p. 7.

[49] *Ibid.*, p. 91.

[50] Terman and Oden, *The Gifted Child Grows Up.*

tion. These groups were evaluated twenty-five years after the first testing to determine the possible effects of acceleration. Terman concluded: (1) There was little difference between the groups in intelligence; (2) the accelerates did better in college and graduate work; (3) ratings of occupational success favored the accelerates; and (4) the criticism of acceleration as causing social maladjustment is "greatly exaggerated," since there was no difference in this factor between the two groups.

The Fund for the Advancement of Education provided 1000 scholarships for high school students to attend college.[51] The recipients were below the age of 16.5 years, and the majority had not completed high school. They were selected for the scholarships on the basis of tests of intelligence and achievement and ratings on social and emotional maturity. They were then compared with a group who were two years older on admission, had completed high school, and scored equally with the "scholars" on various measures of scholastic aptitude. The findings of this program indicated that (1) the colleges and parents considered the program of early admission successful; (2) the "scholars" had greater difficulty than the comparison group in adjusting initially, but the problems were resolved; (3) the scholastic record of the younger group was better than that of the older group, and (4) a larger proportion of the "scholars" went to graduate school.

The major objection to acceleration of students, whether by early admission, skipping, or telescoping, has been a fear that acceleration displaces the child from his social and emotional peers and thus affects his subsequent social adjustment. This concern has persisted in spite of the evidence that no serious detriment to social and emotional adjustment results from acceleration. The studies submitting such evidence, however, have dealt primarily with acceleration of one or two years. There is little information on the effects of acceleration of four or five years.

Research studies frequently draw conclusions and inferences for a group as a whole. In the case of gifted children, however, no conclusions can apply to all. In a school situation decisions on acceleration have to be made for each individual separately. Deciding on the procedure for the adaptation of instruction for a gifted child should not depend upon the fact of his giftedness alone. It must take into account (1) his deviation from the class in which he is placed and (2) the discrepancies in growth patterns within himself.

The growth pattern of George shown in Figure 8 depicts a boy who is physically, socially, mentally, and educationally accelerated above his chronological age and grade placement. This boy could probably be accelerated one to two years without untoward effects. The profile shows

[51] Fund for the Advancement of Education, *They Went to College Early* (New York: The Fund, 1957).

that he is physically and socially more like 11- and 12-year-old children than like the 10-year-old group in which he is placed. He also is able to achieve adequately at the seventh-grade level. Placing him in the sixth or seventh grade would not be detrimental to his development.

But Ignatius, who is of the same age and IQ as George, shows a different growth pattern. Physically and socially he is more like 10-year-old children, even though in academic achievement he also rates at the sixth- and seventh-grade level. Advancing Ignatius to the sixth or seventh grade would displace him physically and socially, even though his academic achievement is high. Retaining him in the regular grades with children who achieve at a lower level academically is also a displacement. In other words, neither acceleration nor retention in the regular grades is necessarily the answer for Ignatius. Some other solution must be found, perhaps in keeping the child with his age group but providing him with other activities such as interest clubs with children of his intellectual ability and academic achievement or special classes for children who show this kind of discrepancy.

From the arguments for and against acceleration it would appear that those in favor of acceleration are thinking primarily of the Georges in Figure 8 while those against it focus primarily on the Ignatiuses. Therefore we cannot say that acceleration is either good or bad, for in some cases it is beneficial and in others it is detrimental. The research in the field is not clear-cut, since the studies have combined subjects such as the Georges, the Ignatiuses, and all the other gifted children regardless of their specific characteristics.

Enrichment

If gifted children are not to be accelerated, how can the schools offer them a challenging program with other children of their own age? To some the answer is enrichment of the curriculum for the gifted child. The term "enrichment" has been applied to an adaptation of the regular program to provide educational experiences over and above those in the regular program. Gallagher has defined enrichment as "the type of activity devoted to the further development of the particular intellectual skills and talents of the gifted child."[52] He includes in these skills the ability to (1) associate and interrelate concepts, (2) evaluate facts and arguments critically, (3) create new ideas and originate new lines of thought, (4) reason through complex problems, and (5) understand other situations, other times, and other people.

Administratively, such enrichment has been tried through various procedures which include:

[52] Gallagher, *The Gifted Child in the Elementary School*, p. 21.

1. Encouraging teachers in the regular grades to challenge the gifted child with additional readings, extra assignments, and an opportunity to participate in other than class activities.
2. Grouping children in a class, so that the few gifted children are in a group by themselves, and challenging their interests and abilities with problems requiring independent research and thought, rather than memory processes.
3. Offering additional learnings such as the study of a foreign language or typewriting in the elementary school.
4. Employing a special teacher for the gifted in a school system. His duties would be (a) to identify the gifted children who need additional stimulation and instruction, (b) to assist the regular teacher to secure additional materials of instruction and suggest additional assignments and experiences, (c) to counsel with the gifted child regarding his extracurricular activities and supplementary school assignments, and (d) to hold seminars or special classes for a part of the day in special areas of interest for the gifted children in the school.
5. Encouraging teachers to hold high standards of achievement for the gifted child, and to help him develop habits of independent work, initiative, and creativity.

Although enrichment of a program may be a factor in acceleration, and certainly is a major reason for special schools and classes, the term as commonly used has applied primarily to enrichment of the curriculum for the gifted child in the regular grades. Enrichment has been a very popular byword in schools since many feel that the gifted child should remain in a heterogeneous class. This practice will (1) give the child better opportunities for developing leadership, (2) allow him to remain with children of his own age, which is especially valuable for a child who is uneven in development, (3) make every teacher a teacher of the gifted, thus elevating the quality of instruction for all children, and (4) minimize the financial requirements since enrichment in the regular elementary grades does not necessarily add to the expense of running a school.

The program of enrichment in the elementary grades is easier to state than to execute. Teachers generally do not have the time or in some cases the knowledge and skills to provide all the enriched experiences a gifted child needs. With thirty to forty children in a class, the teacher must utilize his time in group instruction for the majority of children. With rare exceptions, enrichment in the regular grades is at the most only partial enrichment.

Special Grouping for Gifted Children — Special Schools and Classes

To adapt and enrich the curriculum for gifted children in the regular school, various forms of grouping have been used. These include (1) grouping the children within a regular class in the elementary school, (2) organizing special sections in the subject matters (e.g., English, science, mathematics, and social studies) in the upper elementary school and in the secondary school, (3) offering advanced courses for superior students in secondary schools, and (4) offering honors courses for superior students in college.

The groupings mentioned above are rather generally accepted; more controversial is the establishment of special schools for gifted children, or self-contained special classes within the regular schools. Three forms of such organization have been used: (1) modified special classes, (2) special classes, and (3) special schools.

Modified Special Classes. In this first grouping the gifted child remains in the regular grades with his peer group but has special instruction for a part of the day with other gifted children. The Colfax Plan[53] in Pittsburgh, Pennsylvania, exemplifies the use of a modified special class. In this large school gifted children are identified in the kindergarten and assigned to a first grade with regular children. This is their home room. For half a day, however, they attend a special class with other gifted children, a workshop for special instruction.

Special Classes. The segregation of gifted children into special classes is practiced in a few city school systems. The children are grouped in grades and progress from one grade to another in a curriculum adapted to their interests, curiosity, and ability. An example of such classes is found in the Major Work Classes in Cleveland, Ohio, which have been in operation as a part of the Cleveland public school system since 1921. They admit children with IQ's of 125 and above. The purpose of these classes in the elementary school is to enrich the program of the grade but not to accelerate. Graduation from the elementary school is at the same age the other children graduate. Here the children learn with gifted children but participate with other children in school activities such as safety patrol, physical education, and other general school programs.

Special Schools. There are few special schools for elementary-school-age gifted children. The Hunter College Elementary School is a special school admitting only gifted children, ages 3 to 11, who are grouped

[53] H. Pregler, "The Colfax Plan," *Exceptional Children,* 20 (September, 1954), 198–201, 222.

by chronological age. In this school children work independently but participate in unit topics and study themes. In addition to special schools there are neighborhoods in which the majority of children in the school are gifted. These constitute a natural homogeneous group of superior children. In some such schools and classes, as in the specially selected class or school, the average IQ is 120 or 125. At the secondary school level, there are a number of schools devoted entirely to the education of superior students. In New York City, for example, the Bronx High School of Science, the Stuyvesant High School, and the High School of Music and Art offer programs emphasizing specialized curriculums for students selected on the basis of ability and interest. At the college level there are some schools with very high selection standards, admitting only those students of superior aptitudes and superior grades.

Evaluation of Special Groupings. The special class or special school for gifted children at the elementary level is not accepted by many school systems. As a matter of fact there has been considerable resistance to it. Havighurst has described the divergent attitudes of two superintendents toward the establishment of special classes for the gifted.[54] One, in a large city, seemed to be very pleased with his organization of classes for the gifted. He had no community opposition and quite a bit of community support. The other, in a smaller community of 20,000, stated that the needs of the gifted children were met without a special program by spending as much money per child on all the children as some communities do on special programs for gifted children. This superintendent felt that the community would not support classes for gifted children and that the way to educate these children was to improve the over-all educational program with better teachers, smaller classes, and expanded facilities. Thus, the type of community and the organization of the school has something to do with the choice between educating gifted children in regular grades or in special classes.

Another reason for resistance to the organization of special classes is the lack of clear-cut experimental evidence that the special class program produces better results than acceleration or enrichment in the regular grades. Sumption evaluated the Major Work Classes in Cleveland with a follow-up questionnaire by means of which he compared three groups, (1) one group with similar IQ's in Cleveland who did not attend the Major Work Classes, (2) one group who attended up to three years, and (3) one group who attended from four to twelve years.[55] In

[54] Robert Havighurst, in *Education for the Gifted, Fifty-seventh Yearbook of the National Society for the Study of Education*, Part II (Chicago: University of Chicago Press, 1958), p. 386.

[55] M. R. Sumption, *Three Hundred Gifted Children* (Yonkers-on-Hudson, N.Y.: World Book Company, 1941).

comparing these groups, Sumption found little difference in physical and mental health or in attitudes toward home or family. The Major Work group did exceed the others in participation in leisure-time activities, in reading, in leadership, and in self-expressive abilities.

Barbe also made a follow-up study of the Cleveland program by means of a questionnaire to those who were graduated between 1938 and 1952.[56] The majority of respondents approved of the Major Work Classes. Only 8 per cent disapproved. In this study the factors listed as best liked were the opportunity to express themselves, the enrichment procedures, and freedom from regimentation. Least liked were the attitudes of other students and teachers and the lack of social contact with other pupils. The girls liked the foreign-language program, while the boys listed foreign language as the least liked.

During the years 1957–1961, the legislature of California appropriated funds for the purpose of studying the effects of special education (acceleration, special classes, and enrichment) on the progress of gifted children.[57] A total of 929 children in elementary and secondary schools, with IQ's of 130 and above, were selected, and educational programs were designed for them. Control groups, without these special provisions, were also established. The results showed marked superiority in academic achievement of the children in the special programs. Although both the control and the experimental groups made notable progress in reading and arithmetic in the first grade, the experimental group made higher gains than the control group.

One surprising finding was the ability indicated on the Graduate Record Examination in social studies, humanities, and natural science. A comparison of both the experimental and the control groups with the scores of college graduates showed that these high school seniors scored higher than the college graduates. Again the experimental group was higher than the control group. The California study has indicated that all special provisions — special classes, acceleration, enrichment — produce results with gifted children.

Adaptations and Recommendations at the Secondary Level

In the preceding sections acceleration, enrichment, and special groups have been discussed as organizational methods by which programs for gifted children can be implemented, especially at the elementary school level. The same basic approaches are found in various combinations in programs at the secondary level. It may be helpful to think of these

[56] W. B. Barbe, "Evaluation of Special Classes for Gifted Children," *Exceptional Children*, 22 (November, 1955), 60–62.

[57] Ruth Martinson. *Educational Programs for Gifted Children* (Sacramento: California State Department of Public Instruction, January, 1961).

approaches to educating the gifted as attempts to provide more content, either in a homogeneous or in a heterogeneous setting (special grouping, enrichment), or to provide for faster coverage (acceleration in any form).

One of the major differences between programs for the gifted at the elementary and secondary levels results from a difference in the organization of curriculums. The child in elementary school attends a self-contained class, generally with one teacher handling all of the subjects. The secondary school does not have self-contained classes and in general allows a more flexible scheduling of students to classes according to their abilities and interests.

Adaptations. The comprehensive high school has been designed to offer a wide variety of educational experiences. In the larger high schools different sections of mathematics, science, and English can be adapted to the abilities and interests of the children. Sections in the various subjects can be made up of slow, average, and bright students. In addition, not all enrollees in the high school need take the same sequences of courses.

Many other adaptations have been initiated. Some of them are listed below:

1. Increase in counseling and guidance activities. This program was recently given added impetus by the provisions of the National Defense Education Act.
2. Offering extracurricular activities — school publications, science clubs, hobby clubs, student government, and so forth.
3. Organization of advanced classes in science, mathematics, English and social studies with emphasis on ideas, concepts, and relationships rather than memory. This is sometimes called an "honors program"; it admits only those superior students who have achieved beyond the minimum requirements.
4. Allowing gifted students to take extra courses each semester to accelerate their graduation from high school.
5. Allowing students to enroll in nearby colleges and universities for courses more advanced than the high school can offer.
6. Allowing students to obtain advanced credit by examination or to enroll in correspondence and television programs for credit by examination.
7. Revision of the sequence and contents of courses in science, mathematics, language arts, social studies, and languages. Such revisions are being made by committees sponsored by professional associations and governmental agencies. An example is the Physical Science Study Committee organized in 1956 at the Massachusetts Institute of Tech-

nology. Composed of university professors, technical specialists, and high school teachers, it has been engaged in revamping a physics curriculum for secondary schools. Similar committees are at work in other subject areas.

Dr. Conant's Recommendations. Recently, Dr. James B. Conant made a study of the American high school and gave some recommendations for provisions which will be of benefit to superior students.[58] These are some of his recommendations:

1. An expanded counseling system where every student will be counseled more intensively than has been true in the past. Dr. Conant recommends one counselor for 250 to 300 high school pupils.
2. An individualized program, based on the abilities and disabilities of the student. Students should not be placed in one category and remain in a fixed curriculum such as "college preparatory" or "vocational" for the rest of their high school careers. Even within these categories there should be variation and option to fit the individual interests and abilities of the students.
3. Groupings according to ability, subject by subject, not curriculum by curriculum. In the courses there should be three types of classes, one for the very able, another for the large group with average intelligence, and a third for the slow students.
4. Four years of mathematics, four years of one foreign language, three years of science, four years of English, and three years of social studies for the able students. Conant urges even extra courses for the more able.
5. A special course of advanced study in special subjects in the high school if there are enough highly gifted students to take it; if not, a special guidance officer or counselor to act as a tutor and keep in close touch with the work of these few students.
6. Summer school for the bright and ambitious student who wishes to progress at a more rapid rate.
7. Heterogeneous grouping in home rooms in order to avoid complete segregation of the gifted. In the home rooms all levels of ability are to be included. These are the social units of the school and deal primarily with the social program and community interests.
8. Organization of the school day into seven or eight periods rather than the six periods commonly employed. This provides the gifted student much more flexibility in electing a wide range of academic subjects.

[58] James Bryant Conant, *The American High School Today* (New York: McGraw-Hill Book Company, 1959).

Educating Special Groups of Gifted Children

It has been repeatedly emphasized that gifted children are not a homogeneous group, and that one or two patterns of education will not be suitable to all of them. There are three types of deviating gifted children who will require special attention over and above the provisions which are being made for gifted children in general. These are (1) the underachieving gifted child, (2) the highly gifted child, and (3) the gifted child with a handicap.

The Underachieving Gifted Child

Some children with high intellectual ability do not achieve. Some are actually failures in school. This fact indicates that it takes more than intelligence to succeed in school as well as in life.

Studies of underachieving gifted children have been made by various investigators. Gowan has summarized these studies and has concluded that the following factors are related to underachievement.[59]

1. Lack of clearness and definiteness of academic and occupational choice.
2. Weak ego controls.
3. Withdrawal and self-sufficiency.
4. Poor uses of time and money.
5. Neurotic tendencies.
6. Authoritarianism in the parental home or the individual himself.
7. Dominant, autocratic, or laissez-faire parents.
8. No goals or impossible demands by parents.
9. Lack of maturity and irresponsibility.
10. Disinterest in other people.
11. Lack of dominance, persuasiveness, and self-confidence.
12. Apathetic and withdrawing view of life.

Gowan speculates that the gifted underachiever is "a kind of intellectual delinquent who withdraws from goals, activities, and active social participation generally. As a child his initial attempts at creative accomplishment may not have been seen by others as 'worthwhile' but only as 'queer' or 'different.'"[60] Gowan believes that this blocking of rewards for deviant achievement has blunted his work drives and stifled his creativity.

[59] John Curtis Gowan, "Dynamics of the Underachievement of Gifted Students," *Exceptional Children*, 24 (November, 1957), 98–101.
[60] *Ibid.*, p. 101.

Gallagher, after surveying the literature concerning underachievers, presents a combination of events which leads to underachievement among children of superior intelligence.

1. The underachieving child grows up in, or belongs to, a cultural group which does not value education, independence, or individual achievement.

2. He has poor parental relationships, in which the parents, especially the father, either show limited interest in academic matters or try to put undue pressure on their children to succeed.

3. The child, unable to obtain satisfaction from parental contacts, seeks out his peer group for satisfying human relationships. Since he searches for others of the same interests as himself he will often find himself allied with other rebellious and angry children.

4. These children will be faced by teachers and other school officials who ask them to meet standards of behavior which are not possible for them, and who treat these children, in many ways, as their parents do. The children thus place the teacher and the school in the same authority category as parents and reject them and their program.

5. The school, in its attempt to deal with these nonconforming and angry children, is likely to take more strict and repressive measures which will turn the children even more emphatically against the school.[61]

This would suggest that the causes of underachievement are outside of the school. The question is: What can the school do to compensate for these out-of-school factors? Numerous suggestions have been made, but few have provided adequate answers.

It would appear that if schools are going to help underachieving bright children a more drastic shift in emphasis will have to be made. This may include:

1. Identifying underachieving gifted children during the early years in school.
2. Assigning tutors to be supportive and to motivate the children through success in academic achievement. This can be done more readily on a one-to-one basis than in a classroom situation.
3. Counseling with the parents concerning the problems of the child and attempting to produce better home relations.
4. Rewarding the child by praise and recognition in school for efforts and achievement in academic work.
5. Organizing small special classes for the underachieving gifted children with special teachers, preferably male if the predominance of such children are mostly boys.

[61] Gallagher, *Analysis of Research on the Education of Gifted Children*, pp. 42–43.

Highly Gifted Children

Children with IQ's of 170 and above are, of course, extremely rare. DeHaan and Havighurst state that there are about one in a thousand who have IQ's of 160 and above.[62] Hollingworth estimated that one in a million have IQ's above 180.[63]

Since most of the studies on the gifted have considered children with IQ's of 130 to 160 there is a question as to whether having an IQ above 170 creates *qualitative* rather than just *quantitative* differences. Because so few children are found with these extreme IQ's, not a sufficient number have been studied for us to understand them. Hollingworth studied twelve children whose IQ's were 180 and above.[64] The early physical development of this group was not unusual. Walking and teething were at average ages. The big difference showed up in the verbal area. They talked somewhat earlier than usual and in reading they showed extreme precocity, learning to read on the average at 3 years of age (only one as late as 4.5 years). On the whole these children were very acceleratd in school but presented difficult educational problems. When these problems were identified early and adequately handled through sound educational guidance and fostering of development, the children became well articulated to school and to society. The cases of clearest adjustment came when the exceptional child attended classes with others approximately of his kind. Hollingworth felt that the problems in personality development and social adjustment were an outgrowth of the deviation between the child's intellectual development and his relative immaturity in other areas.

Terman and Oden compared eighty-one children with IQ's of 170 and above with the rest of the gifted children in the Stanford studies.[65] Like Hollingworth's findings, this study noted achievement in reading at the age of 3, 4, or 5 and marked acceleration in elementary school. Although many of these subjects received high grades in college, 25 per cent received only fair or poor grades. Furthermore, those with the highest IQ's did not receive the highest ratings in social adjustment. They were poor mixers and tended to participate in solitary activities. Two-thirds of the women with IQ's of 170 and above were office workers or housewives.

It is rather apparent from the few studies available that the child with an extremely high IQ may have a more difficult time making personal and social adjustments than one with an IQ between 130 and 150 unless

---

[62] DeHaan and Havighurst, *op. cit.*, p. 229.
[63] Hollingworth, *op. cit.*
[64] *Ibid.*
[65] Terman and Oden, *The Gifted Child Grows Up.*

he is given special attention by his parents and teachers. A variety of reasons may be postulated for this difficulty, including the effects of ignorant or thoughtless adults, rejection by peers who may think him peculiar, and divergence from the rest of society in his value system. But the difficulties in adjustment can most easily be explained by internal discrepancies in growth. The child's intellectual abilities are growing nearly twice as fast as is usual, and it is too much to expect physical and emotional processes to keep pace with such rapid development. With this irregular development, the child is going to be out of place in any group of average children. If he is placed according to his intellectual level he will be out of line physically, socially, and/or emotionally. If he is placed with his age peers he will be out of line intellectually. Furthermore, the greatest deviation occurs at a time when he is least able to understand and handle it, that is, during the early school years. At 5 a child with an IQ of 160 has a deviation of three years between his 8-year mental ability and that of his age peers. A 5-year-old child finds it physically and emotionally difficult to compete with 8-year-olds, yet a child with third-grade abilities would be equally out of place living and working with 5-year-olds. At the age of about 20 the young person begins to catch up with himself, since he has reached physical and social maturity and is probably associating with others more nearly like himself.

The educational procedures used with this type of child are undoubtedly of supreme importance. It will be recalled that Hollingworth found the best adjustment among children who had been included in experimental groups for gifted children. Many of our outstanding men of history have not had to face the problem of adjusting to average children in school because they were tutored at home. Some of Hollingworth's subjects were also tutored. There are other cases of successful individuals who received tutoring during their earlier years either in conjunction with formalized schooling or without it until they were ready for high school or the university. DeHaan and Havighurst have recommended giving the extremely gifted child two groups to deal with — one group not more than a year or two older with whom he can play and associate outside of school and another group closer to his mental age for intellectual pursuits.[66] It may be that for the extremely gifted child tutoring is essential unless there is available a class of high-level gifted children with whom he can have enough in common to stimulate his social, emotional, and educational development. Another possibility is half-day placement in school for physical education, art, and some aspects of school life, and tutoring at home for the rest of the day in academic pursuits.

[66] DeHaan and Havighurst, *op. cit.*, p. 241.

The Gifted Child with a Handicap

The fact that gifted children as a group are superior in physique and health does not mean that all gifted children are healthy, have perfect eyesight and hearing, and are good athletes. The purpose of this section is to point out that there are intellectually gifted among the handicapped.

Helen Keller was both deaf and blind, and had it not been for her superior intelligence and excellent tutelage, she could not have succeeded in scholarly endeavors. Franklin D. Roosevelt was crippled with poliomyelitis. The great physicist Steinmetz was orthopedically handicapped. Beethoven composed music even after he became deaf.

Schools for the physically handicapped and institutions for the emotionally disturbed and for delinquents have within them children who test high on intelligence tests adapted to their handicaps. In general, high intelligence becomes a great asset to a child with a handicap. The education of children with various handicaps will be discussed in later chapters.

General Principles — Administration and Instruction

The educational purpose of studying the development and characteristics of gifted children is to assist us in organizing for their education and devising instructional procedures which will be conducive to more effective development.

Administration

It is obvious that there is no *one* plan for the education of all gifted children. Each gifted child is unique unto himself, and as a group gifted children cannot be organized under a single plan of education. Efforts to properly educate these children by one specific plan, such as acceleration, special classes, or enrichment in the regular grades, are found inadequate in some situations.

A decision on where to place a gifted child, how to organize for his education, and what teaching techniques and materials to use depends largely upon the pattern of development of that particular child and the provisions for all children in the school system. It is therefore necessary that a gifted child be evaluated in terms of his abilities, disabilities, interests, habits, home environment, and community values. The educational program for the child can be better determined on the basis of this evaluation than by setting up an educational program and fitting all gifted children into it.

Some of the adaptations and adjustments which should be taken into consideration are the following:

1. When a child's patterns of growth in physical, social, mental, and educational areas are all accelerated beyond the chronological age, acceleration in grade placement can be considered.

2. When the physical, social, and emotional areas are equal to the chronological age, but the educational achievement is advanced, a special class can be considered.

3. When the school system is too small (not providing sufficient gifted children of a particular kind for a special class), enrichment, tutoring, or special sections within the class for the gifted children in the regular classroom is necessary.

4. When the class in which a gifted child is placed contains a preponderance of children of superior intelligence, even though it is not designated as a class for the gifted, enrichment of the program is probably more desirable than special classes or acceleration, neither of which may be necessary.

5. When the child is gifted but underachieving, special attention to his social and emotional problems or possible areas of weakness is called for. Intensive counseling and parent education or even remedial instruction may be more important for this child than his placement.

6. When inner discrepancies in growth are quite marked, as we often find in children with extremely high IQ's, a tutorial or individualized method of instruction may be necessary if the child is found to be unable to adjust to other situations.

7. When school systems feel that enrichment in the regular grades is the most feasible plan, a special teacher or coordinator for gifted children is advisable. Many feel that it is unrealistic to expect every teacher to furnish enrichment in the regular grades. Teachers need the help of a specialist or consultant.

8. Since the research cited earlier indicates that acceleration by early school admission, skipping or telescoping grades, or early admission to college is not detrimental to the social and emotional development of most of the gifted children, consideration should be given to these procedures. Establishing a fixed chronological age as an entrance requirement, as is done in most school systems, is not taking into account the mental maturity of gifted children, whose mental level may be beyond 7, 8, or 9 when they are allowed to enter school.

Suggestions for Instructional Practices

Gifted children have particular mental qualifications for achievement, particularly in the academic subjects of the elementary school. Certain instructional modifications and changes in materials are necessary if a child's program is to be adequate either in a special class, under acceleration, or in the regular grades. The following suggestions for instructional practices are based on qualitative or quantitative differences between gifted and average children:

1. *Gifted children learn faster than the average child and therefore require less repetition in order to learn the same material.* If a gifted child takes his first-grade reader home some night and finishes it, he should not be required to go over it page by page with the rest of the class but should be allowed to go ahead with supplementary reading, even though the teacher must take precautions to see that he has actually acquired the necessary learning she expects from the basic reader.

Gifted children do need drill on some things, but usually less of it. Not having had to go through endless drill in order to learn things, they are often impatient with excessive drill on mechanical operations such as arithmetic computation facts. They prefer problem-solving exercises to mechanical drill periods. They would usually prefer to figure out why 7 and 8 are 15 than to memorize $7 + 8 = 15$. They tend to learn rationally rather than by sheer memory and sometimes need to be helped to appreciate the efficiency acquired by learning some things automatically, even though that entails the boring task of repetitive memorizing of facts and tables of numbers. Often the drill can be concealed in assignments which have a meaningful appeal. In learning number facts, for instance, some of the drill may take the form of finding out how many ways 10 may be broken up, or playing games which require number combinations.

2. *The reasoning ability of gifted children is superior to that of other children. They see relationships and grasp ideas more readily.* Wonderful as this is, it creates certain pitfalls for the teacher:

The child often demands an explanation and a reason which goes into greater detail than the teacher is able to give or is ready to present to the rest of the class. Gifted children would like to be able to reason problems through and understand them, and the teacher must be prepared to help them do so.

The inverse situation is also true at times, when the gifted child must be helped to analyze the steps by which he arrived at a certain result or conclusion. His reasoning ability is sometimes so quick that he derives an answer without going through the routine steps required by the average child. This is particularly the case in some arithmetical problems. The child sometimes needs help in analyzing the thinking process and understanding a routine when he has to apply it later to more complicated situations.

The gifted child's ability to perceive relationships quickly makes it possible for him to complete assignments faster than other children. He may finish in ten minutes what he is allowed thirty minutes to do. Teachers should be on the alert and see that he is not permitted to just sit or get into mischief and distract others.

His reasoning ability creates greater depth of understanding. He is often able to delve deeper into problems, is able to sense more subtle relationships, and comes up with conclusions and generalizations beyond those expected of a child of his age. This trait should not be overlooked but fostered and developed.

3. *Gifted children usually have a large vocabulary and good verbal ability.* They are interested in using them in communication with the teacher and the class. Even though what they say may be above the level of comprehension of the rest of the class, gifted children should be given an opportunity to express themselves, particularly in writing, in reports, and in explanations and discussions in a classroom.

4. *The gifted child has a broad fund of information.* Because of his keen memory and ability to relate and retain information, he may be expected to know more than other children. One teacher complained, "This child brings many facts which are not explained in the textbook. I don't know where he gets them." She was not prepared to handle this additional information. Because the child had read and remembered a great deal, he did not stick to the assigned textbook but covered the topic in a much broader way, disconcerting the teacher, who wanted the class to learn a particular lesson in a particular textbook. The teacher should encourage such broader approaches, although it may mean some additional homework for herself.

5. *The gifted child has insatiable curiosity.* He is fascinated with imaginative activities, interested in science; he wants to know the whys and wherefores of many things. The instructional procedure for this child is not to try to keep him from delving into new problems but to utilize this curiosity as a motivating factor in further study.

6. *The gifted child has a wide range of interests.* His intellectual abilities drive him in many directions, particularly in the intellectual fields. Sometimes he does not wish to do the routine lesson of the school because of his interest in other topics. The way this is handled depends upon the rigidity of the class organization. If the teacher expects each child to complete identical assignments, whether or not they are of value to all, she may have difficulty with her gifted children. But if individual interest can be utilized to develop the tools and abilities, the gifted child may be able to "kill two birds with one stone." The task of the teacher here is to relate the interests to the developmental area. A particular child who has already mastered a certain technique can be excused from a routine assignment and allowed to take up some other

interest. There are times, of course, when routine tasks must be ac· complished before more appealing activities are pursued.

7. *Gifted children are generally socially adjusted and popular with other children.* They are not odd or maladjusted, as is believed by many. They may, however, be made that way if their creative abilities, deviant behavior, and sometimes lack of conformity are dampened. They may develop a self-concept of being eccentric and different and then attempt to isolate themselves from the group. Teachers can assist a great deal in fostering a worth-while self-concept in children who have these bents.

8. *The gifted child may be critical and dissatisfied with his own achievements.* Auto-criticism is an asset, provided the individual does not become critical of everything he does and cease to produce because he cannot be satisfied with his own production. Teachers should watch for marked auto-criticism and should help the child become satisfied with what he can do at a particular stage of development.

9. *Gifted children are generally observant.* They perceive many things to which other children are oblivious in the same experience. They grasp many more phenomena from a particular experience and relate them to each other and to other experiences. Taking advantage of this tendency, teachers should allow them to go beyond the class on the same assignment.

10. *Many gifted children show creative abilities.* These creative spurts may appear to the teacher and other children as deviant and not fitting into the regular program of the school. As stated earlier, we do not know how much creative imagination the regular program is dulling because of the teacher's desire to produce a certain degree of conformity to the program of the school. Teachers should watch for flashes of creativity in children and encourage them, even at the risk of some deviant behavior. This deviantly expressed creativity should be recognized, and directed if possible into constructive channels.

Whether a school provides for its gifted through special schools and classes, through acceleration, or through enrichment in the regular grades, an effort is made to expand the horizons and extend the abilities of these children.

In the light of current research in creative thinking, Guilford's analysis of the thinking process demands recognition.[67] In classifying the components of intelligence, he has enumerated five basic operations: (1) cognition (recognition or discovery); (2) memory (retention of what is cognized); (3) divergent thinking (reorganizing known facts into new

[67] J. P. Guilford, "Three Faces of Intellect," *American Psychologist,* 14 (August, 1959), 469–479.

relationships); (4) convergent thinking (arriving at more conventional conclusions); and (5) evaluation (reaching decisions as to correctness or adequacy of what is known). All of these operations play an important part in the intellectual process.

An effective program will develop the ability to think by means of these five processes, utilizing productive thinking as well as the knowing and remembering of facts. In enriching the program for gifted children we are interested in more than their scores on standardized tests. We want more than the ability to recognize and memorize facts. Ability in productive thinking is of utmost importance. One aspect of productive thinking is divergent thinking, which plays a big role in an area recently receiving more and more attention. This is the area of creativity. The school must do more than pass on to new generations the facts and ideas it has acquired; it has the added responsibility of developing the ability to create new ideas and evolve new facts and relationships.

Wilson[68] has some suggestions for the development of creative thinking in children, some of which follow:

Brainstorming. First the rules are set down: (1) no criticism of any idea presented; (2) the wilder the idea the better; and (3) the greater the number of ideas the better. Then a question is posed, such as: What can we do to make school more interesting?

Stimulating sensitivity to problems. The children are asked to discuss what would happen if everyone in the world became deaf, or if we all had three fingers, or if someone invented a pill as a substitute for all food.

Encouraging ideational fluency. The children are asked to list all the ways a brick can be used, or in how many ways water can be made to work for one.

Encouraging originality. Activities and assignments in class can deliberately seek to produce uncommon or unusual responses. Pupils are asked to look for a different way of doing something.

Encouraging redefinition ability. In this activity the pupil is faced with a problem such as: If you went to a picnic and forgot a frying pan what would you use instead?

These approaches illustrate some attempts which can be made to develop creativity in gifted children. How effective they are must await the results of current and future research.

[68] Robert C. Wilson, "Creativity," *Education for the Gifted, Fifty-seventh Yearbook of the National Society for the Study of Education,* Part II, pp. 108–128.

Summary

1. Gifted children have been defined as those who have superior ability to deal with facts, ideas, and relationships. Talented children and youth have been defined as those who have special aptitudes in specific areas such as music, art, social leadership, mechanics, and so forth. These are not distinct differences since talented children usually are gifted intellectually, and most intellectually gifted children have talent in some area.

2. The prevalence of gifted children in a school system is contingent upon the criteria used and the socioeconomic status of the community. The prevalence is estimated to be one-half of one per cent (in an average community if an IQ of 140 and above is taken as a criterion) to 16 to 20 per cent (if an IQ of 115 is the criterion).

3. Identification of gifted children is accomplished by a combination of procedures — teacher's referral, achievement in school, and group and individual intelligence tests.

4. Adaptation of a school program to a gifted child can best be accomplished by noting his discrepancies in physical, social, emotional, intellectual, and academic growth.

5. The studies on gifted children, particularly those of Terman, who defined giftedness as having an IQ above 140, indicated that (a) in physical and health characteristics they were superior to the general population; (b) they were advanced in school subjects two to four years beyond the average; (c) their intellectual maturity was maintained in adulthood; (d) their interests were more in abstract than in practical subjects; (e) their mental health and adjustment were superior to those of other children while in school, and fewer of them developed serious maladjustment or delinquency; and (f) eight times more gifted men entered the professions than was true for the general population.

6. Dissatisfaction with the IQ as the sole measure of giftedness is growing. Newer instruments are being developed to measure creative or productive thinking.

7. The three organizational procedures which have been used to adapt instruction for the gifted are (a) acceleration, (b) enrichment, and (c) special schools and classes. All of these methods have proved to be of value.

8. Special attention is directed to special groups of intellectually gifted children such as underachievers, children with very high IQ's, and gifted children with handicaps.

9. Principles of organization and teaching and various programs for elementary and secondary schools have been described.

DISCUSSION QUESTIONS

1. What developments have there been since World War II which have encouraged more gifted students to attend institutions of higher learning?

2. What social, economic, and political factors are currently encouraging acceleration of programs for gifted individuals?

3. It is generally agreed that intellectual superiority is the essential ingredient for "giftedness." What are some other traits, in order of importance, which help us define giftedness?

4. Table III indicates variations in the prevalence of giftedness among communities of different sociocultural levels. How do you explain this variation?

5. What advances in testing and knowledge about the traits of gifted children make it possible for schools to identify gifted children more accurately now than fifty years ago?

6. Which of our modern educational programs would have been most suitable for men such as John Stuart Mill? Norbert Wiener? Wernher von Braun? Albert Einstein? Thomas Edison? Would you recommend any programs not commonly found in our schools today?

7. What basic assumptions underlie modern educators' reluctance to accelerate gifted children like Ignatius (see Figure 7) whose social and physical development lags behind their academic achievement? Are these assumptions valid?

8. Suppose that further research establishes that the differences Terman found between gifted and normal children are the result of socioeconomic status rather than of intelligence. If this is so, what research questions would educators then have to ask about giftedness?

9. What types of community would tend to favor each of the following kinds of programs for the gifted: acceleration, special classes, enrichment in the regular grades?

10. List and justify specific ultimate goals for the highly gifted individual in contemporary American society.

11. In view of the principles of instruction and the discussion of the development of creativity in your text, which kinds of games and leisure-time activities would you recommend which would further develop the abilities of gifted children, and which kinds would you discourage?

SELECTED REFERENCES

Abraham, Willard. *Common Sense About Gifted Children.* New York: Harper & Brothers, 1958.

American Association for Gifted Children. *The Gifted Child,* Paul Witty, ed. Boston: D. C. Heath and Company, 1951.

Bentley, John E. *Superior Children, Their Physiological, Psychological and Social Development.* New York: W. W. Norton and Company, 1937.

Bish, Charles E. *Can We Provide a Better Program for the Able Student?* National Association of Secondary School Principals, Bulletin No. 42. Washington: National Education Association, December, 1958.

Brandwein, Paul F. *The Gifted Student as Future Scientist.* New York: Harcourt, Brace and Company, 1955.

Cutts, Norma E., and Nicholas Moseley. *Bright Children: A Guide for Parents.* New York: G. P. Putnam's Sons, 1953.

Cutts, Norma E., and Nicholas Moseley. *Teaching the Bright and Gifted.* Englewood Cliffs, N.J.: Prentice-Hall, Inc., 1957.

DeHaan, Robert F., and Robert J. Havighurst. *Educating Gifted Children.* Chicago: University of Chicago Press, 1957.

Fliegler, Louis A. *Curriculum Planning for the Gifted.* Englewood Cliffs, N.J.: Prentice-Hall, Inc., 1961.

French, Joseph L. *Educating the Gifted; A Book of Readings.* New York: Henry Holt and Company, 1959.

Gallagher, James J. *The Gifted Child in the Elementary School.* Washington: American Educational Research Association, National Education Association, 1959.

Gallagher, James J. *Analysis of Research on the Education of Gifted Children.* Springfield, Ill.: Office of the Superintendent of Public Instruction, 1960.

Havighurst, Robert J., Eugene Stivers, and Robert F. DeHaan. *A Survey of the Education of Gifted Children.* Supplementary Educational Monograph No. 83. Chicago: University of Chicago Press, 1955.

Hildreth, Gertrude. *Educating Gifted Children at Hunter College Elementary School.* New York: Harper & Brothers, 1952.

Hollingworth, Leta. *Children Above 180 IQ.* Yonkers-on-Hudson, N. Y.: World Book Company, 1942.

McClelland, David C. *Talent and Society.* Princeton, N.J.: D. Van Nostrand Company, 1958.

National Society for the Study of Education. *Education for the Gifted, Fifty-seventh Yearbook.* Chicago: University of Chicago Press, 1958.

Passow, A. Harry. *Planning for Talented Youth.* New York: Teachers College, Columbia University, 1955.

Pressey, Sidney L. *Educational Acceleration: Appraisals and Basic Problems.* Monograph No. 31. Columbus: Bureau of Educational Research, Ohio State University, 1949.

Scheifele, Marian. *The Gifted Child in the Regular Classroom.* New York: Teachers College, Columbia University, 1953.

Sumption, Merle R., and Evelyn M. Luecking. *Education of the Gifted.* New York: Ronald Press Company, 1960.

Terman, Lewis M., B. T. Baldwin, and Edith Bronson, eds. *Genetic Studies of Genius.* Vol. I, *Mental and Physical Traits of a Thousand Gifted Children.* Stanford, Calif.: Stanford University Press, 1925.

Terman, Lewis M., ed., and Catharine M. Cox, assisted by Lela O. Gillan, Ruth H. Livesay, and Lewis M. Terman. *Genetic Studies of Genius.* Vol. II, *The Early Mental Traits of 300 Geniuses.* Stanford, Calif.: Stanford University Press, 1926.

Terman, Lewis M., Barbara S. Burks, and Dortha W. Jensen. *Genetic Studies of Genius.* Vol. III, *The Promise of Youth: Follow-up Studies of 1000 Gifted Children.* Stanford, Calif.: Stanford University Press, 1930.

Terman, Lewis M., and Melita H. Oden, eds. *Genetic Studies of Genius.* Vol. IV, *The Gifted Child Grows Up: Twenty-five Years Follow-up of a Superior Group.* Stanford, Calif.: Stanford University Press, 1947.

Terman, Lewis M., and Melita H. Oden, eds. *Genetic Studies of Genius.* Vol. V, *The Gifted Group at Mid-Life: Thirty-five Years Follow-up of the Superior Child.* Stanford, Calif.: Stanford University Press, 1959.

They Went to College Early. New York: Fund for the Advancement of Education, 1957.

Worcester, Dean A. *The Education of Children of Above-Average Mentality.* Lincoln: University of Nebraska Press, 1956.

3

Children with Low Intelligence

In Chapter 1, Figure 1 was presented to show the distribution of intelligence according to the Stanford Revision of the Binet Scale. It will be recalled that the lower end of the distribution of intelligence included the slow learner and various degrees of mental retardation. This chapter is devoted to a further study of those children whose learning ability and general adaptation to society are below the average.

Children with low intelligence have been classified in various ways. Every profession has its own groupings for its own purpose. The physician tends to classify children according to the type of physical defect, if the child has one, such as mongolism, cretinism, and so forth. He may also classify according to cause of the defect. The social worker tends to categorize the child according to his degree of adjustment or independence: as independent, marginally independent, or dependent. The psychologist classifies the child according to his degree of psychological deficit as indicated by the IQ and other measures. The educator uses rate of learning or degree of defect as the basis for organizing an educational program for the child. Categories used most frequently by educators have included (1) the slow learner, (2) the educable mentally retarded, (3) the trainable mentally retarded, and (4) the totally dependent mentally retarded.

The slow-learning child is not considered mentally retarded because he is capable of achieving a moderate degree of academic success even though at a slower rate than the average child. He is educated in the regular classes without special provisions except an adaptation of the regular class program to fit his slower learning ability. At the adult level he is usually self-supporting, independent, and socially adjusted.

The educable mentally retarded child is one who, because of slow mental development, is unable to profit to any great degree from the programs of the regular schools, but who has these potentialities for development: (1) minimum educability in reading, writing, spelling, arithmetic, and so forth; (2) capacity for social adjustment to a point where he can get along independently in the community; and (3) minimum occupational adequacy such that he can later support himself partially or totally at a marginal level. The term "educability" then refers to minimum educability in the academic, social, and occupational areas.

The trainable mentally retarded child is defined as a child who is so subnormal in intelligence that he is unable to profit from the program of the classes for educable mentally retarded children, but who has potentialities in three areas: (1) learning self-care in activities such as eating, dressing, undressing, toileting, and sleeping; (2) learning to adjust in the home or neighborhood, though not to the total community; and (3) learning economic usefulness in the home, a sheltered workshop, or an institution.

The totally dependent mentally retarded child is one who, because of markedly subnormal intelligence, is unable to be trained in self-care, socialization, or economic usefulness, and who needs continuing help in taking care of his personal needs. Such a child requires almost complete supervision throughout his life since he is unable to survive without help.

The Developmental Patterns of Children with Low Intelligence

Children with varying degrees of low intelligence present different growth patterns. In Figure 10 four children of differing degrees of retardation are represented. Each child is 10 years old. The chronological age is the only point on the profile which is the same for all four children. Case A is a slow learner; Case B, an educable mentally retarded child; Case C, a trainable retarded child; and Case D, a totally dependent retarded child.

It will be noted that the 10-year-old slow-learning child (Case A) is quite a bit like the average 10-year-old in the physical areas of height, weight, and motor coordination. With an IQ of 87 he is a little more than a year retarded mentally below his chronological age, about half a year in social maturity, and between one and two years on all other characteristics. His reading, for example, is at a third-grade level although he is placed in the fifth grade in school. This child is able to get along in the regular grades even though he is below his grade placement in general educational achievement. In most fifth grades there are a number of children who are doing third-grade work, a few more who

FIGURE 10

Profiles of Four Children of Differing Degrees of Mental Retardation

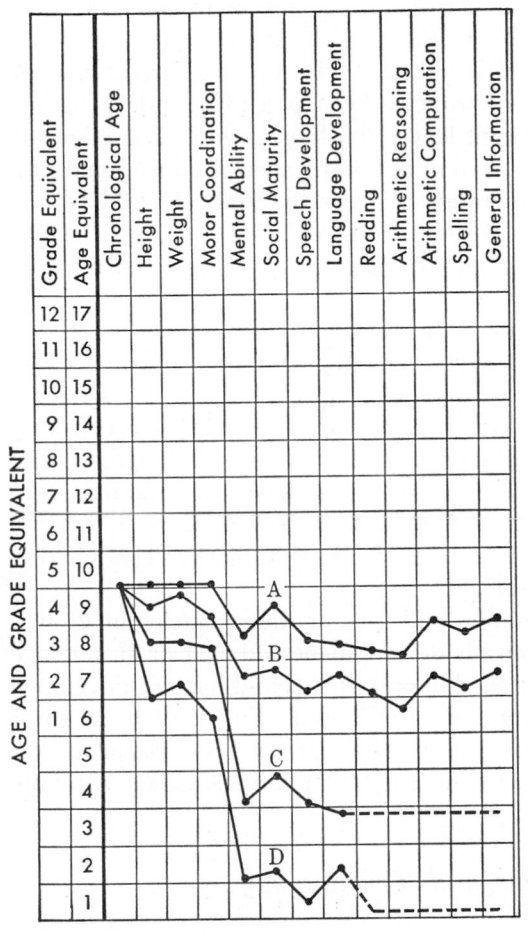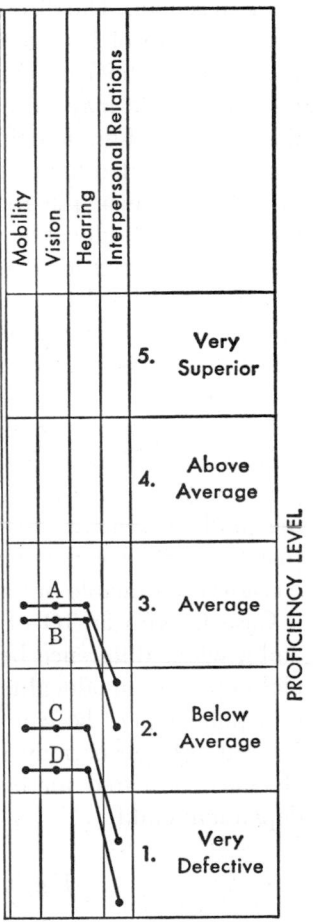

A, slow learner
B, educable mentally retarded child
C, trainable mentally retarded child
D, totally dependent mentally retarded child

are doing fourth-grade work, many who are doing fifth-grade work, some who are doing sixth-grade work, and even a few who may be doing seventh- and eighth-grade work. Thus a fifth grade in the regular school has an achievement range of about two years below to two years above that grade. We expect the regular grade to provide instruction adapted to children within this range of ability. For that reason, slow-learning children tend to remain in the regular grades rather than being placed in special classes, particularly in the elementary school.

The 10-year-old educable mentally retarded child in Figure 10 (Case B) has a Binet IQ of 72. This child is doing beginning second-grade work in school. The discrepancy between his achievement and that of the average child of his age is quite marked and he is unable to cope with the regular school program. Although a child with third-grade reading and arithmetic may be able to struggle through a fifth-grade program, first- or second-grade achievement leaves too large a gap. The educable mentally retarded child therefore requires some special educational provisions outside of the regular grades. This is the kind of child who is considered an educable or a high-grade mental defective, but he can learn to get along in society, maintain a job at a later age, and function at a minimal level in unskilled work.

The profile of a trainable mentally retarded child (Case C) shows discrepancies in growth much wider than those of the educable child. Here we find an IQ of 40 and a mental level of 4 years. Physical development in terms of height and motor coordination are also considerably retarded, but not as much as mental ability. Speech, language, and general information are also close to the 4-year level. In reading, spelling, and arithmetic the profile is shown with broken lines, indicating that the child has not begun to achieve in these subjects. This child is considered trainable but not educable.

Case D with an IQ of 20 shows still greater discrepancies in growth and a wider difference between his development and that of an average child or even an educable or trainable one. This child has not developed to a point where he can do anything for himself. Even as late as 16 or 17 years of age he may not be able to take care of his personal needs. He must be cared for by others and for that reason is called a totally dependent child.

Definitions and Terminology

The problem of finding a general definition of mental retardation has been difficult for educators, psychologists, psychiatrists, and others. Mental retardation is not a disease, like cancer or tuberculosis, but a condition. A general definition must describe those manifestations of the condition which pertain in all cases. The difficulty of finding a general definition is obvious when one tries to define a heterogeneous group of types and degrees on a continuum. For example, how do we define a "small man"? Are small men all those who are less than five feet in height? Suppose some men below five feet weigh more than some men above six feet. Are they still "small men"? Or do we add a weight criterion and say all men below five feet who weigh less than 120 pounds are considered small men? Similarly, in defining mental retardation we must include many criteria and thus arrive at a multidimensional definition. We must concern ourselves with overlapping medical, social, psychological, economic, physical, and educational factors. Some of the terms commonly used in this field are described below:

A *mental defective* is defined by Doll as a person who is (1) socially incompetent, (2) mentally subnormal, (3) retarded intellectually from birth or at an early age, (4) retarded at maturity, (5) deficient as a result of constitutional origin (heredity or disease), and (6) essentially incurable.[1]

Feeble-mindedness is used by most American authorities synonymously with mental deficiency. In general, it is a legal term used mostly in the earlier statutes. Very common at one time, it is not currently used as extensively because of the legal stigma attached to it in this country. In England the term refers to the high grades or less severe degrees of mental deficiency.

Oligophrenia is the French term for mental deficiency and is occasionally used in America by some authors, especially in a medical context.

Mental Retardation Versus Mental Deficiency

Sarason and Gladwin have attempted to differentiate between mental deficiency and mental retardation.[2] They conceive of mental deficiency as requiring the presence of a central nervous system pathology of a kind and degree which renders the individual incapable of normal social and intellectual functioning. On the other hand, they think of the mentally retarded as those of a higher intellectual level in special classes and institutions who usually come from the lower social classes and who "presumably do not have any central nervous system pathology." While this type of a distinction may be of importance to the medical diagnostician, the educator finds it more helpful to delineate degree rather than cause of defect. He is more interested in terms relating to ability level than to etiology. Brain injury, for example, is not definitive of the

---

[1] Edgar A. Doll, "The Essentials of an Inclusive Concept of Mental Deficiency," *American Journal of Mental Deficiency*, 46 (October, 1941), 214–219.

[2] Seymour B. Sarason, *Psychological Problems in Mental Deficiency* (New York: Harper & Brothers, 3rd ed., 1959), p. 404.

child's capabilities. Two children may both have brain damage, but one may be a custodial case and the other respond readily to education.

Terminology Related to Degree

The terms "mental retardation," "mental deficiency," "feeble-mindedness," and "oligophrenia" are general terms including all degrees of defect and applicable to all kinds of children with subnormal intelligence. More specific terms refer to definite degrees of retardation. The following is a list of these terms categorized according to the type of program provided:

Nursing Care	*Trainable Classes*	*Educable Classes*	*Regular Classes*
Idiot	Imbecile	Moron	Dull-normal
Dependent	Semidependent	Marginally independent	Independent
Totally dependent	Trainable	Educable	Slow learner
Low grade	Middle grade	High grade	Borderline
IQ 0–25	IQ 25–50	IQ 50–75	IQ 75–90

For educational purposes the categories of slow learner, educable, trainable, and totally dependent appear to be adequate. The differentiation between mental deficiency and mental retardation suggested by Sarason and Gladwin on the basis of central nervous system pathology may not be of value to the educator.

The Prevalence of Children with Low Intelligence

The numerous surveys of various populations to determine the prevalence of children with low intelligence have shown a wide range of incidence estimates. One reason for the divergence is the fact that different investigators used different criteria for the groups they called mentally retarded.

An example of the difference in prevalence rates given by different authors is presented in Table IV. It is obvious from the figures summarized by Pintner that wide variations exist in surveys and estimates. The British Royal Commission of 1908, with an estimate of less than one-half of one per cent (0.40%), is one-fifteenth the estimate of X County, Minnesota, of over 6 per cent.

Another way of estimating the prevalence of children with low intelligence is to use the normal curve of intelligence test scores. This gives us a theoretical estimate.

TABLE IV

Estimates of the Prevalence of Feeble-Mindedness

Authority	Percentage
British Royal Commission, 1908	0.40
Oregon Survey, Carlisle, 1921	0.50
United States, Baily and Haber, 1920	0.65
Wisconsin Schools, Cary, 1916–18	0.70
British Mental Deficiency Committee, 1929	0.73
Oneida County, N.Y., Carlisle, 1918	0.73
Porter County, Ind., Clark, 1916	0.90
Rural County, Ohio, Sessions, 1918	1.80
Rural Survey, Del., Mullan, 1916	1.80
Toronto Schools, Smith 1920	2.00
Goddard's estimate, 1914	2.00
Terman's estimate, 1916	2.00
Cleveland Survey, Mitchell, 1916	3.00
Popenoe's estimate for U.S.A., 1929	4.00
X County, Calif., Terman, 1918	4.24
Eight Minnesota towns, Kuhlmann, 1923	4.70
X County, Minn., Anderson, 1922	6.10

Source: Rudolf Pintner, "The Feebleminded Child," *Handbook of Child Psychology,* C. Murchison, ed. (Worcester, Mass.: Clark University Press, 1933), p. 811.

Figure 11 assumes that the average child has an IQ of 100 and is represented on the normal curve and on the standard deviation scale at 0. This curve would indicate that 0.13 per cent or 1⅓ child per 1000 has an IQ below 55. Actual studies show a higher prevalence in the population,

FIGURE 11

Theoretical Distribution of Intelligence Test Scores

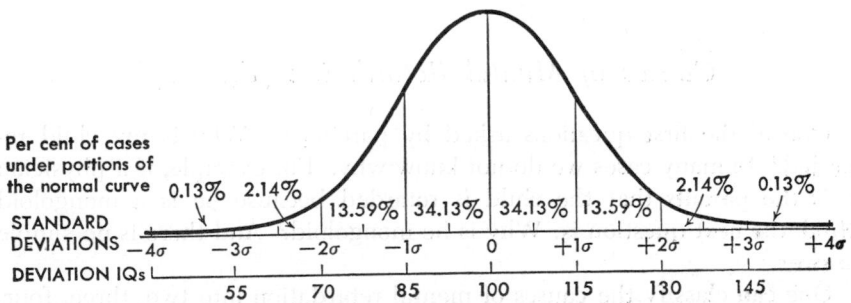

Source: Adapted from *Test Service Bulletin No. 48* (New York: Psychological Corporation, January, 1955).

91

since the theoretical curve does not allow for that mental retardation caused by abnormal physical conditions such as mongolism, cretinism, and brain injury. According to the normal curve, 2.14 per cent or 21 in 1000 children should have IQ's between 55 and 70. In some communities there are more than this figure while in other communities it has been difficult to find 1 per cent or 10 in 1000 in this range of intelligence. The summary of Pintner (Table IV) shows many deviations from this theoretical estimate.

When we attempt to give the prevalence for each level — the totally dependent, the trainable, the educable, and the slow learner — our studies do not yield clear-cut figures. Taking into consideration the surveys made in England and in various parts of the United States, and also considering the socioeconomic and cultural levels of the community, we can estimate the rates shown in Table V.

TABLE V
Estimated Rate per 1000 School-Age Children

Level of Community	Totally Dependent	Trainable	Educable	Slow Learner
Low	1	4	50	300
Middle	1	4	25	170
High	1	4	10	50

It will be noted from Table V that the prevalence of totally dependent or trainable children does not differ between the low, middle, and high socioeconomic communities. This indicates that pathological conditions, such as mongolism, occur with the same frequency regardless of the cultural level of the family. The differences in frequency of retardation between communities occur primarily among the educable retarded and slow learners. Studies relating to these differences are discussed later.

Causes of Mental Retardation (Etiology)

One of the first questions asked by parents is: Why is my child retarded? In many cases we do not know why. For example, if a physician tells the parents that the child is retarded because he is a mongoloid child, the next question is: Why is he mongoloid? And there is no simple answer.

One can classify the causes of mental retardation into two, three, four, or a dozen categories. For example, Tredgold attempted to divide mental retardation into two groups according to causes, namely, (1) primary amentia and (2) secondary amentia.[3] By primary amentia he meant mental retardation which was inherited. By secondary amentia he meant retardation caused by external factors, i.e., resulting from disease or other conditions.

Doll accepted two kinds of causes: (1) endogenous and (2) exogenous.[4] The endogenous type is the result of "hereditary transmission of psycho-biological insufficiency," while the exogenous type includes "pathological alterations of normal development as well as some relatively rare hereditary types of pathological morphology represented by the clinical varieties of mental deficiency."

Davenport discussed the causes of mental retardation in seven categories based on developmental stages: (1) defects arising in the germ plasma, (2) defects resulting during fertilization of the egg, (3) defects connected with implantation, (4) defects arising in the embryo, (5) defects arising in the fetus, (6) defects arising from birth injuries, and (7) defects arising in infancy and later childhood.[5]

In this chapter the causes of mental retardation will be discussed under three major categories: (1) organic, (2) genetic, and (3) cultural.

Acquired Organic Causes

Organically caused mental retardation is characterized by definite central nervous system pathology which is not hereditary. The defect or abnormality in the brain or nervous system may arise before birth (prenatal), during birth (perinatal), or after birth (postnatal) as a result of injury, disease, toxic conditions, and so forth. It is hard sometimes to differentiate among genetic (hereditary), environmental, and organic factors affecting the fetus during embryological development. The organic factors may involve a genetic predisposition which is manifest only when the fetus is affected by certain environmental conditions.

Masland has discussed this relationship:

> Accurate data are not now available by which to determine to what extent maldevelopment of the nervous system is attributable to hereditary factors, to what extent to environmental factors, and to what extent to a combination of the two. The search for specific environmental factors is thus of particular importance. The problem of the detection of agents operative before birth is complicated by the fact that the results are not evident until a long time after the agent may have ceased to be operative. Although pathological examination may give some clue as to the ap-

[3] A. F. Tregold and R. F. Tregold, A *Textbook of Mental Deficiency* (Baltimore, Md.: Williams and Wilkins Company, 8th ed., 1952).

[4] Doll, *op. cit.*

[5] Charles B. Davenport, "Causes of Retarded and Incomplete Development," *Proceedings of the American Association on Mental Deficiency*, 41 (May, 1936), 208–214.

proximate time when the injury occurred, the fact that the actual maldevelopment occurred at a specific time during pregnancy does not necessarily indicate that the primary factor responsible was operative then rather than previous to that time. Because of the great latency between the time of occurrence of the insult and the time when the diagnosis can eventually be established, the relationship between cause and effect is not often an evident one. Until such a relationship has been established, the relevant data on which to establish such a relationship may be overlooked and may not even be included in the data relative to the pregnancy or previous history of the pregnant woman. This problem is also complicated by the fact that certain factors operating in the production of maldevelopment may be operative before the pregnancy itself occurs, and they may actually be taking place throughout the early life of the prospective mother.

A second factor which complicates the detection of the causative agents in maldevelopment is the frequent interplay of factors and the difficulty of distinguishing cause from effect. It has been demonstrated, for example, that hemorrhage during pregnancy, toxemia, and prematurity are all factors which are associated with an increased incidence of mental retardation in the offspring. It is difficult to determine, however, to what extent the retardation is the result of the maldevelopment of the fetus which in itself caused the "complication of pregnancy" and to what extent the complication of pregnancy caused injury to the fetus at the time of its occurrence.[6]

Prenatal and Perinatal Causes. The conditions which affect the embryo and produce central nervous system involvement with mental retardation are known as prenatal causes.

Maldevelopment of the embryo or fetus can be the result of *infection* in the mother during pregnancy. A classic example is the case of German measles (rubella). If the mother contracts German measles during the first trimester of pregnancy, the child may be born mentally retarded and/or with other abnormalities. Toxemia, syphilis, influenza, encephalitis, and other diseases are likely to produce a defect in the embryo.

Studies have indicated that there are more *premature births* among the retarded than among the normal. Masland quotes Alm as stating that "'Among those prematurely born children who survived the first two or three years of life, there is a moderately higher incidence of such disorders as are usually considered to be associated with birth injuries, than among the controls.'"[7] Masland asserts that "It is probable that a considerable reduction of mental retardation secondary to prematurity has resulted from improved management of the premature child."[8]

[6] Richard L. Masland, Seymour B. Sarason, and T. Gladwin, *Mental Subnormality* (New York: Basic Books, Inc., 1958), pp. 53–54.
[7] *Ibid.,* p. 101.   [8] *Ibid.,* p. 103.

Birth injuries are a possible cause of mental retardation. During the process of birth a number of factors account for damage to the central nervous system. One is known as "anoxia." Under this condition the child does not receive enough oxygen and some of the brain cells are likely to be destroyed. The child, if he survives, may be a "blue baby." Schreiber stated that the brain cannot function without an adequate supply of oxygen.[9] When the oxygen supply to the brain is blocked for more than a few minutes, irreparable damage to the brain cells results. During pregnancy or birth there are a number of conditions which cause oxygen deprivation and thus cell destruction and consequent mental deficiency. According to Masland, "Important changes in the chemistry of the body occur during conditions of asphyxia, and evidence is presented to suggest that some of the secondary changes occurring during asphyxia are of more serious concern than is the oxygen deprivation *per se*."[10]

Mental retardation is sometimes associated with incompatibility between the *Rh factor* of the mothers' blood and that of the child. The Rh factor was discovered in 1940 by Landsteiner and Wiener, who reproduced the condition of incompatibility by injecting blood from the rhesus monkey into the rabbit.[11] The Rh-positive factor is found in 86 per cent of human beings. The 14 per cent who do not have the Rh factor are known as Rh negative. The incompatibility of Rh-positive and Rh-negative blood produces agglutinin, which prevents blood cells from maturing in the bone marrow. This condition appears to be more common in the mentally retarded than among normals. When obstetricians know that the parents are Rh incompatible, they are alerted to the condition and can prevent mental retardation or cerebral palsy by transfusing the baby's blood at birth.

Postnatal Causes. Mental retardation can be caused by disease and injury after birth and during the period of infancy or early childhood. Many such conditions are not too well understood and their effect on mental retardation in humans is a matter of speculation based on studies with animals. The fact that the central nervous system after birth resists infections may lower the incidence of postnatal as compared to prenatal causes.

One postnatal disease known to cause mental retardation in some cases is encephalitis — or brain fever. This includes many conditions but refers primarily to a virus infection which produces a high fever and

---

[9] Frederick Schreiber, "Mental Deficiency from Paranatal Asphyxia," *Proceedings of the American Association on Mental Deficiency*, 44 (May, 1939), 95–106.

[10] Masland, *op. cit.*, p. 108.

[11] Reported by R. R. Gates, *Human Genetics* (New York: The Macmillan Company, 1946), I, 700–709.

possibly causes destruction of brain cells. Cases have been reported in which it was believed that a very high fever caused by other diseases resulted in brain damage and mental retardation.

Genetic Causes

Although it is sometimes impossible to differentiate genetic or hereditary factors from the acquired organic factors just discussed or from environmental or cultural factors, research workers have attempted to determine the relative significance of each.

Studies on the inheritance of mental retardation fall into two major areas: (1) biological research and (2) social research. Biological research has been discussed by Allen,[12] who classified the conditions of mental deficiency into four groups according to the genetic mechanisms of causation:

1. For the first group there is little or no evidence of genetic causation. Allen cited mongolism as an example, but since then it has been discovered that mongolism may actually have a genetic origin. It has recently been reported that in mongoloids an extra or a deviant chromosome is present.[13]

2. In the second group are conditions such as *phenylketonuria* which appear to have a fairly definite genetic basis, according to Allen. *Phenylketonuria* results from an inborn error of metabolism and is associated with mental retardation. In this condition the individual has too much phenylalanine, which is easily detected by simple tests that can be routinely administered to infants. The condition is inherited and for each phenylketonuric there are 300 carriers. At present there is a test which promises reliable identification of the carrier. Armstrong has found that giving an infant who has phenylalanine in his urine (indicating phenylketonuria) a phenylalanine-free diet has produced normal development in some instances.[14] This discovery has major implications even if it applies only to a few retarded children. It means that even though a child inherits a condition which leads to mental retardation science may be able to change it and thus prevent mental deficiency.

3. Allen's third group consists of the condition known as *neurofibromatosis*. About 10 per cent of the patients having this condition are mentally defective. It has been traced to an "irregular dominant inheritance."

4. In a fourth group Allen classifies *familial mental deficiency,* by

[12] Gordon Allen, "Patterns of Discovery in the Genetics of Mental Deficiency," *American Journal of Mental Deficiency,* 62 (March, 1958), 840–849.

[13] Josef Warkany, "Etiology of Mongolism," *Journal of Pediatrics,* 56 (March, 1960), 412–419.

[14] M. Armstrong, in *Etiological Factors in Mental Retardation,* Report of the Twenty-third Ross Pediatric Research Conference (Columbus, Ohio: Ross Laboratories, 1956).

which he means quantitative variation. For example, in the measurement of height of men there will be "by nature" some at the short end and some at the very tall end, with the majority in the middle. Similarly, some individuals are at the lower end of the intelligence scale, owing to hereditary biological variation, and are thus retarded.

For many years it was believed that most cases of mental retardation were the result of the inheritance of defects. This idea was given credence by the studies of Goddard,[15] who traced the descendants of a Martin Kallikak. During the Revolutionary War, Kallikak mated with a barmaid who was considered mentally defective. After the war he married an intelligent woman and from a study of their descendants Goddard was able to make a comparison with Kallikak's other progeny. He traced both lines of descendants for a number of generations back, beginning with one of the patients at the Vineland Training School. There were many more social degenerates and feeble-minded individuals among the descendants of the feeble-minded barmaid than among those of Kallikak and his intelligent mate. Goddard concluded from this study that feeble-mindedness is inherited. He claimed that 77 per cent of mentally defective individuals show some mental deficiency or feeble-mindedness in their ancestry.

Since the studies of Goddard there have been many investigations and new discoveries. At the present time we are not asking: Is mental retardation inherited? We are asking: If there is an inheritance of mental retardation, just what is it? The amount of mental deficiency which is inherited, according to surveys, has ranged from 29 per cent to 90 per cent. In other words, many feel that some mental deficiency is inherited, but how much is not known.

As long ago as 1934, Adolph Myerson stated:

> The study of feeble-mindedness has suffered from the overemphasis laid upon certain exceptional sociological situations, namely, the occurrence of so-called families who really represented ecological groups and who have come down in history as the great paradigms of the sociological and biological threat and danger to the race by the feeble-minded. The Nams, the Kallikaks, the Tribes of Ishmael, the Virginians, and others of the royal families of the feeble-minded became the basis of generalizations which were, as a matter of fact, based on flimsy evidence, on what may really be called statisticalized gossip. . . .
>
> It may be stated that in those groups of the feeble-minded concerning which we have some definite knowledge, heredity does not appear to be a factor of any real importance; that in those groups where we

[15] H. H. Goddard, *The Kallikak Family* (New York: The Macmillan Company, 1912); H. H. Goddard, *Feeble-mindedness: Its Causes and Consequences* (New York: The Macmillan Company, 1914).

have little real understanding, and where the appearance of the individual corresponds more to that of the so-called normal, heredity appears to be of great importance. It may safely be stated that there is some correspondence, on the whole, between diffuse bodily defect and inferiority, on the one hand, and mental inferiority, on the other. It also appears quite certain that we are not yet at the point in understanding where we can speak of feeble-mindedness as anything like a biological unit for which we may expect Mendelian ratios.[16]

Cultural Factors

Cultural factors in the etiology of mental retardation refer to causative factors in the social environment. It should be recalled that reference has been made to environmental factors surrounding the fetus and to the effects of infections of the mother and other conditions on it. Environmental factors also play a part after birth or during the postnatal period of mothering in child-rearing practices and in the socioeconomic level of the home. Siblings are a part of the social environment of the growing infant and child. It is postulated that environment has some effect on depressing the child's intelligence or accelerating it, within the range of his inheritance.

The studies on the influence of environment or "nurture" have dealt with heredity and environment, or nature and nurture. While the literature in this field is voluminous, as yet we do not know exactly which environmental conditions depress or accelerate development.

Clarke and Clarke, in a section on the genetic and environmental studies of intelligence, state:

> It may be assumed that heredity plays an essential part in determining the limits of intellectual development, but these limits are considerably wider than was formerly thought. With moderate uniformity of environment, individual differences result largely from genetic variations. The feeble-minded [educable mentally retarded], however, more than any other group in western culture have been reared in most adverse circumstances, followed in many cases by further lengthy periods of residential schools and institutions, with all that this implies. Thus the feeble-minded in such conditions seem likely to be functioning towards the lower end of their spectrum of potentialities, while normals under ordinary conditions of life approximate more closely to their upper limits.[17]

Allen does not agree with the concept of a ceiling imposed by heredity.[18] He believes that this concept is misleading, and cites the cases of

[16] A. Meyerson, "Medical Psychiatry," *The Problem of Mental Disorder,* Madison Bentley, ed. (New York: McGraw-Hill Book Company, 1934), pp. 36–37.

[17] Ann M. Clarke and A. D. B. Clarke, *Mental Deficiency: The Changing Outlook* (Glencoe, Ill.: The Free Press, 1958), p. 119.

[18] Allen, *op. cit.*

phenylketonuria who, though destined by heredity to mental deficiency, can avoid this condition with a special diet. Hence, he contends, heredity does not set a ceiling. He feels that education, likewise, need not consider a ceiling.

Sarason has reviewed extensively the cultural and psychological factors in mental subnormality. He presents specific evidence of the relation of adverse socioeconomic and cultural factors to the incidence of mental retardation and concludes:

> Most of this report has been concerned with what we have termed the mentally retarded individual. Such individuals, of somewhat staggering numbers in our population, come largely from the lowest social classes, or from culturally distinct minority groups, or from regions with conspicuously poor educational facilities or standards. Because the condition is so highly correlated with social class and cultural factors we have insisted on distinguishing it from mental deficiency, where such relationships do not obtain and where, in contrast to mental retardation, there is demonstrable central nervous system pathology which effectively precludes an independent social existence. Regardless of theoretical bent, no responsible investigator has denied that the level and quality of the functioning of the mentally retarded reflects social and cultural factors. *What has not been systematically studied is how these kinds of factors operate so as to have an interfering effect on development.* The question of the degree of influence of these factors can not be answered until we understand how and when they exert their influence.[19]

Kirk has summarized the studies of the effects of environment on mentally retarded children.[20] Of the four groups of studies the first includes case studies of children who had a deprived environment, such as the study by Itard of the Wild Boy of Aveyron. This and other case studies appear somewhat ambiguous and do not show necessarily that a change of environment changed the status of the cases perceptibly. A second approach used by researchers is that of changing the environment by placing children in foster homes. In general the results show that intellectual development of children is affected in varying degrees by the type of home in which they are placed. A third approach has been the comparison of the intellectual level of children from different environments. These studies do not point to any clear conclusions because many of the variables involved could not be controlled. A fourth approach is the investigation of the effects of environmental enrichment and school programs on the development of retarded children. The studies here

[19] Sarason, *op. cit.*, p. 644.
[20] S. A. Kirk, *Early Education of the Mentally Retarded* (Urbana: University of Illinois Press, 1958).

are also controversial, with some concluding that altering rate of development through environmental enrichment or school is possible while others contend that it is impossible.

To test the varying points of view Kirk conducted a longitudinal study on the effects of preschool education on the development of educable mentally retarded children.[21] He studied 81 children whose IQ's ranged initially from 45 to 80. Twenty-eight children in a community were enrolled in a preschool while 26 were examined but not placed in the preschool situation. Kirk trained 15 children in an institution and examined but did not train 12 others who remained on the wards. At the age of 6, all children entered either a community or an institutional school. They were then followed up for periods ranging from one to four years.

Kirk concluded that:

1. Preschool training tended to increase the developmental rate of retarded children.

2. Although half of the children with organic pathologies increased their rate of development, their improvement was less marked than that of children without organic diagnoses.

3. Children from psychosocially deprived homes tended to either retain their rate of development or increase the rate during and after the preschool period, while those who did not receive preschool experience tended to drop or remain the same in rate of development.

4. Children in the institution who received training at the preschool level showed marked gains in rate of growth, while those who were not given preschool experience and remained on the wards tended to drop in rate of growth.

5. Children placed in foster homes and also in the preschool changed markedly in rate of growth.

6. Children from relatively adequate homes, not given preschool experience, tended to hold their rate of growth during the preschool period but increased their rate when they entered school at the age of 6. This indicated that the age of 6 is not too late for increasing developmental rate, provided the children come from relatively adequate homes.

In reference to the effects of early schooling, Kirk concluded that:

> The evidence presented indicates that, with reference to mental development, either (a) the deprivation of the children in this experiment displaced their inherent rate of growth one level downward and school experience restored it later, or (b) the first diagnosis represents the inherent rate of growth, and the school experience displaced this rate of growth one level upward. . . .
>
> . . . It would appear that, although the upper limits of development

21 *Ibid.*

for an individual are genetically or organically determined, the functional level or rate of development may be accelerated or depressed within the limits set by the organism. Somatopsychological factors and the cultural milieu (including schooling) are capable of influencing the functional level within these limits.[22]

Relation of Etiology to Degrees of Low Intelligence

There are some relationships between degree of subnormal intelligence and causal factors. These relationships have been suggested in previous sections.

The defect in a totally dependent mentally retarded child almost always has an acquired organic or genetic cause. Whether the cause is genetic or acquired through disease or injury, the child has a central nervous system involvement with accompanying physical disabilities which renders him incapable of adjusting or learning sufficiently to take care of himself. The organic or genetic cause, whatever it may be, is responsible for the inability of the child to function.

The cause of much retardation at the trainable level is also organic. Pathological conditions in these trainable children are apparent in most of the cases. In classes for trainable children, for example, it has been found that one-third of the enrollment consists of mongoloid children, approximately another one-third consists of brain-injured children, and the other third is usually of unknown etiology.

The educable mentally retarded group consists of children of mixed etiologies. A small proportion may have a diagnosis of organic pathology, such as minimal brain injury. The majority, however, show biological variation (the lower end of the scale of intelligence) or cultural factors causing the retardation, or a combination of heredity and subcultural environments. This group is more amenable to education and environmental enrichment.

For the most part the slow-learning group is subcultural, with a cultural factor postulated as the cause of slow learning ability. There are a small number who have minor organic pathologies, such as minimal brain damage, but the large majority of them come from subcultural homes.

Summary

1. Children with low intelligence have been classified for educational purposes as (a) slow learners, (b) educable mentally retarded, (c) trainable mentally retarded, and (d) totally dependent. Other terms

[22] *Ibid.*, p. 213.

used primarily by the medical and psychological professions include "idiot," "imbecile," "moron," "mentally deficient," "feeble-minded," and "oliogophrenic."

2. It is estimated that in an average community the prevalence of mental retardation for each 1000 school-age children will be approximately 1 totally dependent, 4 trainable mentally retarded, 25 educable mentally retarded, and 170 slow-learning children.

3. The causes of mental retardation may be classified as (a) organic (before, during, and after birth), (b) genetic or inherited, and (c) cultural or environmental.

4. The organic and genetic factors in mental retardation are primarily in the domain of the medical and biological sciences. Education is concerned primarily with the cultural and environmental factors, since adequate education and social management can compensate to some extent for deprived environmental situations. How much can be done to improve or compensate for poor heredity or organic pathology remains for future researchers in the biological and social sciences to determine.

DISCUSSION QUESTIONS

1. Why does it seem necessary for the different disciplines to evolve their own terminologies and classifications for children with low intelligence, instead of combining them into one set of terms or one system of classification which would be equally useful to medicine, psychology, social work or sociology, and education?

2. How can you account for the absence of difference in prevalence of totally dependent and trainable mentally retarded among the different sociocultural levels in a community, and the marked difference in prevalence of the educable and slow learners among the different socioeconomic levels (Table V)?

3. From the different classifications given in your text, which one do you prefer, and why?

4. In view of current knowledge about heredity and mental deficiency, how useful do you believe sterilization would be as a means of decreasing the prevalence of mental deficiency (ignoring any moral or religious issues)?

5. Assuming that the studies on deprivation have established a social-environmental factor as a cause of mental retardation, what should our society do about it? To decrease this cause of retardation, would you advocate (a) taking children out of inadequate homes and placing them in good foster homes at state expense, (b) establishing nursery schools and day-care centers in all depressed areas, (c) giving free medical attention to all children in underprivileged areas, (d) subsidizing through state or federal ap-

propriations slum clearance, adult education, and extensive recreational facilities?

6. What advice might you expect would be given to couples who are concerned about the effects of the following situations on the intelligence of their children: (*a*) husband's brother is epileptic; (*b*) wife is Rh negative; (*c*) wife's sister is mongoloid; (*d*) husband's father attended school twelve years but never achieved above a fourth-grade level.

7. Two estimates of the prevalence of mental deficiency are made for the same isolated rural area. One study uses an IQ criterion for the definition of mental deficiency, and the other uses a social competency criterion. How would you expect the results to compare?

8. Your text states that a cultural factor may cause slow learning ability. Name some specific cultural factors that might do so, and explain how.

9. If Doll's six criteria for mental deficiency, including incurability, are accepted, then how can special education programs for this group be justified?

Selected References

Abel, T. M., and E. F. Kinder. *The Subnormal Adolescent Girl*. New York: Columbia University Press, 1942.

Benda, C. E. *Mongolism and Cretinism*. New York: Grune and Stratton, 1946.

Binet, A., and T. Simon. *Mentally Defective Children*. New York: Longmans, Green and Company, 1914.

Clarke, Ann M., and A. D. B. Clarke. *Mental Deficiency: The Changing Outlook*. Glencoe, Ill.: The Free Press, 1958.

Davies, Stanley P. *Social Control of Mentally Deficient*. New York: Thomas Y. Crowell Company, 1930.

Gallagher, J. J. *A Comparison of Brain-Injured and Non Brain-Injured Mentally Retarded Children on Several Psychological Variables*. Monograph of the Society for Research in Child Development. Vol. 22, No. 2, 1957.

Goddard, H. H. *The Kallikak Family: A Study of the Heredity of Feeble-mindedness*. New York: The Macmillan Company, 1912.

Goddard, H. H. *Feeble-Mindedness: Its Causes and Consequences*. New York: The Macmillan Company, 1914.

Itard, Jean Marc Gaspard. *The Wild Boy of Aveyron*. Translated by George and Muriel Humphrey. New York: Appleton Century-Crofts, Inc., 1932.

Jordan, Thomas. *The Mentally Retarded*. Columbus, Ohio: Charles E. Merrill Books, Inc., 1961.

Kirk, S. A. *Early Education of the Mentally Retarded.* Urbana: University of Illinois Press, 1958.

Oster, Jakob. *Mongolism.* Copenhagen: Danish Science Press, 1953.

Masland, R. L., S. B. Sarason, and T. Gladwin. *Mental Subnormality.* New York: Basic Books, Inc., 1958.

Penrose, Lionel S. *The Biology of Mental Defect.* New York: Grune and Stratton, 1949.

Sarason, S. B. *Psychological Problems in Mental Deficiency.* New York: Harper & Brothers, 3rd ed., 1959.

Strauss, A. A., and Laura E. Lehtinen. *Psychopathology and Education of the Brain-Injured Child.* New York: Grune and Stratton, 1947.

Tredgold, A. F. and R. F. Tredgold. *A Textbook of Mental Deficiency.* Baltimore, Md.: Williams and Wilkins Company, 8th ed., 1952.

Wallin, J. E. Wallace. *Children with Mental and Physical Handicaps.* New York: Prentice-Hall, Inc., 1949.

4

The Educable Mentally Retarded Child

The educable mentally retarded child has been defined as one who has potentialities for development in (1) minimum educability in the academic subjects of the school, (2) social adjustment to such a point that he can get along independently in the community, and (3) minimum occupational adequacy to such a degree that he can later support himself partially or totally at the adult level.

Educable mentally retarded children are usually not recognized as mentally retarded at the preschool level. Although they are slightly delayed in talking, language, and sometimes walking, the retardation is not so great as to cause alarm on the part of the parents. Most of these children are not known to be mentally retarded until they enter school and begin to fail in learning the required subject matter. An example of the life of an educable mentally retarded child may be illustrated with the case of Billy.

A Case Study

Billy was the first-born child of a family of mediocre income and education. The father had left school at the age of 15 after completing the sixth grade. The mother was reported to have left school in the ninth grade at the age of 16. The father was employed sporadically at laboring jobs, currently ground maintenance in a small plant. The mother, at the time Billy entered school, was occupied as a housewife with three children. They lived in a small house of two bedrooms in the poorer area of a middle-sized city. The family had been known to social agencies at a time when the father was unemployed and relief was requested.

When Billy was 6 years old he entered school and was placed in the first grade as other children were. On the Stanford-Binet test he obtained an IQ of 68 and a mental age of 4 years, 1 month. Most of the children in the class had mental levels of around 6 and were able to cope with the instruction in reading and other school subjects. But Billy was not ready for first grade. He completed the first year without even beginning to learn to read. Because of this failure, he was retained in the first grade for a second year, when he was 7 years of age.

At the age of 8 Billy still could not read. However, the school had retained him in the first grade once and was reluctant to keep an 8-year-old child with beginning 6-year-olds. Consequently, they placed him in the second grade even though his mental age (5 years, 5 months) was still below that required for reading. At the end of the year Billy was still unable to read although he had picked up a few words. He had now attended school for three years without beginning to read. At the age of 9, Billy was retained in the second grade because he could not read. His mental level was now 6 years, 1 month; mentally he was ready to begin reading like normal 6-year-olds. At the end of the second year in second grade he had picked up a little reading and was sent into the third grade, since the school did not wish to retain him in the second grade for a third year. By this time Billy was 10 years old, but he was unable to keep up with 8-year-old children doing third-grade work. Although he began to do some reading and number work and to participate in the oral activities of the class, he felt inferior. At this time he became unpopular with the children because he took advantage of his size, strength, and physical abilities and became a bully. Children did not seek him out as a friend.

The third-grade teacher became frustrated with Billy because of his nonachievement in class. She wondered why he was placed in the third grade when he could barely do first-grade work. She had to devote considerable attention to his problems with other children, and it was necessary to prepare special lessons which could occupy him while she taught the rest of the class.

At this time the school personnel began facing the problem of the educable mentally retarded like Billy and decided to organize a special class. As finally set up, the class had fourteen children in it, aged from 9 to 14 and with IQ's ranging from 55 to 80. Billy was placed in this class and remained in it until the age of 16, when he left school. By this time he was achieving academically at the beginning fourth-grade level, and his social adjustment to his classmates was fair. Obtaining a part-time job during the summer as an usher in the theater he wanted to continue it during the year and so quit school. By the age of 22 Billy had tried seven different part-time or full-time jobs. At this time he was drafted into the army, where he made satisfactory adjustment in the infantry. He was discharged after his period of military service as a private first-class.

The example just given is only an illustration of the problems facing an educable mentally retarded child in the regular grades and through postadolescence. In the regular classes he was misplaced according to both age and academic achievement yet was unable to profit sufficiently from the regular grades to warrant his retention there.

Billy's social maturity and social adjustment also were retarded. He was not able to get along adequately with children of his own age because their play interests and activities were beyond his. He tended to play with younger children. In spite of such discrepancies it was important for the school to allow him to go through the growing stages, to learn to get along with individuals, learn to respect property rights, learn to respect the rights of others, learn to give and take with other children, so that at the adult level he could participate in the activities of the community, go to work by himself, and do the many things which the average person does for himself. For this reason special classes for the educable mentally retarded have been organized, where children of roughly the same age, same capacities, and similar achievements can learn together in a classroom situation.

The Growth Pattern

The profile of an educable mentally retarded child given in Chapter 3 (Case B) represents an average educable mentally retarded child. It does not represent a particular individual, since a single person has many more discrepancies. The profile is the smoothed curve of averages in these characteristics. To more adequately represent the educable mentally retarded child the profile should be a band rather than a line. Using such a band, Figure 12 shows the range of development in each area for children usually labeled educable. On each characteristic most of these children will fall somewhere within the shaded area. They range in IQ from 50 or 55 up to 75 or 80. An educable mentally retarded child of 12 will therefore have a mental age between 6 and 9 years, as indicated by the shaded area.

FIGURE 12

Profile Showing Range of Abilities in a Group of Educable Mentally Retarded Children

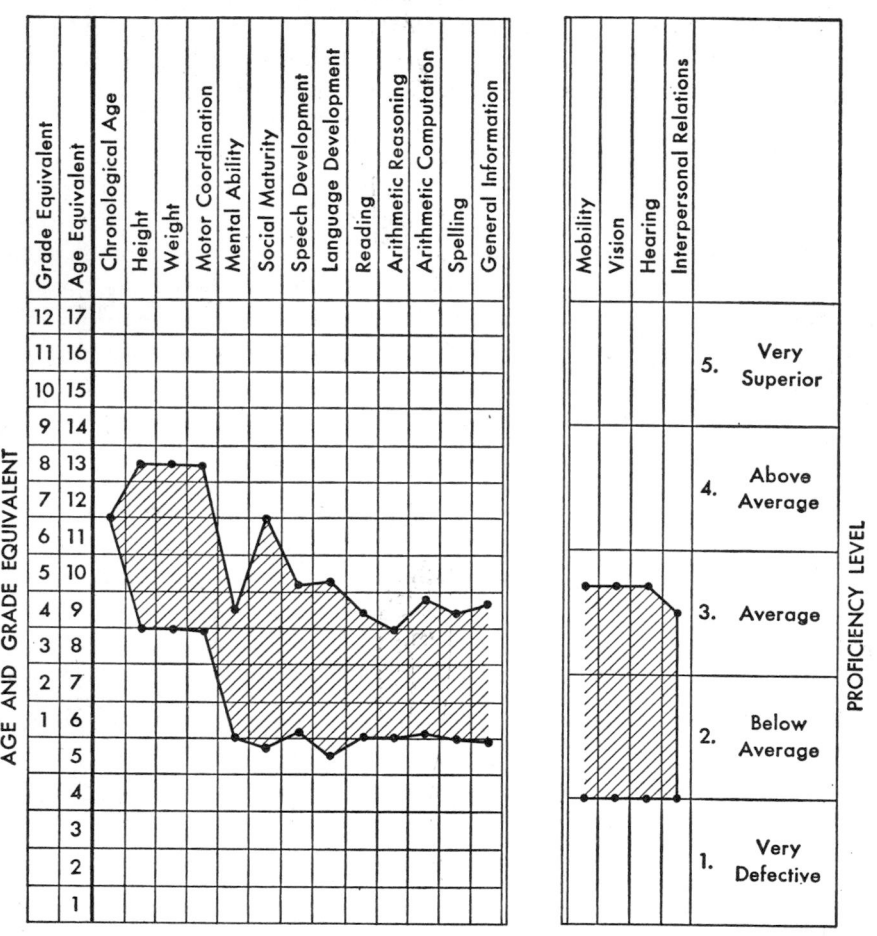

It should be noted that in height, weight, and motor coordination some of the retarded children are higher than average children but the majority of them are average or below. In other words, for physical characteristics there is an overlap between the educable mentally retarded and the average child.

On mental age there is no overlap since all, by definition, are below average. On social maturity there is a wider discrepancy. Some educable mentally retarded children are near average in social maturity, but the large majority are below average. On speech and language development and reading and other academic subjects there is no overlap; the educable mentally retarded child is definitely below the average. On other characteristics the overlap is considerable, for although on the whole there are more defects in ability to see and hear and in mobility among the educable mentally retarded than among the average, many of the former are quite normal in these respects. Similarly there is an overlap in interpersonal relations; some of the educable mentally retarded are near average but the majority are below average.

Characteristics

It is difficult to list characteristics found in all educable mentally retarded children. No single child has all of the characteristics, for some are peculiar to only a certain group. Nevertheless, a teacher or diagnostician should keep the following in mind in identifying or teaching the educable mentally retarded.

Physical Characteristics

1. In height, weight, and motor coordination most educable mentally retarded children approximate normal children.

2. Because a small number have organic causes for the retardation, such as brain injury, these few are likely to be physically inferior to normal children.

3. More handicaps of vision, hearing, and motor coordination are found among the educable mentally retarded. However, a substantial number do not have such defects.

4. Many retarded children come from substandard homes, which are generally inferior in sanitation and attention to health matters.

Intellectual Characteristics

1. The mentally retarded child shows low performance on verbal and nonverbal intelligence tests. His IQ will be in the range from 50 or 55 to 75 or 80. This implies a rate of mental development approximately one-half to three-fourths that of an average child.

2. Retarded mental development may include slowness in maturation of specific intellectual functions needed for school work, such as being significantly low in memory for auditory and visual materials, generalizing ability, language ability, conceptual and perceptual abilities, imagination and creative abilities, and other functions considered basically intellectual.

Academic Characteristics

1. The educable mentally retarded child is not ready for reading, writing, spelling, and arithmetic when he enters school at the age of 6. He does not begin to acquire these skills until he is about 8 years old or even, perhaps, until he is 11. This delay in learning is related to mental age, not to chronological age.

2. The rate at which the child progresses in school is comparable to his rate of mental development, that is, about one-half to three-quarters the rate of the average child. He should not be expected to cover a year's material in a year's time, as do average children.

3. At the end of his formal school career his academic achievement will probably have reached second- to sixth-grade level, depending upon his mental maturation.

Personal and Social Characteristics

There are no basic social traits which differentiate the educable mentally retarded from the average child. Negative social or interpersonal traits sometimes attributed to the former are usually related to situations in which they are placed. These social characteristics are by-products of the difference between the expectancies of society and the abilities of the mentally retarded to cope with the requirements.

1. Short attention span or lack of concentration and participation of the mentally retarded child in a regular classroom is often engendered by expecting him to respond like other children to materials he cannot learn or understand in a classroom situation. This characteristic, quite prevalent when retarded children are in the regular grades, tends to disappear when materials and methods are geared to their ability to succeed.

2. Low frustration tolerance has been ascribed to the mentally retarded. It is also related to repeated failure experiences in life and in school since the child is expected to function according to his chronological age. Tolerance for frustration can be increased by a home or school environment which will avoid failure and substitute success experiences.

3. Social values and attitudes generally correspond to those of the home and neighborhood associates and are, in many instances, typical of low socioeconomic areas and areas of substandard housing.

4. The retarded child's play interests correspond more closely to those of children of his own mental age than of similar chronological age.

5. There are more behavior problems and there is slightly more delinquency among the retarded in proportion to their numbers than among children of average intelligence. This may be partially the result of

the substandard environment in which a large percentage of these children live. Since behavior problems also stem from the discrepancy between the child's capacity to perform and the requirements of the environment, a finding dramatically evident among retarded children, it is important that the environment of the latter, both home and school, be harmonized with their capacity to perform and to learn. This, of course, is one of the reasons why special classes are organized.

Occupational Characteristics

1. The educable mentally retarded can learn to do skilled and semiskilled work at the adult level.

2. Their success in unskilled occupational tasks is generally related to personality, social, and interpersonal characteristics rather than to the ability to execute the task assigned.

3. Employment records of the educable mentally retarded show that approximately 80 per cent eventually adjust to occupations of an unskilled or semiskilled nature and partially or totally support themselves. The occupational adjustment of the retarded is further discussed later in this chapter.

Purposes and Objectives of Education of the Mentally Retarded

In organizing an educational program for the educable mentally retarded, the first task is to determine its basic goals. Actually, they do not differ from the general objectives for all children. For example, the Educational Policies Commission has listed four major objectives of education: (1) self-realization, (2) human relationships, (3) economic efficiency, and (4) civic responsibility.[1] These apply to the educable mentally retarded as well as the normal. The chief differences are the addition of more specific objectives, the limits which the educability of these children imposes on the attainment of the objectives, and the adaptations in instruction needed to attain the more limited objectives.

Kirk and Johnson have listed the purposes of a program for the educable mentally retarded:

1. They should be educated to get along with their fellow men; i.e., they should develop social competence through numerous social experiences.

2. They should learn to participate in work for the purpose of earning

---

[1] Educational Policies Commission, *The Purposes of Education in American Democracy* (Washington: National Education Association, 1938), p. 47.

their own living; i.e., they should develop occupational competence through efficient vocational guidance and training as a part of their school experience.

3. They should develop emotional security and independence in the school and in the home through a good mental hygiene program.

4. They should develop habits of health and sanitation through a good program of health education.

5. They should learn the minimum essentials of the tool subjects, even though their academic limits are third to fifth grade.

6. They should learn to occupy themselves in wholesome leisure time activities through an educational program that teaches them to enjoy recreational and leisure time activities.

7. They should learn to become adequate members of a family and a home through an educational program that emphasizes home membership as a function of the curriculum.

8. They should learn to become adequate members of a community through a school program that emphasizes community participation.[2]

Stated in different words and in broader concepts, the program should stress the development of (1) social competence, (2) personal adequacy, and (3) occupational competence. Social competence refers primarily to the ability of the individual to get along with his fellow men, that is, his family, his school and neighborhood mates, and other members of the community. Personal adequacy refers to his ability to live with himself in some sort of equilibrium. Occupational competence refers to his ability to support himself partially or totally in some productive activity.

Goldstein and Seigle have compiled a curriculum guide utilizing multidimensional objectives. They have delineated ten life functions, which persist throughout the life of the individual: (1) citizenship, (2) communicating, (3) home and family, (4) leisure time, (5) management of materials and money, (6) occupational adequacy, (7) physical and mental health, (8) safety, (9) social adjustment, and (10) travel.

> The Life Functions lend themselves to a further breakdown within an educational frame of reference. Identifiable within each Life Function are the behaviors and skills necessary to their performance. These behaviors and skills can be viewed as proficiencies in subject matter to be acquired in the course of school participation.[3]

Goldstein and Seigle's curriculum guide was further subdivided into the traditional academic areas of learning: (1) arithmetic, (2) fine arts,

[2] Samuel A. Kirk and Orville Johnson, *Educating the Retarded Child* (Boston: Houghton Mifflin Company, 1951), p. 118.

[3] Herbert Goldstein and Dorothy Seigle, *A Curriculum Guide for Teachers of the Educable Mentally Handicapped*, Circular Series B-3, No. 12, (Springfield, Ill.: Office of the Superintendent of Public Instruction, 1958), p. 1.

(3) language arts, (4) physical education, (5) practical arts, (6) science, and (7) social relationships.

The third phase of the curriculum guide divides the traditional learnings into developmental sequences for (1) the primary class, (2) the intermediate class, and (3) the advanced or secondary class.

By (1) defining life functions, (2) delineating the necessary academic learnings for the educable mentally retarded, and (3) listing the specific activities on a sequential and developmental level, Goldstein and Seigle have produced a guide from which a teacher can organize her own course of study.

Adjustment in the Community

The ultimate purpose of educating mentally retarded children is to help them adjust to the community at the adult level as social participants and wage earners.

During earlier days many of the educable mentally retarded were committed to institutions. It was believed that they could obtain training there and later be paroled to the community as rehabilitated individuals. But the institutions were not being built fast enough to accommodate all the educable mentally retarded as well as those who were more severely retarded. The organization of special classes in the public schools, beginning in about 1900, was aimed at educating the retarded in the community where they would later live and work. At the same time, the institutions were not even keeping pace with admission applications for the trainable and totally dependent. Most institutions do not now admit the educable retarded unless the situation is complicated by other serious problems such as dependency or delinquency. Overcrowded conditions permit them to admit only emergency cases. The problem of the educable mentally retarded has therefore become a problem for the schools and the community.

What Success Has Been Achieved?

To determine how well the educable mentally retarded adjust socially and occupationally at the adult level, numerous follow-up studies have been conducted.

One of the first of these was made by Channing.[4] She followed up 1000 special class graduates in ten large cities in the United States, approximately five years after they had left school, and found that a

[4] Alice Channing, *Employment of Mentally Deficient Boys and Girls*, Department of Labor, Bureau Publication No. 210 (Washington: Government Printing Office, 1932).

large proportion of them were employed and earned wages not far below those of their normal peers. Specifically, 20 per cent of the boys and 34 per cent of the girls were out of work half the time as compared to 8 per cent of unselected boys and 11 per cent of unselected girls of comparable age. Channing pointed out that the subnormal can obtain employment but that their employment records are less satisfactory than those for an unselected group.

Kennedy compared 356 individuals who had been diagnosed as mentally subnormal when they were in school with 129 adults of normal IQ, matched for age, sex, and socioeconomic status.[5] Since the study was conducted during a period of high employment, better work records were found among the retarded than those shown by Channing in the late 1920's. Kennedy found that (1) there were no differences in marriage rate among the two groups, (2) the retarded had a higher divorce rate, and (3) there was a tendency for the retarded to have an unsatisfactory work record, but little difference in wages earned. The conclusion was that there were many more similarities between the educable retarded and the normals than there were differences. Some of the adjustment differences noted indicated that the retarded participated less in recreational activities (theater, sports, dancing) and read less. Their jobs were primarily of the unskilled type, while many of the normal adults had office jobs requiring some academic education.

The most extensive long-term follow-up study was conducted by Baller[6] in 1935 and followed up by Charles[7] in 1953. Originally Baller selected 206 individuals who had previously been classified as mentally deficient and enrolled in special classes in Lincoln, Nebraska. He compared their social and economic status with that of a group of others of the same age who as children had been considered normal. He found many more infractions of the law and considerable job instability. Charles found 75 per cent of this group fifteen years after they had been studied by Baller. At the time of Baller's study, the United States was in a depression and there was much unemployment. When Charles made his study, unemployment was at a minimum. His findings were as follows:

1. Eighty per cent of the sample found were married.

2. Twenty-one per cent of the married group had been divorced. These marriage and divorce rates were lower than the national averages.

[5] Ruby Jo Kennedy, *The Social Adjustment of Morons in a Connecticut City* (Hartford, Conn.: Mansfield-Southbury Training Schools Social Service Department, 1948).

[6] W. R. Baller, "A Study of the Present Social Status of a Group of Adults Who, When They Were in Elementary Schools, Were Classified as Mentally Deficient," *Genetic Psychology Monographs,* 18 (1936), 165–244.

[7] D. C. Charles, "Ability and Accomplishment of Persons Earlier Judged Mentally Deficient," *Genetic Psychology Monographs,* 47 (1953), 3–71.

3. About 80 per cent of the married subjects had children; the average number of children per family was 2.03. The national average at that time was 2.62.

4. Their children were, on the whole, making satisfactory progress in school. The average IQ of the 73 children tested was 95 and IQ's ranged from 50 to 138.

5. Eighty-three per cent of the group located were self-supporting, some living in shacks and some in expensive new homes.

6. Laboring occupations for the males and housekeeping for the females constituted the majority of occupations. A few had managerial positions.

7. Twenty-four of the subjects were retested with the Wechsler-Bellevue Intelligence Scale. The average verbal IQ was 72, the performance IQ was 88, and the total scale was 81. These scores were considerably higher than the original Binet ratings.

8. Sixty per cent of the men had violated the law. Most of the offenses, however, were traffic or civil violations of some kind. None was serious.

The numerous studies on the social and vocational adjustment of the educable mentally retarded which have been reported show that the large majority do adjust to society and become self-supporting citizens. The degree of their adjustment is contingent upon a number of factors beyond the control of the mentally retarded. These include the economic condition of the country. In periods of high employment the mentally retarded obtain jobs and contribute their skills to society. In periods of unemployment a larger proportion of them, as compared to their normal peers, become unemployed.

In conclusion it may be stated that the educable mentally retarded are able to adjust to society and lead a normal life in the community if the social conditions of the community are conducive to their adjustment. It is the problem of schools and society to educate these children and assist them in becoming self-supporting and contributing members of society.

The Organization of Special Schools and Classes

If educable mentally retarded children are unable to cope successfully with the curriculum of the regular grades, what kind of organization is necessary for their maximum growth and development?

The regular school is organized by grade levels. In general, the normal children placed in grades are of approximately the same chronological age. It is assumed that these children develop at about the same rate and that the regular classroom instruction can be adapted to the individual differences within a grade. But as has been indicated earlier, the educable mentally retarded child is too far below the average child to adjust in the regular grade. For that reason, throughout the world[8] various forms of special school and classroom organization have evolved in school systems.

The Segregated Departmentalized Special School

In a few school systems the mentally retarded have been housed in one school, a special school with different groupings according to age, mental age, and achievement level. Here a departmental organization is usually found in which children go to various teachers for physical education, arithmetic, reading, social studies, arts and crafts, and so forth at different periods of the day.

Special segrated schools, although relatively common in earlier days, are at present quite rare owing to a changing philosophy and to certain organizational problems. They have often been stigmatized as "dummy schools." Parents have objected to sending their children to a special school, preferring to have them go to the neighborhood school. Although there are some advantages to segregated schools of this type, most educators believe that such an organization is not a suitable one for the educable mentally retarded child. It tends to become institutionalized and certainly reduces the child's opportunities to associate with average children. In Europe the special school is quite common.[9]

The Ungraded Special Class

The ungraded special class is frequently used in a school system with only a small group of educable mentally retarded children. If there are eight to fifteen children in a school system (not sufficient to form several classes), they may be grouped in one ungraded class, where ages range between 8 and 16 and mental abilities are widely divergent. These classes tend to be smaller than homogeneous classes but they are actually not ideal, since the children must be grouped within the class at very different achievement levels.

The Modified Special Class

Some school systems are so small that they do not have a sufficient number of children for a homogeneous or even an ungraded class. Various forms of organization may be used in this situation. Basically, they involve including the mentally retarded children in a special class for part of the day and assigning them to the regular classes the rest of the day.

[8] *Organization of Special Education for Mentally Deficient Children,* Publication No. 214 (Geneva: International Bureau of Education, 1960).
[9] *Ibid.*

This allows the special class teacher to include not only educable mentally retarded children but some educationally retarded children also. These classes are not entirely satisfactory since they often become "dumping grounds" for all types of children with various problems, including cases of reading difficulty, slow learners, behavior problems, and some educable mentally retarded. A teacher of such a class cannot organize a consistent developmental program for the mentally retarded child.

The Itinerant Teacher Program

A few school systems have tried to provide for the educable mentally retarded by allowing them to remain in the regular grades while employing an itinerant teacher to go from class to class to help the child and the regular teacher with materials and methods. This is to some extent a compromise program and is applicable to widely dispersed rural areas where it is difficult to organize a central class. Although having itinerant tutors for children with a specific disability such as a speech problem or reading disability is sound, such a program for the mentally retarded is not equally appropriate. These children require a total educational program rather than tutoring in one subject, such as reading, which is the usual activity of an itinerant teacher for the mentally retarded.

The Homogeneous Special Class

The homogeneous special class is the organization preferred by most special educators. It is made up of educable mentally retarded children with a small range of chronological ages (two to four years) and mental ages (one to two years). It is more efficient for a teacher to conduct a program for children whose chronological ages range from 6 to 9 and whose mental ages range from 4 to 6 than to plan for a range twice this large.

Principles of Organizing Special Classes

Organizing special classes is not to be accomplished without planning. It requires the identification of mentally retarded children by means of teacher referral, individual psychological examinations, social histories, and medical evaluation. It requires the selection of a properly qualified teacher. It requires decisions on the kinds of classes there will be, where they will be located, how big they will be, and how parent cooperation can be maximized.

Kirk and Johnson have listed the principles which should be followed in organizing special classes.[10] The following is a condensation of their formulations:

[10] Kirk and Johnson, *op. cit.*, pp. 126–128.

1. *The younger the children, the smaller the class.* Based on this principle, a primary class for young retarded children should have an enrollment of eight to twelve, while a class of adolescent children in the secondary school, where they are more self-sufficient and where some of them are sent to other classes, could have an enrollment of twelve to eighteen children per teacher depending upon the organization of the class.

2. *The more heterogeneous the group, the smaller the class.* Based on this principle, a class with a wide range of ages and mental abilities is more difficult to organize and teach than would be the case if the children were all of about the same age and mental level. If the group is homogeneous, a larger class can be adequately handled.

3. *Special classes for mentally retarded children should be organized within regular elementary and secondary schools.* In school systems one elementary school from among three or four can be selected to house one or two special classes. It is preferable to have the children go to their neighborhood school rather than to one central school. This principle is not consistent with the plan of organizing just one special school housing only mentally retarded children.

4. *The teacher selected to plan for and educate the mentally retarded should be thoroughly trained.* To modify the school program and adapt instructional materials and techniques is a professional task requiring special training.

5. *Adequate diagnosis of these children should be made before they are placed in the special class.* Special classes for educable mentally retarded children should not be dumping grounds for all school failures in a public school system. It is necessary that the children be properly diagnosed and their assets and liabilities be discovered before they are placed in a special class.

6. *Cooperation of the parents should be solicited before their children are assigned to a special class.* It is necessary for the school personnel to explain to parents the mental development of the child and to seek their cooperation before placing him in a special class. Going ahead without the consent and cooperation of the parents sometimes leads to difficulties in the program for the child.

7. *Enrollment in newly organized classes should be increased gradually.* When a new class is being initiated it is best started with a small group of children. The teacher can then more easily become acquainted with the children and the children will have an opportunity to become acquainted with each other. Placing twelve or fifteen children, most of whom are strangers to each other and to the teacher, in a new class all at once makes it difficult for both the pupils and the teacher.

8. *The teacher of the special class should be given considerable lati-*

tude in organizing the curriculum according to the needs and abilities of the children. Special classes do not ordinarily follow a standard curriculum because of the diverse nature and characteristics of the children involved. It is necessary for the teacher, as the trained specialist, to have freedom to organize the class according to the abilities and needs of the particular children assigned to her. This of course does not mean that she lacks a program, but rather that she is flexible enough to suit the curriculum to the children.

Principles of Instruction in Special Education

In Chapter 1 special education was defined as the part of education which is extra or in addition to that ordinarily offered to the average children in a school. A legitimate question would be: What additional practices and procedures are used in a special class for the mentally retarded?

Besides the formulation of specific objectives and the organization of a special class, there are certain adaptations of instructional materials and procedures, which we shall examine.

Assessment

The mentally retarded child must have a special diagnosis including medical, social, psychological, and educational evaluations before he is assigned to a special class. A reassessment should be made at periodic intervals thereafter. His level of development in various areas should be evaluated as was done for each of the children represented in the developmental profiles. This kind of assessment, together with the medical and social history, will give the teacher an indication of the child's assets and liabilities, an insight into his abilities and achievements as shown by his developmental pattern, and facts about his physical and social status before she begins instruction. It will give her a good beginning on the ongoing evaluation she must make. Modifications of educational and instructional practices are to a large extent dependent upon the adequate assessment of the child. This is one feature which differentiates the education of the retarded child from that of the average, since the normal child does not usually need such a comprehensive and thorough evaluation.

Special Materials.

Educable mentally retarded children need special materials. The physical size of the classroom, the desks, and the furnishings are not different from those of a regular grade, but the instructional materials must be different. For example, the reading books used in regular classes are geared to the development of an average child. Whereas it may take seventeen repetitions of a word before the average child can learn it in a primer or preprimer, the retarded child may need twenty-five or thirty repetitions before he will learn it. This means that the primer or first reader goes a little too fast for efficient instruction of the retarded child, and the teacher must find supplementary material, fill in with additional instructional materials, and use specialized instructional procedures in a variety of situations if the child is to learn efficiently. It is necessary to improvise, adapt, and adjust books and materials to the rate of learning.

Special Remediation

Some mentally retarded children develop relatively evenly but substantially below the normal in many areas. For instance, a retarded child may be below the average in language, speech, and arithmetic but may not have special disabilities. He is retarded in general. On the other hand, some educable mentally retarded children have specific disabilities over and beyond their developmental retardation. This is illustrated in the case of Johnny, who was developing evenly in most areas at a 9-year level but who had not been able to learn to read. With reading about two and a half years below his other competencies, he had a specific disability in reading in addition to his mental retardation. Some children may have specific disabilities in communication, or in arithmetic, or in relating abstract ideas. It is therefore necessary for the teacher to find these special lacks in the retarded, to secure more detailed diagnoses, and to introduce remedial procedures.

Throughout the last century there have been attempts to discover specific disabilities and to find appropriate clinical teaching procedures which will remedy them. Strauss and Lehtinen developed special clinical teaching procedures for certain kinds of brain-damaged children.[11] Hegge, Kirk, and Kirk developed the *Remedial Reading Drills* for educable mentally retarded children with reading disabilities.[12] Decroly, Montessori, and others all attempted to develop special clinical methods. At present our diagnostic procedures and methods of remediation are still in the developmental stages, but work is under way to find special methods in differential diagnosis and special clinical teaching procedures for the deficits discovered.

Special Learning Principles

The primary characteristic of mentally retarded children is that they

[11] A. A. Strauss and L. E. Lehtinen, *Psychopathology and Education of the Brain-Injured Child* (New York: Grune and Stratton, 1947).

[12] T. G. Hegge, S. A. Kirk, and W. D. Kirk, *Remedial Reading Drills* (Ann Arbor, Mich.: George Wahr Publishing Company, 1940).

do not learn as readily as others of the same chronological age by the methods ordinarily used. Instruction therefore must utilize the best practices in learning, as follows:

1. Progress is from the known to the unknown, using concrete materials to foster understanding of more abstract facts.

2. The child is helped to transfer known abilities from one situation to another, rather than being expected to make generalizations spontaneously.

3. The teacher uses many repetitions in a variety of experiences.

4. Learning is stimulated through exciting situations.

5. Inhibitions are avoided by presenting one idea at a time and presenting learning situations by sequential steps.

6. Learning is reinforced through using a variety of sense modalities — visual, vocal, auditory, kinesthetic.

Systematic Instruction

Educable mentally retarded children lack a high level of generalization and are usually unable to learn material incidentally, without instruction, as the average child learns it. Much of the knowledge and skills acquired by the average child is learned without specific instruction by the teacher. But for the retarded child instruction needs to be systematically presented without too much reliance on incidental learning. Learning should be programmed in sequence and presented in such a way that the child will learn at a rate compatible with his development. Systematic instruction in every area requires time, planning, and insight, the essentials in a special education program for the educable mentally retarded child.

Individualized Instruction

The term "individualized instruction" has two meanings. In the regular grades it means that the teacher adapts instruction to individual differences. The organization of the special class with its philosophy results in a kind of individualization which is not workable in the regular grades. It includes both the adaptation of instruction and materials to the achievement level of each child and also clinical educational teaching for special disabilities. The latter is more feasible in a special class because of the special assessment furnished the teacher by the psychologist and the smaller size of the class.

Success Experiences

Educable mentally retarded children who have failed in the regular grades and then been placed in a special class may have developed low frustration tolerance, negative attitudes toward school work, and possibly some compensatory behavior problems which make them socially unpopular. The best way to cope with these problems is to organize a *day-to-day* program presenting the child with short-range as well as long-range tasks in which he succeeds. The self-concept and the self-evaluation of the child are dependent upon how well he succeeds in the assignments given to him. Thus a special class teacher must be very careful to see not only that the child does not fail but also that he experiences positive success and knows that he has succeeded. Although this principle is applicable to all children it is particularly necessary with children who are retarded. They face enough failures in school and in life without having to repeat them over and over again in a classroom situation.

Grouping the Mentally Retarded

In the regular school, children are grouped according to chronological age since other abilities and achievements correlate with age. The mentally retarded, however, because of their discrepancies in growth, require a different kind of grouping.

Since there are usually not enough retarded children of the same mental, social, physical, and chronological age in any one school to warrant a strictly homogeneous grouping, compromises are made. For instructional purposes there are usually five levels: (1) a preschool class, (2) an elementary primary class, (3) an elementary intermediate class, (4) a junior and/or senior secondary school class, and (5) a postschool vocational training and placement program. These programs will be discussed briefly.

The Preschool Class

Although many educable mentally retarded children below the age of 6 are enrolled in regular kindergartens and nursery schools, kindergarten or nursery school attendance is not compulsory. Parents from the lower socioeconomic levels cannot afford to avail themselves of these facilities for their children. Studies by Skeels,[13] Kirk,[14] and others[15] have presented strong evidence that mentally retarded children from lower socioeconomic areas and cultural levels may be functioning at a low intellectual level because of cultural deprivation. In these cases preschools tend

---

[13] Harold M. Skeels, "A Study of the Effects of Differential Stimulation on Mentally Retarded Children: A Follow-up Report," *American Journal of Mental Deficiency,* 46 (January, 1942), 340–350.

[14] S. A. Kirk, *Early Education of the Mentally Retarded* (Urbana: University of Illinois Press, 1958).

[15] S. B. Sarason, *Psychological Problems in Mental Deficiency* (New York: Harper & Brothers, 3rd ed., 1959).

to raise the rate of development. It is unfortunate in our society that those children who need preschools most are not given the opportunity to attend them, while those from the higher cultural and economic levels who have maximum nurture at home, and probably need it less, are the ones who do receive preschool education.

Preschool classes for the educable mentally retarded are not common. One reason is that these children are not identified as retarded at an early age unless the retardation is associated with lack of speech or some physical manifestation such as cerebral palsy. It is the school environment which brings the retardation to light.

The program of a preschool for educable mentally retarded children, whose chronological ages are between 3 and 6 years and whose mental ages range between 2 and 4, is very similar to that of any other nursery school or kindergarten. It is designed to develop the mental and social abilities of the children. Generally it is organized as an environment with numerous centers of interest. The teachers allow the child to react to the environment, and through additions of materials or verbal suggestions attempt to elevate or improve his various mental and social abilities.

The Elementary Primary Class

One of the more common classes for the mentally retarded in school systems is the primary class. Here we find children who are 6 to 10 years of age and whose mental levels range from 3 or 4 to 6. This grouping draws together those children who are ready for a social and academic program. Since they are not yet sufficiently mature to learn the elements of reading, the program aims at furthering their social, psychological, and physical readiness for the next stage of development.

The primary class program is generally more structured than is that of a preschool. At this stage the children learn by means of games and activities of short duration, which can be structured for the purpose of developing (1) confidence through successful accomplishment, (2) habits of physical health and safety, (3) language and speech skills, (4) beginnings in quantitative concepts, (5) visual and auditory abilities, (6) thinking abilities, and (7) general work habits and attitudes which will permit them to benefit from group participation.[16]

The Elementary Intermediate Class

The intermediate special class in the elementary school is the most frequently found special class. In most schools, the child attends the regular grades until he has failed for several years. Then he is referred

[16] The reader is referred to the bibliography at the end of the chapter for detailed curriculums and descriptions of programs in elementary and secondary classes.

for examination, tested, and assigned to a special class. Children in this group are from 9 to 12 or 13 years of age and have mental ages between 6 and 9.

In the intermediate class the child (1) learns the tool subjects of reading, writing, and arithmetic, (2) adjusts to and learns about his physical environment (the community, the state, the nation), (3) learns about his social environment (people, customs, and institutions), and (4) learns about himself and his drives, desires, and aspirations.

Skills in the tool subjects are developed during periods of systematic instruction and during periods of application of the skills to life situations. Work units or experience units have been used extensively in classes for the mentally retarded. These have been found most useful in teaching the children about their physical, social, and personal environment.

The Secondary School Class

In the past, the educable mentally retarded child who attended the intermediate elementary class remained in that class until he left school at the end of the compulsory school age. Recently, however, school systems have organized special classes at both the junior and senior high school levels. Children are admitted to the junior high school special class at ages 13 and 14, and to the senior high school class at age 15 or 16. Special classes in senior high school have tended to increase the school's holding power for these children until the age of 18 or 19.

A special class in the high school usually involves the assignment of the children to one special teacher for a part of the day. In this extended home room the pupils continue with instruction in the tool subjects but they go to some classes with other high school pupils — for example, beginning classes in home economics, industrial education, physical education, art, and music.

The curriculum for educable mentally retarded children in the secondary school emphasizes:

1. Experiences to extend their efficiency in the tool subjects of reading, arithmetic, spelling, and writing. Since this is terminal academic education for the educable retarded child, he should learn to utilize these tool subjects in everyday activities.
2. Development of "home building" skills. During this terminal education the pupils should learn to become participating members of a family and to be responsible for family activities. Home economics for the girls and household mechanics for the boys are important aspects of the secondary school curriculum.
3. Occupational education including such attitudes and skills as manners, appearance, methods of getting along with the "boss" or fellow work-

ers, following directions, expressing vocational goals and skills, general job training, and acquiring vocational information. Occupational education should not be confused with vocational education or specific trade training. These children do not necessarily go into the skilled trades and consequently are not placed in vocational schools for that purpose.

4. Getting along in society, holding a job, and participating in community life. This requires adequate social relationships and is an important goal of the secondary school curriculum. The educable mentally retarded youth should have experiences which develop good interpersonal relations with others in the community.

5. Understanding of physical and mental health. This includes good personal hygiene, attractive appearance, following of health rules, using leisure time well, establishing adequate values, acquiring a sense of achievement, accepting one's own limitations, good personal conduct, establishment of security, and pride in accomplishment.

Postschool Program

In the past, most educable mentally retarded youth could obtain unskilled jobs and partially or totally support themselves. This situation continues to some extent. However, because of the increasing complexity of our society, it is becoming more necessary to give additional training and assistance in the placement of the mentally retarded in jobs suitable to their abilities and educational level.

Job training, placement, and follow-up after the school years have been facilitated by Public Law 113, passed by the United States Congress in 1943. Prior to that time the Civilian Vocational Rehabilitation Program was confined to the physically handicapped. Under the new law the vocational rehabilitation program is also allowed to train, place, and follow up educable mentally retarded youth.

This law provides a link between school training and the vocational rehabilitation divisions which exist in all states. The school can provide the general education, and the vocational rehabilitation counselor can carry on from there. Some schools are now incorporating supervised part-time job placement with the terminal school program whenever vocational rehabilitation and the school can cooperate. These new programs are more necessary now than ever before because it is more difficult for the mentally retarded to adjust socially and vocationally in present-day society. In the first place, society is becoming more urban and more complex. In the second place, automation is decreasing the number of unskilled jobs. Our culture now places a premium on intelligence, management ability, technical progress, and machine operation. The mentally retarded will require more help in the future to adjust to a society that emphasizes service positions, professional competence, and technical skill.

Effectiveness of the Curriculum

The development of programs for the educable mentally retarded has not progressed without controversy. Research has attempted to answer some questions and to settle some controversies regarding the effectiveness of special classes and the degree of achievement of mentally retarded children in reading, arithmetic, language and speech, art and music, and physical education. Kirk has summarized the research literature in this area,[17] the results of which will be discussed below.

Are Special Classes Beneficial?

A number of studies have attempted to determine whether it is better to place retarded children in special classes or leave them in the regular grades. All of these studies compared children assigned to special classes with children of comparable IQ's remaining in the regular grades. The results have indicated that (1) except for children at the lower range of educability (IQ's in the 50's and 60's) children left in the regular grades are generally superior academically to those assigned to the special classes, but (2) the social adjustment of retarded children in the special classes is superior to those left in the regular grades, and (3) children who are left in the regular grades tend to be rejected and isolated by the average children in these classes.

Studies measuring academic progress must be viewed with caution, for finding that retarded children of the same IQ in the regular grades are academically superior may only mean that those who were most educationally retarded in a school system were the ones who were placed in the special class. It is natural for a regular teacher to refer to a special class the child who is most retarded educationally and who is the greatest problem in class.

The sociometric studies of the retarded children in the regular grades have shown quite definitely that these children are isolated and rejected by their peer group.[18] Even the studies which show low academic progress of special class children suggest a better social adjustment in the special class.

[17] Samuel A. Kirk, "Research in Education of the Mentally Retarded," *Mental Retardation 1961: A Review of Research* (Chicago: University of Chicago Press, in press).

[18] G. O. Johnson, "A Study of the Social Position of Mentally Handicapped Children in the Regular Grades," *American Journal of Mental Deficiency*, 55 (July, 1950), 60–89.

How Do Retarded Children Read?

Considerable research has been conducted on (1) the level at which mentally retarded children read and (2) what process is most successful in teaching these children to read.[19] These studies yield some interesting conclusions:

1. Mentally retarded children do not read up to their mental-age-reading-grade expectancy, probably because teachers emphasize their social adjustment rather than their academic achievement, and also because the child who is most retarded educationally is referred to the special class.

2. Research on reading methods has not shown the superiority of any one method over others. Some authors found success with the phonic method, some with the experience or other methods. Experiments testing the effectiveness of a particular procedure have been conducted on retarded children who were significantly below their mental-age-grade expectancy. These children made rapid progress during the initial stages of training, then tapered off as they approached their mental-age-grade expectancy.

3. Brain-injured children with perceptual disturbances are able to learn to read as well as non-brain-injured retarded children when emphasis is placed on reading and special methods are used.

What Are the Arithmetic Achievements of Retarded Children?

The studies on arithmetic achievement indicate that retarded children achieve in harmony with their mental-age-grade expectancy in arithmetic fundamentals but are below this expectancy in arithmetic reasoning. It appears that, according to present methods of teaching, the retarded child is able to achieve at a higher grade level in the more mechanical computational skills than in arithmetic reasoning. This may be a reflection of the methods of teaching, since it is easier to drill on computational problems than to develop insights into quantitative concepts.

Some of the differences which have been found in the processes of arithmetic suggest that retarded children are inferior to average children of the same mental age in (1) solving arithmetic problems presented verbally, (2) establishing mature habits such as eliminating "counting on fingers," (3) decreasing careless mechanical errors and errors in reading, and (4) understanding the abstract terms of mathematics, space, time, and quantity. As in reading, research workers have not been able to find

[19] L. M. Dunn and R. J. Capobianco, "Studies of Reading and Arithmetic in Mentally Retarded Boys," *Monographs of the Society for Research in Child Development,* 1954, Vol. 19, No. 1 (Lafayette, Ind.: Child Development Publications, 1956).

a significant difference between the arithmetic abilities of brain-injured and non-brain-injured retarded children.

What Are the Speech and Language Problems?

As in other areas of achievement, speech and language appear to be highly correlated with mental age. It has been found that speech defects are more prevalent in the mentally retarded than in average children and that the greater the mental defect, the greater the prevalence of speech defects. It has been difficult to show substantial improvement in retarded children's speech as a result of speech therapy.

Like speech, reading, and arithmetic, language development is related to mental age, possibly because language is a factor in intelligence tests of the verbal type. Some studies have shown, however, that language development is also related to opportunities for language usage, and that some socially deprived children have improved in language development when they were placed in more favorable environments or received special training.

Do Retarded Children Have Artistic or Musical Abilities?

Since industrial education and art and music education are standard parts of the curriculum for the mentally retarded, this phase of their education has been evaluated by some researchers.

The consensus of most workers is that art and music competence, like achievement in other areas, is related to mental age. The mentally retarded are slower to learn and remain longer at each stage. It is rare to find a mentally retarded child who has exceptional ability in art or music, although there is wide variation among the mentally retarded as a group and considerable overlap with normal children in ability.

What Are the Physical Abilities of the Retarded?

A few studies have been conducted on the motor proficiency and physical education achievements of the retarded. These studies[20] indicate that in motor proficiency retarded children are inferior to normals. Studies on the effects of physical education programs in improving motor proficiency have been inconclusive.

In some cases, however, retarded children have achieved above the average in sports like baseball and boxing. Again, there is a great deal of overlapping in ability with normal children, some mentally retarded being far above some average and gifted children in these areas; but most of them are below normal children in motor proficiency.

[20] R. J. Francis and L. Rarick, *Motor Characteristics of the Mentally Retarded,* Cooperative Research Monograph No. 1 (Washington: U.S. Department of Health, Education and Welfare, 1960).

Summary

1. Educable mentally retarded children are considered minimally educable in (a) the academic areas of the school, (b) social adjustment in the community, and (c) in the occupational field at an unskilled or semi-skilled level.

2. Although their rate of growth in the physical traits of height, weight, and motor coordination is close to that of average children, their rate of development in mental, social, and academic areas is one-half to three-fourths that of the average child.

3. With adequate education and training, the majority of educable retarded children become marginally or totally self-supporting at the adult level.

4. Special education of the mentally retarded includes the organization of special classes, adequate diagnosis of abilities and disabilities, special materials, and special instruction.

5. Special schools and classes have been organized for these children at the preschool, primary, intermediate, and secondary levels. Vocational rehabilitation services are available to them after the age of 16.

DISCUSSION QUESTIONS

1. What rate of progress in school subjects would you expect of an educable mentally retarded child whose IQ was about 70? For example, at what grade level should he be reading at age 10? 14? 16?

2. Your text states that the rate of mental development of an educable mentally retarded child is one-half to three-fourths the rate of a normal child. Does the same rate apply to educational development. Why or why not?

3. Some of the personality characteristics attributable to the educable mentally retarded include short attention span and low frustration tolerance. Are these characteristics the result of difficulty in adjustment to a difficult environment or an inevitable or inherent characteristic of mental retardation?

4. It has been stated that any grade should be flexible enough to adapt instruction to the educable mentally retarded and that the segregation of children in special classes is contrary to the principles of democracy. Debate both sides of this controversy.

5. What is "special" in a special program for the educable mentally retarded?

6. Since our society is becoming more complex, and since automation is replacing the unskilled worker, what are the future employment possibilities for the educable mentally retarded?

7. What are the relative weights of mental age, IQ, chronological age, height, weight, and personality on the prediction of performance in reading, arithmetic, art, music, and other school subjects?

8. If further research confirms the present suggestion that educable mentally retarded children in special classes adjust better socially, but do less well academically than educable mentally retarded children left in regular classes, what effect might this have on future planning for the education of the retarded?

SELECTED REFERENCES

Anderson, Meta L. *Education of Defectives in the Public Schools.* New York: World Book Company, 1917.

Burt, Cyril. *The Backward Child.* New York: Appleton-Century Company, 1937.

Davis, Guy P. *What Shall the Public Do for the Feebleminded?* A Plan for Special-School Training Under Public School Auspices. Cambridge: Harvard University Press, 1927.

Descoeudres, Alice. *The Education of Mentally Defective Children.* Boston: D. C. Heath and Company, 1928.

Duncan, John. *The Education of the Ordinary Child.* New York: Ronald Press Company, 1943.

Featherstone, William B. *Teaching the Slow Learner.* New York: Teachers College, Columbia University, 1951.

Goddard, H. H. *School Training of Defective Children.* New York: World Book Company, 4th ed., 1923.

Goldstein, Herbert, and Dorothy Seigle. *The Illinois Plan for Special Education of Exceptional Children: A Curriculum Guide for Teachers of the Educable Mentally Handicapped.* Circular Series B-3, No. 12. Springfield, Ill.: State Department of Public Instruction, 1958.

Hood, Oreste E. *Your Child or Mine.* New York: Harper & Brothers, 1957.

Ingram, Christine P. *Education of the Slow-Learning Child.* New York: The Ronald Press Company, 3rd ed., 1960.

Inskeep, Annie. *Teaching Dull and Retarded Children.* New York: The Macmillan Company, 1930.

Kennedy-Fraser, David. *Education of the Backward Child.* London: University of London Press, 1932.

Kirk, S. A. *Teaching Reading to Slow-Learning Children.* Boston: Houghton Mifflin Company, 1940.

Kirk, S. A. *Early Education of the Mentally Retarded.* Urbana: University of Illinois Press, 1958.

Kirk, S. A., M. E. Black, R. M. Duffin, I. K. Garrison, and G. O. Johnson. *Educating the Mentally Handicapped in the Secondary Schools.* Springfield, Ill.: State Superintendent of Public Instruction, Circular Series A, No. 51, Illinois Secondary School Curriculum Bulletin No. 12, 1951.

Kirk, S. A., and G. O. Johnson. *Educating the Retarded Child.* Boston: Houghton Mifflin Company, 1951.

Lewis, Richard S. *The Other Child; The Brain-Injured Child.* New York: Grune and Stratton, 1951.

Lloyd, Frances. *Educating the Subnormal Child.* New York: Philosophical Library, 1953.

Loewy, Herta. *The Retarded Child: A Guide for Parents and Teachers.* New York: Philosophical Library, 1951.

Pennsylvania University, Psychological Laboratory and Clinic. *Special Class for Backward Children.* Reported by Lightner Witmer. Philadelphia: Psychological Clinical Press, 1911.

Smith, Marion F. *Teaching the Slow Learning Child.* New York: Harper & Brothers, 1954.

Strauss, Alfred A., and Laura E. Lehtinen. *Psychopathology and Education of the Brain-Injured Child.* New York: Grune and Stratton, 1947.

Tansley, A. E., and R. Guilliford. *The Education of Slow Learning Children.* London: Routledge & Kegan Paul, 1960.

U.S. Office of Education. "Curriculum Adjustment for the Mentally Retarded." Bulletin No. 2. Washington: Government Printing Office, 1950.

Wallin, J. E. Wallace. *Education of Mentally Handicapped Children.* New York: Harper & Brothers, 1955.

5

The Trainable
Mentally Retarded Child

The trainable mentally retarded child has been defined as one who, because of subnormal intelligence, is not capable of learning in classes for the educable mentally retarded but who does have potentialities for learning (1) self-care, (2) adjustment to the home or neighborhood, and (3) economic usefulness in the home, a sheltered workshop, or an institution.

Other terms have been used to denote the *trainable child*. The terms "imbecile," "semi-dependent," "severely retarded," "middle-grade defective," and "child with an IQ between about 25 and 50" are somewhat synonomous with "trainable." The term "trainable" appears to be most widely preferred. The World Health Organization discussed the problem of terminology at length and concluded, "These children are often called 'ineducable' although the term 'trainable' has been suggested as an alternative, and this term is preferred by the Committee."[1]

Kirk has surveyed the definitions given by the various states which have established programs for trainable children and summarized the characteristics of these definitions into a composite statement for school purposes. According to this formulation, a trainable child is one who is

[1] World Health Organization, *The Mentally Subnormal Child*, Technical Report Series No. 75 (Geneva: Palais des Nations, April, 1954), pp. 23–24.

(1) of school age; (2) developing at the rate of one-third to one-half that of the normal child (IQ's on individual examinations roughly between 30 and 50); (3) of retarded mental development to such an extent that he is ineligible for classes for the educable mentally retarded but will, however, not be custodial, totally dependent, or require nursing care throughout his life; (4) capable of learning self-care tasks (such as dressing, eating, toileting) and capable of learning to protect himself from common dangers in the home, school, or neighborhood; (5) capable of learning social adjustment in the home or neighborhood and learning to share, respect property rights, and cooperate in a family unit and with the neighbors; and (6) capable of learning economic usefulness in the home and neighborhood by assisting in chores around the house or in doing routine tasks in a sheltered environment under supervision, even though he will require some care, supervision, and economic support throughout his life.[2]

The Prevalence of Trainable Mentally Retarded Children

A study of Illinois communities indicated that there are approximately 1.5 trainable children per 1000 school-age children living at home.[3] The institutions had received from these same communities less than one child per 1000. This meant that there were more children of the trainable type in a community than in institutions, but that both combined would be between two and three per 1000 school-age children.

A similar study was made in Michigan in three communities.[4] Here there appeared to be an average of 1.7 trainable children per 1000 school-age children in the community and 1.6 from those communities in institutions. Thus here there were between three and four children per 1000 school population.

Another study by Bienenstock and Coxe in New York, found that there were 1.1 trainable children per 1000 in the community and 1.7 trainable and totally dependent in institutions.[5]

The results of these studies (Table VI) indicate that there are approximately two to four children of the trainable type in a population of 1000 school-age children, and that one to two out of 1000 are in a com-

---

[2] Samuel A. Kirk, *Public School Provisions for Severely Retarded Children* (Albany: New York State Interdepartmental Health Resources Board, 1957), p. 13.

[3] *Report on Study Projects for Trainable Mentally Handicapped Children* (Springfield, Ill.: Office of the Superintendent of Public Instruction, November, 1954).

[4] *Interim Report: The Michigan Demonstration Research Project for the Severely Mentally Retarded* (Lansing: State Department of Public Instruction, October, 1955).

[5] T. Bienenstock and W. W. Coxe, *Census of Severely Retarded Children in New York State* (Albany: Interdepartmental Health Resources Board, 1956), p. 62.

munity and eligible for classes for trainable children. In terms of the organization of classes this means that there usually has to be a population of about 7000 school-age children, or a total population of 25,000 to 30,000 individuals in a community, before one class for the trainable is feasible. Such a community usually has between seven and twelve children eligible for such a class. The other trainable children would be in institutions.

TABLE VI
Rate of Trainable Children in
1000 School-Age Population

Study	In Community	In Institution	Total
Illinois Study[a]	1.49	.85	2.34
Michigan Study[b]	1.70	1.60	3.40 [sic]
New York Study[c]	1.10	1.70[d]	2.80

[a] *Report on Study Projects for Trainable Mentally Handicapped Children* (Springfield, Ill.: Superintendent of Public Instruction, November, 1954).
[b] *Interim Report of the Michigan Demonstration Project for Severely Mentally Retarded* (Lansing: State Department of Public Instruction, October, 1955).
[c] T. Bienenstock and W. W. Coxe, *Census of Severely Retarded Children in New York State* (Albany: Interdepartmental Health Resources Board, 1956), p. 62.
[d] Includes children below 25 IQ.

Provisions for Trainable Children

Institutional Provisions

The first institution for the mentally retarded in the United States was organized in Massachusetts in 1848. Since that date institutions have been built in most of the states, some states having as many as seven.

The original purpose of most of the institutions was to train the mentally retarded and return them to the community. Some states did not originally admit totally dependent children but accepted only children who were trainable and educable. Few of these institutions, however, could actually refuse admission to emergency cases of totally dependent children. As time went on, all of them began to accept children of all grades of defect, and those remaining in the institution for life were of the lowest abilities.

Thus the admissions to most of the public institutions consisted of children with all grades of mental defect. Originally, and for many years, the admissions to institutions included a larger proportion of educable than of trainable children, and more trainable than totally dependent.

Goldstein tabulated the first admissions of individuals into institutions from 1900 to 1952.[6] He found that from 1922 to 1939 the institutions admitted approximately 45 per cent morons (educable), about 30 per cent imbeciles (trainable), and approximately 17 per cent idiots (totally dependent). By 1952 the picture had changed. The moron group had dropped to approximately 35 per cent while the imbecile group had increased to 37 per cent and the idiot admissions to over 20 per cent. These figures indicate that the residential institutions are gradually becoming less like training institutions, as they were originally intended, and more like hospitals or life-care institutions.

As classes for the educable increase in the public schools, the rate of commitment to institutions of this group of the mentally retarded tends to decrease. Henderson has shown this tendency in Illinois institutions.[7] He also found that the educable child who is sent to an institution from a community is usually dependent or delinquent. The reason for removal from a community, therefore, is not only mental retardation but also an inadequate home or a tendency toward delinquency. If the child were not retarded, he would probably have been sent either to a home for dependent children or to an institution for delinquent children.

During the depression of the 1930's and, following that, World War II, with its shortages of materials and manpower, few institutions were built or expanded. As population increased (and consequently the numbers of mentally retarded), those in existence were unable to house the number applying for admission. Waiting lists became longer and longer, and the institutions which were built or expanded were far from sufficient to accomodate the new requests and also take care of the backlog of children requiring admission. This situation, together with other factors, caused parents to organize and to request provisions for their retarded children in the community.

Community Classes

It appears, from the large waiting lists, that our society is not willing to build sufficient institutions to take care of all of the trainable children in the community. Furthermore, many parents do not want to send their retarded children to institutions but would rather support them at home. This is a personal problem which in each case must be settled on its own merits.

[6] Herbert Goldstein, "Population Trends in U.S. Public Institutions for the Mentally Deficient," *American Journal of Mental Deficiency,* 63 (January, 1959), 599–604.

[7] Robert Henderson, "Factors in Commitment of Educable Mentally Handicapped Children to Illinois State Schools," doctoral dissertation, University of Illinois, 1957.

Many parents who had accepted the responsibility for keeping their children at home instead of having them committed to an institution felt the need for some kind of group activity and for some kind of organized training program. At first they met together to set up their own classes for the children, hiring their own teachers (often not adequately qualified), procuring their own supplies, and organizing classes in homes, in basements, in churches, or wherever they could find space. At the same time, they tried to make the public aware of their needs and sought the support of social agencies and state legislatures and local school boards. Some communities became cognizant of the problem and accepted the responsibility for helping to support these classes. Some communities incorporated them into the school system, thereby making it possible to improve the standards for teachers, housing, and programs. Better criteria were established for the admission of children which made possible a more homogeneous grouping.

There remains a controversy, however, as to whether training these children fits into the functions of a school or whether it is impossible for a school to offer the children experiences which will be profitable to their growth and development and which cannot be provided adequately by the family or other agencies.

The parents have argued that they, as taxpayers, have helped to pay for the public schools and that their children should not be deprived of the benefits just because they were born or have become less fortunate. They have pointed out that the statutes in many states provide that all children are entitled to an education and that school districts are required by law to supply schools for all children, not just a certain segment of the children. These statutes were drawn up before the advent of the concept of the IQ or the concept that schools can provide for many kinds of children. For that reason it is practically mandatory for schools to admit the mentally retarded and provide adequate training for them just as they provide adequate, though different, training for other children. Some states have provisions for the exclusion of children who disrupt the classroom, who are behavior problems, or who are a danger to themselves and others, but it is recognized that most of the trainable children do not fall into these categories. Thus the schools have found it difficult to exclude them on a legal basis.

On the other hand, some educators and many parents of normal children maintain that public schools should not organize classes for trainable children because this changes the concept of the role of a school. They feel that it is the function of a school to teach academic subjects and that schools should be limited to those who are educable and who can profit even at a minimum level from such a program in order to become socially and economically independent at the adult level. If a child cannot be educated to become relatively independent at the adult level, they believe, the problem is outside the scope of an educational institution.

The two points of view are exemplified by Goldberg and Cruickshank in the debate which is quoted in part below:

Yes!

By I. Ignacy Goldberg

There is growing recognition that children who are characterized as "trainable mentally retarded" are individuals with potentialities that deserve to be developed to the fullest extent.

Whether or not the public schools should provide training for this type of school-age child is a rather academic question, since many school systems have already introduced services for these children.

It was estimated that in the Fall of 1956, there were about 7,000 trainable children receiving education (or training) in over 600 public-school day classes.

In the Fall of 1958, 10 states had mandatory legislation and 15 had permissive legislation for the inclusion in the public schools of the trainable mentally retarded. Four additional states interpreted the existing statutes for exceptional children to include the trainable without further legislation. . . .

Ongoing programs for trainable children are still in such an early stage of development that it is difficult to evaluate their full success. However, several research projects initiated and financed by the U.S. Office of Education and other state, local, and private agencies are investigating the effects of school training on the subsequent adjustment of these children.

In a democracy, such children have the right to be trained to the maximum of their ability, regardless of whether they live at home or in an institution. Thus they should be: (1) educationally diagnosed; (2) placed in the best educational environment; (3) trained by qualified personnel; (4) periodically evaluated to determine progress; (5) recommended for further training and placement after "graduation" from the special class; and (6) followed up to assure optimal placement and adjustment.

What agency in our society is better qualified and equipped to assume leadership and co-ordination of the above mentioned services than the public school? And what agency is better qualified to initiate and conduct parent-education programs, educational research, and curriculum development or to regulate professional standards of teachers who work with these children?

In my opinion, there is no doubt that the public school has a responsibility to extend these programs further and, through a concentrated effort over a period of years, to decide what contribution it can make to the growth and welfare of trainable children.

No!

By William M. Cruickshank

For a number of reasons, I do not believe that the responsibility for severely retarded children should be assigned to the public schools.

First of all, public schools were established to educate those who have the ability to learn, and the severely retarded are unable to benefit from education (as distinguished from training).

Education, as defined by Dewey and others, demands the ability to generalize; to reason and make judgments; to remember and to form new concepts out of previous learning; to solve problems; to abstract and to deal with abstractions; to utilize language concepts. Obviously, the severely retarded child lacks these abilities.

Secondly, public education in the United States has been seen as a medium through which citizens could be prepared to reach a level of effective understanding of and participation in civic matters and thus return something tangible or intangible to the state.

Only by the broadest stretch of the imagination can the severely retarded child be regarded as capable of returning anything to the community.

Public education is also based on the belief that as a result of learning, the individual will be able to assume a self-directed role in society and that he will probably assume responsibility for others — his wife and children or parents.

This goal is unattainable by the severely retarded, who throughout life will be dependent upon others, even when they have had optimum training opportunities.

Thirdly, when the severely retarded are placed in the public schools, it is only natural that both parents and the community infer that such children are going to learn to do what most other pupils do in school. Such placement carries false implications of normalcy that can result only in disillusionment. There is no real advancement possible either for individual children or for society as a whole in providing public school education for the severely retarded.[8]

Regardless of the relative merits of the two points of view cited, state legislators have become aware of the problem, and in many states there are now provisions for helping — and in some cases for requiring — schools to provide facilities for trainable children. The large majority of children in any community are already under the auspices of the schools, and it has been felt that the schools, therefore, are in a better position to make the provisions necessary for this additional group.

One reason why state legislatures are willing to help provide for these children is that it is cheaper for society to provide public school classes

[8] I. Ignacy Goldberg and William M. Cruickshank, "Trainable but Noneducable," *National Educational Association Journal,* 47 (December, 1958), 622–623.

than it is to provide both education and maintenance in a state school for the mentally retarded. Ordinarily, however, state schools do not provide teachers and educational programs for trainable children in institutions because it is difficult enough to provide the necessary number of teachers and educational programs for the educable children committed to their care. Therefore it is hard to compare the cost of community training for these children with institutional training and maintenance. On the surface it would appear that if the children remained at home, with their parents providing board and room and clothing, society could more cheaply organize classes for them within the community. On this problem Kirk makes the following statement:

> It appears that the per capita cost of educating a severely retarded child in the public schools for a full day program is around $900 per child plus or minus $300. The costs are high when schools in general are high and when all items of expenses are included in cost accounting. Costs are lower when class size is increased, when classes operate on a one-half day program, and when aides are used instead of teachers.[9]

As compared to the cost of institutions, the figures just given do not indicate that the cost of classes within a public school are substantially below the cost required for institutionalization. The argument that it is cheaper to provide for these children in community classes, which require transportation and other costs, is not necessarily a tenable one. If, however, the institution provided the same kind of training and education as the public school, plus the maintenance, it would naturally be more expensive to send a child to an institution than to keep him at home and send him to a public school class.

The Organization of Community Classes

Remarkable progress in the quality and organization of classes for the trainable has been made in a decade of trial and error. Beginning with a spontaneous, haphazard program in which parents operated classes on a shoestring in whatever location they could buy, beg, or borrow, classes for the trainable have acquired professional status and financial support. There is considerable variation in the organization and procedure, depending on the location and in large part on the composition of the classes. As criteria for admission became more clearly delineated and as the objectives were better understood, the program became more meaningful.

Admission Requirements

The admission requirements for school classes for trainable children

[9] Kirk, *Public School Provisions for Severely Retarded Children,* p. 54.

have been formulated in many states. The following represent those most generally in effect.

1. The age of admission for trainable retarded children in the public school classes is generally the same as for other children. In most instances this age is 6.

2. The objective criterion which appears to be the most valid for admission is the IQ based on individual psychometric tests administered by a psychologist trained and experienced in the diagnosis of mental retardation. The usual IQ range for these classes is between 30 or 35 and 50 or 55 and the IQ's are derived from such tests as the Stanford-Binet Intelligence Scale, the Minnesota Preschool Scale, the Merrill-Palmer Scale, and the Kuhlmann Tests of Mental Development.

3. Most children admitted into the classes are required to have a medical examination to determine their physical ability to participate in the program.

4. Not all children with IQ's between 35 and 50 are admitted. Other criteria include ability to get along in the class and a minimum ability to take care of their needs, such as toileting, partial dressing, and so forth. Schools tend to exclude children who are a danger to themselves or others and those whose behavior is likely to disrupt the classroom program.

5. Children admitted to these classes must have some minimum communication ability in the form of either speech or gestures. Most trainable children above the age of 6 with IQ's over 30 have these abilities.

6. The general procedure for admission is to have a committee composed of a psychologist, a social worker, teachers, and other school personnel accept or reject the children.

Size of Class

The size of class for trainable children varies from about six to fifteen. At first, when the children have not been accustomed to being away from their mothers, the classes should be small; they can gradually be increased in size as the children learn the routines. A homogeneous class of children of approximately the same age and abilities can be larger than a heterogeneous class of children. Another factor determining the size of the class is the age and school experience of the children. Young inexperienced children require more attention from the teacher; hence their class should be small. Older children who have had school experience can be grouped in a larger class, since they will not require as much personal care by the teacher.

Transportation

Because of the geographic distribution of trainable children in a community and their inability to go to school unattended, it is necessary to provide transportation for all trainable children. This is a major item which adds to the expense of operating classes for them.

Qualifications of Teachers

Because classes for trainable children are so new in public schools, no general agreement on the qualification of teachers has been reached. Kirk has surveyed the certification standards of a number of states and asserts:

> A survey of state certification standards and qualifications of teachers of the severely retarded leads to the following conclusions:
>
> 1. Since colleges and universities have not established training programs for the preparation of teachers of severely retarded children, local school systems have been forced to employ certified teachers without specific training in teaching the severely mentally retarded.
>
> 2. State administrators require a general teaching certificate and, through in-service training, experience, workshops and courses in college in related areas, expect to develop adequate teachers of the severely retarded.
>
> 3. No specific set of standards of skills and knowledges has been established by state departments or by colleges for teachers of the severely retarded.
>
> 4. Matrons and aides are necessary for large classes of young severely retarded children (under 10 years of age). They relieve the teacher of care problems in a classroom.
>
> 5. Parents of severely retarded children do not generally succeed [as helpers] in classes in which their own child is enrolled.
>
> 6. Temporary volunteer parent helpers are not advisable. The severely retarded child needs consistent training by one person. Adjustment to many personalities in a class is difficult for him.
>
> A perusal of the skills and knowledges required by teachers of the severely retarded over and above the courses required for a general teaching certificate would lead to the following recommendations:
>
> 1. Teachers of the severely retarded should have instruction in the characteristics of mongoloid and brain-damaged children. About one-third of the children in the classes are mongoloid children. A large proportion of the other two-thirds are brain-damaged.
>
> 2. Skills in arts and crafts, music, industrial arts, recreational games, and homemaking are valuable tools in classes for the severely retarded. Methods of teaching reading, arithmetic, or other school subjects are necessary for the elementary teacher and for the teacher of the educable mentally handicapped, but not for the teacher of trainable children.
>
> 3. Courses in child development commonly given to nursery school and

141

kindergarten teachers are of value to teachers of the severely retarded.

4. A study of the goals, objectives, and activities included in a curriculum for the severely retarded is necessary.

5. Special attention to parent problems is necessary for all teachers of severely retarded children. Methods of interviewing and counseling parents are important.

6. Teachers who do not expect immediate results or who are not frustrated because children do not learn are suitable as teachers of the severely retarded. One who can appreciate small gains instead of no gains tends to be successful.

7. Practice teaching or experience under supervision with the severely retarded is essential. Such experience is the only way one can determine whether a teacher has insight into the limitations and abilities of the children, is able to relate to them, and is able to create programs and activities suitable to the growth and development of the children.[10]

The Curriculum and Course of Study

The Goals of the Curriculum

In defining an educational program for any group of children, it is necessary to define the general objectives of the curriculum and then to give the specific elements required in a course of study. The general objectives of the curriculum for a trainable child are inherent in the definition, namely, (1) the objective of developing self-care or self-help, (2) the objective of developing social adjustment in the home and neighborhood, and (3) the objective of developing economic usefulness in the home or in a sheltered environment. These constitute the broad goals of the educational program for trainable mentally retarded children.

Self-Help. The major characteristic which differentiates the trainable mentally retarded from the dependent mentally retarded is self-care. If a child can learn to dress and undress himself, eat properly, to take care of himself in the bathroom, and to follow sleep routines, he is not dependent on someone else for his personal needs. In a restricted sense he becomes independent as far as taking care of himself is concerned. Although such independence is common among normal children after the age of babyhood, it is necessary to educate the trainable child in the elements of self-care.

Social Adjustment in the Home and Neighborhood. It is not expected that the trainable child will become independent in the community — that is, learn to go around the community by himself or be in charge of his affairs outside of the home. He is, however, expected to get along in

[10] *Ibid.,* pp. 60–61.

the home and in his immediate neighborhood. This particular learning achievement includes language development, sharing with others, waiting his turn, obeying, following directions, sensing the feelings of others, and other aspects of interpersonal relationships, especially those concerned with daily associations. Social adjustment is not a subject which is taught like chemistry or physics. It is an intangible type of development which comes about through recreation and play, singing, dramatics, and working and living with others.

Economic Usefulness. The term "economic usefulness" is applied to the trainable child to differentiate this ability from occupational or vocational activities which are within the capacity of educable children. It is expected that the trainable child will be of some use in the home, the school, or a sheltered environment in either community or institution. In the home, economic usefulness means helping with housework and yard work. These activities can be developed in the classroom through many of the programs which require care of the room, cooking, washing and wiping dishes, arts and crafts, woodwork, and the ability to complete simple tasks under minimum supervision. This kind of objective is more attainable with older trainable children in school than with younger ones.

The Elements of the Curriculum

The mental ages in classes for trainable children range between about 3 and 7 years. At this mental level the academic program prescribed for educable or for normal children is not warranted. It would be well here to discuss some limitations of and possibilities for these children.

Reading. In general, trainable children do not learn to read from even first-grade books. Their ability is limited to reading and recognizing their names, isolated words and phrases, common words used for their protection, such as "danger," "stop," "men," "women," and other signs which they encounter in a community. Teaching them to read these signs and labels should not begin when they are young but should be introduced before they leave the school.

Arithmetic. Trainable children are not taught formal arithmetic as it is taught in the primary grades. They can learn some quantitative concepts, however, such as more and less, big and little, and the vocabulary of quantitative thinking. They are also taught to count up to 10 and to recognize differences between groupings. The older children can learn to write numbers from 1 to 10 and some of them can learn time concepts, telling time by the clock and possibly understanding the calendar. Some can recognize and remember telephone numbers, their own ages, and some simple money concepts.

Arts and Crafts. Activities in this area include coloring, drawing, painting, simple woodwork, pasting and cutting, and making simple craft objects. Such activities may help in developing motor control, appreciation of color and form, and the ability to complete a task.

Dramatization. Classes for trainable children use considerable dramatization such as acting out a story or a song, playing make-believe, shadow playing, and using gestures with songs, stories, and rhymes.

Physical Hygiene. The routine of a classroom includes drinking juice or milk, discussion about the kinds of food eaten at different meals, the care of the teeth, cleanliness, safety, and posture. These health habits usually need to be fostered both in the school and at home.

Language. This program includes the development of speech and the understanding of verbal concepts. It also includes listening skills, listening to stories, roll calls, discussing pictures, and other activities familiar to the children in the classroom.

Mental Development. Mental activity can be stimulated through experiences. The teacher attempts to keep in mind the development of imagination, concept building, problem solving, and the ability to discriminate and to remember visual and auditory patterns. The latter is sometimes called sensory training.

Practical Arts. Under this heading are included cooking, sewing, dishwashing, cleaning, gardening, setting the table, chores around the classroom, preparing foods, and learning to help with home activities. This program is best limited to older trainable children.

Motor Development. Motor development is best stimulated through games, recreational activities, various manipulative skills, playing, outdoor recreation, and similar activities.

Self-Help. Self-help includes grooming, toileting, dressing, undressing, eating, brushing teeth, washing, and care of clothes and other personal belongings.

Socialization. It is important for the children to learn certain skills which will assist their socialization, such as greeting people with "Hello," shaking hands with visitors, learning to be quiet while someone else is talking, having acceptable table manners, getting along with classmates in school, helping others who need help, and other activities of an interpersonal nature.

Social Studies. The important area of study here is the home and the way it participates in the community. This includes learning about holidays, transportation, church, knowing the months and days of the week, and so forth.

Music. Music is a medium through which trainable children can learn many things. Singing, rhythm bands, musical games, and other activities help release energy and also serve as a form of expression and a socializing influence.

Is Training Effective?

The results of a training program for trainable mentally retarded children should be evaluated in relation to the goals stated earlier: independence in self care, social adjustment in the home and neighborhood, and economic usefulness at the adult level in home, sheltered workshop or institution. To make such an evaluation one would have to set up a series of programs within the public schools and follow them up for twenty-five or thirty years. There has not yet been time for this kind of follow-up and only studies covering shorter periods are available. These do help to answer some questions:

Are Children from Trainable Classes Eventually Institutionalized?

Studies on this question indicate that many of the children in trainable classes later become institutionalized. Lorenz followed up a group of children eighteen years after their admission into a public school special class for trainable children.[11] She found that 47 per cent of the 66 children studied were institutionalized upon leaving the special class. Boys had a higher percentage of institutionalization than girls. Those institutionalized usually came from the average or below average socioeconomic levels. Tisdall followed up a group of 126 trainable children five years after their enrollment in a special class.[12] He found that during this period 12 per cent had already been institutionalized. In another study Saenger found that 26 per cent were institutionalized.[13] Accurate knowledge of the number that will be institutionalized must await a study which lasts a generation, since the percentages given above seem to depend on how long after the children left school the study was made.

[11] Marcella H. Lorenz, "Follow-up Studies of the Severely Retarded," *A Study of Public School Children with Severe Mental Retardation*, M. C. Reynolds, J. R. Kiland, and R. E. Ellis, eds., Research Project No. 6 (St. Paul, Minn.: Statistical Division, State Department of Education, 1953).

[12] William Tisdall, "A Follow-up Study of Trainable Mentally Handicapped Children in Illinois," *American Journal of Mental Deficiency*, 65 (July, 1960), 11–16.

[13] G. Saenger, *The Adjustment of Severely Retarded Adults in the Community* (Albany: New York State Interdepartmental Health Resources Board, October, 1957).

It appears that many of the children will eventually be in institutions unless a new program evolves which will retain them in the home and community. Such programs are currently being tried in a number of centers, and it is claimed that the past record of institutionalization will not obtain in the future when these become adequate. A community program includes sheltered workshops, recreational centers, and parent counseling.

Does a Class for the Trainable Assist the Parents?

Many people feel that the organization of a class for trainable children has been justified because of its great value to parents. First, it relieves the mother of the constant care of the child. Second, it gives the parents a chance to become more objective by having an opportunity to see what the child can learn outside of the home. And third, it helps the parents to become more realistic concerning the developmental limitations of the child. Reynolds and Kiland found that after the children were in the classes for some time the parents reduced their expectations for the children's learning of the academic subjects.[14] Similarly, in the Illinois Study[15] the parents tended to become more realistic about their children's abilities and limitations. They began to realize that although the children improved in self-care skills they would not become self-supporting.

Do the Children Become Economically Useful?

One of the alleged purposes of a class is to help the children become economically useful. Both the Lorenz and the Tisdall studies found that about one-third of the children who were beyond school age and remained at home were considered economically useful in the home or in a sheltered workshop.

Saenger found that about one-quarter of the group residing in the community earned some pay.[16] Saenger's group, however, was intellectually at the borderline level between trainable and educable. Lorenz found that two of the sixty-six children were employed for remuneration outside of the home,[17] while Tisdall found only one of his sample working in the community.[18] These children had IQ's in the 50's and were borderline trainable-educable. The figures confirm the prediction that trainable children are not able to hold a job in the community or to be occupationally adequate but can be of some nonremunerative help in a limited environment.

14 Reynolds, Kiland, and Ellis, *op. cit.*
15 Cited in note 3.
16 Saenger, *op. cit.*
17 Lorenz, *op. cit.*
18 Tisdall, *op. cit.*

The figures on economic usefulness of trainable children do not give us the true picture. Their degree of usefulness will depend on proper selection of such children for the special classes, an adequate training program, and facilities in the home and community for their adjustment. A community, for instance, which does not provide a sheltered workshop in effect requests the parents to either keep these children at home or send them to an institution. Unless proper facilities and programs are available it is impossible to evaluate accurately the economic usefulness of trainable children.

Do Classes for Trainable Children Fulfill Expectations?

There have been numerous studies evaluating the results of programs. Invariably the children improve from year to year, but whether the improvement stemmed from the programs or from maturation was not known. Two studies each used two groups of children, one of which was placed in a training program while the other (the control group) remained at home or in an institutional environment. Hottel compared twenty-one matched pairs of children.[19] He found that although both the experimental and the control (home) groups improved in mental and social age and other measures, the experimental group did not improve more than the control group. Cain and Levine compared four groups: (1) an institution school group, (2) an institution nonschool group, (3) a community public school group, and (4) a community nonschool group.[20] They found no difference in gain scores in social competence between the school and home groups, but there was a difference in gain scores between the two institution and two community groups in favor of the community children.

Summary

1. Trainable mentally retarded children are those children whose limits of educability have been defined as (a) competence in self-care skills, (b) adjustment in the home and neighborhood, and (c) economic usefulness in the home or sheltered environment.

2. It is estimated that there are approximately three to four trainable

---

[19] J. V. Hottel, *An Evaluation of Tennessee's Day Class Program for Severely Mentally Retarded Children* (Nashville: George Peabody College for Teachers, 1958).

[20] Leo F. Cain and Samuel Levine, *A Study of the Effects of Community and Institutional School Classes for Trainable Mentally Retarded Children*, U.S. Office of Education, Cooperative Research Project No. SAE 8257 (San Francisco: San Francisco State College, June, 1961).

children per 1000 school children, residing at home or in institutions.

3. Provisions for trainable children have been made in residential institutions, public school classes, and day-care centers under parent or welfare auspices. The problems of the trainable child appear to be partly the responsibility of education and partly that of welfare agencies. This dual responsibility has raised a controversy concerning which agency of government shall have charge of the care, education, and management of the trainable mentally retarded.

4. In the future there will probably be a comprehensive program for this group of retarded which will include preschool classes, day-care and training classes during the school-age period, and sheltered workshops and residential institutions during the postschool period.

DISCUSSION QUESTIONS

1. The term "trainable" has been criticized because, according to one point of view, training and education are synonymous. How can this term be justified for one group of mentally retarded?

2. Which one of the following plans is most acceptable for severely retarded children: (*a*) accept all in institutions, (*b*) provide for them in public school classes, (*c*) provide for trainable children with IQ's of 40 to 55 in public school classes, and those children below in community or state day-school classes not under public school auspices, (*d*) provide for such children in community day-care classes not under public school auspices, or (*e*) leave the problem to the parents to organize and operate their own schools.

3. If you were asked to give a speech to a group of parents of trainable children, outline what you would tell them about these children.

4. If you were asked to give a speech to an elementary-school P.T.A., outline what you would tell them about trainable retarded children.

5. In an average community of 4000 school children, how many trainable children are you likely to find in the community, and how many classes would you organize?

6. Self-help, social adjustment, and economic usefulness were cited as the three goals of training. Discuss the importance of these three accomplishments in the life of the child and his family.

7. Since many trainable children eventually become institutionalized, discuss the merits of establishing school classes for them while they are children.

8. What community facilities might be expected to reduce or delay the necessity for institutionalization?

Selected References

All Day Institute. "Mongolism: A Symposium," reprinted from *Quarterly Review of Pediatrics*, May, August, November, 1953.

Baumgartner, Bernice B. *The Illinois Plan for Special Education of Exceptional Children: A Curriculum Guide for Teachers of Trainable Mentally Handicapped Children.* Circular Series B-2. Springfield, Ill.: State Department of Public Instruction, 1955.

Baumgartner, Bernice B. *Helping the Trainable Mentally Retarded Child; a Handbook for Teachers, Parents, and Administrators.* New York: Teachers College, Columbia University, 1960.

Capa, Cornell, and Maya Pines. *Retarded Children Can Be Helped.* Great Neck, N.Y.: Channel Press, 1957.

Carlson, Bernice W., and David R. Ginglend. *Play Activities for the Retarded Child.* Nashville: Abingdon Press, 1961.

Farber, Bernard. "Family Organization and Crisis: Maintenance of Integration in Families with a Severely Mentally Retarded Child," *Monographs of the Society for Research in Child Development*, Vol. 25, No. 1. Lafayette, Ind.: Child Development Publications, 1960.

Farber, Bernard, William C. Jenne, and Romolo Toigo. "Family Crisis and the Decision to Institutionalize the Retarded Child," *Council for Exceptional Children Research Monograph*, Series A, No. 1, 1960.

French, Edward L., and J. Clifford Scott. *Child in the Shadows.* Philadelphia: J. B. Lippincott Company, 1960.

Gunzburg, Herbert C. *Social Rehabilitation of the Subnormal.* London: Bailliere, Tindall and Cox, 1960.

Hill, Arthur S. *The Forward Look: The Severely Retarded Child Goes to School.* Bulletin No. 11. Washington: Federal Security Agency, Office of Education, 1952.

Hood, Oreste E. *Your Child or Mine.* New York: Harper & Brothers, 1957.

Kirk, Samuel A. *Public School Provisions for Severely Retarded Children.* Albany: New York State Interdepartmental Health Resources Board, 1957.

Kirk, Samuel A., Merle B. Karnes, and Winifred D. Kirk. *You and Your Retarded Child.* New York: The Macmillan Company, 1955.

Levinson, Abraham. *The Mentally Retarded Child.* New York: The John Day Company, 1952.

Loewy, Herta. *The Retarded Child: A Guide for Parents and Teachers.* New York: Philosophical Library, 1951.

National Association for Retarded Children, Inc. *The Evaluation and Treatment of the Mentally Retarded Child in Clinics*. New York: The Association, 1956.

Rosenzweig, Louis E., and Julia Long. *Understanding and Teaching the Dependent Retarded Child*. Darien, Conn.: Educational Publishing Corporation, 1960.

Schonell, Fred J., J. A. Richardson, and Thelma S. McConnel. *The Subnormal Child at Home*. London: Macmillan and Company, 1958.

Theodore, Sister Mary. *The Challenge of the Retarded Child*. Milwaukee: Bruce Publishing Company, 1959.

6

Children with Auditory Handicaps

Individuals with auditory handicaps may have difficulty hearing in one or both ears or may not hear at all. Professionals and laymen alike have used various terms: "hard-of-hearing," "deaf," "deaf-mute," "deafened," "partially deaf," and "partially hearing." Most of these terms came into use as a means of differentiating some of the auditorily handicapped children from others. "Deafened," for instance, usually refers to someone who once had hearing and developed language and speech, and later became deaf. Such an individual's reactions in the field of learning and communication are quite different from those of a person who was born deaf and never learned to speak or to communicate verbally, sometimes called a deaf-mute.

Streng gives the following definitions:

> The child who is born with little or no hearing, or who has suffered the loss early in infancy before speech and language patterns are acquired is said to be deaf. One who is born with normal hearing and reaches the age where he can produce and comprehend speech but subsequently loses his hearing is described as deafened. The hard of hearing are those with reduced hearing acuity either since birth or acquired at any time during life.[1]

[1] Alice Streng, Waring J. Fitch, LeRoy D. Hedgecock, James W. Phillips, and James A. Carrell, *Hearing Therapy for Children* (New York: Grune and Stratton, 2nd ed., 1958), p. 9.

Classification

Because of the confusion in terminology and because training programs differ according to the type of problem, the Conference of Executives of American Schools for the Deaf has made the following classification:

1. THE DEAF: Those in whom the sense of hearing is nonfunctional for the ordinary purposes of life. This general group is made up of two distinct classes based entirely on the time the loss of hearing occurred. These include:
a. *The congenitally deaf* — those who were born deaf.
b. *The adventitiously deaf* — those who were born with normal hearing but in whom the sense of hearing became nonfunctional later through illness or accident.
2. THE HARD OF HEARING: Those in whom the sense of hearing, although defective, is functional with or without a hearing aid.[2]

For the purposes of educational organization, auditorily handicapped children have been classified according to degrees of hearing loss. In general, two educational programs are practiced, one for hard-of-hearing children and the other for deaf children.

Hard-of-hearing children have been classified by Streng as follows:[3]

Children with mild losses are those who have a 20 to 30 decibel loss in the better ear in the speech range. Their speech develops spontaneously through the use of the ear and their hearing borders on normal. Such children require little specialized attention from the school system except favorable seating in the classroom and an awareness of the difficulty on the part of the teacher.

Children with marginal losses are those who have hearing losses of 30 to 40 decibels. It is hard for them to understand speech by ear at normal distances and sometimes they have difficulty in following group conversations. Such children require instruction in auditory training and sometimes in speech and the use of hearing aids.

Children with moderate losses are those with 40 to 60 decibel losses. They have enough hearing to learn language and speech especially through the use of hearing aids. Their educational program includes amplification of auditory material and an increased use of visual aids.

Children with severe losses are those having hearing losses of 60 to 75 decibels and retaining what is known as residual hearing. They can learn

[2] Committee on Nomenclature, Conference of Executives of American Schools for the Deaf, *American Annals of the Deaf*, 83 (September, 1938), 1–3.
[3] Streng et al., *op. cit.*, pp. 164–165.

language and speech but only with specialized techniques and hearing aids. Because they do not learn language and speech spontaneously at a younger age, they are sometimes called "educationally deaf," meaning that they are to be educated like the profoundly deaf. Their instruction is, therefore, in classes for the deaf. Sometimes these children can be trained to hear with hearing aids and can later be classified as hard of hearing.

Children with profound losses are those with hearing losses greater than 75 decibels. Even with amplification of sound they cannot use hearing to understand language. These are the children who require intensive specialized instruction in all areas without major use of the sense of hearing.

Both of the classification systems just given relate to the degree of hearing loss. Loss of hearing may also be classified according to the time of onset. This is particularly important from an educational point of view because if an individual has already acquired speech before the loss of hearing, the whole communication and educational process is different from that used with persons who have never known speech and language. Therefore the term "deafened" is used in referring to the former. It will be noted that the definition quoted earlier from the Conference of Executives of American Schools for the Deaf included a distinction between *congenitally deaf* and *adventitiously deaf*. This is also an effort to classify according to the time of onset of deafness.

There are many variables to be considered in describing the deaf and hard of hearing. Because of this multidimensional nature of the problem any classification may be of doubtful value since it cannot take into account all variables. No group of deaf or hard of hearing is homogeneous unless the following variables are considered: (1) degree of hearing loss, (2) age at onset, (3) type of hearing loss — whether sensory-neural, conductive, central, or psychogenic. (These will be discussed later.)

Case Illustration

Many hard-of-hearing children have found social adjustment difficult because they could not interact socially as hearing children do. In school, likewise, progress is likely to be uneven if they hear only part of the material presented. Thus a hearing loss may interfere with social adjustment and educational progress especially in the areas of speech and language. The amount of difficulty will vary with the degree of hearing loss and also with other factors. Figure 13 illustrates the different effects of varying degrees of hearing loss.

FIGURE 13

Profiles of Three Children of Differing Degrees of Hearing Loss

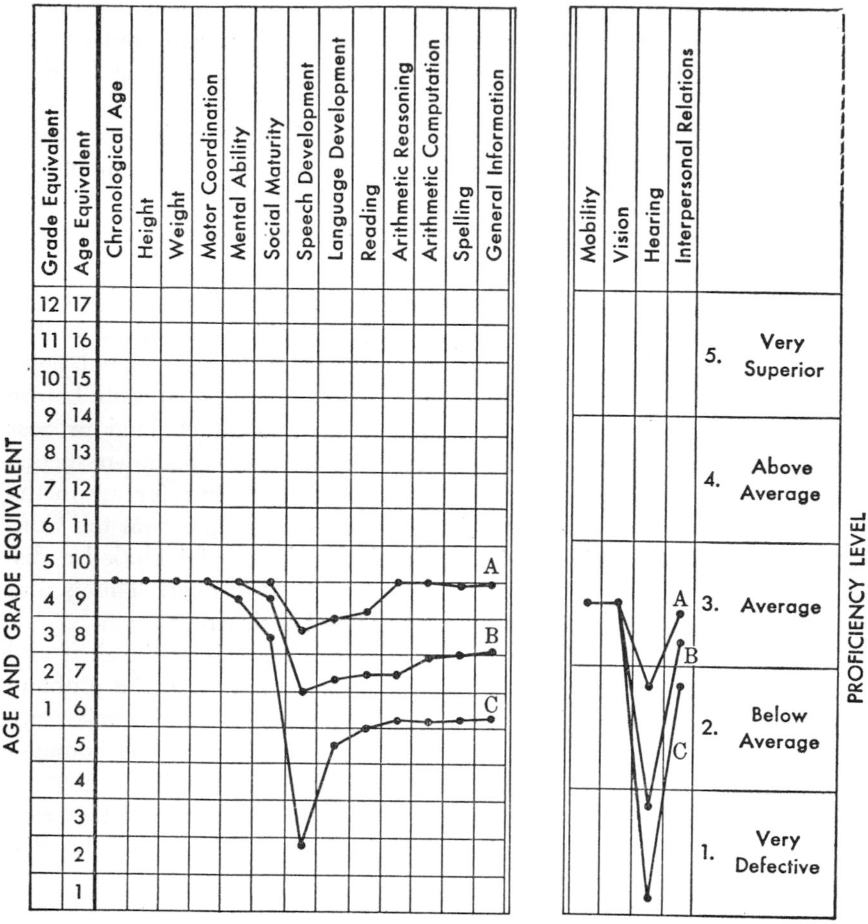

A, hard-of-hearing child
B, deafened child
C, deaf child

Case A

Figure 13 presents three development profiles. The upper one, labeled A, represents a child with a marginal loss of hearing of 35 decibels. It will be noticed from the upper profile that the hard-of-hearing child is 10 years of age and is physically (in terms of height, weight, and motor coordination) average. In mental ability and in social maturity there appears to be no difference between him and the average. In speech development the child is slightly retarded in that he has some difficulty in articulation and requires speech correction. His language development and reading are only slightly retarded while his achievement in arithmetic, spelling, and general information is approximately average. The only difference between this child and an average child is a slight difficulty in speech development, language development, and reading.

Fortunately, this hard-of-hearing child has been fitted with a hearing aid, and has received speech correction. The only special education he has needed is some help in the use of his hearing aid, in speech correction, and in lip reading. Otherwise, he is so much like the average child that he has functioned adequately in the regular grades. An itinerant speech correctionist has given him speech correction, auditory training, and lip-reading lessons once a week for the last year.

Case B

The next profile on the chart (B) presents the developmental pattern of a child with a severe hearing loss. He is classified as educationally deaf. Approximately normal in intelligence, social maturity, and physical ability, he is quite retarded in speech development. Actually, this child was born with normal hearing but at the age of 4 suffered a serious hearing loss in both ears. On the audiometric test he had a 65 decibel loss. Fortunately, however, he had learned to talk quite normally before his loss of hearing and had developed considerable language ability, so that now he still can learn through the auditory channel with the help of hearing aids. His retardation in speech is a result of his not having developed normally in speech and language since the age of 4. At present his language is below the 7-year (second-grade) level and his reading and other academic abilities are also around the second-grade level. The hearing loss had interfered considerably with his educational progress, but with the use of hearing aids, speech development, and other specialized techniques in a classroom for the deaf, he is progressing, though at an understandably slower rate than Case A.

Case C

The third profile is of a child with a profound hearing loss which existed at birth. This child has never heard sounds and cannot be helped with a hearing aid. He must be in a special class for the deaf.

In speech development, this child is still quite defective. He does not talk as well as a child of 2½ years, even though he has had some instruction. His language development is at about the 5-year level. His reading and other academic subjects are at the beginning first-grade level even though he is now 10 years of age. We would consider him about four years retarded educationally.

Although these three profiles all represent auditorily handicapped children, they differ considerably. They show the progress such children make, depending upon the age at onset of deafness, the intelligence, the degree of hearing loss, and the amount of intensive instruction which has been received during the growing stages.

Prevalence of Hearing Loss

The prevalence of defective hearing is difficult to estimate, although many surveys have been made. The rate of occurrence appears to be partly dependent on the method of testing, the criteria used by the investigator, the community, and other factors. For example, Farber found that in the literature estimates ranged from 1.5 per cent to 5 per cent of the school population.[4] Yet in Farber's own study the teachers in Illinois reported only .48 per cent of the school population as having hearing losses. This figure includes children already placed in classes for the hard of hearing and probably represents the prevalence of moderate and severe hearing losses, losses large enough so that teachers are able to recognize them. Mild hearing losses are not detected by teachers very readily. Curry found that teachers refer only 7.4 per cent of children with hearing losses,[5] and Warwick reports that teachers referred fourteen out of a group of sixty-three children with impaired hearing.[6]

According to Silverman a rough estimate of the prevalence of hearing loss is that 5 per cent of school children have a hearing impairment, and that one or two out of ten in this group or about five in a thousand will require special educational attention.[7]

Methods of Measuring Hearing Loss

The identification of hearing losses has become a technical problem. Whereas very severe or profound loss is rather easily recognized, children with mild or moderate hearing losses are hard to identify. Teachers may feel that the child just does not pay attention or is mentally handicapped or stubborn.

[4] Bernard Farber, *The Prevalence of Exceptional Children in Illinois*, Circular, Census 14 (Springfield, Ill.: Office of the Superintendent of Public Instruction, 1959).

[5] E. Thayer Curry, "The Efficiency of Teacher Referral in a School Hearing Testing Program," *Journal of Speech and Hearing Disorders*, 15 (September, 1950), 211–214.

[6] Harold L. Warwick, "Hearing Tests in Public Schools of Fort Worth," *Volta Review*, 30 (November, 1928), 641–643.

[7] Richard Silverman, "Education of the Deaf," *Handbook of Speech Pathology*, Lee E. Travis, ed. (New York: Appleton-Century-Crofts, Inc., 1957), p. 393.

It is important for a classroom teacher to be aware of some of the symptoms which may be misinterpreted, such as those displayed by (1) the child who ignores, confuses, or does not comply with directions; (2) the child who daydreams a great deal; (3) the child who is educationally retarded; (4) the child with a slight speech defect; (5) the child who is "lazy"; (6) the child who seems dull.

Informal Methods of Testing Hearing

There are several informal ways to test a child's hearing before referring him for a more thorough examination. Before the advent of the electric audiometer these cruder methods were frequently used, and a teacher may still find them helpful in making a rough appraisal of a child's hearing.

The Conversational Test. In this test the child is placed about twenty feet from the teacher and is asked questions in a conversational voice. If he cannot respond, the examiner moves closer and closer until the child can hear and respond. Ordinarily, a normal conversational voice is heard at twenty feet. The examiner can test one ear, then the other, to determine the relative acuity of each ear. This kind of test is very rough but can be used if a hearing loss is suspected. It does not tell the examiner what degree of loss exists or whether it is a central, conductive, or nerve loss. If the child has difficulty in hearing at ten to twenty feet he should be referred for an examination.

The Whisper Test. As in the conversational test the child may be placed twenty feet from the examiner and asked to repeat two numbers, such as 2 — 4 or 6 — 3, presented to him in a whisper. Or the examiner may whisper a list of words. This test is similar to the conversation test except that the examiner uses a whisper.

The Watch-Tick Test. In the watch-tick test the examiner uses a watch with a louder tick than the ordinary wristwatch has. It is brought closer and closer to the ear until the child states that he hears it. Since the watch-tick has a higher frequency than the voice, it sometimes enables one to detect high-frequency loss. This is a very subjective test, since the distance at which the tick can normally be heard depends on the loudness of the particular watch.

The Coin-Click Test. Like the watch-tick test, the coin-click test detects high-frequency losses, since some children who have a high-frequency loss will hear a conversational voice but be unable to hear a coin click.

Formal Testing

The informal tests are used by teachers and psychological examiners to obtain a crude measure of hearing ability. The most accurate method of testing is with an electric pure-tone audiometer, which produces pure tones of known intensity and frequency.

These two dimensions — frequency and intensity — are necessary for evaluating a hearing loss. *Frequency* refers to the number of vibrations (or cycles) per second of a given sound wave: the greater the frequency, the higher the pitch. An individual may have difficulty hearing sounds of certain frequencies whereas those of other frequencies are quite audible to him. The frequencies most important for the understanding of speech range between 500 and 2000 vibrations per second. *Intensity*, on the other hand, refers to the relative loudness of a sound.

To determine an individual's level of hearing it is necessary to know what intensity of sound is needed to cross his threshold of hearing at each of the frequency levels. The pure-tone audiometer presents the individual with sounds of known intensity and frequency and asks him to respond when he hears the tone. The degree of hearing loss is recorded on an audiogram from −10 to 100 decibels. The hearing in each ear is plotted separately. A hearing level of 30 decibels indicates a mild hearing loss; an 80-decibel level indicates profound deafness.

Routine audiometric procedures cannot be used with infants and young children, but clinical testing of young children can be accomplished by electrodermal and other procedures in audiology clinics. Generally, however, hearing loss in a young child is detected by informal means such as observing his behavior and ability to react to sounds in his environment. Does he respond to music? to noise? or to voices? Gesell has given a list of signs suggestive of deafness in young children.

Signs Suggestive of Deafness in Infants and Young Children[8]

I. *Hearing and Comprehension of Speech*
   General indifference to sound
   Lack of response to spoken word
   Response to noises as opposed to words

II. *Vocalizations and Sound Production*
   Monotonal quality
   Indistinct
   Lessened laughter
   Meager experimental sound play and squealing
   Vocal play for vibratory sensation
   Head banging, foot stamping for vibratory sensation
   Yelling, screeching to express pleasure, annoyance or need

[8] Arnold Gesell and C. S. Amatruda, *Developmental Diagnosis* (New York: Harper & Brothers, 1947), p. 278.

III. *Visual Attention and Reciprocal Comprehension*

    Augmented visual vigilance and attentiveness
    Alertness to gesture and movement
    Marked imitativeness in play
    Vehemence of gestures

IV. *Social Rapport and Adaptations*

    Subnormal rapport in vocal nursery games
    Intensified preoccupation with things rather than persons
    Inquiring, sometimes confused or thwarted facial expression
    Puzzled and unhappy episodes in social situations
    Suspicious alertness, alternating with co-operation
    Markedly reactive to praise and affection

V. *Emotional Behavior*

    Tantrums to call attention to self or need
    Tensions, tantrums, resistances due to lack of comprehension
    Frequent obstinacies, teasing tendencies
    Irritability at not making self understood
    Explosions due to self-vexation
    Impulsive and avalanche initiatives

Causes of Hearing Defects

Deafness is a symptom of a defect in the hearing mechanism. Much of the diagnosis is made by inference, and often the exact nature and origin of the defect are unknown. In roughly one-third of the cases the cause cannot be determined with certainty. Some hearing defects are predetermined by the genetic structure of the individual and may be present at birth or develop later in life. Some are acquired through disease, trauma, or other insults to the organism.

Causes Occurring Before Birth

Prenatal infections and toxic conditions of the mother may create auditory defects in the child. The viruses of mumps and influenza, for example, especially during the early months of pregnancy may cause degeneration of important nerve cells that results in deafness. German measles afflicting the mother during the first three months of pregnancy often has quite serious effects.

Some diseases specific to the functioning of the auditory mechanism may occur at any stage in life, including the period *in utero*. In *otosclerosis,* for example, spongy bone is formed in the middle and inner ear, occasionally at birth but usually not until later in life.

Some *malformations* are present at birth, such as abnormalities of the external auditory canal which prevent sound from being carried into the mechanism of the ear. The eardrum or some of the structures of the middle ear may be deformed or absent, and development of the neural mechanism of the inner ear may be arrested.

Hereditary degenerative nerve deafness may also be present at birth or occur soon after.

Traumatic and Other Conditions at Birth

During delivery certain *traumatic experiences,* such as pelvic pressure, use of forceps, and intracranial hemorrhage, may cause damage to the nervous system resulting in auditory and other defects. Fortunately such problems are becoming increasingly rare.

Another untoward condition at the time of birth is prolonged *lack of oxygen* available to the infant as in prolonged labor, heavy sedation, or blockage of the infant's respiratory passages. This may produce rapid degeneration in some of the more delicate neural mechanisms of the ear as well as those of other sensory organs or of the central nervous system itself.

Of fairly recent discovery is the effect of *blood incompatibility* between the mother and infant. The best-known incompatibility is that of the Rh factor, but current research has indicated similar effects from other types of blood incompatibility.

Causes Occurring After Birth

Postnatal diseases and *accidents* account for a large percentage of hearing loss. If they occur early in life, before the acquisition of speech and language, the implications, educationally, are the same as if the child had been born deaf.

Childhood diseases take their toll in hearing defects but their frequency and severity have been lessened by advances in immunization and antibiotics. At one time such infectious diseases as scarlet fever, mumps, diphtheria, whooping cough, measles, typhoid fever, pneumonia, and influenza accounted for a great deal of deafness. Meningitis is still reported as a frequent cause of hearing defects, but this too is becoming more amenable to control. *Otitis media,* which is common to many upper respiratory diseases, may cause loss of hearing through infection in the middle ear. Davis and Fowler state, "Pus in the middle ear is a more frequent cause of hearing loss than any other except perhaps senility."[9] The presence of *infected adenoids, tonsils,* and *sinuses* favors the produc-

[9] H. Davis and E. P. Fowler, "Hearing and Deafness," *Hearing and Deafness,* H. Davis and S. R. Silverman, eds. (New York: Holt, Rinehart and Winston, Inc., rev. ed., 1960), p. 95.

tion of infection in the middle ear and is therefore an indirect cause of hearing loss.

If acute infections of the middle ear are not properly treated, *chronic otitis media* may follow. If this is extended or recurs frequently, adhesions may form and destroy the eardrum or the bony structure of the middle ear. If the infection extends into the mastoid process of the temporal bone, a *mastoidectomy* may be necessitated. A "simple" mastoidectomy removes only the diseased portion of the mastoid bone; in a "radical" mastoidectomy it is also necessary to remove the bony canal wall plus whatever is left of the eardrum and other diseased parts. The "simple" mastoidectomy does not cause an appreciable hearing loss. The "radical" operation usually leaves a hearing level of 35 to 40 decibels because the middle ear is destroyed either by the operation or by the previous infection.[10]

Otosclerosis has been mentioned as a hereditary disease which may affect hearing at any stage of life. Similarly, there is a *degeneration of the auditory nerve* which seems to be hereditary and may affect the individual at any age. Although little is known about this condition, it is stated that ". . . if *both* parents have true hereditary deafness . . . their children will almost certainly be born deaf or soon become deaf."[11] Even if the parents themselves have normal hearing, but there is a history of such deafness on both sides, the children may have defective hearing.

Concussions on certain parts of the head may cause temporary or permanent loss of hearing. Subjection to prolonged *high-frequency sounds*, as in certain industrial conditions or military experiences, may likewise have a traumatic effect on the nervous mechanism of the ear. Other forms of insult to the auditory nerve may come from *intracranial tumors*, from *cerebral hemorrhage*, or from the *toxic effect of certain drugs*.

Old age creates a deterioration in hearing known as *presbycusis* and is possibly the most common of all causes of hearing loss.

Cortical defects as in some of the aphasias may cause defects in hearing or in understanding what is heard. Many impairments of hearing which cannot be explained by other abnormalities are attributed to abnormal functioning of the central nervous system.

Psychological and emotional factors also play a role in some forms of hearing loss. Auditory defects of psychogenic origin include hysterical

---

[10] T. E. Walsh, "The Surgical Treatment of Hearing Loss," *Hearing and Deafness*, H. Davis and S. R. Silverman, eds. (New York: Holt, Rinehart and Winston, Inc., rev. ed., 1960), pp. 145–148. Victor Goodhill, "Pathology, Diagnosis, and Therapy of Deafness," *Handbook of Speech Pathology*, Lee E. Travis, ed. (New York: Appleton-Century-Crofts, Inc., 1957), pp. 331–333.

[11] Davis and Fowler, *op. cit.*, p. 110.

deafness, in which an individual finds it easier to resolve a deep unconscious emotional conflict by elimination of hearing than by other forms of adjustment. Often military experiences are such a shock to the sensibilities that functional deafness ensues.

Davis and Fowler report data from Hoff General Hospital (United States Army) showing that, of the last 500 cases admitted for auditory rehabilitation toward the end of World War II, 15 per cent had psychogenic factors as all or part of the cause of loss of hearing.[12] In many cases there is some loss or a temporary loss which is exaggerated or prolonged for psychological reasons.

Psychogenic deafness must not be confused with malingering, in which the individual pretends to be unable to hear. Usually the malingerer can be detected by special tests.

Extensive current statistics are not available giving number and proportions of the various causes and classifications of hearing defects. The most comprehensive study of its kind was made in 1928 by Shambaugh.[13] Approximately one-half of his cases were profoundly deaf while the other half had severe hearing losses. Hearing loss was of congenital origin in 61.8 per cent of the cases and was acquired in 38.2 per cent.

In a National Study of the psychological effects of deafness Myklebust found 39.1 per cent exogenous (acquired), 22.6 per cent endogenous (hereditary), and 38.3 per cent of unknown origin.[14]

Types of Hearing Defects

Because of the complicated structure and functioning of the ear, defects in hearing may occur in many different forms. Basically these defects are of three main types: (1) conductive losses, (2) sensory-neural or perceptive losses, and (3) central deafness.

A *conductive hearing loss* is one which reduces the intensity of sound reaching the inner ear, where the auditory nerve begins. To reach the inner ear sound waves in the air must pass through the external canal of the *outer ear* to the eardrum, where the vibrations are picked up by a series of bonelike structures in the *middle ear* and passed on to the *inner ear*. This sequence of vibrations may be blocked anywhere along the line. Wax or malformations may block the external canal; the eardrum may be broken or unable to vibrate; the movement of the bones in the middle ear may be obstructed. Any condition hindering the sequence

[12] *Ibid.*, pp. 119–120.

[13] G. E. Shambaugh, Sr., *et al.*, "Causes of Deafness in 3120 Children in Public Schools for the Deaf," *Archives of Otolaryngology*, 7 (1928), 424.

[14] Helmer R. Myklebust, *The Psychology of Deafness* (New York: Grune and Stratton, 1960).

of vibrations or preventing them from reaching the auditory nerve is considered a conduction loss.

This type of defect seldom causes a hearing loss of more than 50 to 60 decibels, since there will still be available the vibrations carried by the bone to the inner ear. The audiometer has a bone-conduction receiver as well as an air-conduction receiver and can therefore measure the ability of the individual to pick up sound through bone conduction.

Figure 14 shows the audiogram of a child with a conductive hearing loss. On the audiometer he heard air-borne sounds at the 30 to 40 decibel level at all frequencies. When using a bone-conduction receiver, however, he responded normally; his difficulty was due to a defect or obstruction in the outer or middle ear rather than in the sensory nerve of the inner ear. As might be expected, the audiogram of this type of hearing loss is fairly even at all frequencies.

A *sensory-neural or perceptive hearing loss* is caused by defects of the inner ear or of the auditory nerve transmitting the impulse to the brain. Sensory-neural hearing loss may be complete or partial, and it may affect some frequencies (especially the high ones) more than others. Thus in Figure 15 the audiogram shows profound loss at the high frequencies and severe loss at the frequencies below 1000 cycles. High-frequency loss is often associated with sensory-neural deafness. The bone-conduction

FIGURE 14

Audiogram of Child with a Conductive Hearing Loss

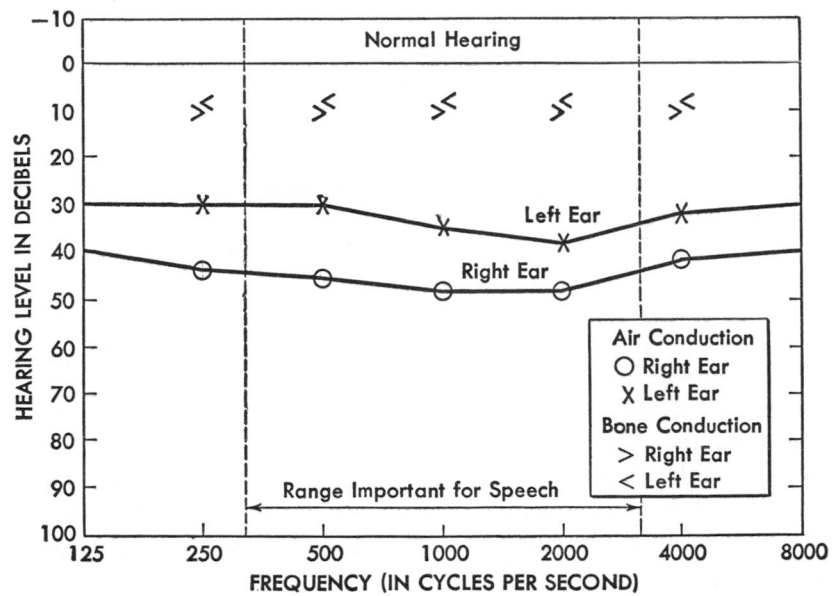

FIGURE 15

Audiogram of Child with a Sensory-Neural or Perceptive Hearing Loss

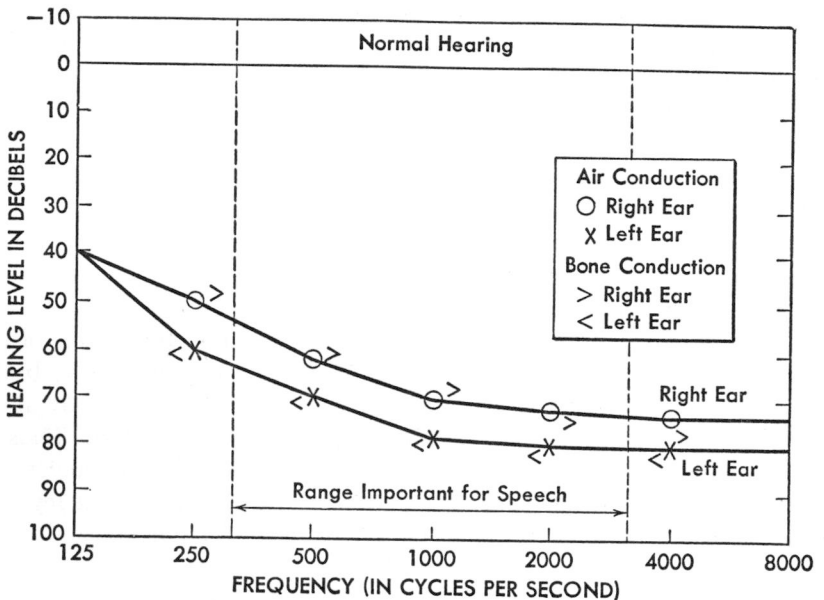

receiver in this case gave no better reception since the defect was in the nerve, not in the mechanism which carried the vibrations to the nerve.

In *central deafness* the peripheral or receiving mechanism of hearing is functioning properly, but still the individual does not hear, owing to some injury or abnormality of the central nervous system. This kind of defect includes the condition in which a person hears sounds but is unable to interpret them — often referred to as auditory aphasia or sensory aphasia or word deafness.

We may also include in this category deafness of psychogenic origin in which the receptive organs are functioning adequately and there is no damage to the central nervous system, but in which the individual does not hear for deep-seated emotional reasons. The deafness of autistic children would be an example of hearing loss of a psychogenic origin.

The proper diagnosis of a hearing defect is a very important and very technical matter. The treatment, the educational program, and even the selection of a hearing aid are dependent upon it. It is obvious, for example, that a bone-conduction hearing aid would not help the child whose audiogram is presented in Figure 15, whereas it probably would help the child represented in Figure 14.

Summary

1. Children with hearing losses are affected in their development in various ways, chiefly in speech and language.

2. Two groupings are made for educational purposes: (a) *Hard-of-hearing* children are classified as children with slight losses, marginal losses, and moderate losses; they are educated through the auditory channel. (b) *Deaf* children are classified as those with severe losses and those with profound losses; they are educated primarily through sense modalities other than the ear.

3. The development of speech and language is dependent upon (a) degree of hearing loss, (b) age at onset of loss, and (c) intelligence.

4. The kinds of hearing loss found in children are conductive loss, sensory-neural loss, and central loss.

5. The estimates of prevalence of hearing loss among school children range from 2 to 5 per cent.

DISCUSSION QUESTIONS

1. What is the purpose of classifying auditorily handicapped children into the deaf, the deafened, and the various degrees of hard of hearing? Explain the controversial nature of these classifications.

2. Of a school population of 18,000, (a) how many children will suffer from a hearing loss? (b) How many can be served by an itinerant speech teacher? (c) How many will require special class placement? (d) How many can remain in the regular class with differential treatment by the classroom teacher?

3. As a teacher, how would you determine when a child should be referred for a hearing examination?

4. Make a table comparing the etiological factors in hearing loss and mental retardation, and note (a) causes unique to mental retardation, (b) causes unique to hearing loss, and (c) causes common to both.

5. What would be the major differences in organizing educational procedures for Cases A and C in Figure 12?

6. State a meaningful proposition which would show the positive or negative relationships of the following pairs of attributes. For example, "hearing loss — speech development" could lead to the proposition: All other factors being equal, the greater the hearing loss the more retarded the speech development.
   (a) Hearing loss — language
   (b) Severely hard-of-hearing children — age at onset

(c) Intelligence — speech and language
(d) Conductive hearing loss — frequency of sound
(e) Sensory-neural loss — high frequencies
(f) Bone conduction hearing aid — sensory-neural hearing loss
(g) Central deafness — psychogenic deafness

Selected References

Davis, Hallowell, and S. Richard Silverman, eds. *Hearing and Deafness*. New York: Holt, Rinehart and Winston, Inc., rev. ed., 1960.

Gates, Arthur I., and Rose E. Kushner. *Learning to Use Hearing Aids*. New York: Teachers College, Columbia University, 1946.

Kelly, James C. *Clinicians' Handbook for Auditory Training*. Dubuque: William C. Brown Company, 1953.

Madden, Richard. *The School Status of the Hard-of-Hearing Child*. New York: Columbia University, 1931.

Myklebust, Helmer R. *Auditory Disorders in Children*. New York: Grune and Stratton, 1954.

Myklebust, Helmer R. *The Psychology of Deafness*. New York: Grune and Stratton, 1960.

Stevens, Stanley S., and Hallowell Davis. *Hearing, Its Psychology and Physiology*. New York: John Wiley and Sons, 1938.

Streng, Alice, Waring J. Fitch, Le Roy D. Hedgecock, James W. Phillips, and James A. Carrell. *Hearing Therapy for Children*. New York: Grune and Stratton, 2nd ed., 1958.

Travis, Lee Edward, ed. *Handbook of Speech Pathology*. New York: Appleton-Century-Crofts, Inc., 1957.

7

Educating Deaf and Hard-of-Hearing Children

The educational provisions for and techniques of teaching deaf children are significantly different from those utilized with hard-of-hearing children. Because hard-of-hearing children have the ability to acquire speech and language through hearing, the problem in teaching them is mainly one of making it possible for them to learn through the methods and techniques used with hearing children. With hearing aids, some individual help in speech, speech reading, auditory training, and a few special arrangements, most of these children can acquire an education through the usual channels and generally in classes with hearing children.

The deaf child faces quite a different problem. Because he never hears speech, he does not normally acquire language or the subtleties of meaning which are more readily acquired through the sense of hearing. The important factor to remember in educating deaf children is that their major deficiency is not so much lack of hearing as inability to develop speech and language through the sense of hearing. Their education, therefore, is probably the most technical area in the whole field of special education. It requires more specialized training on the part of the teacher than any other form of education.

This chapter will first discuss the less technical problem of providing special educational adaptations for hard-of-hearing children and then describe the procedures in educating deaf children.

Educational Provisions for the Hard of Hearing

In fulfilling its responsibilities to hard-of-hearing children, the school has to (1) identify those needing help, (2) see that they are adequately diagnosed and given whatever medical treatment is necessary, and (3) provide an appropriate educational program.

Identification

The first problem the school faces is that of locating the children needing help. It has already been shown that locating them in a haphazard manner by teacher referrals or parent requests brings to light only a small proportion of the children with hearing difficulties. Often a child with a hearing loss of 30 or 40 decibels is not detected by parents or teachers since he hears conversational speech and probably learned to talk at an average age. Sometimes deviant behavior is not recognized as related to hearing loss but is attributed to other factors (such as low intelligence, emotional problems, lack of interest) which may or may not be pertinent. A systematic attempt to find the auditorily handicapped would include a screening test for all children and an individual test for those who fail to pass the screening test.

A group audiometric test can be given to all classes in a school system. Each child in a class is given earphones and makes appropriate responses when he hears the controlled stimulus produced by the audiometer. Instead of a group screening test an individual sweep-check audiometric test may be administered — usually by the school nurse or hearing specialist. The term "identification audiometry" is preferred by some specialists for these screening procedures.

Many children who indicate a hearing loss on a screening test are found not to have a loss when given an individual test. Inattention, poor understanding, and other irrelevant factors sometimes make a child respond poorly in a group setting.

Assessment

Children found to have a hearing loss are referred to an otologist, who determines the exact nature of the disability and if possible administers medical treatment. For example, he may find wax in the ears, infected adenoids or tonsils, or some other abnormality which can be corrected. His diagnosis may also determine the type of hearing aid or the kind of program which is necessary.

Programming

As was suggested earlier, the educational program is not the same for all cases of hearing handicap. The child with a severe hearing loss needs specialized techniques and materials, which will be discussed in the next section. At present we are dealing with the philosophy and methods of teaching hard-of-hearing children who, despite their handicap, can make some use of auditory stimuli.

For many years hard-of-hearing children were taught in special classes. These classes had some advantages in that the class number was kept small, there was an increased use of visual aids, and auditory training and lip reading could be an integral part of the program. Since the recent improvements in hearing aids, however, it has been found that most of these children gain more from being with normal children. They are usually able to keep up with the work if given a little assistance in the areas of special need.

Hard-of-hearing children (as shown in Fig. 13) are not very different from their classmates. Except in speech, language, and reading they are not seriously retarded academically. Special classes are provided for those with marked variation or with variations in many areas, but when a discrepancy occurs in only one or two remediable areas, it is advisable to keep the child in the regular grades and allow him to leave the class for short periods for specific tutoring in his regions of difficulty. For this reason, special classes for the hard of hearing are decreasing in school systems.

More widely recommended is enrollment in the regular grades and provision of itinerant teachers to help the children individually or in small groups for a half-hour or an hour a day. This instruction would consist of (1) training in the use of hearing aids, (2) auditory training, (3) lip reading, and (4) speech correction.

Instruction in the Use of Hearing Aids. With young children considerable care should be used in introducing the hearing aid. At the outset a child should not wear a hearing aid all day. The best procedure is to start using a hearing aid only in the tutoring session and under the supervision of the speech and hearing teacher. It should be used for short periods of time under instruction and the periods gradually increased, so that the child will learn to use the hearing aid profitably.

Auditory Training. Training the child to listen to and discriminate between different sounds is called auditory training. Before the advent of hearing aids, auditory training involved speaking into the ear or using tubes to amplify the sound. Now that the vacuum-tube hearing aid and the transistor type of hearing aid are available, these are extensively used in auditory training.

Modern electronics has vastly improved hearing aids. Specific frequencies can be emphasized, tone quality has been improved to make reproduction more natural and speech more intelligible, adjustments can be made by the wearer, and packaging has become more convenient. With the application of transistors to hearing aids, the size has been diminished until now the necessary mechanisms can even be put in an eyeglass frame.

The major aim of auditory training is to help the child at as early an age as possible to learn to discriminate between sounds. This kind of instruction is given to the hard-of-hearing child by an itinerant hearing specialist in school in accordance with the needs of the child. Of great importance for this type of training is home instruction, particularly during the preschool period. Parents can aid a great deal in auditory training, and one of the goals of the hearing specialist is to so instruct the parents and obtain their cooperation.

Lip Reading (Speech Reading). Although we use the auditory sense to understand the spoken word, most of us can hear and understand another person better if we are looking directly at his face. Certain facial expressions and movements add meaning to what he says. That is why television, which uses both auditory and visual aids, is more effective than a radio. If you turn on your television so that the picture shows clearly, but tune down the voice to the point where it is only partially audible from where you are sitting, you will experience what cues a hard-of-hearing person uses. In this situation you will begin to rely on the facial and lip movements of the speaker to supplement the faint voice you hear. If you turn off the visual picture but leave the faint voice on, you will understand less of what the speaker is saying.

Lip-reading or speech-reading lessons are given to hard-of-hearing children to sharpen their understanding of what is said to them.[1] By directing their attention to certain cues in lip and facial movements they can learn to fill in from context the sounds they do not hear and the words which are indistinct. Many words look much alike to the lip reader — words such as "cup" and "up." These cannot be discriminated visually. But words like "fish" and "ball" are rather easy to differentiate. It is also fortunate that the vowels, which are harder to tell apart visually, are easier to discriminate auditorily since they belong to the lower-frequency ranges. Some of the consonants, like *s*, are harder to hear because they belong to the high-frequency ranges in

[1] John J. O'Neill and Herbert J. Oyer, *Visual Communication for the Hard of Hearing* (Englewood Cliffs, N.J.: Prentice-Hall, Inc., 1961).

speech, where a deficit in sensory-neural or perceptive deafness is more common.

By giving a hard-of-hearing child some help outside of the regular classroom in auditory training, speech reading, and the use of a hearing aid, the itinerant teacher is helping him understand more effectively the speakers who surround him — the teacher, the children in class, and his parents.

In general, three methods of teaching lip reading have been used. The first emphasizes the analysis of details in a word. This is a phonetic approach to lip reading. Instruction is programmed with a series of exercises in phonics, in which the child learns to distinguish phonetic elements by seeing them and repeating them to himself. In one such system, the Jena method, the child memorizes vowel series, then combines vowels with consonants and later uses words and sentences.[2]

A second method, the whole method of teaching lip reading, does not use a phonetic or syllable approach but emphasizes thought units as a whole.[3] The child is told stories even though he understands only parts of them. Nitchie first advocated a phonic method but later developed a whole method of lip-reading instruction.[4] Her methods of teaching involved the synthesis of what was read.

A third method, described by Bruhn, is based on the German Mueller-Walle Method.[5] In her lessons with children she presents the most visible sounds first and the less visible sounds at a later time. The lessons begin with syllables and move on to sentences.

Speech Training. Many children who are hard of hearing have not heard certain sounds accurately and so have developed speech with sound substitutions and other articulatory defects. In addition, because they sometimes do not hear background noises, they fail to adjust the loudness of their voices to surrounding noises. Some speak too loudly because they cannot hear their own voice, owing to a perceptive loss; others do not speak loudly enough because, having a conductive loss, they can hear their own voices through bone conduction much better than they hear others.

The usual procedure for speech training is first to find out what errors a child makes in speech. Errors can be tabulated in a more formal way

[2] Anna M. Bunger, *Speech Reading — Jena Method* (Danville, Ill.: The Interstate Press, 2nd ed., 1952).

[3] Agnes Stowell, Estelle Samuelson, and Ann Lehman, *Lip Reading for the Deafened Child* (New York: The Macmillan Company, 1928).

[4] Elizabeth H. Nitchie, *New Lessons in Lip Reading* (Philadelphia: J. B. Lippincott Company, 1950).

[5] Martha E. Bruhn. *The Mueller-Walle Method of Lip Reading for the Hard of Hearing* (Boston: M. H. Leavis, 1947).

by using an articulation test. A child is asked to label or name pictures or objects, and the teacher notes whether the child adds or omits sounds and whether his distortions or substitutions occur in the initial, medial, or final positions. In addition, the teacher will note the voice quality and any abnormalities in speaking.

Following the detection of specific errors, corrective measures can be initiated. In school it is best for the child to remain in the regular grades for his educational program, while the special teachers help him with his speaking and hearing problems in an individual situation or in a small group. Most effective results are obtained when such training is integrated with the work of the regular class and when the parents will cooperate with the program at home.

Educational Provisions for the Deaf

Although we may find differences of opinion in all areas of education, people concerned with the education of the deaf have been sharply divided into opposing camps. The controversy has continued for many years and although tempered by time it goes on today in modified form. The two methods of education of the deaf are commonly known as *oralism* and *manualism*.

The oral method develops communication through speech and lip reading without the use of signs or gestures. The language of signs, or the manual method, achieves communication by conventional gestures of the hands or arms to express thoughts. Another form of manual language uses the manual alphabet, in which there is a fixed position of the fingers or hands for each letter of the alphabet. This is a kind of writing in the air.

The Development of Educational Programs for the Deaf

According to Wallin, the pioneers in the education of the deaf were Juan Pablo Bonet and Jacob Rodrigues Pereire, Spaniards of the seventeenth century.[6] Bonet originated the manual alphabet for the deaf, published in Madrid in 1620. This was a major innovation in the field since it gave the deaf a means of communication with those who knew the manual alphabet. Pereire extended Bonet's alphabet and added to it the manual sign language.

But Pereire also expanded a more far-reaching technique known as *lip reading* or the oral method of teaching the deaf by having them acquire meaning from the movements of other people's lips and facial

[6] J. E. Wallace Wallin, *The Education of Handicapped Children* (Boston: Houghton Mifflin Company, 1924), pp. 6–9.

muscles and form their own words from what they had seen. According to Wallin, Pereire held to the theory that touch is the primitive sense and that all special senses are modifications of touch. Through the tactual sense, he tried to produce voices in deaf children. Thus, through visual apprehension of the movements of the visible speech organs and through the vibrations which could be felt by the deaf child, Pereire introduced the oral method.

Because of Pereire's contribution he was awarded a pension by Louis XV, and the oral method received the official commendation of a committee of the Parisian Academy of Science. Wallin asserts,

> There has perhaps been no achievement in the whole realm of remedial pedagogy or educational rehabilitation quite equal to the feat of teaching a deaf child who may never have heard a spoken word and who is even unable to hear his own voice, to speak and apprehend speech. It is much more difficult to reach the deaf than the blind, for the deaf are deprived of the greatest stimulus to mental growth, namely, spoken language.[7]

According to Silverman, it was the Abbé Charles Michel de l'Épée in France and Samuel Heinicke in Germany who advanced the cause of deaf education on the continent in the eighteenth century.[8] De l'Épée founded the first public school for the deaf in 1755 in Paris, where he taught by the manual method. De l'Épée's contemporary, Samuel Heinicke, founded the first public school for the deaf in Germany, using the oral method. Thus the two methods of teaching the deaf received impetus at about the same time — de l'Épée favoring signs and manualism, Heinicke advocating speech and speech reading.

The first school for the deaf in the British Isles was opened in Edinburgh in 1760 by Thomas Braidwood, who became well known for his oral methods of teaching deaf children. His reputation spread to the United States and stimulated Thomas Hopkins Gallaudet, a divinity student in Hartford, Connecticut, to go to Scotland to study the oral method. He was disappointed with what he obtained there. Braidwood was supposedly getting good results from his use of the oral method with deaf children but he was secretive about his methods. Gallaudet therefore crossed the channel to France and studied the manual approach of de l'Épée under Sicard, de l'Épée's successor. After his return to the United States, Gallaudet in 1817 opened at Hartford, Connecticut, the first school for the deaf in this country, where education was, of course, by the manual method. Gallaudet was also responsible for bringing to Hartford Laurent Clerc, who himself was deaf. At the Hartford school,

---

[7] *Ibid.*, p. 8.

[8] S. R. Silverman, "From Aristotle to Bell," *Hearing and Deafness*, Hallowell Davis and S. R. Silverman eds. (New York: Holt, Rinehart and Winston, Inc., rev. ed., 1960), pp. 405–412.

then called the American Asylum for the Education and Instruction of the Deaf and Dumb, Clerc became the first deaf teacher of the deaf in the United States.

Although the Hartford school was supported privately, it soon won public support and became the forerunner of state-supported schools throughout the United States, most of which combine oral and manual methods. Private residential schools like the Clarke School for the Deaf in Northhampton, Massachusetts, the Lexington School for the Deaf in New York, and the Central Institute for the Deaf in St. Louis, Missouri, were organized and continue to function as advocates of the oral method. The federally sponsored College for the Deaf in Washington, D.C., where the work was carried on by Gallaudet's son, Edward Minor Gallaudet, bears the name of Gallaudet.

In this country Alexander Graham Bell also opened up new channels for teaching speech to the deaf. His method of "Visible Speech" helped the child understand the placement of his speech organs in producing speech. His invention of the telephone led to the development and use of hearing aids and to greater emphasis on the use of amplification of sound in teaching speech to children with severely defective hearing. These inventions advanced oral methods of teaching the deaf and made it possible for many children to understand speech and language who previously could not have done so. Bell was also responsible for founding the Volta Bureau of information on deafness.

The oral method has had many advocates in the United States, although advancement of this technique came somewhat later than teaching by the manual method. The first public day school utilizing the oral method was established in Boston in 1869. Horace Mann, who had studied the education of the deaf in Germany, was influential in this undertaking.

Both the oral and the manual methods are in use today. Most authorities agree that there is a place for each or for a combined method. No group insists that all deaf children should be taught by the manual method. Both residential and day schools advocate the oral method for those children who are capable of learning by it. In many residential schools, for instance, most children are given an opportunity to learn the oral method at first, but if they do not make progress they are then taught by the manual method. In most residential schools a combined manual and oral method is used as the instructional technique for a large proportion of the children. In addition, when a group of deaf children congregate, as in a residential school, they naturally learn from each other, and the manual method becomes the common denominator of communication because there are some children who never do learn oral speech. Younger children especially rely on the manual method, for adequate lip reading and speech require many years of training and considerable facility.

In general, day schools for the deaf and some of the private residential schools are strictly oral schools and frankly discourage the use of the sign language or finger spelling. The state residential schools use both methods, but communication among the children themselves in the residential units is mostly by the manual method.

Day and Residential Schools

At present there are residential schools, day schools, and special classes in city schools for deaf children. Table VII shows that approximately two-thirds of deaf children who are receiving education in this country go to the residential schools, either privately or publicly operated. The state schools are administered by a state authority and offer education and maintenance without charge. The education of children in day schools is of two types: either a segregated school is devoted entirely to deaf children or one or more classes are provided for the deaf in a school housing hearing children. The size of the classes ranges from five to ten children. Most of the residential schools combine oralism and manualism, but as indicated earlier a few schools (such as the Central Institute for the Deaf in St. Louis, Clarke School for the Deaf in Massachusetts,

TABLE VII

Enrollment in Schools and Classes for the Deaf and Hard of Hearing, 1955 and 1960

Kind of School	1955[a]			1960[b]		
	Number of Schools	Deaf	Hard of Hearing	Number of Schools	Deaf	Hard of Hearing
Public residential schools	72	12,436	1,665	72	13,911	1,778
Day schools	10	1,147	325	10	1,714	346
Day classes in public schools	200	2,866	1,408	254	4,282	2,671
Denominational and private residential schools and classes	50	1,540	273	64	1,676	473
Schools and classes for the multiple handicapped	11			15		
Total	343	17,989	3,671	415	21,583	5,268

[a] *American Annals of the Deaf*, 101 (January, 1956), 222.
[b] *Ibid.*, 106 (January, 1961), 162.

and the Lexington School for the Deaf in New York) use the oral method exclusively. The advantages claimed for each kind of school are presented for comparative evaluation.

Advantages of Residential School Placement	*Advantages of Day School Placement*
The child may be overprotected at home, but in a dormitory he has to learn to get along with other children and accept his own responsibility.	The child is the responsibility of his parents and should remain at home like other children.
The whole program can be geared to the educational program for the deaf without contradictory training by parents and others.	He needs the warmth and affection of family life.
A total program of training can be effected since cottage parents and teachers serve together as guidance personnel.	
A residential school can concentrate the efforts of specialized teachers for children of all ages.	The oral method can be emphasized in the day school, at home, and in the community. There will be little opportunity for manualism in a day school, since most of the children with whom the deaf child associates are hearing children.
Because deaf children are too few, school systems cannot organize homogeneous classes. In a residential school with more children, children can be grouped according to age, ability, and interests in a more effective manner than is done in day schools.	There is an opportunity to integrate some of the activities of the deaf child with those of hearing children; in future life he will, after all, be living in a hearing world.

There has been very little research to evaluate the relative advantages of day schools and residential schools or their effects on the future lives of their pupils. Upshall, comparing the development of children in institutions and children in day schools, found that the intelligence of those in institutions was somewhat lower than that of day school students.[9] Similarly, in comparing 311 day school pupils with 1470 residential school

[9] C. C. Upshall, *Day Schools Versus Institutions for the Deaf*, Teachers College Contributions to Education, No. 389 (New York: Bureau of Publications, Teachers College, Columbia University, 1929).

pupils he found that the achievement of the former was somewhat higher than that of the latter.

The results of Upshall's study do not determine which method is best. All they indicate is that those who are enrolled in day schools tend to have a higher nonlanguage intelligence test score and higher educational achievement. A selection factor may be operative here, since in some instances day schools refer those with poor learning ability to residential schools. Upshall also discovered that the day schools had a greater proportion of children with better hearing and more who had become deaf later in life. These children also spend more years in school. When Upshall matched cases in day schools with cases in residential schools for age, intelligence, onset of deafness, and degree of hearing loss, he still found a slight educational superiority for those in day schools, but the difference was not statistically significant.

Quigley and Frisina conducted a different kind of an experiment, matching 120 residential school children with 120 children living at home (day pupils) but attending the same residential schools.[10] The day pupils were found to be superior in speech and speech reading, but there was no difference in finger spelling ability or vocabulary. In some of the adjustment evaluations the resident pupils scored slightly higher than the day pupils. This difference was more evident among boys than among girls.

Whether to send a child to a day school or to a residential school for the deaf depends upon many factors. If adequate provisions exist in the community, the child should probably go to the day school. If, on the other hand, there are few deaf children in the community and no place to educate them, it is usually better for the child to be in a residential institution. Therefore, the question is not whether day schools are more effective than residential schools, or vice versa, but what is most beneficial for a particular child in a particular community.

Factors Influencing Educational Development of Deaf Children

As with all children, there are many environmental influences and factors which produce individual differences in development among deaf children. The more tangible and important factors are (1) intelligence, (2) degree of deafness (severe or profound), and (3) age at onset of deafness.

Intelligence. The progress of a deaf child in school is partially dependent upon his intelligence, his rate of learning, and his ability to gen-

---

[10] Stephen P. Quigley and D. R. Frisina, "Institutionalization and Psychoeducational Development of Deaf Children," *Council for Exceptional Children Research Monograph No. 3* (Washington: National Education Association, 1961).

eralize, draw conclusions, and make use of subtle cues. There are found some deaf children who are superior in intelligence, many who are average, and some who are mentally retarded. Performance on non-language intelligence tests (where the deaf child's language difficulty is minimized) indicates that the IQ's of deaf children attending school range from 60 to 160.

Pinter surveyed the results of various nonlanguage and performance intelligence tests given to deaf children mostly in residential schools. He states, "Our best estimate at present, therefore, is that the average I.Q. of the deaf does not quite reach 90."[11] In general, however, children attending oral schools and public day schools tend to be close to 100 IQ while the larger group attending residential schools averages around 90 IQ. This difference is not necessarily attributable to the teaching methods since there is a selection factor in effect. The more intelligent children are less likely to be sent to a residential institution, whereas the ones who find it difficult to function in the day schools are often referred to the residential schools.

Myklebust points out in his study of deafness and mental development that although the deaf seem to be inferior to hearing children on some intellectual tasks, they are equal or superior on other tasks.[12] For example, he found that the deaf are superior to hearing children on memory for designs, tactual memory, and memory for movement. But they were inferior to hearing children on digit span, picture span, and memory for dots.

Degrees of Deafness. Children placed in classes and schools for the deaf have either (1) a severe loss of hearing in the speech range (60 to 75 decibel level) or (2) a profound hearing loss at a level of over 75 decibels.

The severely deaf child has considerable residual hearing and can profit in most instances from a hearing aid. Such a child is sometimes called *educationally deaf;* that is, he is not completely deaf but needs the specialized training of a deaf child. In other words, for instructional purposes he *is* deaf. Without intensive training, hearing aids, special techniques, and individual help, he will not develop language and speech. With such help children with this defect usually do develop language and speech. In some instances and with proper instruction they can be reclassified as hard of hearing and can move into the program for hard-of-hearing children; that is, they can be placed in a regular class with additional tutoring by a special teacher part of the day.

[11] Rudolph Pintner, Jon Eisenson, and Mildred Stanton, *The Psychology of the Physically Handicapped* (New York: F. S. Crofts and Company, 1941), p. 127.

[12] Helmer R. Myklebust, *The Psychology of Deafness* (New York: Grune and Stratton, 1960).

The profoundly deaf, however, cannot profit as much from a hearing aid and frequently find it very difficult to acquire speech and language. They make slower progress in language, speech, and school subjects than do the severely deaf children.

Age at Onset of Deafness. It has been emphasized that the age at which a child becomes deaf has a significant influence on his language and speech development. If a child does not lose his hearing until after he has acquired some speech and language, he at least has some concept of the process of communication and a base on which to build more speech and understanding of language. If he is born deaf or loses his hearing before he has learned to talk, he progresses much more slowly in these areas. Of course, the older the child is when he loses his hearing and the more advanced his speech, the easier his education will be later. To illustrate this point, Figure 16 gives the educational profiles of Carl, who was born with normal hearing, and Jim, who was born deaf.

Carl developed normally until the age of 7. He entered school when he was 6, and his intellectual ability was slightly above average. His school achievement was comparable to that of the average child. At the age of 7, however, he contracted meningitis, and when the disease subsided, Carl was unable to hear. Believing that this was a temporary condition, the parents waited for Carl's hearing to return. But it did not return, and he was diagnosed as having a total hearing loss of a sensory-neural type. There was nothing that could be done for him medically.

At the age of 10 Carl was given a series of physical, educational, and mental tests, the results of which are presented in Figure 16. It will be noticed that he was average in height and weight, and slightly above average in motor coordination and mental ability. In social maturity he was average. In speech development his progress had been slowed down by his loss of hearing and he was considered to have the speech development of a child less than 9 years old. Language development was somewhat better; much of this could be gained from reading, in which, because of a good start in first and second grade, he was able to continue to progress at an average rate. He relied a great deal on reading since this was his best channel for obtaining information. In his other school subjects he was also progressing normally. This profile shows that Carl's major difficulty is in speech and language, which though handicapped by his loss of hearing were sufficiently well established at the time of his illness to permit him to gain ideas through written language.

Jim's profile reveals a much greater retardation. Jim was born deaf; the cause of his disability was unknown. It will be seen from the pro-

FIGURE 16

Profiles of Two Deaf Boys, One Born with Normal Hearing, One Born Deaf

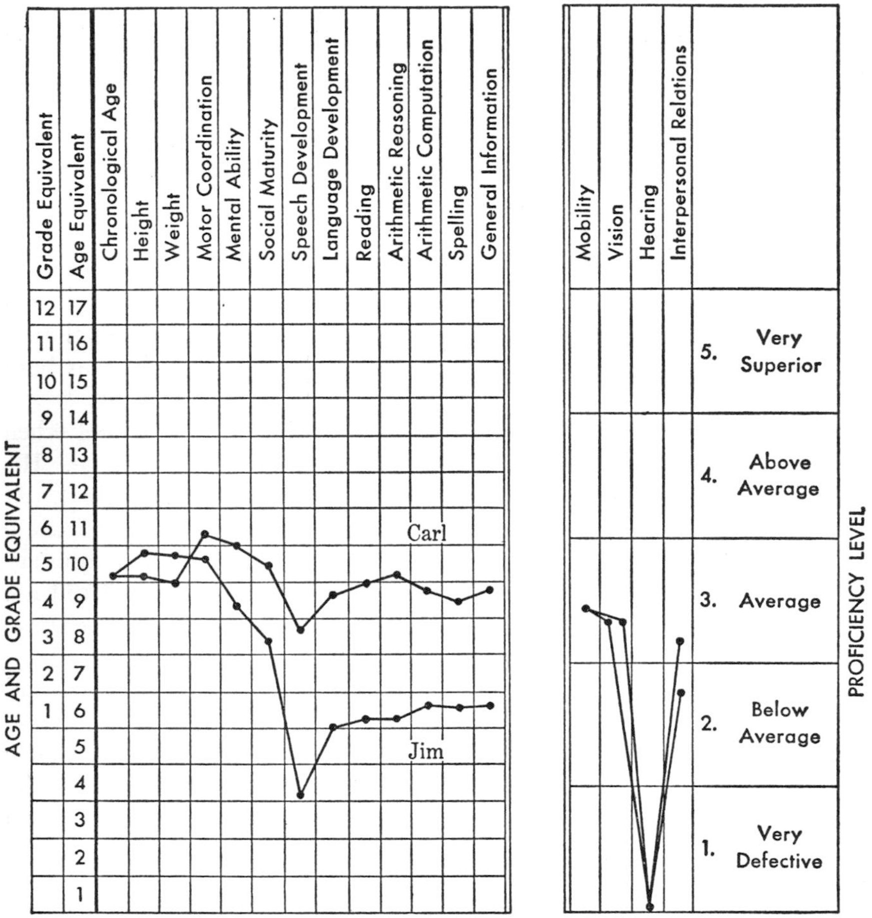

Grade Equivalent	Age Equivalent	Chronological Age	Height	Weight	Motor Coordination	Mental Ability	Social Maturity	Speech Development	Language Development	Reading	Arithmetic Reasoning	Arithmetic Computation	Spelling	General Information		Mobility	Vision	Hearing	Interpersonal Relations			Proficiency Level
12	17																					
11	16																			5.	Very Superior	
10	15																					
9	14																					
8	13																			4.	Above Average	
7	12																					
6	11												Carl									
5	10																					
4	9																			3.	Average	
3	8																					
2	7																					
1	6																			2.	Below Average	
	5										Jim											
	4																					
	3																			1.	Very Defective	
	2																					
	1																					

AGE AND GRADE EQUIVALENT

PROFICIENCY LEVEL

file that at the age of 10 Jim was slightly above average in height, weight, and motor coordination and average in intelligence. In social maturity he showed some retardation, but in speech and in language development the retardation was marked. This handicap, of course, took its toll in other school subjects so that when he was 10 Jim was doing only first-grade reading and slightly better in other school subjects. Even this ability was due to the fact that he had been fortunate enough to attend nursery school, where he was taught some speech and speech reading. Had he not had a consistent program for the deaf, he would probably have learned no speech, no oral language skills, and no reading. The discrepancy between his school achievement and his physical, mental, and social abilities had been decreased because of the educational program.

Figure 16 demonstrates the effect of the early loss of hearing. Both boys were profoundly deaf, with hearing losses of 80 to 90 decibels in each ear due to sensory-neural deafness. But Jim, whose educational retardation was very great, had been born deaf, whereas Carl had acquired his deafness after speech and language had had seven years to develop.

Specialized Curriculum for Deaf Children

In Chapter 6 a deaf child was defined as one whose hearing loss is so great that it interferes with the development of speech and language. With a lesser degree of hearing loss the child is designated hard of hearing. The hard-of-hearing child has many difficulties socially and educationally, but because he has some hearing he is able to learn to communicate with others and to gain meaning from written language. His education progresses through a modification of methods and techniques used with normal children. For a deaf child, however, the basic disability — loss of hearing — creates a chain of difficulties. Without hearing he does not naturally acquire speech and language; without speech and language he does not acquire knowledge and understanding of other subject matter. Because of the variety of deficits and because of the nature of the techniques necessary to teach the deaf, he needs a small special class and a teacher who understands the problems and is skilled in giving specialized training.

The specialized curriculum of a class for the deaf includes: (1) speech development, (2) speech reading and auditory training, (3) language development, (4) reading, and (5) other school subjects.

Speech Development

As the hearing child learns to speak, the observer can recognize a series of stages. At first the child extends his gurgling and swallowing sounds into babbling. He toys with these sounds and experiments with his voice, and as he babbles he hears himself and sometimes repeats the same sound over and over again. Later he may repeat the sounds that someone else says if they are in his repertoire. This is the stage of imitation which at first is only echoing or imitating his own babbling sounds or the sounds his parents make. He may say "ma ma ma" or "da da da" just as repetition of sound, without attaching any meaning to it. As "da da da" is repeated over and over again in the presence of his father, he connects the two and moves into a higher stage in learning to talk: associating meaning with certain sounds. When the mother says "da da" he looks for his father, or when he says "da da" his father comes to him. By these stages the hearing child turns his babbling into meaningful words, and meaningful speech is then well on its way.

But the deaf child cannot hear his own babbling and it soon stops. He does not hear the words of his parents and hence neither imitates them nor attaches meaning to them. In short, he does not learn to speak by ordinary channels. If he is to learn to speak, it must be by other routes which are tedious, less efficient, and extremely slow in developing. But it has been found that a totally deaf child can learn to speak if properly taught by skilled parents and teachers. The intonation and expression may not be those of a hearing child, but he can learn to make himself understood. Vibrations and the sense of touch, visual aids, kinesthetic and proprioceptive cues, and the use of any residual hearing through a hearing aid are all part of the process as he learns to speak. Though often used together, they will be discussed separately.

Speech Training Through Vibration and the Sense of Touch. The tactile sense was used intensively by Kate and Sophia Alcorn in teaching deaf-blind children and also in teaching deaf-seeing children.[13] With his eyes closed the child feels speech vibrations by placing his hand on the teacher's cheek, near the mouth, and so begins to discriminate between sounds, words, and sentences. He develops comprehension through touch before he is required to speak, just as a normal child understands through hearing before he speaks. Understanding of ideas precedes expression of ideas.

In all methods of teaching the profoundly deaf, the sense of touch is an important factor. Through touch, the child feels the teacher's voice when his hand is in front of her mouth as she articulates consonants such as *b* and *p*. He feels vibrations of some sounds when his hand is on her cheek and other sounds when his hand is on her throat. With his hand on his own cheek, nose, or throat he tries to reproduce the same vibrations and gradually learns to pronounce sounds and words in correct order when he feels the face of the teacher and then his own face. Through these tactile cues the deaf child begins to articulate even though he does not hear. The steps in developing speech from the beginning stages to more complex phases are highly technical and require a teacher who is thoroughly trained. The process is very different from that used in correcting speech in a hearing child.

[13] Kate Alcorn, "Speech Developed Through Vibration," *Volta Review,* 40 (November, 1938) 633–637. Sophia K. Alcorn, "Development of Speech by the Tadoma Method," *Proceedings of the Thirty-Second Meeting of the Convention of American Instructors of the Deaf* (Washington: Government Printing Office, 1942), pp. 241–243.

Speech Training Through the Use of Visual Aids. Although deaf-blind children rely primarily on the tactile sense, the deaf-seeing child is taught to use visual cues in addition to tactile cues. He learns to read other people's speech and by watching the face of the teacher and using a mirror he learns to reproduce what he sees as well as what he feels. The Alcorn system described earlier uses visual cues at a later stage when it combines speech reading with speech. Visual symbols representing the form of the mouth are presented, such as:

for *a* as in c*a*t,

or

for *o* as in b*oa*t.

Speech Training Through Kinesthetic or Proprioceptive Cues. In addition to vision and touch (both responding to external cues), the child learns to control his speech by sensing the muscular movements within his own mouth, jaw, tongue, lips, larynx, and so forth. Through practice his use of these kinesthetic cues eventually becomes automatic. Initially, however, he must be made conscious of these internal cues. He will eventually learn to control his voice and articulation, not because he hears them, but because he feels them internally.

Speech Training Through the Use of Hearing Aids. Many deaf children have some residual hearing even though not sufficient to understand or learn speech. Through powerful hearing aids their residual hearing can help them to discriminate differences and is used in teaching speech. This is a supplementary help to the training of speech which must utilize the tactile, visual, and kinesthetic methods. Thus hearing aids are used in classes for the deaf even though profoundly deaf children are not able to understand speech by them.

The highly technical task of teaching speech to deaf children is only part of the curriculum. Teaching speech is related to teaching language, speech reading, reading, and the content subjects.

Speech Reading or Lip Reading

Deaf children must rely heavily on their ability to interpret the lip and face movements of other people in order to understand their speech. For this reason lip reading is emphasized from a very young age. As in other areas of education, various methods of teaching deaf children to read speech have developed.

Lip reading requires the ability to interpret speech by seeing a few clues to a word or sentence. Those who are able to lip-read well "fill in," so to speak, most of the speech they read. For example, one can see the articulatory movements in sounds such as *th, p,* and *f.* But the articulation of sounds such as *k* or *h* or *g* is not visible. Some sounds such as *n* and *t* cannot be visually differentiated. The vowel sounds of *ee* and *ay* are indistinguishable visually. Hence the lip reader must infer the sounds he cannot see from those he can see. Likewise words in a sentence must at times be inferred from the content, since words such as *man* and *bat* are not easily distinguishable by sight.

A combination of various methods is usually used by most teachers of the deaf. When the child is young, the teacher or the parent talks to him in whole sentences. Initially he obtains vague impressions of the idea through the whole or synthetic approach. At first he may not obtain any clues, but as the parent or teacher repeats the same expression over and over again in the same relationship to something which the child is experiencing — an object or an act or a feeling — the child begins to get an idea of what is being said. At a later stage these vague whole impressions are converted into lessons which emphasize details. Exercises are given to aid the child in discriminating between different words and between sounds. For example, two pictures may be presented, one of a ball and another of a boat. The child is taught to "point to the ball," or "point to the boat."

Lip reading for deaf children in special classes for the deaf is used in teaching language, speech, and the regular school subjects. It is not, like arithmetic, taught at certain hours of the day. It permeates the whole class day, whenever the teacher talks to the children. When hearing aids are used it is combined with auditory training.

Language Development

One of the major by-products of deafness is the deficit which results from the inability to hear language spoken by others. Language is one of the most complex of human skills. It involves many facets, including concept formation. It may be easy to teach a child the concept of a ball through lip reading, and whether the ball is large or small, or gray or white.. But how can one develop the idea of "intangibility" or "the" or "of" or "for"? Concrete objects like "comb" and "ball" or action verbs such as "sit" and "jump" can be demonstrated, but the more complex forms of language and particularly the different shades of meaning of the same word are difficult to teach. For example, the word "run" has many meanings: "the boy runs" or "the river is running" or "a road runs in front of the house" or a "run in a stocking."

Reading and language are combined because the deaf child learns language through reading, and reading primarily through language. As a matter of fact, deaf children who develop language of a complex nature usually derive their comprehension primarily from reading and experience.

Howard Hofsteater, who never learned speech or speech reading, was taught finger spelling by his deaf parents when he was very young. He learned to read and thus developed written rather than spoken language including a high degree of abstract conceptualization. This is his description of how he developed reading and language:

> As soon as my parents became convinced that I had irretrievably lost my hearing, they were confronted with the question of what next to do with me. . . . Quite normally they argued that if a normal hearing child effortlessly acquires spoken language by hearing it and imitating it, a deaf child should be able to do exactly the same by seeing it used. They saw no psychological — nor physiological — difference between a baby's using its vocal cords, tongue, and lips to imitate spoken language and a baby's using his hands to imitate movements of finger-spelled words. . . .
>
> The idea that whenever they manipulated their fingers in my direction would in some way affect my well-being must have percolated through somehow, for I developed at a rather early age the faculty of *concentrated visual attention* — subject, of course, to my fluctuating desire to listen. . . .[14]

It is obvious from these extracts from Mr. Hofsteater's autobiography that he has developed fluent use of the English language. This conceptual and abstract process was developed by extensive reading throughout his school years and after.

Hearing children learn the grammatical forms of their language by hearing words repeated in certain relationships over and over in their daily lives. One of the most effective principles of learning is that of *contiguity.* When two things have been presented together many times, the presentation of the first brings to mind the second. Thus a child repeatedly hearing the expressions "one boy" and "two boys" later responds "boy" when he means one boy and "boys" when he means two boys. He similarly learns to use the more complicated types of plurals such as "men" and "mice" and various verb forms which are learned by use rather than logic.

But the deaf child cannot experience these subtle differences through lip reading. For that reason there have evolved a number of systems of teaching language to deaf children, using a more mechanical approach to language forms and utilizing logical and visual techniques.

[14] Howard T. Hofsteater, *An Experiment in Preschool Education, An Autobiographical Case Study,* Bulletin No. 3, Vol. VIII (Washington: Gallaudet College, February, 1959), pp. 10–12.

The best-known system is the Fitzgerald Key.[15] It is used after children have learned some language forms in a natural way, without crutches or mechanical devices. The teacher introduces this series of symbols and structured sentences with questions: "Who?" "What?" "How many?" and "Where?" in relation to the grammatical structure of their sentences. These four questions are the key words of the method. By a systematic procedure the children gradually develop an understanding of grammar. When this becomes automatic in speech and writing they have acquired intelligible language.

Such keys are initially "crutches" which the child uses to follow some sequence or pattern in language. It is necessary for him to develop a vocabulary, to understand and produce different shades of meaning for words in a sentence, and to express relationships. This slow and laborious process cannot be accomplished through lip reading or other activities alone. The greatest aid to the development of language in its higher forms is through the skills of reading and writing.

Very commonly used is the so-called *natural method* of teaching language. Groht[16] is one of the advocates of this method, which uses language in natural situations through lip reading and writing, then later presents language principles formally. The method is inductive and is more in harmony with the principles of learning language used by hearing children.

Teachers emphasize different methods at different stages of development. Silverman has given some general principles:

1. Language teaching should be related to significant and meaningful experiences of children.

2. Language should constantly be made to serve a purpose for the child.

3. All sensory channels should be used to teach language.

4. Teachers need to be alert to ideas that are developing in children so that they may furnish the language to express them.

5. Children need many varied contacts with the same language in order to make it theirs.

6. Many children need formal, systematic aids to acquisition of language. Many shun language when they feel insecure in its use.

7. Schools and homes should create an atmosphere where language is used and where books are read regularly.[17]

---

[15] Edith Fitzgerald, *Straight Language for the Deaf: A System of Instruction for Deaf Children* (Washington: The Volta Bureau, 2nd ed., 1954).

[16] Mildred Groht, *Natural Language for Deaf Children* (Washington: The Volta Bureau, 1958).

[17] S. R. Silverman, "Clinical and Educational Procedures for the Deaf," *Handbook of Speech Pathology*, Lee E. Travis, ed. (New York: Appleton-Century-Crofts, Inc., 1957), p. 418.

Reading

Language development for the deaf child is slow and laborious. Reading achievement is likewise slow and laborious. Surveys of reading achievement show that deaf children are markedly retarded below their chronological and mental ages.

Pugh studied the reading ability of deaf children in a large number of schools for the deaf by administering the Iowa Silent Reading Test and the Durrell-Sullivan Reading Achievement Test.[18] She found that as a group the deaf are notably retarded at the older ages, less so at the younger ages. That is, they become more and more retarded as the language requirements for understanding increase in complexity. Pugh found some deaf children, however, reading at a high level, exceeding the norms for hearing children of their age. This means that some deaf children can learn to read like hearing children if they are properly taught and possess adequate intellectual abilities.

Thompson conducted an experiment with ten 6½-year-old children.[19] She used a systematic, visual, picture-association technique, teaching the children for an hour a day over a period of one year. Comparing their progress with that of ten similar children taught by the usual methods, she found that for the first year those taught by her method exceeded the control group by two and one half times, as tested by a picture-word association reading test. She did not follow up these children to determine whether the early gains on picture-word association were maintained. Nor has anyone since then conducted such a longitudinal study. Much research will be necessary before we can know what specific techniques of reading are most effective with deaf children throughout the grades.

The teaching of speech, speech reading, language, and reading creates conflicting problems for the teacher of the deaf. An understanding of language, for example, is necessary for progress in reading, yet it is through reading that a deaf child best learns to understand language. Reading comprehension is dependent on language comprehension, and language development is dependent upon the child's developing grammatical sequences, relationships, and nuances of meanings through context clues derived from reading. No shortcut system for teaching language has been devised that will give the deaf child what the hearing child gains through his ears.

[18] Gladys Pugh, "Summaries from 'Appraisal of the Silent Reading Abilities of Accoustically Handicapped Children,'" *American Annals of the Deaf*, 91 (September, 1946), 331–349.

[19] Helen Thompson, *An Experimental Study of the Beginning Reading of Deaf-mutes*, Teachers College Contributions to Education, No. 254 (New York: Teachers College, Columbia University, 1927).

Other School Subjects

In oral schools much class time is devoted to speech development, speech reading, language, and reading. But the curriculum also includes arithmetic, spelling, writing, literature, and the social and physical sciences, just as it does for hearing children.

Many schools utilize the unit plan for these school subjects. The children are given concrete experiences and activities, trips, dramatics, and demonstrations to assist them in understanding. There are no textbooks designed especially for the deaf, since they learn to utilize the books intended for hearing children. The specialized teaching techniques of communication used to teach the content subjects differ from age to age in a developmental sequence for the nursery school, kindergarten, elementary school, and high school.

Education at Different Developmental Levels

Early Home Training. Educators of the deaf emphasize early training in the communication skills as soon as a child is known to be deaf. At first the child learns to communicate at home, partly by facial expressions, gestures, and movements. Those who advocate oralism suggest that the parents not gesture with their hands, but rather talk to the child so that he will watch for clues in facial expression instead of watching hand movements.

Thus even the child in the crib obtains clues from his mother through her manner of handling him (tactile and kinesthetic) and through her facial expressions (visual). As the mother says "no," she shakes her head; when she says "yes," she has a different facial expression and nods. The child soon learns to respond to the lip movements and the facial expression or head movement. Through the tactual sense he obtains communication clues by feeling the vibrations of his mother's voice as she sings to him, or by feeling her face and throat as she talks.

Parents are generally instructed to use a whole or natural method of communicating with a deaf child, rather than a special system. They are asked to talk-talk-talk to the child, even though at first, like hearing babies, he does not understand. He will note in time that lip movements, head movements, facial expressions, and vibrations have some communicative meaning. This develops very slowly, but faster if the parent continues to communicate in a natural way without excessive use of signs and gestures.

Parents can get valuable suggestions from teachers of the deaf in school systems or hearing clinics even before the child is enrolled in the school. In addition, a correspondence course has been developed by the John

Tracy Clinic to assist parents with the problems and especially the communication problems of young deaf children.[20]

The Nursery School and Kindergarten. Many schools for the deaf admit children as young as 2½ to 3 years of age. The reason for such early admission is the greater need these children have for opportunities to practice socialization in a group situation and to develop skills in communication. The play activities of the nursery school and kindergarten foster growth in the communication skills through speech reading and in other ways. Although the children cannot hear, rhythm activities use pianos, drums, and other musical instruments, to which they can respond by feeling the vibrations. At a later age speech too will be developed partly through responses to vibration.

In addition, the teacher talks to the children when they are watching her face. They learn, for example, to recognize their names. They learn to jump, or stop, or walk, or dance, in response to the verbal request of the teacher. In this way a beginning is made in language as well as a start in speech reading. At the 5-year level the children begin to respond to words and phrases written on flashcards or on the board. This kind of reading is usually initiated earlier with deaf children than with the hearing child. Whereas the latter relies on hearing and speech for communication, the young deaf child has to rely heavily on vision. Hence the emphasis on beginning reading at an earlier age. Ordinarily, the same vocabulary is used in developing speech, speech reading, and reading.

The major purposes of nursery schools and kindergartens for young deaf children between the ages of 3 and 6 are: (1) to give the child experiences with other children in sharing, playing, and taking turns (a socialization process); (2) to develop language, speech, and speech-reading ability; (3) to help the child take advantage of his residual hearing through the use of hearing aids and amplified sounds; (4) to develop in the child elementary number concepts; (5) to develop a readiness for reading words and phrases; and (6) to provide parent education.

The Elementary Years. The elementary school for deaf children is divided generally into a primary level and an upper elementary level. The primary-level instruction for deaf children between ages 6 and 10 is much more highly structured than that in the kindergarten. Training in language, speech, reading, and speech reading permeate all activities and all content subjects. If the child does not learn speech and speech

[20] *Correspondence Course for Parents of Little Deaf Children* (Los Angeles, Calif.: John Tracy Clinic, 1954).

reading at this age level, it is unlikely that he will acquire these skills later.

In some residential schools all deaf children are given instruction by the oral method until the age of 9 or 10. If they acquire speech at this level the emphasis on oralism continues. If speech and speech reading have not developed, however, instruction in manual communication by means of signs and finger spelling is generally given. Language, reading, and the content subjects are pursued through sign language and finger spelling. In many residential schools deaf teachers of the deaf are employed for instruction in the manual department.

The upper elementary level in schools for the deaf enrolls children of ages 9 or 10 to 16. Since deaf children are generally from two to four years retarded educationally, the instruction is keyed to the content subjects of the fourth through the eighth grades. The large majority of deaf children consequently do not complete the eighth grade.

High School and College. Deaf children continue from the elementary school into high school in public school systems and residential institutions. In day schools many of them are assigned to regular classes in the high school rather than to special classes but have an itinerant teacher who helps them understand what they miss from class discussion. With such assistance some of the severely and profoundly deaf are able to complete high school.

A small percentage, much smaller than in the hearing group, reaches college. Some continue and graduate from regular colleges. Others attend Gallaudet College in Washington, D.C. The profoundly deaf, especially from residential schools, tend to go to Gallaudet, where instruction is in finger spelling and in the manual language.

Fusfeld tested 134 applicants to Gallaudet College, all of whom had graduated from residential schools for the deaf.[21] He found that their median grade achievement on the Stanford Achievement Test was Grade 9.2, with a range from fourth grade to twelfth grade. Because high school graduates from residential schools are usually about three years retarded educationally, Gallaudet College offers a preparatory course for those who need it.

Pintner has summarized the educational achievement of deaf children and stated that it is three to four years below that of the hearing child.[22] Those who became deaf after age 4 and who had already acquired some language scored higher on achievement tests than those who were born deaf. Silverman, however, states that at the Central Institute for the Deaf

---

[21] Irving Fusfeld, "The Academic Programs of Schools for the Deaf," *Volta Review,* 57 (February, 1955), 63–70.

[22] Pintner, Eisenson, and Stanton, *op. cit.,* chap. V.

(a private residential school) the children showed only a two- to three-year retardation.[23] Whereas Pintner gives an educational quotient (EQ)[24] of 70 for the national average, Silverman found an EQ of 77.8 at the Central Institute. The IQ's of the children at the Central Institute appear higher than the national average from residential schools for the deaf.

Occupational Adjustment

Deaf adults adjust to practically any kind of job which does not have as a prerequisite the ability to hear. The deaf are found in professions, managerial positions, and skilled, semiskilled, and laboring jobs. The most extensive survey was made during the depression of the 1930's by Elise Martens of the United States Office of Education.[25] Of 3786 employed men who were profoundly deaf, about one-third (1173) were operatives in mills or factories, 533 were unskilled laborers, 330 were typesetters (a trade frequently taught in schools for the deaf), and all types of other occupations were represented: shoemaker, teacher, painter, forester, farmer, carpenter, cabinetmaker, and so forth. Engineering, medicine, law, real estate and the ministry were listed for from one to seven men. Out of 1151 profoundly deaf women, 574 were employed as operatives in mills or factories, 120 as hotel or domestic servants, 75 as teachers, and 65 as dressmakers. One was a real-estate agent, one was a trained nurse, and several were managers, librarians, bookkeepers, or cashiers. The others had positions as cook, typist, waitress, housekeeper, clerk, and welfare worker.

In a more recent study, Lunde and Bigman, in cooperation with the National Association for the Deaf (an association for deaf adults), distributed a questionnaire to deaf individuals throughout the United States. Ten thousand one hundred and one completed schedules were received. Of these, 97 per cent were from white respondents, 86 per cent of whom ranged in age from 20 to 59. Of the total group responding, 7920, or four-fifths, were employed. The rest were housewives, retired persons, and others.

The occupational distribution of the employed deaf in this study[26] is shown in the following:

[23] S. Richard Silverman and H. S. Lane, "Deaf Children," *Hearing and Deafness,* H. R. Davis, ed. (New York: Murray Hill Books, 1947), p. 376.

[24] The EQ is derived by dividing the educational age by the chronological age and multiplying by 100.

[25] Elise H. Martens, *The Deaf and Hard-of-Hearing in the Occupational World,* Bulletin No. 13 (Washington: Office of Education, 1936).

[26] Anders S. Lunde and Stanley K. Bigman, *Occupational Conditions Among the Deaf* (Washington, D.C.: Gallaudet College, 1959).

191

	Employed Deaf	In U.S. (1957) Population
Professional, technical, and similar workers	6.6%	10.6%
Managers, officials, and proprietors	3.2	15.5
Clerical, sales, and similar workers	7.2	20.7
Craftsmen, foremen, and similar workers	35.9	13.4
Operatives and similar workers	35.2	20.1
Others — i.e. service workers, laborers, etc.	11.9	19.7

It is interesting to note from this distribution of occupations that, as compared to the general population, there were fewer deaf in the professional fields, managerial positions, and clerical and sales positions, because of the necessity of communication in these jobs. There were greater numbers of deaf serving as skilled and semi-skilled workers and machine operators, and in similar jobs. The industrial stronghold of deaf male respondents was in the printing and publishing industries.

The national surveys have indicated that 85 per cent of the deaf workers are successful in their occupations. Observations of others also indicate that deafness as such does not preclude successful employment and independence, especially in occupations that do not require oral communication skills.

Summary

1. Hard-of-hearing children are generally educated in the regular grades with an itinerant teacher helping them in the specific areas of (a) use of hearing aid, (b) auditory training, (c) speech reading, and (d) speech training. Deaf children are generally educated in a special class or school for the deaf.

2. For educational purposes, *deaf* children are those who were born without hearing or who lost their hearing before they acquired speech and language. Children who lose their hearing after the acquisition of speech and language are classified as *deafened*.

3. Deaf children are educated in public or private residential schools or in day schools and classes which are usually part of public school systems.

4. Two methods of teaching the deaf have existed for many years: (a) the manual method, which utilizes signs and finger spelling, and (b) the oral method which relies on speech and speech reading for communication.

5. On nonverbal intelligence tests, the deaf range from mentally retarded to superior with the average possibly slightly below 100 IQ.

6. Intelligence, degree of hearing loss, and age at onset of deafness are related to the educational progress of deaf children.

7. The greatest handicap created by the loss of hearing is the difficulty of developing speech and language.

8. The methods of instruction for deaf children differ markedly from those used with hearing children and concentrate on developing (a) speech, (b) speech reading, (c) reading, and (d) language.

9. The curriculum for deaf children is similar to the curriculum for normal children but includes the necessary teaching of techniques of communication.

10. Because of the handicap in speech and language, deaf children are from two to five years retarded in educational subjects.

11. In adult life the deaf are employed in all types of work not requiring hearing, from professional to unskilled labor, with the majority holding semiskilled and unskilled jobs. They are considered satisfactory employees.

DISCUSSION QUESTIONS

1. What do you consider to be the major differences in educational organization and procedures for (a) deaf and (b) hard-of-hearing children?

2. Give the advantages and disadvantages of (a) special classes and (b) itinerant teacher service for hard-of-hearing children.

3. It has been found that in the early stages of learning a child responds to learning tasks as vague wholes; later he responds to differential parts of the learning tasks; and still later he responds to the sum of these parts as an integrated whole. With this developmental theory in mind, when would you use the Jena, Nitchie, or Mueller-Walle method of teaching speech reading?

4. Give as many reasons as you can think of for the persistence of the controversy between oralism and manualism in the teaching of deaf children.

5. List all the disadvantages of residential schools. What are the disadvantages of day schools?

6. In residential schools the children are first given an opportunity to learn by the oral method. If they are not successful they are then taught by the manual method or the combined method. What advantages and disadvantages do you see in this approach? Can you suggest an alternate approach and justify it?

7. According to Table VII, the largest growth in enrollment in the five-year period 1955–1960 was in day classes for both the deaf and hard of hearing. Predict the enrollment in 1970 and justify your predictions with specific facts and trends.

8. Your text has indicated that the educational progress of deaf children is dependent upon (*a*) intelligence, (*b*) degree of deafness, and (*c*) age at onset of deafness. Evaluate the relative importance of each of these three factors.

9. Many of the deaf who have been trained by the oral method revert to the manual method of communication as adults. Speculate on some of the reasons why this happens.

10. Evaluate the relative importance and effectiveness of the different methods of teaching speech to deaf children. When would one procedure be emphasized over the others?

11. If language can best be developed through the process of reading, why do those who advocate the oral method insist that the child develop language through speech and lip reading at an early age?

12. In many areas of exceptional children the enrollment in public day school classes exceeds the enrollment of such children in institutions. This is not the case in the field of the deaf, as is shown in Table VII. Give as many reasons as you can to show that this ratio will not change.

Selected References

Alcorn, Sophia K. "Development of Speech by the Tadoma Method," *Proceedings of the Thirty-Second Meeting of the Convention of American Instructors of the Deaf.* Washington: Government Printing Office, 1942.

Avondino, Josephine. *The Babbling Method: A System of Syllable Drills for Natural Development of Speech.* Washington: The Volta Bureau, 1924.

Barry, Katherine E. *The Five Slate System: A System of Objective Language Teaching.* Philadelphia: Sherman, 1899.

Bender, Ruth E. *The Conquest of Deafness.* Cleveland, Ohio: The Press of Western Reserve University, 1960.

Best, H. *Deafness and the Deaf in the United States.* New York: The Macmillan Company, 1943.

Brunschwig, L. *A Study of Some Personality Aspects of Deaf Children.* New York: Columbia University, 1936.

Bunger, Anna M. *Speech Reading — Jena Method.* Danville, Ill.: The Interstate Press, 2nd ed., 1952.

Davis, Hallowell, and S. Richard Silverman, eds. *Hearing and Deafness.* New York: Holt, Rinehart and Winston, Inc., rev. ed., 1960.

Groht, Mildred. *Natural Language for Deaf Children.* Washington: The Volta Bureau, 1958.

Heider, Fritz, and Grace Heider. "Studies in the Psychology of the Deaf, *Psychological Monographs*, 1940, Vol. 52, No. 1.

Heider, Fritz, and Grace Heider. "Studies in the Psychology of the Deaf, No. 2," *Psychological Monographs*, 1941, Vol. 53, No. 5.

Keller, Helen. *The Story of My Life*. New York: Doubleday and Company, 1954.

Kinzie, C. E., and R. Kinzie. *Lip Reading for the Deafened Adult*. Philadelphia: John C. Winston Company, 1931.

Lassman, Grace. *Language for the Preschool Deaf Child*. New York: Grune and Stratton, 1950.

Levine, Edna. *Youth in a Soundless World*. New York: New York University Press, 1957.

Morkovin, B., and L. Moore. *Life Situation Speech Reading Through Cooperation of the Senses*. Los Angeles: University of Southern California Press, 1948.

Myklebust, H. R. *Auditory Disorders in Children*. New York: Grune and Stratton, 1954.

Myklebust, H. R. *The Psychology of Deafness*. New York: Grune and Stratton, 1960.

Nitchie, Elizabeth. *New Lessons in Lip Reading*. Philadelphia: J. B. Lippincott Company, 1950.

O'Neill, John J., and Herbert J. Oyer, *Visual Communication for the Hard of Hearing*. Englewood Cliffs, N.J.: Prentice-Hall, Inc., 1961.

Stowell, Agnes, E. E. Samuelson, and A. Lehman. *Lip Reading for the Deafened Child*. New York: The Macmillan Company, 1928.

Streng, Alice, J. Fitch, L. D. Hedgecock, J. W. Phillips, and J. A. Carrell. *Hearing Therapy for Children*. New York: Grune and Stratton, 2nd ed., 1958.

Travis, L. E., ed. *Handbook of Speech Pathology*. New York: Appleton-Century-Crofts, Inc., 1957.

Whildin, Olive A., and M. A. Scally. *The Newer Method in Speech Reading for the Hard-of-Hearing Child*. Westminster, Md.: John William Eckenrode, 1939.

8

The Visually Handicapped Child:
The Partially Sighted

Children with marked visual defects, like those with auditory impairments, are classified educationally in two major categories: (1) the blind, who are educated through channels other than vision, and (2) the partially sighted, who are able to utilize vision in acquiring educational skills. The differentiation between normal vision, partial sight, and blindness is made, at least theoretically, on the basis of visual acuity. Throughout this discussion it must be kept in mind that no really adequate definition of degree of disability is possible, because measured sense organ defect is only one of many factors which determine level or efficiency of function in that area.

The term "partial sight" means seriously defective vision and is usually defined as less than 20/70 acuity in the better eye after correction, or as a progressive eye disorder that will probably reduce vision below 20/70, or as some other serious visual malfunction such as tunnel vision (peripheral vision subtending an angle less than 20 degrees). Hathaway has elaborated this definition in educational terms and includes as partially sighted (1) children having a visual acuity of 20/70 or less in the better eye after all necessary medical or surgical treatment has been given and compensating lenses have been provided when the need for them is indicated (such children must, however, have a residue of sight that makes it possible to use this as the chief avenue of approach to the brain), and (2) children with a visual deviation from the normal who, in the opinion of the eye specialist, can benefit from the special educational facilities provided for the partially seeing.[1]

In addition to the children meeting these general criteria Hathaway includes (1) those who have undergone eye operations and require readaptation of the eye and psychological adjustment to such conditions as enucleation (removal of an eye) and (2) those with muscle anomalies and other conditions which necessitate re-education of the abnormal eye.

The prevalence of mild visual defect is very high. A typical estimate is that one out of every four children has some visual anomaly. Dalton tested 5821 school children in California and found that 22 per cent of elementary school children and 31 per cent of high school students had some visual defect.[2] The great majority of these defects are correctable, but it is estimated that about one in 500 has a visual defect serious enough (even with maximum possible correction) so that he is classified as partially seeing. The most accurate estimates indicate that in 1955 there were 68,000 to 70,000 partially seeing children in the school and preschool age groups.[3] At this time approximately 8000 children were enrolled in about 700 classes or other facilities for the partially sighted. Thus about one partially sighted child out of every eight or nine is receiving the appropriately adapted educational program.

The lower limit of vision for educational purposes is difficult to define. It must be kept in mind that measurements of the kind obtained from the Snellen chart refer only to central, distance visual acuity, which is but one of several aspects of vision and not a crucial one for most school work. This will be discussed later under identification of partially seeing children.

Kerby surveyed 7310 children enrolled in over 600 classes for the partially sighted and found that less than 30 per cent of the children fitted the visual acuity limits used in defining partially seeing children — that is, between 20/70 and 20/200 after correction.[4] This finding illustrates the importance of remembering that, educationally speaking, the crucial factor in distinguishing between partial sight and blindness is that partially sighted children can utilize vision as an important channel of

[1] Winifred Hathaway, *Education and Health of the Partially Seeing Child* (New York: Columbia University Press, 4th ed., 1959), p. 16.

[2] M. M. Dalton, "A Visual Survey of 5000 School Children," *Journal of Educational Research*, 37 (October, 1943), 81–94.

[3] American Public Health Association, Committee on Child Health, and the National Society for Prevention of Blindness, *Services for Children with Vision and Eye Problems* (New York: American Public Health Association, 1956).

[4] C. Edith Kerby, "A Report on Visual Handicaps of Partially Seeing Children," *Journal of Exceptional Children*, 18 (February, 1952), 137–142.

learning, while the blind must rely on other approaches, primarily auditory and tactile-kinesthetic.

Some Kinds of Visual Defects Found Among Partially Seeing Children

In a national survey of the visual defects found in 600 classes for partially seeing children made by the National Society for the Prevention of Blindness, Kerby reports the following types and percentages of defective vision:

Refractive errors (myopia, hyperopia, etc.)	49 per cent
Developmental anomalies of structure (cataracts, albinism, etc.)	22 per cent
Defects of muscle function (strabismus, nystagmus, etc.)	17 per cent
Disease or defects of the eye (due to infection, injuries, etc.)	11 per cent
Others, causes undetermined	1 per cent

Refractive Errors

It will be seen from the table above that refractive errors constitute approximately one-half of all visual defects. In the normal eye (emmetropic) the size, shape, and refractive media are such that the image of an object focuses directly on the retina. In the mature normal eye no muscular effort or accommodation of the lens is necessary to clearly see objects 20 feet or more away. The cornea, the lens, and the fluids within the eyeball make is possible for the image to focus accurately on the light-sensitive membrane on the back of the eyeball known as the retina. When the eye looks at an object closer than 20 feet, the muscles in the eye increase the convex curvature of the lens so that the image of the closer object will still focus on the retina. The increase of the lens curvature through the use of the ciliary muscles is called accommodation.

When the eye is not normal (ametropic), the image does not focus on the retina at 20 feet. In these cases of refractive abnormality the eye is hyperopic, myopic, or astigmatic, or a combination thereof.

Hyperopia, or farsightedness, is a condition in which the eye is too short from front to back, so that the rays of light focus behind the retina, forming a blurred and unclear image on it. To correct this condition a convex lens is placed before the eye to increase the "bending" of the light rays and bring them to a focus within a shorter distance, that is, on the retina rather than behind it. The term "farsightedness" implies only that distant objects can be seen with less strain on the muscles of lens accommodation than can near objects, and does not mean, as is often thought, that the hyperope can see farther or more clearly at a given distance than can the emmetrope.

Myopia, or nearsightedness, is a refractive error opposite in kind to hyperopia. In myopia the eye is too long from front to back or the refractive media bend the light rays too much. In either case the rays of light focus in front of the retina when the eye is at rest and viewing an object 20 or more feet distant. Correction for this type of refractive error is made with a concave lens, which spreads or diverts the rays of light, focusing them farther back in the eye and directly on the retina.

Astigmatism is a refractive error resulting from an irregularity in the curvature of the cornea or lens of the eye. The light rays from any given object or point do not all focus at the same point on the retina. Parts of the image may fall behind the retina, and parts in front, so that vision is blurred. The eye attempts to clarify the image through accommodation, but this affects the entire lens equally, and cannot influence corneal irregularities at all. Most astigmatism is more or less regular and is correctable. Irregular astigmatism is only partially correctable.

Defects of Muscle Function

Another type of visual defect found in children is abnormality in the external ocular muscles which control the movement of the entire eyeball in its orbit. These muscles are not to be confused with the internal muscles of lens accommodation discussed above.

Strabismus, or crossed eyes, is caused by a lack of coordination of eye muscles; the two eyes do not simultaneously focus on the same object. In most cases one eye turns inward toward the nose, while the other focuses on the object being viewed. When, as in this case, the deviating eye rotates inward, it is called *internal strabismus* or *convergent squint.* When the deviating eye turns outward it is called *exterial strabismus.* Occasionally, *alternating strabismus* is found, in which the eye turns alternately in and out. Strabismus can be constant or intermittent.

Heterophoria is a defect in muscular balance of the eyes in which the deviation of the eyes is not apparent, as in strabismus, but latent. In this condition there is (1) a tendency for the eyes to deviate from the normal position for binocular fixation, and (2) a partially counterbalancing tendency toward simultaneous fixation through forced muscular effort. When the eyes tend to pull toward the nose, it is called *esophoria,* and when they tend to pull away from the nose it is *exophoria.* When the eyes tend to pull upward or downward it is *hyperphoria.* Heterophoria tends to cause difficulties in visual fusion, that is, in the ability to coordinate or fuse the two images from both eyes into a single image.

Developmental Anomalies

Developmental anomalies of the structure of the eye are less frequent than refractive errors.

Albinism is a hereditary, congenital condition characterized by relative absence of pigment from the skin, hair, choroid coat, and iris. It is often accompanied by refractive errors, lowered visual acuity, nystagmus (quick jerky movement of the eyes, usually lateral, but occasionally in a rotary or vertical direction), and photophobia (extreme sensitivity to light).

A *cataract* is a condition of the eye in which the crystalline lens or its capsule becomes opaque, with resultant loss of visual acuity. Cataracts are sometimes removed successfully through surgery by removing the lens or by a "needling" process in which the opacity is broken up and then absorbed. In either case vision is affected. When the entire lens has been removed it is often impossible to achieve normal central acuity by means of external lenses alone, and almost inevitably peripheral vision is distorted.

Diseases Affecting the Eye, and Other Pathological Conditions

Many diseases and conditions other than those already mentioned can attack the eyeball, cornea, lens, vitreous humor, choroid, retina, or optic nerve and cause marked visual deficiencies or total blindness. Common among these diseases are diabetes, syphilis, glaucoma, and keratitis. Retrolental fibroplasia is one of the most important and will be discussed in the chapter on blind children.

Identifying Visual Impairments

Total blindness is relatively easy to recognize and is almost always detected in the infant by the time he is a year old, and usually much earlier. Identification of a partially sighted youngster is much more difficult. As a young child, he has little concept of vision which is better than or different from his own; thus it is difficult for him to report his visual problems. Often he may appear awkward, clumsy, careless, or even mentally slow. It is not unusual for severe visual defects to remain undetected until the child reaches school age. The importance of an adequate vision screening program and systematic observations of visual behavior in school cannot be overestimated. Among preschool and school children the following should be observed and noted as possible indications of visual difficulty:

1. Strabismus; nystagmus.
2. How the child uses his eyes: tilting his head, holding objects close to his eyes, rubbing his eyes, squinting, displaying sensitivity to bright lights, and rolling his eyes.
3. Inattention to visual objects or visual tasks such as looking at pictures or reading.
4. Awkwardness in games requiring eye-hand coordination.
5. Avoidance of tasks that require close eye work.
6. Affinity to tasks that require distance vision.
7. Any complaints about inability to see.

Tests for Visual Efficiency

Observation of the child's behavior can give parents and teachers a hint that there may be some visual difficulty. But there are more efficient and accurate methods. Usually, screening tests are given to identify the presence or absence of visual difficulties, and then if the observations and/or screening tests suggest a defect, tests and examination by an eye specialist make the final determination.

The Snellen Test for visual screening is the most widely used because of the ease and speed with which it can be administered to a child by a nurse or teacher and because it can be used with young children. The Snellen chart measures central distance visual acuity only. It does not give any indication of near point (14–18 inches) vision, peripheral vision, convergence ability, fusion ability, or muscular imbalance. The Snellen chart at 20 feet measures only far point acuity, and this aspect of vision is perhaps one of the least important for the kinds of visual tasks necessary in school work.

For the reasons just mentioned, it is now strongly recommended that school vision screening programs be expanded to include tests in other areas to supplement the Snellen chart. This is in fact being done now in many schools.

The Snellen Test chart consists of rows of letters (or E's in various positions, for use with young children and illiterates), each row in a different size print. Each size letter represents an optical measure. The "20 feet" row is so designated because it has been found that the person with normal vision can read that line at a distance of 20 feet. The notation used to indicate performance on the Snellen chart should be interpreted as follows: This subject sees at a distance of *numerator* feet the line that a person with normal vision sees at a distance of *denominator* feet. Thus 20/70 means that the subject sees at 20 feet what one with normal vision could see at 70 feet.

Snellen's notation and the corresponding percentage of visual efficiency are as follows:

20/20	100.0 per cent
20/35	87.5 per cent
20/70	64.0 per cent
20/100	48.9 per cent
20/200	20.0 per cent

Other Tests

In addition to the Snellen Test, which is the easiest to administer, other more comprehensive visual screening tests are available. Those most suitable for use in schools include the Massachusetts Vision Test, the Keystone Telebinocular, and the Ortho-rater. Informal tests include a sighting test to determine monocular dominance, and the "cover" test for heterophoria.

Tests by Eye Specialists

The primary purposes of screening tests and observations is to identify children suspected of having visual defects in order that they may be referred to an eye specialist (ophthalmologist, oculist, or optometrist). The specialist makes the professional evaluation of the visual condition of the child and determines the diagnosis and treatment or correction. If correction can be made with glasses or other treatment, no special adaptation of instruction is necessary. If correction is not possible, or if only a partial correction can be made, the child is eligible for special instruction.

The Growth Patterns of Partially Seeing Children

The various groups of exceptional children, including the blind, have been surveyed extensively with respect to their physical, social, mental, and educational development. Among the visually handicapped, concentration on research has been primarily with the blind, and surprisingly little has been done with partially seeing children.

Lowenfeld has suggested that this paucity of research may be due to the fact that the partially sighted child is "for all practical purposes a seeing child, and his handicap, if it is one, does not affect him in any different way from other children who slightly deviate from the 'normal.' "[5] The available evidence indicates that the development of par-

[5] Berthold Lowenfeld, "Psychological Problems of Children with Impaired Vision," *Psychology of Exceptional Children and Youth*, William M. Cruickshank, ed. (New York: Prentice-Hall, Inc., 1955), p. 273.

tially sighted children does not deviate from that of seeing children nor does it show discrepancies in growth within the child. For this reason we do not include a developmental profile here.

In the absence of conclusive data, however, it should at least be mentioned that the opposite point of view has been held by some, namely, that a severe deficit in any sensory area does in fact result in total adjustment patterns which are different from those of nonhandicapped persons. Marzolf has stated this somatopsychological viewpoint quite succinctly: "Any degree or kind of visual defect is likely to have consequences for adjustment, and severe handicap is a major problem of adjustment in itself."[6]

Pintner summed up our knowledge about this aspect of partially sighted children when he maintained in 1941, "About the children themselves from a psychological point of view we know practically nothing."[7] Fourteen years later, in summarizing our current knowledge, Lowenfeld stated that ". . . conditions have not changed to any considerable extent."[8]

One of the few extensive studies on children in "sight-saving classes" was conducted by Myers in 1928–1930.[9] He sent questionnaires to such classes existing in the United States at that time, and his findings, and those of others, are as follows:

Sex. Out of 2860 children, Myers found that 50.2 per cent were boys and 49.8 per cent were girls. It is interesting to compare this with Kerby's finding in 1952 that of 7300 children in classes for the partially sighted 57.2 per cent were boys.[10]

Health. Myers found that according to the judgments of teachers, there was no difference in general health between the children in sight-saving classes and normally seeing children.

Intelligence. Myers utilized two approaches to the question of whether the intelligence of children with defective vision is similar to that of the normal child. He asked the teachers to record psychological test data and also to rate the children. On teachers' judgments the children were average or above, while on intelligence test scores they were average or below. Pintner reviewed the studies which have in-

---

[6] Stanley S. Marzolf, "The Physically Handicapped," *An Introduction to Clinical Psychology,* L. A. Pennington and Irwin A. Berg, eds. (New York: Ronald Press Company, 1954), p. 315.

[7] R. Pintner, J. Eisenson, and Mildred Stanton, *The Psychology of the Physically Handicapped* (New York: F. S. Crofts and Company, 1941), p. 260.

[8] Lowenfeld, *op. cit.,* p. 273.

[9] Edward T. Myers, "A Survey of Sight-saving Classes in the Public Schools of the United States," *The Sight-Saving Class Exchange* (New York: National Society for the Prevention of Blindness, 1930).

[10] Kerby, *op. cit.*

vestigated the relationships between intelligence test scores of partially sighted and of normal children and found contradictory results.[11] He stated that our knowledge on this factor is meager and indicated that intelligence tests devised for normally seeing children may be penalizing partially seeing children.

Livingstone administered the Stanford-Binet test to sixty 8- and 9-year-old children in classes for the partially seeing and found their average IQ to be 98.6.[12] Enlarging the test print did not help them to score any higher than they did on the regular size. He concluded that although the visually handicapped were below normal on visually presented tests, they performed like normal children on reasoning, language development, and abstract generalization.

In an earlier study very similar to Livingstone's, Pintner found a mean Stanford-Binet IQ of 95 for a group of 602 partially seeing children.[13] He, too, could not see that enlarging the test materials made any difference.

Educational Achievement. Myers' survey indicated that in educational achievement partially seeing children in the regular grades and in the special classes were not very different, according to teachers' ratings. Peck tested 234 children in Grades 2 to 9 with the Stanford Achievement Reading Tests, using two time intervals — the regular time and an extended period.[14] At all grade levels the partially seeing children scored as well as the seeing children with the regular testing time and increased their scores only slightly when the extra time was allowed. This would seem to indicate that the partially sighted child is not unduly penalized on reading tests. However, a report from London states that although partially sighted children were not penalized in arithmetic they did score lower than normal children in reading.[15]

Several studies have investigated which type size is most easily read. In general, both 18-point and 24-point sizes are legible. The larger print necessarily decreases the number of words included in the eye span and thus decreases the speed of reading. Nolan found the average reading speed of 264 partially sighted children (Grades 4 to 12) to be about 100

[11] Pintner, Eisenson, and Stanton, *op. cit.*, pp. 255–256.

[12] Jerome S. Livingstone, "Evaluation of Enlarged Test Form Used with the Partially Seeing," *Sight-Saving Review*, 28 (Spring, 1958), 37–39.

[13] R. Pintner, "Intelligence Testing of Partially Sighted Children," *Journal of Educational Psychology*, 33 (April, 1942), 265–272.

[14] O. S. Peck, "Reading Ability of Sight-Saving Class Pupils in Cleveland, Ohio," Publication No. 118, National Society for the Prevention of Blindness. Reprinted from the *Sight-Saving Review*, 3 (June, 1933).

[15] Committee on Problems Relating to Partially Sighted Children, *Report of the Committee of Inquiry into Problems Relating to Partially Sighted Children* (London: His Majesty's Stationery Office, 1934).

words per minute, which is less than half the speed of seeing children.[16]

When evaluating research dealing with visual defects and school achievement, especially reading, it is important to keep in mind the possibility that the degree and type of defect, not its presence or absence, may be a vital factor. This is exemplified by the fact that among very bright high-achieving children the incidence of visual defects, particularly myopia, is higher than average. Quite possibly the inclusion of these children in a study of visual defect and achievement could statistically obscure an otherwise significant relationship between some degrees and types of defect and low achievement.

Social Adjustment. Pintner and Forlano administered the Aspects of Personality Test and the Pupil Portraits Test to more than 400 children in classes for the partially sighted and found no consistent differences between them and seeing children.[17]

In a sociometric study of physically handicapped children, including those with visual defects, Force found that the handicapped were less popular than the nonhandicapped.[18] In Murphy's study of attitudes toward the handicapped, educators ranked the visually handicapped as the lowest.[19] The latter also ranked second lowest in terms of teachers' knowledge about them and desire to teach them.

Although severe visual defects have not been established as causal factors in producing personality and social maladjustment, we must recognize that a severe visual defect could have psychological effects. Certainly the basic fact of limitations on what can be seen, the possible physical pain and discomfort of some visual conditions, the possibility of cosmetic disfigurement, the likelihood of undue parental concern, and negative attitudes of children, parents, and teachers could all be sources of personality problems.

Educational Programs for the Partially Sighted

Special school classes for partially seeing children originated in England in 1908, according to Smith.[20] Although as far back as 1885 medical

---

16 C. Y. Nolan, "Readability of Large Types," *International Journal of Education of the Blind,* 9 (1959), 41–44.

17 R. Pintner and G. Forlano, "Personality Tests of Partially Sighted Children," *Journal of Applied Psychology,* 27 (June, 1943), 283–287.

18 Dewey G. Force, Jr., "Social Status of Physically Handicapped Children," *Journal of Exceptional Children,* 23 (December, 1956), 104–107, 132–133.

19 A. T. Murphy, "Attitudes of Educators Toward the Visually Handicapped," *Sight-Saving Review,* 30 (Fall, 1960), 157–161.

20 Helen L. Smith, "Pioneer Work in Sight Saving," *The Sight-Saving Class Exchange* (June, 1938), No. 65.

examiners in England urged specialized education for these children, it was not until 1908 that Dr. James Kerr and Dr. N. Bishop Harmon were able to persuade the educational authorities to establish the first class at Boundary Lane, England. At this time only nearsighted children were admitted to these so-called "myope schools." Soon classes for myopes spread to other schools in England and Scotland.

In the United States the first class for the partially sighted was initiated in Boston in 1913. Miss Helen Smith, the first American teacher of sight-saving classes, has described their beginnings: In 1910 Mr. Allen, Director of the Perkins Institute for the Blind, informed the Massachusetts Commission for the Blind of the work of the myope classes in London. Several years later the School Committee of Boston decided to begin such a class in the Boston schools and selected Miss Smith, from the Perkins Institute, as its teacher. At first named a "semi-blind class," it later was called a "conservation of eye class." This more adequate name was still somewhat awkward, and it was again changed — to "sight-saving class."

Smith reports that it was not easy to convince parents that their children would benefit from special class placement. Many of the parents interviewed declined to permit their children to leave the grades in which they had been placed to enter a special class. After much work, the class was started with six pupils. Once well established, however, it became known to other parents, who voluntarily applied to have their children admitted.

Other cities heard about the myope classes in England, and shortly after the opening of the Boston class one was opened in Cleveland, Ohio. More classes followed in other cities and states.

Organization of Programs

Several different methods of organizing programs for partially seeing children have evolved, differing with the size of the community and with the administrative philosophy. These methods include: (1) the segregated class, (2) the cooperative plan, (3) the itinerant teacher plan, and (4) the resource room.

1. The first class organized in Boston was *segregated;* the children were assigned to the sight-saving class for the whole day. One teacher organized and taught children of all grades. This type of organization is now rarely used since educators feel that these children can and should participate for part of the day with regular class children.

2. The most common program that has been in operation is called the *cooperative plan,* in which the children are assigned to the special class for close eye work and to the regular grades for other kinds of work where oral instruction predominates. This was the type of class

organized in Cleveland in 1913, about six months after the opening of the Boston class. There are advantages to this type of organization, since children of different grade levels assigned to a class for the partially seeing for close eye work can remain with their regular grades for other work. The differences in grade levels do not interfere with the progress of the class since the work is individualized.

3. The *itinerant teacher* plan is used in smaller communities and rural areas and in some larger communities. Under this plan the partially seeing child is enrolled in the regular grades. An itinerant teacher, traveling from school to school, furnishes special materials, instructs the regular teacher in their use, helps the child keep up with his class, and counsels him with respect to his adjustment.

4. Another plan utilizes the *resource room*. The child is assigned to the regular class but goes to a resource room for special tutoring and special materials as needed. The idea is to adjust the child to the regular class and to help him keep up with children of his own age. This plan is now replacing the cooperative plan.

The Classroom

The first requisite in establishing a class for partially seeing children is to set up a suitable physical environment.

1. A school should be selected which is centrally located, since the children may have to be transported from various parts of the community.

2. The school should contain grades of the same levels as the children in the special class. For example, children achieving at the level of Grades 2, 3, 4, and 5 should be housed in an elementary school so that they can be assigned to their respective grades.

3. The location of the class in a school depends on (a) the location of the grades and (b) the classroom that offers the most effective natural lighting. Second-floor rooms may be preferable to first-floor rooms because of the lighting factor.

4. Lighting is very important for partially seeing children. Illumination must be free from glare and direct sunlight and evenly distributed throughout the room. Artificial illumination must be available for use at different times of the day. Other factors to be considered include the amount and height of window space, adequacy of artificial illumination, and coloring of walls and ceilings.

Equipment and Materials

In addition to physical requisites of the classroom itself, classes for partially seeing children require special equipment and special materials designed to facilitate instruction and learning. These include the following:

Movable and Adjustable Desks. Movable desks should be adjustable for height, angle, and position. It is preferable to raise the top of a desk for a nearsighted child rather than to have the child lean over in his seat to see visual materials. Different angles are needed for different activities. The desks should be placed at a 30-degree angle to the windows to avoid glare and to preclude facing the window directly. The child should be seated in such a position that the light will fall evenly on his desk. All desks, seats, and tables should be of light neutral color, with a somewhat dull finish.

Chalkboards. Black chalkboards are not recommended for partially seeing children. Instead a gray or gray-green chalkboard is generally used; it reflects more light and still gives adequate contrast to white chalk. The purpose of this combination, like all materials and equipment in a class for the partially seeing, is to avoid glare and to make seeing as comfortable as possible.

Pencils and Paper. Special care in selecting paper and pencils is desirable. The paper is of cream color, unglazed, and slightly rough. The pencils are of heavy lead (thicker than the ordinary pencil lead) and soft.

Typewriters. Children in resource rooms or classes for the partially seeing can use primary typewriters equipped with larger type than the usual typewriter. The teacher prepares lessons on this typewriter, and the pupils also use it for many purposes.

Dictaphones and Record Players. Since partially seeing children learn a great deal aurally, instead of relying only on reading for information, special classes and resource rooms include dictaphones and phonographs for presenting lessons and stories and data of many kinds. Teachers may give special assignments, partly in writing and partly on the dictaphone. In addition, much information may be obtained from talking books (ordinarily used with the blind) and other educational audio materials.

Books and Reading Materials. Classes for partially seeing children contain books with large type, usually 18 to 24 points instead of the usual 12 to 14. Other materials such as large maps, enlarged graphs, and special globes with raised relief surfaces are also included in the equipment for a special class. Enlarged phonic charts in classes where phonics is taught are also helpful.

Projection and Magnifying Equipment. Projection equipment which will enlarge charts, maps, and reading material is needed. Care should be taken to adjust this type of equipment so that distortions are avoided and proper contrast results. Magnifying bars or glasses placed directly over the pages of a book printed in regular type are frequently used.

The General Program and Curriculum

The late Mrs. Winifred Hathaway has been responsible to a large extent for the philosophy and program for the cooperative plan of educating partially seeing children.[21] Her emphasis on the importance of contact with normally seeing children has now been extended into the resource-room plan. Under both of these plans (cooperative and resource-room) the special teacher and the regular teacher share responsibility for the child's program and instruction. In the cooperative plan the special teacher has the primary responsibility and the child is actually assigned to the special room as his home room. The reverse is true in the resource-room program where the regular teacher has the responsibility and the child goes to the resource room only for specialized help.

In practice, a child, upon assignment to a class or resource room for partially seeing children, is studied in terms of his level of achievement in school subjects. A program is designed for him and he goes part time to the special class for close eye work and part time to a regular grade of children of his age and level of achievement. The program for him is discussed by the two teachers involved, who agree on the area of instruction for which each is to be responsible.

Since the goals and purposes of education for partially seeing children are the same as for other children, the curricular program is also the same. Special education focuses primarily on the mode of presentation. The environment of the classroom, the special equipment, and the special teacher are all provided to compensate for the visual defects, not to change the curriculum. Partially sighted children learn what other children learn, but are aided through media which facilitate their learning. Occasionally, the physical education program is modified slightly for a youngster whose vision might be harmed by strenuous activity or by sudden movement, as in the case of a partially detached retina.

Earlier the special classes for these children were called "sight-saving classes." The general purpose was to educate the child and at the same time save his sight. Actually the special class *does not improve* the vision of the child but may improve his ability to *use* his vision. The term "sight-saving" has in general been discarded for these classes; they are now called "classes for the partially sighted." In addition, the early emphasis on avoidance of reading and other close work thought to be harmful to eyes has been found unnecessary. Children's eyes are not

[21] Hathaway, *op. cit.*, p. 201.

hurt by reading small print, but they can probably learn more efficiently if the type is easier to see. For that reason partially seeing children are being encouraged more and more to participate in the regular grades and with materials other children use as soon as they can do so. Thus the cooperative plan is being replaced by the resource room, in which the child is assigned to a regular grade and comes to the resource room only to use the equipment and materials better suited to him at his stage of development. Here, with the help of the special teacher, he learns to use the equipment and obtains special help in areas which are difficult for him in the regular grade.

In an earlier section it was pointed out that the achievement of partially seeing children in school is not markedly retarded as compared to that of seeing children. On the other hand, like seeing children, some of them have difficulties in learning to read, write, spell, or understand arithmetic, disabilities which are easily interpreted by teachers as being a result of the visual defect. This is not always the case, and teachers should look for other factors inhibiting the learning of reading. Since the ability to read is dependent upon mental processes, as long as the child is able to discriminate and perceive the visual symbols he will be able to read if inhibiting factors in the learning process are not present. Factors which inhibit learning will be discussed in Chapter 10.

The adjustment of the partially sighted child in school, whether he is assigned to a regular grade with extra assistance in a resource room or to a special class for the partially sighted, will depend on many factors, among which are his visual acuity, his interests and abilities, his orientation to class activities, the size of the class, the attitudes and skills of the teacher or teachers, and the availability of suitable materials and physical surroundings which will enable him to utilize his limited vision.

Summary

1. Partially seeing children are those who have seriously defective vision after correction and who require adaptations of visual materials and special methods of instruction.

2. The deviation in vision does not cause marked discrepancies in growth patterns. Hence the partially seeing child can be educated with seeing children if some adaptations are made in materials and instructional procedures.

3. Partially seeing children are educated (a) in a regular grade with the aid of an itinerant teacher, (b) by assignment to a regular grade with the aid of a resource room, and (c) under a cooperative plan of assignment to a special class and a regular grade.

4. The special arrangements and equipment in a class for the partially seeing include the selection of a centrally located school, uniform lighting, special adjustable desks, gray-green chalkboards, special unglazed rough paper and special pencils, typewriters, record players, dictaphones, large-type books, and magnifying and projection equipment.

DISCUSSION QUESTIONS

1. Those classes which are now called special classes for the partially sighted were previously called "sight-saving" classes. What changes in thinking have brought about this shift in terminology?

2. Which types of visual defects can be expected to have the greatest effect upon academic progress? Which will have the least impact?

3. Research has produced confusing answers to the question of the effect of visual defects on reading. How can you account for this confusion?

4. Statistics show that seven out of eight visually handicapped children do not receive an adapted educational program. Do you think this is neglect, or that these children receive adequate education in the regular grades? Why?

5. Plot a profile of a typical partially seeing child who has the proper educational program, keeping in mind what research has pointed out about the growth patterns of these children.

6. Which do you think is the greater handicap: moderate degree of hearing loss or partial loss of sight? Give reasons for your choice.

7. Evaluate the three organizational procedures that are being used to educate partially seeing children. Is there any evidence that one is superior to another? If not, how are the organizational plans justified?

8. What would you delineate as "special" (over and above, or in addition to, the program offered the ordinary child) in the educational program for the partially seeing child?

SELECTED REFERENCES

Galisdorfer, Lorraine. *Educational Reading Guide for Partially Seeing Children.* Buffalo, N.Y.: Foster & Stewart Corporation, 1951.

Galisdorfer, Lorraine. *A New Selected Bibliography of Literature on the Partially Seeing.* Kenmore, N.Y.: the Author, 1951.

Hathaway, Winifred. *Education and Health of the Partially Seeing Child.* Revised by F. M. Foote, Dorothy Bryan, and Helen Gibbons. New York: Columbia University Press, 1959.

Henderson, Florence. *Structure and Function of the Eye, A Handbook for Nurses and Teachers.* San Francisco: Gutenberg Press, 1957.

Mackie, Romaine. *Education of Visually Handicapped Children.* Federal Security Office, Bulletin No. 20. Washington: Government Printing Office, 1951.

Mackie, Romaine P., and Edith Cohoe. *Teachers of Children Who Are Partially Seeing.* U.S. Department of Health, Education and Welfare, Bulletin No. 4. Washington: Government Printing Office, 1956.

Mann, I., and A. Pirie. *The Science of Seeing.* New York: Penguin Books, 1950.

Merry, Ralph Vickers. *Problems in the Education of Visually Handicapped Children.* Cambridge, Mass.: Harvard University Press, 1933.

New York State Education Department. *The Adjustment of the Partially Seeing Child in the Regular Classroom.* Albany: University of the State of New York, 1957.

Sight-Saving Review. New York: National Society for the Prevention of Blindness. Published quarterly.

9

The Visually Handicapped Child: The Blind

Throughout the ages, blindness has been regarded as one of the most severe and most traumatic of physical handicaps. Unfortunately there has been a great deal of emotionality, especially sympathy and pity, connected with blindness.

It is therefore not surprising that the care of the blind is hardly a new venture but one which has existed in most societies throughout history. In spite of the relatively small number of blind persons in comparison to those with other handicapping conditions, our society has made social, legislative, and educational provisions for them on a scale proportionately greater than for any other type of exceptionality. As mentioned in the previous chapter, the blind have also been the subject of a great deal of research.

Definitions

Total blindness is an obvious condition, easy to recognize and define, but lesser degrees of blindness are another matter. Any definition, of necessity, depends upon the purpose for which it is made. Thus today there is "medical blindness," "legal blindness," "occupational blindness," "educational blindness," and so forth.

For educational purposes a blind person is one whose vision is so defective that he cannot be educated through visual methods. This category includes persons with light-dark and gross-form discrimination only, as well as the totally blind. Legally, the blind are those who have a visual acuity of 20/200 or less in the better eye after maximum correction, or who have a visual field which subtends an angle of 20 degrees or less in the widest diameter. Some children who are legally blind may read large type and function as partially sighted. Some have motion, light, or object perception which aids in travel but is not adequate for use in academic learning situations.

Abel summarized the deliberations of the Committee on Statistics of the Blind and gave a so-called layman's description of blindness:

1. people who are totally blind or have light perception, up to but not including 2/200 would be unable to perceive motion or hand movements at a distance of three feet;
2. the blind individual having motion or form perception might perceive up to 5/200 and would be unable to count fingers at a distance of three feet;
3. those people who might be expected to have travel vision would perceive up to 10/200 and would be unable to read large letters similar to those in the headlines of a newspaper;
4. those who would be expected to read large headlines might be measured on the Snellen Chart up to 20/200; they would not, however, be expected to read 14-point or smaller type;
5. individuals having borderline vision might have a visual acuity of 20/200 or more but they would not have sufficient vision for activities in which eyesight is essential; these individuals are further described as unable to read 10-point type, or if they read it all, they would do so with a marked handicap.[1]

For educational purposes, the major factor to consider in determining whether to assign a child to a class for the partially seeing or to a class for the blind is whether the child can see enough after the provision of medical correction and optical aids to be presented educational materials visually, or whether he must be taught through the auditory and tactile senses. The degree of blindness and age at onset must both be considered in planning for the education of a blind child. A child who was born blind depends upon hearing and touch for his knowledge and imagery. On the other hand, a child who became blind after birth might retain visual imagery and correlate what he hears or touches with it. For that reason Lowenfeld categorizes visual handicaps in six groups:

[1] Georgie Lee Abel, "The Education of Blind Children," *Education of Exceptional Children and Youth*, W. M. Cruickshank and G. O. Johnson, eds. (Englewood Cliffs, N.J.: Prentice-Hall, Inc., 1958), p. 297.

1. Total blindness, congenital or acquired before the age of five years.
2. Total blindness, acquired after five years of age.
3. Partial blindness, congenital.
4. Partial blindness, acquired.
5. Partial sight, congenital.
6. Partial sight, acquired.[2]

Those in the first four categories come within the definition of blindness and should be considered blind for educational purposes. Lowenfeld feels that those who lose their sight before the age of 5 are not able to retain any useful visual imagery. This theory has been experimentally tested by Schlaegel, who found that visual imagery disappeared in those who lost their vision before 6 years of age.[3]

Prevalence

Estimates of the number of blind children of preschool and school age vary from 10,000 to 15,000. The total number of blind persons in this country was estimated to be 347,688 in 1958.[4] At least two-thirds of all blind persons are in the 65-and-older age group. It is anticipated that the number of blind people over 65 will continue to increase as the average life span increases. On the other hand, the incidence of blindness among preschool children has dropped sharply with the prevention of retrolental fibroplasia, which accounted for over half of all blindness in preschoolers during the years 1945–1955.

Kerby stated that there were 7000 blind children attending schools and classes for the blind in 1954–1955, an estimated prevalence rate of 20 per 100,000 school children.[5] By 1959, there were 13,491 children enrolled in residential and public schools, of which 51 per cent were receiving specialized educational services in day classes for the blind or in classes for sighted children.[6] This increase in blind pupils in school was mainly attributed to the coming of school age of children who had been made blind by retrolental fibroplasia.

[2] Berthold Lowenfeld, "Psychological Problems of Children with Impaired Vision," *Psychology of Exceptional Children and Youth,* William M. Cruickshank, ed. (Englewood Cliffs, N.J.: Prentice-Hall, Inc., 1955), p. 219.

[3] T. F. Schlaegel, Jr., "The Dominant Method of Imagery in Blind as Compared to Sighted Adolescents," *Journal of Genetic Psychology,* 83 (1953), 265–277.

[4] Samuel Ashcroft, "The Blind and Partially Seeing," *Review of Educational Research,* 29 (December, 1959), 519–528.

[5] C. Edith Kerby, "Causes of Blindness in Children of School Age," *Sight-Saving Review,* 28 (Spring, 1958), 10–21.

[6] "Education of the Blind," *Britannica Book of the Year 1960* (Chicago: Encyclopaedia Britannica, Inc., 1960), p. 109.

Causes of Blindness

The major causes of blindness have been listed in broad categories: infectious diseases, accidents and injuries, poisoning, tumors, general diseases, and prenatal influences including heredity.

In 1954, Kerby surveyed the statistics on causes of blindness among 4426 blind children in residential schools.[7] Of the major causes, infectious diseases accounted for 7.4 per cent; injuries, 4.9 per cent; tumors, 5.1 per cent; heredity, 14.3 per cent; poisoning, including excessive oxygen, 19.3 per cent; and prenatal causes unspecified, accounting for the largest group, 41.8 per cent.

Some of the important factors relating to etiology (causes) of blindness and incidence over the years are as follows:

1. Public health measures have been effective in reducing blindness due to infectious diseases. According to Kerby there were 75 per cent fewer cases of blindness from infectious diseases between 1933–1934 and 1954–1955. A large part of this decrease is due to mandatory state public health laws requiring the use of prophylactic drops in the eyes of newborn babies. In 1907 ophthalmia neonatorum (caused by gonococcus or other micro-organisms) accounted for 28.2 per cent of blindness. By 1954 the preventive measures imposed by public health departments had reduced the prevalence to one-tenth of one per cent among pupils in schools for the blind. The treatment for syphilis and the requirement of premarital blood tests have resulted in 73 per cent fewer cases of blindness due to syphilis in the school-age group.

2. Public and parent education in safety measures, together with the legislative prohibitions against fireworks and guns for children, has reduced the rate of blindness due to accidents. According to Kerby, there have been 47 per cent fewer cases of blindness in this category among children between 1937–1938 and 1954–1955.

3. There was no perceptible change in the prevalence of those reported as blind as a result of genetic factors. This etiological category has always been difficult to establish and is generally based on a history of blindness in the family.

4. The decreases in blindness in some categories would have been expected to decrease the total rate of blindness among school-age children. But unfortunately, reduction in some categories was offset by an increase in blindness due to the appearance of a new disease causing blindness in children — retrolental fibroplasia, listed under "poisoning." Kerby's data show that in 1943 there were 1114 preschool children listed as

[7] Kerby, *op. cit.*, pp. 10–21.

having other causes of blindness and 81 as having retrolental fibroplasia.[8] In 1950 there were 636 preschool children with retrolental fibroplasia and 681 blind from all other causes. Because of this high prevalence of retrolental fibroplasia a decade ago, it was responsible for approximately one-half of the blindness in preschool children in 1954. (This figure is in contrast to Kerby's 19.1 per cent due to poisoning, since the latter figure included blindness at all age levels.)

Because of its dramatic rise and fall, and because it represents an example of how a medical advance in one area can produce a handicapping condition and thus create a social and educational problem, retrolental fibroplasia will be discussed in more detail.

The Dramatic Story of Retrolental Fibroplasia

Seldom has a disease had a more spectacular history than that of retrolental fibroplasia. It was nonexistent prior to 1938, was not named or diagnosed as a clinical entity until 1942, and had virtually disappeared by 1955, leaving in its wake thousands of blinded children.

Literally, retrolental fibroplasia means "fibrous tissue behind the lens." This eye disease was so named in 1942 by Dr. T. L. Terry, a Boston ophthalmologist.[9] Later study has shown that the name is not entirely accurate. Dr. Terry had initially observed only cases in the late stages of the disease, and what he saw as "fibrous tissue" was in fact the completely detached retina, which had floated toward the lens. The disease, thus, is primarily one of the retina.

It was originally noted by Terry that this new and previously unknown type of maldeveloped eye was occurring only in premature babies. Sixty-five per cent of the cases of retrolental fibroplasia were diagnosed by 6 months of age, and only very rarely as late as a year.

Beginning in about 1944 the incidence of the disease increased at an alarming rate, reaching its peak in 1952–1953, at which time it accounted for well over half of all the blindness in preschool children. In some hospitals the disease was striking as many as one out of every eight premature babies.[10]

[8] C. Edith Kerby, "Blindness in Preschool Children," *Sight-Saving Review*, 24 (Spring, 1954), 15–29.

[9] T. L. Terry, "Extreme Prematurity and Fibroblastic Overgrowth of Persistent Vascular Sheath Behind Each Crystalline Lens: Preliminary Report," *American Journal of Ophthalmology*, 25 (February, 1942), 203–204. T. L. Terry, "Fibroblastic Overgrowth of Persistent Tunica Vasculosca Lentis in Infants Born Prematurely," *American Journal of Ophthalmology*, 25 (December, 1942), 1409–1423.

[10] V. E. Kinsey, "Retrolental Fibroplasia; A Cooperative Study of Retrolental Fibroplasia and Use of Oxygen," *Archives of Ophthalmology*, 56 (October, 1956), 481–543.

In 1952, ten long research-filled years after retrolental fibroplasia was first diagnosed, evidence began to accumulate suggesting that the increased concentration of oxygen (then possible owing to improved incubators) to which premature youngsters were routinely subjected was the culprit. Very quickly it was established that this was the case, and, even more important, that the concentration and duration of oxygen therapy could be significantly reduced without increasing the mortality rate.

In an extensive study of 586 premature infants, Kinsey showed conclusively that the length of time the premature infant was kept in the oxygen-enriched environment was the important factor in the incidence of retrolental fibroplasia.[11] The findings on the cause of retrolental fibroplasia were rapidly circulated and by 1955–1956 the disease was occurring only very rarely, as shown in Figure 17.

Now that we have looked briefly at the history of retrolental fibroplasia, let us examine some of the results of its short, but too long, existence. Comprehensive figures and data on its incidence are not yet available, but some idea can be obtained from scattered sources. Between 1942 and 1954, 497 blind youngsters were reported to the California School for the Blind and the Variety Club (a California organization for preschool counseling of the blind).[12] Of these, 384 (77 per cent) were blind because of retrolental fibroplasia.

Among statistics currently available are those from the state of New York which are based on the census of blind children as of December 31, 1957.[13] The dramatic rise and fall in frequency of retrolental fibroplasia can be seen in Figure 17 showing the incidence, by birth year, in New York State between 1938 and 1956.

It will be noted from Figure 17 that retrolental fibroplasia reached its peak during the years of 1952–1953. The sharp drop in the graph after 1953 highlights the results of the decreased use of oxygen. The low points in 1955 and 1956 might be artificially low because a few cases born in those years had not been reported by 1957, the year of the study. Nevertheless, retrolental fibroplasia accounted for a large proportion of blind children born between 1940 and 1952–1953, and since that date the incidence has dropped abruptly due to better control of oxygen.

Meantime, however, the schools and institutions of our country were suddenly confronted with the problem of planning an educational program, providing materials, training teachers, social workers, and counselors, organizing vocational services, legislative programs, and so forth

[11] *Ibid.*

[12] Data presented by Dr. Berthold Lowenfeld, Superintendent of the California School for the Blind, San Francisco State College, December 4, 1954, mimeo.

[13] William M. Cruickshank and Matthew J. Trippe, *Services to Blind Children in New York State* (Syracuse, N.Y.: Syracuse University Press, 1959), p. 5.

FIGURE 17

Incidence of Retrolental Fibroplasia in New York, 1938–1956

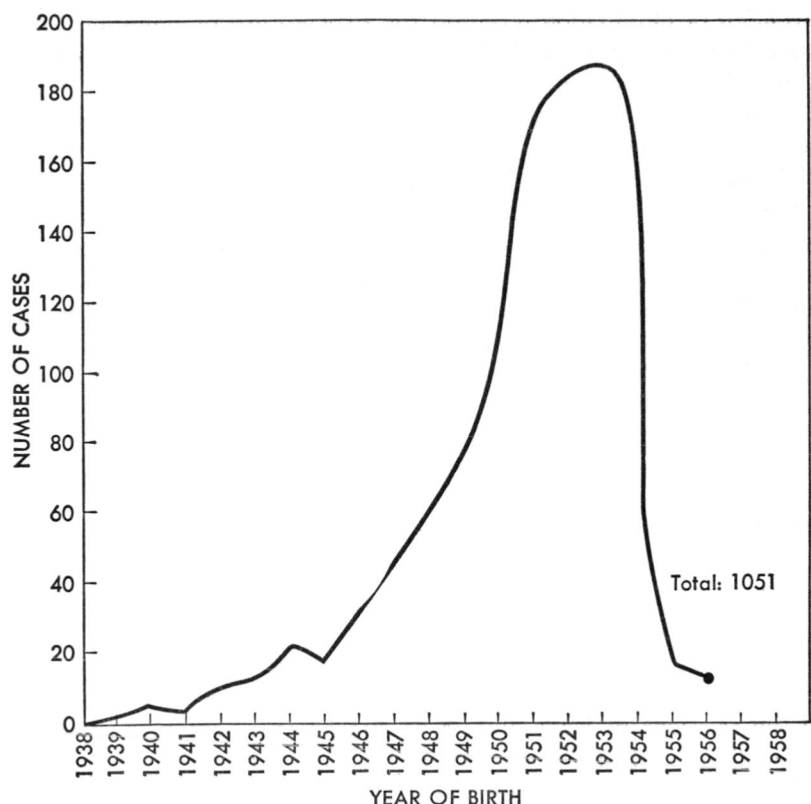

Source: Adapted from William M. Cruickshank and Matthew J. Trippe, *Services to Blind Children in New York State* (Syracuse, N.Y.: Syracuse University Press, 1959), p. 5.

for the thousands of blind children who are now growing up. And this planning had to be done with the realization that by about 1972 these children will have passed through their first twelve educational years, and the need for the programs so hurriedly established will be rapidly disappearing.

This brief glance at retrolental fibroplasia illustrates one of the problems often introduced by technological or scientific advances. The widespread use of oxygen therapy did indeed save the lives of many premature babies, but at the expense of unnecessarily blinding thousands of children. We knew enough to use oxygen therapy, but not enough to use it judiciously. As we advanced with one foot, we retreated with the other.

219

Once again interference by man with the process of nature resulted in an artificially produced disability. The man-made disease of retrolental fibroplasia absorbed the attention of the medical world, and its ultimate prevention or elimination required the expenditure of huge amounts of money, time, and personnel. Now the burden is being felt by families, schools, clinics, and other institutions, and in a few years it will affect the vocational world. Thus, what began as a medical advance to prevent death from prematurity has become a broad educational-psychological-social area of concern. Similarly, today there is considerable speculation on the effects of nuclear bombing and radiation on the incidence of handicapping conditions in children. Will we again witness the spectacle of an advance in one area of physical science producing defects in human development and new social problems? Such a thesis is forcefully presented by the Nobel Prize-winning scientist Linus Pauling.[14] Progress is indeed not made in a straight line.

The Growth Patterns of Blind Children

Blindness affects the development of the child in that the blind child becomes aware of the world through senses other than sight — that is, through the senses of hearing, touch, and smell. Although the tactile sense is primary and is used extensively by young blind children, many objects cannot be perceived through touch either because of physical inaccessibility or because of social restraints. Hills and mountains, space, and the relations of large objects to one another remain a mystery to blind children. Most of these are explained to the child orally and by analogy to what he can hear and feel.

What effect does blindness have on the development of the blind child in the various areas of growth represented earlier for other kinds of exceptional children? Does blindness affect his height, weight, mobility, intelligence, and social behavior? These questions and others have been subjects for research and experiment. When we turn to the literature in an attempt to answer them, we are faced with differences of findings and interpretation, for a number of reasons:

1. Many of the studies do not distinguish between causes of blindness. If a youngster has been blinded by an accident there is no reason to believe his intelligence has been affected. However, in a case of blindness resulting from rubella, which often results in mental retardation also, the chance that intelligence will be affected is much larger.

2. Many of the tests used in assessing personality and social adjustment as well as achievement and intelligence have been designed for and

[14] Linus Pauling, *No More War!* (New York: Dodd, Mead and Company), 1958.

standardized upon sighted subjects. Interpretation of scores obtained by blind subjects is at best equivocal.

3. In very recent years there has been some reason to believe that placement of blind children in residential or public schools is selective. This is not always made clear in research which includes both residential and day school pupils.

4. It is very difficult to know what part of any differences found between blind and sighted subjects is due to the visual deficit and what part to differential treatment accorded to blind children.

Height and Weight

There is no reason to believe that blindness has any effect on the height and weight of individuals. Krause, however, reports that in the early years of retrolental fibroplasia some children were restricted and were not allowed to develop independently.[15] He stated that these children's height and weight were less than the average for that age. But since the children had been premature infants, it may have been the prematurity, rather than blindness, which caused both the height-weight difference and the overprotection.

Motor Coordination

The research by Buell on motor performance showed quite clearly the inferiority of the blind to the partially sighted and the inferiority of both to normals.[16] Norris found a high relationship between blind children's opportunities for learning and their mobility or motor performance.[17] It is highly probable that a group of blind children who had had opportunities to climb trees, roller-skate, and wrestle along with their sighted peers from preschool days would not be found seriously deficient in motor coordination. Similarly, it would be expected that a group of sighted children who had been sedentary and had not taken part in such activities would be somewhat deficient motorically.

Two case studies illustrate the dangers of generalizing in this area. Gesell, Ilg, and Bullis followed the development of a blind child from infancy through the age of 4 and found the sequence of development to be normally progressive in posture, manipulation, locomotion, exploration, language, and social behavior.[18] On the other hand, Wilson and

---

[15] A. C. Krause, "Effect of Retrolental Fibroplasia in Children," *Archives of Ophthalmology*, 53 (April, 1955), 522–529.

[16] Charles Buell, "Motor Performance of Visually Handicapped Children," *Journal of Exceptional Children*, 17 (December, 1950), 69–72.

[17] Miriam Norris, Patricia J. Spaulding, and Fern H. Brodie, *Blindness in Children* (Chicago: University of Chicago Press, 1957).

[18] A. Gesell, F. L. Ilg, and G. E. Bullis, *Vision: Its Development in Infant and Child* (New York: Paul B. Hoeber, Inc., 1950).

Halverson observed another blind child and found general developmental retardation which was most pronounced in motor areas.[19]

Intelligence

Lowenfeld argues that blindness limits perception and cognition in three ways: (1) in the range and variety of experiences, (2) in the ability to get about, and (3) in the control of the environment and of the self in relation to it.[20] These restrictions would be expected to affect intellectual development.

Assessing the intelligence of the blind has been difficult in that standard instruments designed for and standardized on the sighted are often inappropriate. Samuel P. Hayes, a pioneer contributor to the field of psychological testing of the blind, revised the Binet test for this use. The Hayes-Binet Intelligence Test has been one of the few reliable and valid instruments available for testing the blind until recent years. Hayes administered the Hayes-Binet to 2372 blind children in residential schools and found the mean IQ to be slightly below average (98.8).[21] According to this study and others more recent, the percentage of blind children falling in the average range is less than that for seeing children, with fewer in the superior range and notably more in the defective range. No relationship has been found between age at which sight is lost and intelligence or achievement.

There should now be a re-evaluation of the intellectual status of blind children, in view of changing conditions affecting blind children as a result of (1) the increase in preschool blindness due to retrolental fibroplasia, (2) the accelerated movement to enroll blind children in regular classrooms, and (3) the changing attitudes of parents.

One study which has investigated the suggestion that retrolental fibroplasia might also be associated with reduced mental capacity was that of Norris, Spaulding, and Brodie.[22] These investigators tested 300 preschool children in the Chicago area whose blindness was due to retrolental fibroplasia. They found no definite evidence that this group of children had a generalized brain defect. The distribution of test scores appeared to the authors to be essentially normal. It should be noted, however, that the use of modified and adapted tests for blind preschool children is open to serious questions of reliability.

---

[19] J. Wilson and H. M. Halverson, "Development of a Young Blind Child," *Journal of Genetic Psychology*, 71 (1947), 155–175.

[20] B. Lowenfeld, "Psychological Foundations of Special Methods in Teaching Blind Children," *Blindness*, P. A. Zahl, ed. (Princeton, N.J.: Princeton University Press, 1950), pp. 89–108.

[21] S. P. Hayes, *Contributions to a Psychology of Blindness* (New York: American Foundation for the Blind, 1941).

[22] Norris, Spaulding, and Brodie, *op. cit.*

Social Maturity

Social maturity of the blind has been assessed by the Vineland Social Maturity Scale and a revision of it, the Maxfield-Fjeld Scale. Norris, Spaulding, and Brodie found the mean SQ on the Maxfield-Fjeld for 66 young blind children (85 per cent of whom had retrolental fibroplasia) to be 91.9,[23] much higher than is usually reported. Hayes found a mean SQ of 80.9 for 300 blind children.[24] Bradway, testing 73 blind students in an institution setting, found an average SQ of 62.[25] This low figure is not supported by the studies mentioned above, nor by Maxfield and Fjeld, who found a quotient of 83.5 for 101 visually handicapped children.[26]

In general, it may be said that blind children do often receive significantly lower social maturity scores than seeing children, but the reasons may lie in aspects of the blind child's environment rather than in his own lack of sight. The tendency for parents to overprotect a blind child is strong, perhaps out of guilt, hostility, anxiety, or simply lack of knowledge about his capabilities.

Speech Development

Brieland reports the observations commonly made in the literature regarding speech of the blind:

1. The blind show less vocal variety.
2. Lack of modulation is more critical among the blind.
3. The blind tend to talk louder than the sighted.
4. The blind speak at a slower rate.
5. Less effective use of gesture and bodily action is typical of the blind.
6. The blind use less lip movement in articulation of sounds.[27]

Other research fails to substantiate these claims. Stinchfield[28] did find more speech defects among the blind, but Rowe,[29] and Brieland[30] did

[23] *Ibid.*

[24] S. P. Hayes, *First Regional Conference on Mental Measurements of the Blind* (Watertown, Mass.: Perkins Institution, 1952), pp. 26–30.

[25] Katherine P. Bradway, "Social Competence of Exceptional Children: III. The Deaf, the Blind, and the Crippled," *Journal of Exceptional Children,* 4 (November, 1937), 64–69.

[26] Kathryn E. Maxfield and Harriet Fjeld, "The Social Maturity of the Visually Handicapped Preschool Child," *Child Development,* 13 (March, 1942), 1–27.

[27] D. M. Brieland, "A Comparative Study of the Speech of Blind and Sighted Children," *Speech Monographs,* 17 (March, 1950), 99–103.

[28] Sara M. Stinchfield, *The Psychology of Speech* (Boston: Expression Company, 1928).

[29] E. D. Rowe, *Speech Problems of Blind Children* (New York: American Foundation for the Blind, 1958).

[30] Brieland, *op. cit.*

not. In fact the latter authors found superior speech among the blind.

While it is true that the blind do not have the visual imitative cues available which are somtimes utilized by seeing children in developing articulation, this is perhaps not a crucial lack. It is apparently amply compensated for by the greater role that oral and aural communication necessarily plays in the life of the blind.

Language Development

Language of children is studied by aural, written, oral, and reading methods. Cutsforth tested congenitally blind children with a free-association test by giving them a noun and asking them to name its attributes.[31] He found that they responded with words that were unrealistic to them. For example, to "night," some of them said "dark," "black," "blue," "yellow," and only one child out of twenty-six responded "cool." Cutsforth felt that these verbalisms were in terms of learned, associative visual responses rather than of the children's own tactile or hearing experiences. In writing compositions, Hayes observed, blind chlidren were equal to sighted in ability.[32] Maxfield reports a methodological study in which eight blind children were found to mention more things, ask more questions, use more proper names, and give fewer commands than seeing children in a free-play situation.[33] This study suggests that blindness facilitates rather than hinders language development under some circumstances.

In general, one may conclude that the language of blind children (if we exclude concepts which require vision) is not deficient. Since much of language is acquired auditorily, the blind, unlike the deaf, can develop language usage similar to that of seeing individuals.

Reading

Blind children learn to read braille, which is a slower process than reading visually. Reading and achievement tests for seeing individuals have been written in braille for the blind and administered with a much longer time limit. On these tests, as summarized by Pinter, the blind are slower readers than are seeing children reading print.[34] During the first and second grades their retardation is not marked, but by the time they have attended school for eight years their reading of braille is comparable to fifth- or sixth-grade print reading.

[31] T. D. Cutsforth, *The Blind in School and Society* (New York: American Foundation for the Blind, 1951), pp. 65–70.

[32] Hayes, *Contributions to a Psychology of Blindness*, pp. 128–130.

[33] Kathryn E. Maxfield, "The Spoken Language of the Blind Preschool Child," *Archives of Psychology*, 1936, No. 201.

[34] Rudolf Pinter, Jon Eisenson, and Mildred Stanton, *The Psychology of the Physically Handicapped* (New York: F. S. Crofts and Company, 1941), pp. 219–221.

Other School Subjects

In arithmetic, spelling, and general information, blind children are retarded educationally as compared to seeing children. Hayes reports retardation in arithmetic,[35] and in a study of general information he reports marked retardation on the Pressey Test of Practical Information.[36] Nolan and Ashcroft report arithmetic scores for the blind as 16 per cent below the norms for the sighted.[37]

Sensory Perception

Research workers have been interested in the question of how other sense functions are affected by visual deficiency. The doctrine of sensory compensation holds that if one sense avenue such as vision is deficient, other senses will be automatically strengthened. It was believed that the blind could hear better and had better memories than sighted individuals. Yet research has not demonstrated this popular opinion. In a study by Seashore and Ling it was found that there was no difference between blind and seeing subjects in auditory, tactual, or kinesthetic sensitivity.[38]

It is possible that blind people make better use of their abilities in other sense fields. A sighted person may tend to disregard sounds in his environment which necessity has caused to have significance to a blind person. This does not mean that the actual hearing abilities of the two individuals differ.

In a comparison of types of imagery experienced in response to oral words or phrases, Schlaegel found no differences between blind and sighted subjects.[39] Both experienced visual most frequently, then auditory, kinesthetic, tactual-thermal, and olfactory-gustatory in that order. When the blind were subdivided on the basis of amount of remaining vision, however, visual imagery increased with visual acuity to the extent that the subjects who were the *least* blind had *more* visual imagery than the seeing subjects had.

The ability of a blind child to utilize various types of imagery is an important consideration in his total development and especially in his educational program. Much more work is needed in this field, but at present it is known that differences exist in the extent to which blind persons

[35] S. P. Hayes, "What Do Blind Children Know?" *Teachers Forum for the Blind*, 11 (1938), 22–29, 32.

[36] Hayes, *Contributions to a Psychology of Blindness*, pp. 11–124, 127, 281.

[37] C. Y. Nolan and S. C. Ashcroft, "The Stanford Achievement Arithmetic Computation Tests," *International Journal for Education of the Blind*, 8 (1959), 89–92.

[38] C. E. Seashore and T. L. Ling, "The Comparative Sensitiveness of Blind and Seeing Persons," *Psychological Monographs*, 25 (1918), 148–158.

[39] Schlaegel, *op. cit.*

utilize sensory channels, and that the extent of visual loss and the age at which the loss occurs are important variables.

Music

It has often been asserted that music is one area in which the blind have exceptional ability and interest. Although music education is emphasized with the blind, and history gives records of some blind individuals who became noted musicians, there is no evidence that the blind in general are superior in musical ability. For a time one of the vocations recommended for the blind was piano tuning, and indeed some have become efficient at this trade. Nevertheless, music, using primarily the auditory sense, is still included in all curriculums for the blind. Various mechanical devices, including typewriters, have been used for typing musical notes, and braille and other notations have been used for reading music. Memorization, of course, plays a large role in the actual performance of blind musicians.

Profiles of Growth Patterns

Figure 18 shows the developmental profiles of three 12-year-old blind children. William has average intelligence. On the Hayes-Binet Test he obtained an IQ of 95. His school experience, like that of the other two children in the profile, has been in a residential school since the age of 5. Frank is of superior intelligence, having scored 132 IQ on the Hayes-Binet Test. His academic achievement is also superior to that of the other two children. Alice is blind and mentally retarded. Both her blindness and her mental retardation have been attributed to her mother as having contracted German measles (rubella) during the first trimester of pregnancy. All three children were totally blind at birth, and all were enrolled between the ages of 5 and 6 in a residential school for the blind.

These profiles illustrate the differences in development of blind children of different intellectual levels. Other multiple handicaps can produce other kinds of developmental patterns. A deaf-blind child would present a much more retarded picture, although Helen Keller, who was a gifted deaf-blind child, was able to compensate for the multiple handicap by superior instruction, intensive effort, and high intelligence.

Educational Provisions for the Blind

The American Foundation for the Blind recognizes three types of educational provisions for blind children. These are:

1. Education in a public or private residential school for the blind.
2. Education with the sighted in public or private schools with a resource or special class teacher available during the entire school day.

FIGURE 18

Profiles of Three Blind Children of Differing Intelligence Levels

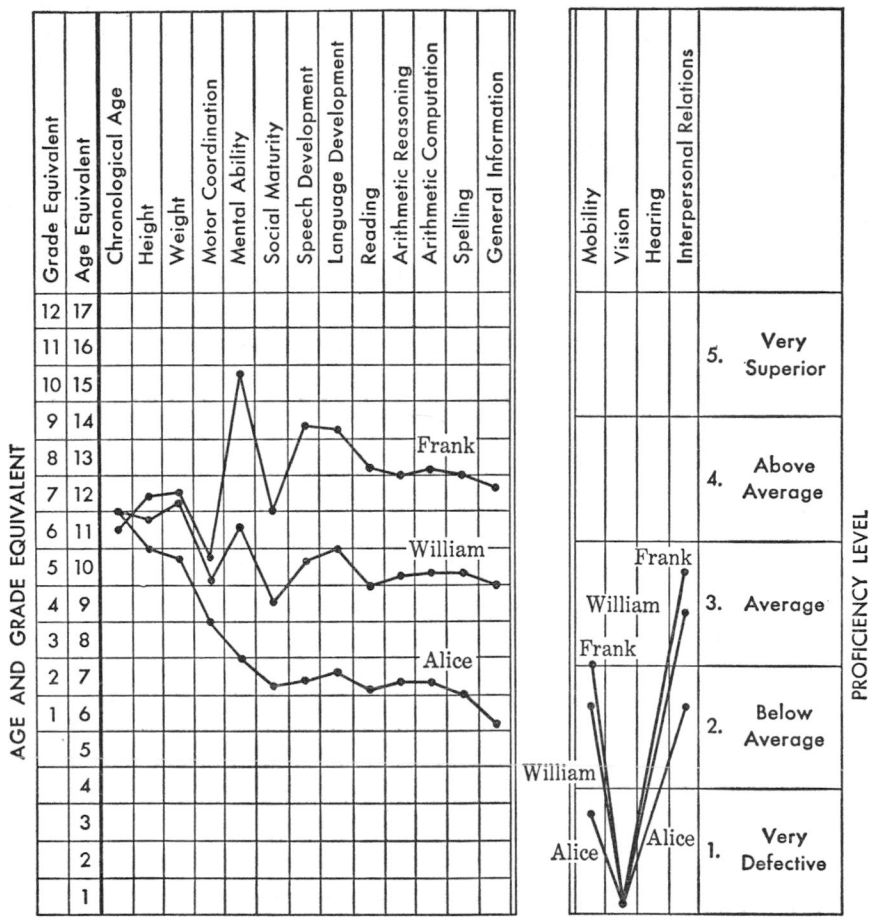

Frank, blind child of superior intelligence, IQ 132
William, blind child of average intelligence, IQ 95
Alice, blind child of retarded mental development, IQ 68

3. Education with the sighted in public or private schools with itinerant teaching service available at regular or needed intervals.

In recognizing these types of education of the blind child of school age, the Foundation is recognizing the important and basic premise *that each blind child should be educated according to his individual needs and that not for a long, long time — if ever — will any one of the three types of education listed above eliminate the other two. . . .*

The Foundation has no hesitancy in stating that some blind children can best be educated with sighted children and that some blind children can best be educated in the residential school. The Foundation has even less hesitancy in stating that any system of educating blind children can be charged with moral guilt if it does not provide for enrolled blind children "an education according to their individual interests and aptitudes, at least *equal* to that which they would have received had they not been blind.". . .[40]

The Residential School

According to Farrell, the first school for the blind was organized in Paris in 1785 by Valentin Haüy.[41] In the United States the first residential school for the blind was organized in 1829. It was named "The New England Asylum for the Blind," now known as the Perkins Institution and the Massachusetts School for the Blind. Since that date most states have established residential schools for the blind, under either private or public auspices.

The residential school is a boarding school for blind children where they generally attend for nine months of the year. Here they live, go to school, and even learn vocations. Such schools often admit children as young as 4 or 5 and terminate their attendance at ages 18 to 21. The residential schools for the blind are not as large as residential schools for other kinds of exceptional children such as the deaf or the mentally retarded. School enrollment ranges from 25 in some states to 200–300 in more populated areas.

Historically, it may be pointed out that in the early nineteenth century, when the first schools for the blind were established in this country, the boarding school was considered the most desirable type of educational facility available, as it was so thought in Europe during this period. Even though it provided an opportunity for thorough training, certain disadvantages of an institutional setting became apparent — routine, formality, segregation, lack of family life, and so forth.

At that time, however, there were only two alternatives — either to send the child to an institution or to train him at home. In spite of the disadvantages of institution living, residential schools offered the benefits of socialization, techniques and facilities, and trained teachers. Even today these advantages must be weighed against the disadvantages and viewed in the light of a particular child's needs and alternative opportunities. The child from a small community which does not have specialized facilities for his education, the child whose home environment is inadequate to cope with his handicap, or the child who has other handi-

[40] *The Pine Brook Report* (New York: American Foundation for the Blind, 1954), pp. 54–55.
[41] Gabriel Farrell, "Blindness in the United States," in Paul A. Zahl, *op. cit.*, pp. 3–25.

caps may find that the advantages of a residential school outweigh the disadvantages.

A different emphasis on the role of the residential schools has been advocated in the Oregon Plan, which is considered desirable by many.[42] There are three essential principles of this plan: First, children who can be educated in the public schools should not be institutionalized; second, the residential school for the blind has as one of its aims returning visually handicapped children to public schools as quickly as possible; and third, each child has a right to individualized services for the optimum maintenance and restoration of vision.

For the most part, blind children are educated with seeing children when feasible, but the residential school will probably continue to serve those who cannot fully benefit from educational services in their home communities.

Public School Day Classes

In 1871, Dr. Samuel Howe stated:

> With a view of lessening all differences between blind and seeing children, I would have the blind attend the common schools in all cases where it is feasible. . . . Depend on it, one of the future reforms in the education of the blind will be to send blind children to the common schools, to be taught with common children in all those branches not absolutely requiring visible illustrations, as spelling, pronunciation, grammar, arithmetic, vocal music and the like. We shall avail ourselves of the special institutions less, and the common schools more.[43]

This prediction by Dr. Howe was not immediately fulfilled, but the proportion of blind children now being educated with the sighted in the public schools is constantly increasing.

Since 1900, when the first public school class was organized in Chicago, special classes for blind children have been seen set up in most of the large cities and in some of the intermediate-sized communities. At the outset, all of the instruction for the blind was conducted in the special class. Gradually, however, blind children in these classes were assigned for part of the day to regular classes.

In a discussion of the trend to include blind children in regular classes, Irwin pointed out that Cincinnati followed Chicago in establishing day school classes for the blind in 1905.[44] The Cincinnati school, however, segregated the children in a special building, thus sacrificing those ad-

---

[42] Berthold Lowenfeld, "The Oregon Plan," *Outlook for the Blind*, 40 (March, 1946), 67–75.

[43] As related by Robert B. Irwin in *As I Saw It* (New York American Foundation for the Blind, 1955), p. 128.

[44] *Ibid.*, pp. 130–131.

vantages which grow out of their association with sighted boys and girls of their own age. In 1920 Seattle organized a class in which the blind children spent part of their day with sighted children. The organization was later changed to a segregated class, but one which lacked much of the special equipment to be found at the state school. The parents felt that if the children were going to be segregated anyway, they would be better off in the state school, so the city class was disbanded.

One further trend should be noted, namely, that of increasing cooperation between the residential schools and the public school system. Many residential schools now send their pupils to public high schools even though the students continue to live at the school for the blind. And increasingly, public school systems avail themselves of special equipment, materials, and training, especially musical and prevocational, which are available at the residential schools.

Organization of day classes for blind children tends to follow procedures described for classes for the partially seeing: (1) the cooperative plan and (2) the integrated plan.[45]

The Cooperative Plan. Under this plan the blind child is enrolled in a special room and is assigned to the regular classrooms for a portion of the school day. The special class becomes the home room, and the teacher of the blind, in cooperation with the regular classroom teachers, plans the educational program for the child.

The Resource Room or Integrated Plan. Under this plan the blind child is enrolled in the regular classroom and has the services not only of his regular teacher but also of a full-time qualified teacher of blind children; in addition, he can use the facilities of a resource room. The regular teachers obtain assistance from the teacher of the blind in planning the child's program, in adapting the classroom procedures, and in providing specialized instruction needed by the blind child in the regular classroom. The child spends as much time as he needs in the resource room with the special teacher utilizing instructional aids.

Itinerant Teacher Program

In this plan the child is sent to a regular school with seeing children. The regular teacher obtains advice and special instruction and materials from an itinerant teacher of the blind employed by a large school unit, by smaller communities jointly, or by a state education agency. The special teacher's responsibilities are to help the regular teacher outline the educational program for the child, to secure appropriate materials, and to give special instruction at specified periods. This includes teaching braille reading and braille writing and providing selected equip-

[45] *The Pine Brook Report,* pp. 1–71.

ment and materials for study, such as recorded texts and study materials identical in content to those used by the seeing children in the class.

The itinerant teacher plan has been used to some extent with the blind for many years, especially at the high school and college levels. Here a blind person has a reader who reads the assignments to him since the materials of many courses are not available in braille. Consultants and libraries are able to provide talking books. The itinerant teacher plan has extended this service downward to the kindergarten and first grade. It is the only practical plan to use in smaller communities when the parents do not wish their child to leave home for attendance at a residential school.

Curriculum

As with all atypical children, the blind child's basic needs and the goals for his education are not different from those of the ordinary child. It is only the means of achieving these goals that are different. The content material and subject matter as well as the attitudes and understandings which are sought are the same as those for seeing children.

Lowenfeld has proposed the following statement as a more specific goal in the education of blind children:

> Education must aim at giving the blind child a knowledge of the realities around him, the confidence to cope with these realities, and the feeling that he is recognized and accepted as an individual in his own right.[46]

Obviously if blind children were exposed only to the educational experiences and materials used with sighted children (which are approximately 85 per cent visual) they would not achieve these goals. Thus special methods, materials, and equipment must be employed, utilizing the senses of hearing, touch, smell, and even taste. The curriculum for the blind must include: (1) adaptations of the general curriculum, (2) some additional or specialized content, and (3) specialized materials and equipment.

Adaptations of the General Curriculum

Most of the adaptations necessary for blind children stem from an effort to provide comparable experiences which do not involve the use of sight or which utilize the limited vision available. That is, the children

[46] Berthold Lowenfeld, "The Child Who Is Blind," *Journal of Exceptional Children,* 19 (December, 1952), 96.

must be given tactual experiences and verbal explanations. The blind child's ability to listen and relate and remember must be developed to its fullest. He must learn efficiency and conservation of time because the techniques he must use to acquire the same information or accomplish the same task are sometimes more cumbersome and time consuming. Therefore the teacher must organize her material better, must be specific in making explanations, and must utilize sound principles of learning.

Teaching, of course, is an art. The ability of the teacher to guide the child in the use of the various adaptations is one of the prime requisites. Lowenfeld has listed five principles suitable to teaching blind children.[47]

1. *Individualization.* Blind children, whether in classes for the blind or in regular classes, differ from each other as much as or more than children in a class for the sighted. The degrees of blindness, ages, home backgrounds, differences in intelligence, and the special teaching problems which they present require an individualized program for each child. For that reason the size of a class for the blind is generally six to eight pupils, and each child's program must be fitted to his particular needs.

2. *Concreteness.* The blind child's knowledge is gained primarily through hearing and touch. But if he is to really understand the world about him, it is necessary that he be presented with concrete objects which can be touched and manipulated. Through tactual observation of models of objects he can learn about their shape, size, weight, hardness, surface qualities, pliability, and temperature. Models of objects are enlargements, if the actual objects are too small, or contractions, if they are too large. This type of presentation, of course, is a distortion of the real object, and its differences should be explained to the child. A model of a house, for example, can be used if its dimensions are explained and related to doors, windows, and other parts of a house which he can touch and feel in reality.

3. *Unified instruction.* Visual experience tends to unify knowledge in its totality. A child entering a grocery store will see the relations of shelves and objects in space. A blind child cannot obtain this unification unless teachers present him with experiences, such as "units of experience" of a farm, post office, or grocery store. It is necessary for the teacher to bring these "wholes" into perspective through actual concrete experience and attempt to unify them through explanation and sequencing.

4. *Additional stimulation.* Left on their own, blind children live a relatively restricted life. To expand their horizons, to develop imagery, and to orient them to a wider environment it is necessary to develop these experiences by systematic stimulation. This requires programming

[47] *Ibid.*, pp. 96–102.

of stimulating experiences from the time the children begin to walk. Mental orientation to their environment can begin by mapping the classroom and having them find their way around it. Later, the orientation is extended to the larger school, and later still to the community through travel instruction.

5. *Self-activity.* For a blind child to learn about his environment it is necessary to initiate self-activity. A blind infant does not reach out for an object, because it does not attract him. He must know of its existence by touch or smell or hearing. Thus his learning is slower. Walking, talking, prehension, feeding, and socialization will be retarded unless training and guidance encourage the development of these behaviors. Maturation must be aided at all stages, and opportunities for doing things himself should be provided and encouraged.

More specific methods of making adaptations in various subject matter fields have been analyzed by Abel from extensive teacher suggestions.[48] These are summarized below:

1. In teaching science, social studies, or other subject matter which requires demonstrations or laboratory experiments, it is important that the teacher: (a) prepare the child for the experience by sufficient previous orientation; (b) arrange for a sighted child to interpret any parts of the experience which were not clear; and (c) evaluate what the blind child derived from the experience.

2. In subjects involving mathematics, number manpulation should be preceded by adequate number experience and an understanding of number concepts.

3. In subjects such as home economics, arts and crafts, and industrial education considerable individual instruction and careful selection of equipment are important. Care must be taken not to develop overdependence. Anyone who has observed blind children working in a machine shop will realize that fear for their safety in such situations is sometimes exaggerated.

4. Physical education for the blind has been emphasized in the literature. Residential schools have demonstrated that a great deal can be done in this area. Public school programs are more and more admitting blind children to physical education classes with the sighted. Careful orientation techniques can alleviate teachers' fear for their safety.

5. Various music subjects have been emphasized. The question has been raised as to whether too much stress has been placed on these subjects regardless of the potentialities of the children. It is important that those with unusual talent be given sufficient opportunity for study and good counseling in relation to a future career. Care should be taken,

[48] Abel, *op. cit.,* pp. 319–320.

however, to see that the blind child does not allow other valuable areas of his curriculum to be neglected because of his music.

Additions to the Curriculum

Because blind children have to acquire their knowledge and abilities through senses other than the visual, a place must be made in their curriculum for learning these extras over and above the general program for seeing children.

Braille is a system of "touch" reading. Embossed characters use different combinations of six dots arranged in a cell two dots wide and three dots high. The symbols are embossed on heavy manila paper in a

left to right order, and the reader usually "reads" with one hand and keeps his place vertically with the other. An advanced reader may use the second hand to orient himself to the next line while he is reading the line above and he may read as much as a third of the line with his left hand. Music, punctuation, and mathematical and scientific notations are based on this same system.

Braille in its original form was developed by Louis Braille, a Frenchman who was himself blind. It was first published in 1829 and further developed five years later. Many other systems have been attempted, including Moon's phonic symbols (modified Roman letters), New York Point (using a cell two dots high and varying in width), American Braille, and British Braille. Each system had its advocates and for many years controversies raged. In an attempt to settle them, a study was undertaken in 1932, which concluded that British Braille was superior to any system being used in this country. One hundred years after Louis Braille first presented his scheme, an agreement was reached on a modified system of British Braille now termed Standard English Braille. Even so, this was not consistently used until about 1950.

Standard English Braille has been developed in several levels differing in the extent to which contractions are used over and above the basic letters and numerals of Grade 1. This is the standard which serves as a common denominator in English-speaking countries.

In 1950 UNESCO adopted a world braille system for all languages, but it has not been highly publicized and there are many details to be worked out. Braille has been adapted in various forms to other languages — Chinese, Esperanto, Spanish, Korean, and many others.

Braille is very bulky. Such works as the Bible or a dictionary require twenty or thirty volumes or more. This presents a storage problem in a school which has an adequate braille library. Fortunately, many braille publications can be borrowed from the American Foundation for the Blind and the Library of Congress.

The eye, of course, is faster than the hand, and as would be expected braille reading is relatively slow, the average speed being about sixty words per minute, or about one-third or one-fourth the rate of sighted readers.

Braille writing is another addition to the curriculum of blind children. It is taught later than braille reading. There are various devices for writing the symbols, easiest and fastest of which is the braille typewriter, or braillewriter machine. This has six keys corresponding to the six dots of the cell. A good braille typist can braille forty to sixty words per minute.

Braille can also be written by hand, using a special slate and stylus. Braille slates, which come in desk and pocket sizes, are boards with a double metal strip, the lower part of which is pitted by cells of six dots each, and the upper punched with corresponding holes. The paper is inserted between the metal strips and the desired dots are embossed by pressing a dull stylus through the appropriate holes. Since this is to be read from the opposite side of the paper, the work must be done in reverse, beginning at the right margin and working toward the left.

Typing, which is seldom included in the elementary curriculum for seeing children, is very important to blind children if they are to communicate with the sighted world, a very small portion of which can read braille. Blind children are taught to use a standard print typewriter as soon as possible, usually in the third or fourth grade. Handwriting is usually very difficult and is no longer emphasized to a great extent, except that an effort is made to teach the writing of one's own signature. The typewriter has all but replaced such devices as wire guide lines, which were needed to help teach handwriting.

Teaching command of the environment is of special importance to the blind child in that both his physical and his social independence are involved. The ease with which he can move about, find objects and places, and orient himself to new or strange physical and social situations will be crucial in determining the role he can assume in peer relations, the types of vocations and avocations that will be open to him as an adult, and his own estimation of himself as an individual.

What can be done to aid the blind child in gaining as much command of his environment, and himself in it, as possible? Certainly from the time he is very young he can be helped to avoid unnecessary fear, both of new experiences and of injury. Sighted children skin their knees, bump their shins, fall from trees, and step in holes. The blind child ought to have the same privileges if he is to experience physical freedom and control of himself and the environment. As he grows older specific training in techniques of traveling — cane, and perhaps guide dog — can be provided.

The factors in the personality and/or background environment of a blind person which are conducive to good travel ability and general mobility are as yet unknown, although they may be dependent upon training and mental imagery. It has been observed that differences in freedom of moving about can be noted between blind children at an early age.

The best "when and how" of formal teaching of travel skills has not yet been determined but is being investigated. Certainly the importance of travel training cannot be overestimated, in that one of the greatest limitations imposed by blindness is on the ability to get about. The situations which force dependence and may cause greatest personality and social problems are very likely to center about mobility. This is perhaps the reason for the current search for electronic devices which will perhaps someday replace the cane, the dog, and the sighted guide.

As part of a heightened awareness of nonvisual cues around him, the blind child must learn to attend to auditory, olfactory, and tactile-kinesthetic cues which the sighted person has no need to notice. For example, the ability of the blind to detect obstacles in their pathway has been found to be a function of the change in pitch of the sound waves reflected by the obstacle as the observer approaches.[49]

The blind child must be taught to feel the difference in the weight of his fork when he has successfully cornered a few peas and when it is still empty. A system of marking his clothing and organizing it is essential for both efficiency and good grooming. These are illustrative of ways in which a blind child can be taught to improve his command of the environment.

The use of models, whether of a room, the Empire State Building, or the child's neighborhood, is generally felt to be helpful in showing the relationship of one place or size to another. But this is not to say that models are approved as a substitute for the experience. Rather, they can help give a perceptual or cognitive map of relations and areas too large to be simultaneously included in direct experience.

The whole area of personal mobility and independence has a particular significance in adolescence when the child is ready to break away from family restraints and overprotection. In his peer relations, security and comfort in controlling himself and his environment are almost essential to the development of poise and independence and to gaining the respect of others.

[49] P. Worchel, J. Mauney, and J. G. Andrew, "The Perception of Obstacles by the Blind," *Journal of Experimental Psychology*, 40 (1950), 746–751.

Teaching social competence is part of the job of the blind child's family, teachers, and friends. The seeing child acquires visually much socially useful information which is not accessible to the blind child, who does not, for instance, know who is in a room as he enters or whether his attire is appropriate and neat, or what visual stimuli may have prompted a burst of laughter from his peers. The skills of successfully determining just what is customary in grooming, eating, etiquette, and the social graces, and then finding ways to implement these customs without visual cues are important to the blind child.

Specialized Materials and Equipment

Any program for the blind must take into account the additional, often very specialized, materials and equipment necessary to provide meaningful experiences to compensate for those the sighted child uses to gain knowledge about the realities around him and to learn to cope with these realities. The ability to use this equipment efficiently is another accomplishment which the curriculum must foster.

Braille materials have already been discussed. It is evident that the use and understanding of these requires a large share of the child's school day.

Audio aids are a basic element in a blind child's quest for knowledge, particularly in the upper elementary grades and beyond. The Talking Book reproducer, other record players, and often a tape recorder may become part of his everyday school life. If he is in the regular grades, the classroom teacher or itinerant teacher may make special explanations or assignments on tape. Textbooks which are not available in braille may be taped or recorded by volunteer workers.

Since braille reading is less than one-third to one-fourth the speed of visual reading, and since the books available in braille are limited, Talking Books have become standard educational media for imparting information to the blind. These long-playing phonograph records of books read by professional readers are heard at the rate of 160–170 words per minute for fiction and about 150 words per minute for texts. The federal government has appropriated funds for their recording and manufacture, and the Library of Congress distributes them free of charge to libraries upon request. Special phonographs are also loaned through libraries. This system makes Talking Books available to blind children and adults in all communities.

In general, the Talking Book has been used for the presentation of fiction rather than for textbooks. Ordinarily, school textbooks are made available through the American Printing House for the Blind, the Library of Congress, or privately.

Talking Books are labeled in braille with a minimum of braille words (to save space), while indicating author, title, and reader. The same information is provided in print for the use of librarians.

Arithmetic aids include an arithmetic board and an adaptation of the abacus. The braillewriter is also used to compute mathematics. Pins and rubber bands are utilized in constructing geometric designs and graphs of various sorts.

Mental arithmetic, of course, is used a great deal in the education of the blind. But higher levels of arithmetic and mathematics require elaborate machines. Calculators can be adapted for use by brailling the dials, or by giving other tactual cues. Similarly, tape measures, rulers, watches, slide rules, compasses, protractors, and so forth have been adapted for use by the blind.

Embossed and relief maps are important in teaching space perception required in understanding geography. Besides braille maps, relief maps, and audible electric maps, jigsaw puzzles and relief globes are also used.

One of the reasons for the importance of maps is not only to supplement the study of geography in general but to help orient the blind to their immediate environment. Mobility around the room or the town requires that the blind person have a mental image of the relation of objects to each other in space. Through sensory cues and the cognitive map he is then able to orient himself, and to move around more freely.

Vocational Adjustment and Rehabilitation

Sheltered workshops have played an important role in the vocational training and employment of the blind. This was even more true in the past than now, as more blind persons are entering competitive fields with the seeing than was the case earlier. Even so, Buell found that 75 per cent of the graduates of the California School for the Blind were employed, half of them in sheltered workshops and the others in competitive jobs.[50]

At one time the vocational emphasis of the workshops was almost exclusively on items like rugs, brooms, and hand-woven ties, but now the shops often subcontract for industrial concerns. The diversification and expansion in vocational pursuits of the blind both in workshop and in competitive jobs reflect (1) the influence of organizations for the blind which have urged that charitable financial assistance be replaced by job opportunities and removal of restrictive legislation, (2) the expansion of the United States Office of Vocational Rehabilitation services for the blind, (3) the demands of wartime industry, which handicapped persons

[50] Josephine Buell, "Employment Status of Former Pupils of the California School for the Blind," *Journal of Exceptional Children*, 23 (December, 1956), 102–103.

met ably, (4) the changed attitudes of the public due to the return of blind veterans, and (5) the increased emphasis on integration of minority and handicapped group members in all walks of life.

Some blind persons are at present engaged very successfully in many different jobs — farming, chemistry, teaching kindergarten through college, osteopathy, and law, to mention only a few. It should not be suggested that blindness imposses no vocational limitations; on the other hand, no blind person should be categorically denied access to a vocation just because of his lack of vision. For years most of our states have had visual acuity requirements for teaching certificates. Very recently a few totally blind teachers of regular classrooms of seeing children have convincingly demonstrated that vision is not after all a prerequisite to good teaching. This kind of experience is being duplicated in other fields which have traditionally been closed to the blind. It is anticipated that as society accepts the blind in competitive employment, and as the blind obtain more opportunities for job training, the proportion of employed in competitive jobs will exceed that in the sheltered workshops.

Summary

1. Throughout the ages, blindness has been considered one of the most traumatic of physical handicaps, and extensive provisions have been made for care and education of the blind.

2. It is estimated that there were approximately 350,000 blind persons in the United States in 1958, that two-thirds of these were over age 65, and that approximately 13,000 blind children are now enrolled in residential and public schools.

3. Blindness among school children from ordinary diseases and injuries has been decreasing over the years, partly owing to public health measures. Recently, however, this decrease was offset by a new man-produced disease called retrolental fibroplasia. The rapid rise of retrolental fibroplasia from 1940 to 1953 has been checked, leaving, however, thousands of blind children in its wake. Approximately one-half of blind children in schools have retrolental fibroplasia.

4. Blindness often affects developmental patterns in the areas of academic learning, mobility, motor coordination, and social maturity.

5. Blind children are educated in residential schools and in public school day classes for sighted children with the assistance of resource rooms and itinerant teachers.

6. In school, specific aids to the blind include (a) the adaptation of the curriculum in terms of special instructional techniques, (b) additions to the curriculum, such as reading and writing braille, learning to type on

regular typewriters, and making special adjustments to the physical and social environments using cues other than sight, and (c) specialized materials such as braille, audio aids, Talking Books, arithmetic aids, embossed and relief maps, and other specially constructed aids to learning.

Discussion Questions

1. In Chapter 7 it was noted that a child who loses his hearing at age five or six retains and improves his speech and language ability. In this chapter it was noted that a child who loses his sight at age five or six (Lowenfeld, Schlaegel) does not retain visual imagery that is usable to him. Why do you think this is so?

2. In the discussion on retrolental fibroplasia it was stated that "progress is indeed not made in a straight line." Illustrate the soundness of this statement by additional examples from other areas of exceptionality discussed in this text.

3. What public health measures are needed to reduce the incidence of blindness still further?

4. Figure 18 gives the growth profiles of three blind children of different intellectual levels. Using the information from the section on "Growth Patterns of Blind Children," draw a profile of two blind children with average intelligence, one of whom was born blind and the other of whom became blind at age six.

5. Do we have the same kind of controversy between residential and day school programs in the field of the blind as we do in the field of the deaf? Why or why not?

6. Evaluate Lowenfeld's five principles of teaching used with blind children. Are these principles unique for blind children, or are they applicable to all children? What are the finer differences, if any?

7. Imagine yourself as blind; then list the methods you would use to study the courses you are now taking, recognizing that your present college textbooks are not written in braille. How do these methods in college differ from the methods used by a third-grade blind child?

8. Of the special methods and materials used in the education of blind children, which ones do you think are most essential? Why?

Selected References

Abel, Georgie Lee. *Resources for Teachers of Blind with Sighted Children.* AFB Publications, Educational Series, No. 9. New York: American Foundation for the Blind, rev. ed., 1957.

Abel, Georgie Lee, compiler. *Concerning the Education of Blind Children.* AFB Publications, Educational Series, No. 12. New York: American Foundation for the Blind, 1959.

Axelrod, Seymour. *Effects of Early Blindness.* AFB Publications, Research Series No. 7. New York: American Foundation for the Blind, 1959.

Chevigny, Hector, and Sydell Braverman. *The Adjustment of the Blind.* New Haven: Yale University Press, 1950.

Cutsforth, Thomas D. *The Blind in School and Society.* New York: American Foundation for the Blind, new ed., 1951.

Farrell, Gabriel. *The Story of Blindness.* Cambridge: Harvard University Press, 1956.

Frampton, Merle E., ed. *Education of the Blind.* New York: World Book Company, 1940.

French, Richard S. *From Homer to Helen Keller.* New York: American Foundation for the Blind, 1932.

Hayes, Samuel P. *Contributions to a Psychology of Blindness.* New York: American Foundation for the Blind, 1941.

Irwin, Robert B. *As I Saw It.* New York: American Foundation for the Blind, 1955.

Lende, Helga. *Books About the Blind.* New York: American Foundation for the Blind, 1953.

Lowenfeld, Berthold, ed. *The Blind Preschool Child.* New York: American Foundation for the Blind, 1947.

Lowenfeld, Berthold. *Our Blind Children.* Springfield, Ill.: Charles C. Thomas, 1956.

Mackie, Romaine P., and Lloyd M. Dunn. *Teachers of Children Who Are Blind.* U.S. Department of Health, Education and Welfare, Bulletin 1955, No. 10. Washington: Government Printing Office, 1955.

Norris, Miriam, Patricia J. Spaulding, and Fern H. Brodie. *Blindness in Children.* Chicago: University of Chicago Press, 1957.

Pelone, Anthony J. *Helping the Visually Handicapped Child in a Regular Class.* Maurice H. Fouracre, ed. Teachers College Series in Special Education. New York: Teachers College, Columbia University, 1957.

The Pine Brook Report, National Work Session on the Education of the Blind with the Sighted. Group Reports No. 2. New York: American Foundation for the Blind, 1954.

Zahl, P. A., ed. *Blindness: Modern Approaches to the Unseen Environment* Princeton, N.J.: Princeton University Press, 1950.

I 0

Cerebral Palsy and
Associated Disorders

The brain is the control center of the body. When something goes wrong with the brain, something happens to the physical, emotional, or mental functions of the organism. The number of things that can happen to the organism are probably as numerous as the nerves and cells of the brain.

Throughout the centuries scientists have been trying to unravel the mysteries of the complex central nervous system. Originally it was believed that the brain functioned as one single organ, like the liver. A little later it was thought that different parts of the brain had separate functions; at one time a so-called science of phrenology emerged in which an individual's personality was analyzed according to the bumps on his head.

Recently, scientists have recognized that there is an integrative function of the central nervous system, and also that different parts of the brain have special functions. The theories of both *mass action* (meaning that the brain functions as a whole) and *localization* (meaning that certain functions are located in certain areas of the brain) have been accepted.

As yet scientists have not been able to specify and precisely locate the functions of the central nervous system sufficiently to explain all

242

behavior on this basis. What we have at present is partial knowledge of the relation of the central nervous system to behavior and to special disabilities.

Cerebral Dysfunction and Disabilities

Figure 19 illustrates attempts to localize brain functions. This is a summary representation of various research and hypothetical conclusions.

FIGURE 19

Summarizing Map of the Areas of Cortical Function

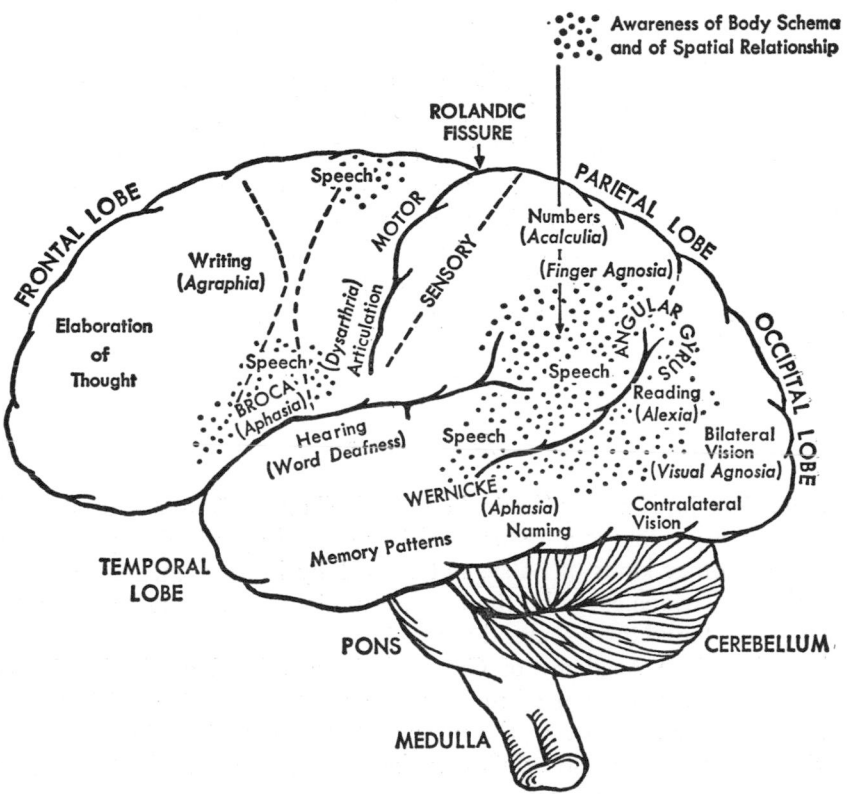

This drawing is based on the conclusions, some hypothetical (e.g., the elaboration zones), others firmly established, in the works of Penfield and Rasmussen (1952) and Penfield and Roberts (1959). The terms agraphia, acalculia, alexia, aphasia, word deafness, visual agnosia, finger agnosia, and dysarthria are terms used by various neurologists to indicate disorders of functions. The localization of these dysfunctions is speculative.

Penfield and Rasmussen, through electrical stimulation of the various parts of the brain in humans during the waking state, were able to produce muscular movements of various parts of the body.[1] In addition, stimulation of the auditory area aroused hearing of tones, and stimulation of the visual areas aroused sensations of color, shape, and other visual representations. When the right temporal lobe was stimulated in one patient there was aroused a memory of being in an office with desks and other people. As a result of these and other studies the brain is being plotted, as shown in Figure 19, to indicate the broad areas which appear to be responsible for certain physical and mental functions.

An injury to the brain, or lack of development of the brain, is likely to result in disabilities of various kinds. Cerebral palsy refers to a "palsy" or motor disability resulting from a deficiency in the cerebrum (brain). But brain damage can also cause other disabilities with or without motor (muscular) handicap.

Injuries to the brain or parts of it before, during, or after birth can cause mental retardation, language disorders (aphasia), reading disabilities (dyslexia), writing disabilities (agraphia), inability to understand words (word deafness), and various forms of motor incoordination including cerebral palsy. The important point to remember is that a brain damage which results in the motor disability called cerebral palsy can also cause language, speech, writing, and other disorders. Furthermore, cerebral disorders can cause these psychological disorders without affecting motor ability.

Definitions

Since "cerebral" means "brain," and "palsy" means "a motor disability," *cerebral palsy* refers to a motor disability caused by a brain dysfunction. There are other kinds of palsy, not caused by brain damage, including spinal palsy, which could be the result of poliomelitis, or end organ palsy such as that found in muscular dystrophy.

The American Academy of Cerebral Palsy defined cerebral palsy as "any abnormal alteration of movement or motor function arising from defect, injury, or disease of the nervous tissues contained in the cranial cavity."[2] A more inclusive definition has been formulated by the United Cerebral Palsy Associations:

[1] W. Penfield and Theodore Rasmussen, *The Cerebral Cortex of Man* (New York: The Macmillan Company, 1952).

[2] Temple Fay, "Desperately Needed Research in Cerebral Palsy," *Cerebral Palsy Review,* 14, (March-April, 1953).

Cerebral palsy embraces the clinical picture created by injury to the brain, in which one of the components is motor disturbance. Thus, cerebral palsy may be described as a group of conditions, usually originating in childhood, characterized by paralysis, weakness, incoordination or any other aberration of motor function caused by pathology of the motor control center of the brain. In addition to such motor dysfunction, cerebral palsy may include learning difficulties, psychological problems, sensory defects, convulsive and behavioral disorders of organic origin.[3]

Thus, the definition of cerebral palsy includes not only the neuromotor component but also many other mental or psychological disabilities of perception, learning, emotions, and speech. The neuromuscular disorder is primarily the responsibility of the medical profession whereas the associated behavioral disorders become the responsibility of the social, educational, psychological, and speech professions. This is why the problem of cerebral palsy requires a team approach by the members of various professions.

It should also be remembered that damage to the brain need not result in neuromuscular disabilities, and that other behavior disabilities can occur in isolation or in combination. To these general disabilities, including cerebral palsy, Denhoff and Robinault have applied the term "cerebral palsy and related dysfunctions."[4] They feel that "cerebral palsy" is too narrow a term and that "cerebral dysfunction" is preferable to "brain-injury" or "brain-damage." The present author will use "cerebral dysfunction" as the general term and "cerebral palsy" in discussing cerebral dysfunction as related only to the neuromuscular disability. It should be pointed out, however, that the majority of cerebral-palsied children have associated handicaps of vision, hearing, and speech, as well as perceptual or behavioral handicaps. In the long run the ultimate treatment or remediation of the associated handicap may be as important as the treatment of the neuromuscular handicap.

Kinds of Cerebral Palsy

Cerebral palsy is not a disease but a condition characterized by a group of concurrent symptoms. This means that, although not like measles or tuberculosis or cancer, it is a describable syndrome and its description is consistent in some ways.

Cerebral palsy takes different forms with different neuromotor disabili-

[3] The United Cerebral Palsy Research and Educational Foundation, *Program for Calendar Year 1958* (New York: The Foundation, 1958), p. 1.

[4] Eric Denhoff and Isabel Robinault, *Cerebral Palsy and Related Disorders* (New York: McGraw-Hill Book Company, 1960).

ties. We differentiate (1) spastic paralysis, (2) athetosis, (3) ataxia, (4) tremor, and (5) rigidity. The first two, the spastic and athetoid groups, comprise the greatest number of cerebral-palsied individuals.

Spasticity

In 1861, Dr. Little in London described a condition in children as a spastic syndrome. This condition was later called "Little's disease" and has since been variously termed cerebrospastic, infantile cerebral spastic, birth injured, and simply cerebral palsied. Use of the word "cerebral" indicates that the paralysis is the result of a damaged brain, to be differentiated from other kinds of paralysis such as that found in poliomyelitis.

In the spastic condition one or more limbs of the body may be affected. The cerebral cortex (particularly the motor cortex), the pyramidal tracts, and possibly some extrapyramidal tracts which deal with the control of voluntary movements are defective. (The pyramidal tracts are in between the sensory and motor regions of the cortex in Figure 19, and the extrapyramidal tracts are below the cortical level, deeper in the brain.) Certain areas of the brain suppress certain impulses, contractions, or stimulations and are therefore called suppressors. When one of these is damaged, suppression does not occur, and the muscles remain in a state of spasticity or tension. Normally there is a balance between the suppressors and the antagonistic muscles. In the condition of spasticity the balance is absent and instead of a smooth movement there are jerky, uncontrolled movements with the spasmodic contraction of the muscles. The child is able to move the affected muscle voluntarily, since the muscle is normal, but the movement is slow, explosive, and poorly performed. Different groups of muscles can be affected by this paralysis: In *monoplegia, one* limb is spastic. In *hemiplegia, one side* of the body, that is, both the arm and the leg, is affected. In *triplegia, three* limbs are involved, generally two legs and one arm. In *paraplegia,* the disability occurs in *both* legs. In *quadriplegia,* all *four* limbs are affected; many times the head and trunk are also involved.

In describing cerebral palsy, a diagnostic team tends to indicate (1) the general condition — cerebral palsy; (2) the parts of the body affected (right monoplegia, left hemiplegia, quadriplegia, and so forth); (3) the degree of involvement, such as mild or severe; and (4) associated disabilities of vision, hearing, intelligence, speech, and learning.

Athetosis

Spastic paralysis has been ascribed to a lesion in the *pyramidal tract,* which is in the motor cortex, while athetosis results from a lesion in the *extrapyramidal* system, located in the forebrain or midbrain. These are not clear-cut areas of deficit, since spasticity may also involve the extrapyramidal system. Although not fully understood, the extrapyramidal system is believed to mediate inhibitory or restraining effects on muscular activity and to control the complex automatic acts like walking and making facial expressions. Children with athetosis walk in a lurching, writhing, and stumbly manner. Their movements are not rhythmical and do not seem to follow any sequence. Their postural attitude is uncontrolled, and many of them writhe and wriggle in variable fashion.

The athetoid individual is able to put his hand to his mouth, but in so doing he goes through various uncontrollable movements, in the extreme case showing squirming gestures and marked facial grimaces. During sleep, however, the athetoid does not writhe or squirm. These movements occur only in the conscious state. As conscious effort and emotionality increase, the athetotic movements become intensified.

Ataxia

This particular condition, less prevalent than spasticity or athetosis, is due to a lesion in the cerebellum, which normally controls balance and muscle coordination. The ataxic child is unsteady in his movements, walks with a high step, and falls easily. Sometimes the eyes are uncoordinated and nystagmus (jerky movement of the eye) is common. Ordinarily, ataxia is not detected at birth but is apparent when grasping and walking begin. As in spasticity and athetosis, there are varying degrees of ataxia, from mild (barely detectable) to very severe, depending on the extent of damage in the cerebellum.

Tremor and Rigidity

Tremor and rigidity are also, like atheosis, the result of injury to the extrapyramidal system. They occur in a small proportion of cerebral-palsied children. *Tremor* cerebral palsy is sometimes detected at an early age when the whole body shows involuntary vibrating movements of irregular nature. These result from an interference in the normal balance between antagonistic muscle groups. The child is generally consistent and predictable and is able to direct his activities toward a goal more adequately than is the athetoid or spastic. *Rigidity* refers to interference with the postural tone and is the result of resistance of agonist and antagonist muscles. There is more of a diminished motion than abnormal motion. These cases, however, are not very common and can be distinguished from the spastics in that their tremor or rigidity is generally even.

Mixed Types

Although different kinds of cerebral palsy can be identified and classified many cerebral palsy cases are mixed types, with some characteristics

of spasticity and athetosis, or spasticity and ataxia, or other combinations.

The Prevalence of Cerebral Palsy

As with many other kinds of exceptionality, it is difficult to determine
very accurately the prevalence of cerebral palsy among children. Many
mild cases go undiagnosed and undetected. If the condition is associated
with the handicap of mental deficiency, for example, the children tend
to be enrolled in institutions for the mentally defective, and are so classified, instead of being classified as cerebral palsied.

Various attempts, however, have been made to estimate the prevalence
of cerebral palsy in different populations. Schonell's study of four county
boroughs in England gives the following incidences per 10,000 population:[5]

Birmingham	7.6
Stoke	5.8
Coventry	9.4
Walsall	7.7

Schonell observed that there were a number of cases in institutions which
were not included in these surveys and indicated that the overall figure,
adding those in institutions, would be an estimated 9 cerebral-palsied individuals per 10,000 population.

Cardwell has summarized the studies which attempted to determine
the incidence and prevalence of cerebral palsy in the population.[6] The
studies vary widely, depending on whether they are giving the number
in 10,000 population as did Schonell or are estimating the number per
1000 births. Cardwell quotes Wishik as stating that there are between
15 and 30 per 10,000 total population, a much higher figure than that
given by Schonell. As with other types of exceptional children, surveys
vary in their definitions and criteria; hence the wide variation in estimates of prevalence.

Another aspect of the prevalence of cerebral palsy is the frequency
with which each type occurs. Various surveys agree that spasticity ac-
counts for roughly one-half of the cases and athetosis for about a fourth.
Typical of these studies is the one by Hopkins, Bice, and Colton, whose

[5] F. E. Schonell, *Educating Spastic Children* (Edinburgh: Oliver and Boyd,
1956), p. 35.
[6] Viola E. Cardwell, *Cerebral Palsy: Advances in Understanding and Care* (New
York: Association for the Aid of Crippled Children, 1956), p. 475.

FIGURE 20

Types of Cerebral Palsy

(Analysis of 1406 Cases Examined by the New Jersey
Crippled Children's Commission Between 1936 and 1951)

Type	Number of Cases	Per Cent of Types
Spastic	645	45.9
Athetoid	333	23.7
Rigidity	177	12.6
Ataxic	152	10.8
Tremor	27	1.9
Mixed Cases	48	3.4
Rare Cases	24	1.7

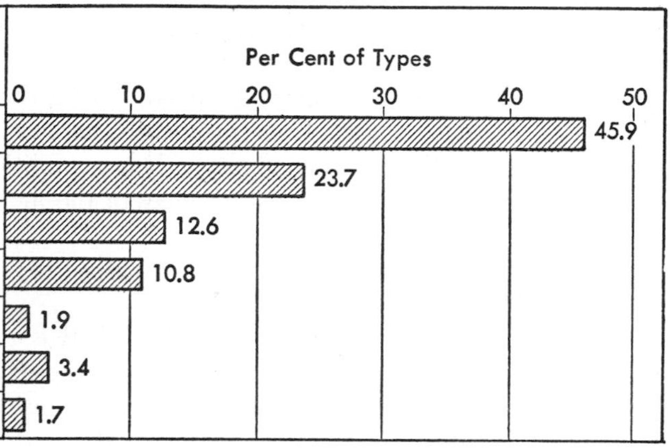

Source: T. W. Hopkins, H. V. Bice, and K. C. Colton, *Evaluation and Education of the Cerebral Palsied Child* (Washington: International Council for Exceptional Children, 1954), p. 3.

data are presented in Figure 20.[7] These data are based on an analysis of 1406 cases examined by the New Jersey Crippled Children's Commission between 1936 and 1951.

The Causes of Cerebral Palsy

The causes of cerebral palsy appear to be very similar to the causes of some forms of mental deficiency explained in Chapter 3. As Illingworth has aptly asserted, ". . . the causes of cerebral palsy and of mental deficiency are so interwoven, that with only a few exceptions research into the causes of one cannot and should not be separated from research into the causes of the other."[8] Rather than repeat the etiological factors presented in Chapter 3, we shall briefly summarize the causative (etiological) factors.[9]

[7] T. W. Hopkins, H. V. Bice, and Kathryn C. Colton, *Evaluation and Education of the Cerebral Palsied Child* (Washington: International Council for Exceptional Children, 1954), p. 3.

[8] R. S. Illingworth, ed., *Recent Advances in Cerebral Palsy* (London: J. & A. Churchill, Ltd., 1958), p. 17.

[9] The reader is referred to Selected References at the end of the chapter for sources of information on etiological factors.

Cerebral palsy, like other conditions, may be caused by factors operative before birth (prenatal), during birth (natal or perinatal), or after birth (postnatal).

Prenatal Conditions

In this category are found (1) genetic or inherited conditions and (2) conditions during pregnancy which result in a defect in the child's central nervous system.

Some conditions causing cerebral palsy during the prenatal period include (1) prenatal anoxia from premature separation of the placenta, severe anemia in the mother, a serious heart condition, shock, or threatened abortion, (2) metabolic disturbances of the mother, and (3) the Rh factor.

Perinatal Conditions

One cause which has been firmly established is injury at birth. Difficulties with the cord and placenta can reduce the oxygen supply, causing anoxia. So can other mechanical factors such as breech presentation, holding back of the head, and brain hemorrhage during birth.

Postnatal Conditions

As in other conditions, childhood diseases such as meningitis, encephalitis, influenza, and possibly high fevers in typhoid, diphtheria, and pertussis could cause cerebral palsy, as could head injuries from accidents, certain poisoning causing toxic conditions (lead poisoning, anoxia, carbon monoxide poisoning), or strangulation. According to Illingworth it is estimated that about 10 per cent of cerebral palsy is caused by postnatal factors.[10]

In commenting on correlated factors Illingworth stated:

> 1. In a small percentage of cases other than kernicterus and heredofamilial degenerative diseases of the nervous system, there is a history of affected near relatives. There is a higher than average incidence of mental deficiency in siblings and near relatives, and a higher than average incidence of other anomalies in affected children.
>
> 2. There is a higher than average incidence of males (about 57 per cent).
>
> 3. There is a higher than average incidence of multiple pregnancies — about 6 per cent, as compared to an average of 1.2 per cent.
>
> 4. There is a higher incidence of previous miscarriages and stillbirths.
>
> 5. There is an increased incidence of antepartum haemorrhage in the later part of pregnancy and of toxaemia.
>
> 6. There is a high incidence of abnormal labour involving conditions which would be likely to cause anoxia rather than mechanical trauma.

[10] Illingworth, *op. cit.*, p. 14.

7. The condition of affected children in the immediate newborn period is more likely to be poor and to cause concern than that of unaffected babies.

8. Postnatal causes include trauma, encephalitis and meningitis.

9. Anoxia is probably the most important single factor, but other factors are involved.[11]

Associated Handicaps

The cerebral dysfunction resulting in cerebral palsy also may cause a variety of other handicaps, singly or in combinations. As in neuromuscular disabilities, where cerebral palsy can affect one arm (monoplegia), or one leg and one arm (hemiplegia), or both legs and both arms (quadriplegia), a cerebral dysfunction may cause none, one, or a number of psychological anomalies: intellectual defects, left-handedness, deficiencies in vision, hearing, speech, or visual-motor perceptions.

Mental Retardation

Often poor speech and uncontrolled writhing or spastic movements of cerebral-palsied children give the layman an unwarranted impression of mental deficiency. There is actually little direct relation between intelligence and degree of physical impairment in cerebral palsy. An individual with severe writhing or uncontrolled spasticity may be intellectually gifted while one with mild, almost unnoticed physical involvements may be severely mentally retarded.

There have been many articles and books written on the intelligence of the cerebral-palsied child.[12] Individual intelligence tests such as the Stanford-Binet and the Wechsler Intelligence Scale for Children are sometimes used to obtain a minimal estimate of the cerebral-palsied child's intelligence, but most examiners feel that his performance is unduly handicapped by his motor or speech impairments. With these cautions in mind some of the studies using intelligence tests will be summarized:

Hohman and Freedheim, who obtained IQ's on 1003 cases referred to a medical clinic, found that 58.8 per cent of the cerebral-palsied children had IQ's below 70 as compared to a normal distribution showing only 5 per cent in this category.[13] Their distribution of IQ's also

[11] *Ibid.*, p. 17.

[12] Edith Myer Taylor, *Psychological Appraisal of Children with Cerebral Defects* (Cambridge: Harvard University Press, 1959).

[13] Leslie B. Hohman and Donald K. Freedheim, "Further Studies on Intelligence Levels in Cerebral Palsy Children," *American Journal of Physical Medicine*, 37 (April, 1958), 90–97.

shows that 25.1 per cent of the palsied group had IQ's of 70 to 90; 13 per cent had IQ's between 90 and 110, and only 3.1 per cent had IQ's above 110.

Schonell estimated the IQ's of cerebral-palsied children from a sample of 354 cases and compared them with the normals,[14] as did Hohman and Freedheim. This study, done in England, indicates that 45 per cent of the cerebral-palsied children have IQ's below 70. Schonell's distribution of the figures for the group as a whole is shown in Table VIII.

TABLE VIII

Distribution of 354 Estimated IQ's of Cerebral Palsy Group Compared with Normal Child Population

IQ Level	Per Cent of Cerebral Palsy Group	Per Cent in Normal Population
130 +	.6	3
110–129	3.4	24
90–109	20.1	46
70–89	26.8	24
69 and below	45.2	3
Not assessable	3.9	

Table adapted from F. E. Schonell, *Educating Spastic Children* (Edinburgh: Oliver and Boyd, 1956), p. 66.

Hopkins, Bice, and Colton also report the distribution of intelligence on the Stanford Revision of the Binet scale for 992 children in New Jersey.[15] Figure 21 shows the marked difference between the normal distribution and that of the cerebral palsied. This survey indicates that 49 per cent of the cerebral-palsied children fall below 70 IQ, 22.5 per cent are between 70 and 89 IQ, 21.9 per cent fall between 90 and 109 IQ, and 6.6 per cent are above 110 IQ. The median IQ is 70.4. These figures agree quite well with the Schonell figures and are a little more optimistic than those presented by Hohman.

Cardwell has summarized thirteen studies on the intelligence test findings of 3700 cerebral-palsied children.[16] She concludes that of those who come to clinics or are assigned to special classes, (1) about 5 to 6 per cent have superior intelligence, (2) about 25 to 30 per cent have average intelligence, (3) about 20 to 25 per cent have borderline or dull-normal intelligence, and (4) about 40 to 50 per cent have IQ's below 70.

[14] Schonell, *op. cit.*, p. 66.
[15] Hopkins, Bice, Colton, *op. cit.*, p. 38.
[16] Cardwell, *op. cit.*, p. 475.

FIGURE 21

Intelligence Distribution on the Stanford Revision of the Binet Scale for 992 Children in New Jersey

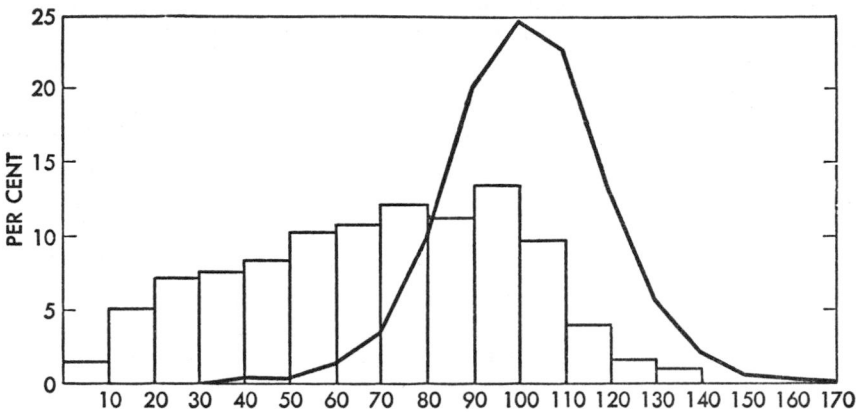

The line graph represents normal distribution (Terman). The bar graph represents total cerebral palsy cases. Median IQ, 70.4.

Source: T. W. Hopkins, H. V. Bice, and K. C. Colton, *Evaluation and Education of the Cerebral Palsied Child* (Washington: International Council for Exceptional Children, 1954), p. 44.

Visual Defects

All of the studies on visual deficiencies in cerebral-palsied children have shown that a substantial number of these children have associated visual anomalies. Hopkins, Bice, and Colton pointed out that in a sample of 939 cases, 72.4 per cent had normal vision while 28.6 per cent had defective or questionable vision.[17] Of the children with visual disabilities 42.7 per cent were ataxic, 27.3 per cent were spastic, and 20.4 per cent were athetoid.

According to Denhoff and Robinault, "various authors agree that over 50 per cent of the cerebral palsied children have oculomotor defects and 25 per cent or more have subnormal vision."[18]

Hearing Defects

Another problem that has faced those who diagnose or treat the cerebral palsied is whether the cerebral damage has affected hearing as it has vision. Since hearing does not have motor functions comparable to those of the eye muscles, hearing defects should be less frequent. Ac-

[17] Hopkins, Bice, and Colton, *op. cit.*, p. 9.
[18] Denhoff and Robinault, *op. cit.*, p. 63.

tually research has found that hearing defects among cerebral-palsied children are not as common as are visual problems.

Hopkins, Bice, and Colton reported that 13.3 per cent of 1121 cases had hearing defects.[19] Of this group the athetoids comprised 22.6 per cent, the spastics only 7.2 per cent. In a survey from England Fish found that 20 per cent of the cerebral-palsied children had hearing losses.[20]

It would appear from these studies that hearing losses among the cerebral palsied, especially among the athetoid group, are greater than among children who are not cerebral palsied, but not as marked as are visual problems.

Speech Defects

Defective speech is the most common type of associated handicap among cerebral-palsied children. In the Hopkins sample of 1224 children, 88.7 per cent of the athetoids and 85.3 per cent of the ataxic group were found to have speech defects.[21] Only 52 per cent of the spastics were diagnosed as having speech problems.

Denhoff and Robinault indicate that, because of neuromuscular disorders, speech involvements exist in 70 per cent of cerebral-palsied children, being more common in athetoids than in spastics.[22] Among the speech defects are *dysarthria,* an articulation defect caused by poor motor control, *delayed speech* due to mental retardation and the cerebral dysfunction, *voice disorders, stuttering,* and the various forms of *aphasia.* These difficulties are explained in greater detail in the section on "Learning Disabilities" in this chapter, and in Chapter 12, "Speech Handicapped Children."

Perceptual Disorders

One of the psychological disabilities commonly attributed to cerebral dysfunction is perceptual disorder. The term "perception" has been defined differently by different authors and includes auditory, visual, tactile, and other sense modalities. With the cerebral palsied, visual perception has had the greatest attention.

Strauss and Lehtinen thought of perception as an intermediate step between sensation and the thinking process.[23] It is a sensation with meaning. Much research has been conducted for the purpose of finding out what kinds of perceptions become distorted in children with cerebral

[19] Hopkins, Bice, and Colton, *op. cit.*

[20] L. Fish, "Deafness in Cerebral Palsied School Children," *Lancet,* 2 (1955), 370–371.

[21] Hopkins, Bice, and Colton, *op. cit.*

[22] Denhoff and Robinault, *op. cit.,* pp. 76–78.

[23] Alfred A. Strauss and Laura E. Lehtinen, *Psychopathology and Education of the Brain-Injured Child* (New York: Grune and Stratton, 1947).

dysfunctions. Cruickshank, Bice, and Wallen have reviewed a part of this extensive literature and have conducted experiments in an attempt to differentiate the perceptual problems of the cerebral palsied from those of children without cerebral palsy, and to determine whether spastics and athetoids differ in their response to visual and visual-motor perceptual tasks.[24] They found that in general both of the latter groups showed poorer performance on most of the tasks, and that the spastics performed more poorly than the athetoids on some of them. They concluded that although the study shows impaired perception in spastic and athetoid children the general picture requires much more research.

Handedness

About 5 to 15 per cent of the general population are left handed. Handedness is determined by the dominance of one cerebral hemisphere over the other. Thus right-handed individuals are left-hemisphere dominant, and left-handed individuals have the control on the right side of the brain. There is also a dominant eye and a dominant foot. Tests of handedness or eyedness are usually referred to as tests of *laterality,* or of *hand or eye preference.*

In the study by Hopkins, Bice, and Colton, it was found that of 1265 cases 24.7 per cent had not developed a hand preference.[25] Out of the 952 cases who had a hand preference 53.9 per cent were right handed and 46.1 per cent were left handed. In a comparative study from eight representative elementary schools, 11.6 per cent of non-cerebral-palsied children were left handed. These figures indicate that there are four times as many left-handed children among the cerebral palsied as among those without cerebral palsy.

Handedness is of particular interest to educators and occupational therapists. It does not always follow that the hand which is least disabled is the dominant or preferred hand. At times the right hand may be preferred in writing even though the child is spastic in the right arm. Forcing the child to write with his left hand is likely to produce reversal tendencies in writing if the left hand is still the nondominant one.

Education and Habilitation Programs

Surveys indicate that many cerebral-palsied children have associated disorders creating multiple handicaps which must be considered in planning an educational program for them. To clarify the needs and

[24] W. M. Cruickshank, Harry V. Bice, and Norman E. Wallen, *Perception and Cerebral Palsy* (Syracuse, N.Y.: Syracuse University Press, 1957).

[25] Hopkins, Bice, and Colton, *op. cit.,* p. 29.

decide on the type of program required, the following classification may be helpful.

An Educational Classification

Since a cerebral-palsied child may be intellectually affected as well as physically disabled, an adequate classification must take into account both his intellectual level and the degree of his physical disability. Since the intellectual level bears more relationship to educational procedures than does the physical handicap, the following six categories are based on intellectual level as the primary determinant and degree of physical disability as secondary.

1. Totally dependent retarded children with (a) severe, (b) moderate, or (c) mild physical handicaps.
2. Trainable mentally retarded children with (a) severe, (b) moderate, or (c) mild physical handicaps.
3. Educable mentally retarded children with (a) severe, (b) moderate, or (c) mild physical handicaps.
4. Intellectually average cerebral-palsied children (including the slow learner) with (a) severe, (b) moderate, or (c) mild physical handicaps.
5. Cerebral-palsied children with adequate intelligence but with associated learning disabilities.
6. Children without cerebral palsy but with learning disabilities resulting from cerebral dysfunction.

Educational Facilities

To provide for the wide range and combinations of intellectual and physical disabilities found among the cerebral palsied, different kinds of educational provisions have evolved. While some cerebral-palsied children with adequate intelligence and a mild physical handicap can adjust in the regular grades, a totally dependent mentally retarded child with severe physical disability will require permanent custodial care. The following types of facilities have been organized for the cerebral palsied.

Home Instruction. This type of instruction is provided for children who are severely physically disabled and cannot attend a school, or who live where a school suitable for them is unavailable. Ordinarily children with normal intelligence are offered this service, and in some situations the educable mentally retarded child with severe physical disabilities is offered education by a home instructor.

Hospital Schools. These schools generally enroll cerebral-palsied children during short-term diagnostic and treatment periods. The children with severe physical handicaps but with normal or near normal intelligence are usually admitted to such schools.

Institutions for the Mentally Retarded. Totally dependent mentally retarded children of all degrees of physical handicaps and trainable mentally retarded children with severe physical handicaps require care and management in an institution if the parents are unable to provide the proper nursing or custodial care at home. No child should be put in this category until he is old enough to be properly diagnosed, which in most instances is not possible before the age of 3 or 4.

Sheltered-Care Facilities. Normal or near normal cerebral-palsied children with severe physical handicaps who cannot be taken care of at home are provided with sheltered-care (residential) facilities and are offered education in these centers.

Special Schools or Classes. Special schools or special classes in regular schools are the most common type of facility for cerebral-palsied children. In many cities these are organized as schools for crippled children and include those with other handicaps than cerebral palsy. The schools accommodate the normal and slow-learning cerebral-palsied child with mild and moderate physical handicaps, and if they have the facilities, as many of them do, they accommodate the severely physically handicapped.

Regular School Classes. The large majority of cerebral-palsied children with normal intelligence and mild physical handicaps attend the regular classes with nonhandicapped children.

Itinerant or Remedial Teacher Program. Whether a cerebral-palsied child is in a regular grade, or in a special school or class, or in a hospital class, he is offered remediation for special learning disabilities. The most common service is speech habilitation, which can be accomplished in the home or in whatever school the child is attending. Provisions for special remediation for other forms of learning disabilities (such as those in language, reading, writing, or arithmetic) are not as common but should apply to cerebral palsied children who have learning disabilities (as defined later) or to children without cerebral palsy whose learning disability is the result of cerebral dysfunction.

Educational Programs[26]

Educational procedures for the cerebral palsied include (1) the organization of programs for different ages and levels: nursery and kinder-

[26] United Cerebral Palsy Associations, *Realistic Educational Planning for Children with Cerebral Palsy,* Maurice Fouracre, ed., Pamphlet 1, 1951; Pamphlet 2, "Pre-Elementary School Level," 1952; Pamphlet 3, "Elementary School Level," 1952; Pamphlet 4, "Post-Elementary Level," 1953; Pamphlet 5, "Psychological Evaluation," 1953; Pamphlet 6, "Guidance and Counseling," 1953 (New York: The Associations).

garten, elementary school, and secondary school; (2) the adaptation and modification of physical facilities and plant to accommodate children with physical disabilities; (3) provisions for general educational activities offered all children; and (4) special individual and small-group remedial instruction for speech, language, reading, writing, and arithmetic disabilities.

The Beginning Years. As soon as a child has been diagnosed as cerebral palsied, whether at 6 months or 2 years of age, steps should be taken to guide the parents in understanding and training him. Although most of the diagnoses are made before school age, and the services of physicians, nurses, and social agencies in the community have been mobilized, there should be some coordination with the school in which the child will be enrolled later. At this stage the parents should be helped to understand cerebral palsy — how it affects mobility, the natural history of its development, and its possible effects on intellectual development. The parents require guidance in facilitating motor activity of the child at a young age, and in developing babbling, understanding of speech, and other forms of communication. Extra effort is needed on the part of the parents and siblings in developing the child's independence in motor and other activities. Although it is quicker and easier for the parents of physically handicapped children to do things for them than to teach and encourage them to do things for themselves, it is important for the child to function as adequately as possible within the limits of his condition. Wherever possible he should be helped to approximate the abilities of the nonhandicapped child in self-care, play, speech, motor activity, intellectual development, and social and emotional adjustment, even though he cannot attain normal development in all of these areas. At this age level the immediate purpose is to make the child as self-sufficient as possible before he enters school.

Preschool Programs Authorities have recommended that an organized school program be offered cerebral-palsied children at the earliest date practicable. Nursery schools and kindergartens have been established in hospitals, in clinic schools, and in private and public schools for 3- to 6-year-old cerebral-palsied children. The general program of the preschool is designed to:

1. Develop motor abilities in the child through special materials, special aids and supports for mobility, and special methods provided by the physiotherapist, the occupational therapist, the recreational therapist, and the special teacher. In the school situation the teacher is the coordinator of the program even though the specific prescriptions are given by the attending pediatrician or orthopedic specialist.

2. Develop language and speech in the cerebral-palsied child, since this is one area where the majority are retarded or defective. This includes the ability to perceive oral language and to express it, to perceive visual stimuli and interpret them, and to express oneself in motor terms. The latter includes both speech and gestures. This phase of the child's development is assisted by a speech correctionist, the parents, and the special teacher.

3. Develop in the child the psychological factors of visual and auditory perception, discrimination, memory, and other factors considered intellectual. These functions are best developed through the school program which includes language usage, listening, planning, problem solving, dramatization, imagination and creative expression (through art and music media), creative rhythms, visual and auditory memory and discrimination, and perception.[27] At this age level an environment with toys, sand tables, doll corners, and so forth, is provided so that the children will learn to respond to the attractions of the environment both physically and mentally. Through the addition of materials and the verbal and manual suggestions of the special teacher the children are helped to progress from one developmental stage to the next.

4. Develop social and emotional adequacy in the child at home and in the school by providing him with opportunities for acquiring emotional security, belongingness, and independence. The school situation is probably superior to the home in not overprotecting the child and in giving him opportunities to do things himself. The environment of the school which includes other children of the same age gives the child an opportunity to learn to interact with others, to share, and to cooperate. It offers him examples of activities which he can imitate, and at the same time the protection and help which he needs when he really needs it.

The Elementary School Program. The elementary school program for cerebral-palsied children with slow learning ability or average intelligence is an extension of the preschool program in provisions for special help, physiotherapy, occupational therapy, recreational therapy, and speech correction. These services generally continue as long as the child is able to profit from them.

Typically, an elementary class has one teacher for about ten children. The ages of the children range from 6 to 10 or 12, or at the upper elementary age group from 10 or 12 to 15 or 16. Their mental levels range from about 5 years to above their chronological ages of 15 or 16. It is

27 Samuel A. Kirk and G. O. Johnson, *Educating the Retarded Child* (Boston: Houghton Mifflin Company, 1951), chap. 7.

difficult to group cerebral-palsied children for instruction since a wide range of abilities and disabilities is usually represented in one class. Within the class individual adaptation of instruction is made, or at best two or three children can be grouped for instruction.

The curriculum is similar to that used for all childen. However, because of physical limitations, sensory defects, some intellectual limitations, and associated psychological disabilities, cerebral-palsied children are generally retarded educationally. Reading progress is hampered by the disabilities mentioned and by learning disabilities, which will be discussed in the next section. Writing is impossible for some and awkward and difficult for many. Larger pencils and paper with widely spaced lines are often provided to facilitate learning to write for those who can achieve in this skill. Schonell includes in the curriculum writing, dramatization, recitation and singing, free activity, nature study, news period, English, literature, art and handwork, history, geography, science, reading, and arithmetic.[28]

The Secondary School and College Programs. Those cerebral-palsied children who are able to achieve academically may attend secondary schools and colleges. At this level they have acquired some degree of independence and have learned to adjust to their physical handicap. Secondary schools do not change their programs of instruction for the cerebral palsied but attempt to make it possible for them to attend, even in wheel chairs, by providing ramps for them to use.

Some universities, especially since World War II, have made a special effort to provide facilities so that very severely handicapped individuals with superior intelligence can attend college. Notable is the University of Illinois at Urbana, Illinois, where a special division for physically handicapped students has been organized, with living quarters, ramps, special transportation, and special parking areas. In 1962 over 185 such students, including both undergraduates and graduates, were enrolled in the program of rehabilitation. The students take courses in many departments of the University. Special recreational facilities are provided for those in wheel chairs. Basketball teams for wheel-chair students (such as the well-known Gizz Kids) compete with other wheel-chair students from other universities.

Auxiliary Educational Program

In addition to the educational program generally supplied by the special teacher, a comprehensive program requires the assistance of parent counselors, speech correctionists, recreation and physical education specialists, and a variety of medical specialists. Such a team is

[28] Schonell, *op. cit.*

necessary to cope with the variety of multiple handicaps found in cerebral-palsied children.

Parent Counseling. Parents faced with the traumatic situation of having a cerebral-palsied child do not readily accept it. They need counseling as they go through the various stages of shock, frustration, exploration, and finally learning to accept the physical and intellectual limitations of their child. Physicians, social workers, and teachers can help them understand and eventually become a member of the team working to help the child develop physically and educationally. Parent counseling is an important part of an educational program, especially for young cerebral-palsied children.

Speech Correction. Since the majority of cerebral-palsied children have speech defects, speech correctionists are indispensable members of the staffs of clinics, hospitals, and schools concerned with these children. This phase of education is discussed in greater detail in Chapter 12, "Speech-Handicapped Children."

Recreation and Physical Education. The drive for play is as strong in the cerebral palsied as it is in other children, even though the former cannot be as physically active. Since recreational and play activities are the natural method of developing muscles, muscle coordination, and eye and hand coordination, play is both a physical habilitation and a mental health activity. It also is a socializing factor, especially for those who are being trained at home.

More than other children, the cerebral palsied need to be taught to play — to play with materials by themselves, and to play with others in a situation requiring social interaction.[29]

Medical Aspects of Habilitation

Following the initial diagnosis by physicians, there are a number of therapies and devices which are provided in clinics, hospitals, and schools for the improvement and physical development of the cerebral-palsied child and for the facilitation of his education.

Control of Seizures. To educate a child in a school program it is necessary to control convulsions which occur in one-quarter to one-third of the afflicted children. Fortunately most seizures can now be controlled with anticonvulsant drugs. Drug therapy to reduce spasticity or athetosis has been only partially successful, but the reduction of anxiety through tranquilizing drugs has reportedly been successful with some children.

[29] Sylvia O'Brien, *More for Fun — A Recreational Handbook* (New York: United Cerebral Palsy Associations, 1960).

Orthopedic Surgery. In some instances orthopedic surgery on arms or legs is performed. Fusing a bone joint or shortening or lengthening a tendon sometimes assists the child to more adequately control his arms or legs.

Braces. Braces are sometimes used after surgery, or to reinforce or stabilize certain muscles while others are being trained. Mechanical devices with splints, casts, and other prosthetic aids can help the children in the use of arms and legs.

Physiotherapy (Physical Therapy). Educating or exercising the muscles, before or after surgery or without surgery, is the responsibility of the physiotherapist. It involves exercises, treatments, and activities for muscle re-education and training in gait, ambulation, and balance. Physiotherapists prefer to begin training in muscle education and movement at a very early age and progress through the stages of development starting with the conditioned reflexes and proceeding developmentally. The use of various methods and equipment such as hydrotherapy, stall bars, sandbags, and stabilizers is common. Physiotherapists also instruct the parents in the handling of the child for the purpose of teaching him independence.

Occupational Therapy. In many schools for cerebral-palsied children occupational therapists serve as both paramedical practitioners and teachers. The occupational therapy program is also involved in the improvement of muscle activity, developing the idea of movement in the child, and teaching him self-help skills. The major aim of the occupational therapist is to evolve activities of interest to the child which will develop adequate motions and improve muscular coordination. Feeding, dressing, and undressing, as well as writing and typewriting, are within the province of the occupational therapist. The parent and the teacher are also involved in these activities, but the occupational therapist has greater knowledge of the relation of certain actions to muscle re-education.

Vision and Hearing Corrections. Since vision and hearing are important channels of communication it is important that defects in either be corrected as much as possible through surgery, orthoptic exercises, or glasses. These defects, especially the visual, are very common in cerebral-palsied children and make the inclusion of eye specialists on the treatment team a necessity.

Learning Disabilities

There are a substantial number of children who are delayed or retarded in learning to talk, who do not develop language facility, or who have great difficulty in learning to read, to spell, to write, or to calculate arithmetic problems.

Not all children with these problems have a learning disability per se. Trainable mentally retarded children, for example, are delayed and retarded in all aspects of communication, not because of a specific learning disability, but because of a generalized mental retardation. Deaf and blind children are retarded in certain communication functions, but their primary handicap is blindness or deafness, not learning disability. Retardation in reading and in other school subjects can be caused by lack of opportunity or poor instruction instead of by a learning disability. Any of these factors may produce delayed or retarded development in the communication processes but the children so affected are not considered to have a learning disability in the sense used here.

A learning disability refers to a retardation, disorder, or delayed development in one or more of the processes of speech, language, reading, spelling, writing, or arithmetic resulting from a possible cerebral dysfunction and/or emotional or behavioral disturbance and not from mental retardation, sensory deprivation, or cultural or instructional factors.

Learning disabilities of various kinds may or may not be associated with cerebral palsy, since some children with cerebral dysfunctions do not have neuromotor difficulties. The neuromotor handicap associated with cerebral palsy is only one of the disabilities which may result from cerebral dysfunction. It is, of course, the easiest to detect and diagnose at a young age.

As in other areas, different professions use different terms for the same disability. In education, a child who has the intellectual capacity to learn to read but who does not learn after adequate instruction is classified as having a reading disability. Similar classifications are made for spelling disabilities, writing disabilities, receptive and expressive language disabilities, and arithmetic disabilities. As will be discussed later, these disabilities refer to a discrepancy between the child's learning capacity (as indicated by aptitude tests) and his achievement, without reference to the cause of the discrepancy between capacity and achievement.

The terminology used in medical literature is different from that of the educator. Members of the medical profession attempt to relate disorders of function in the various communication processes to a cerebral dysfunction. The neurological concern has been with associating specific types of learning disabilities with particular areas of the brain. Figure 19, taken from Penfield and Rasmussen,[30] indicates that some brain areas are perhaps related to reading, word meaning, understanding of speech, auditory memory, and so forth.

[30] *Op. cit.*

Some of the neurological terms and their meanings are listed below:

1. The term *aphasia* has been used in its widest meaning to denote an inability, caused by cerebral dysfunction, to communicate in reading, writing, or speaking or to receive meaning from spoken or written words. Applied to adults, it denotes loss of an ability once possessed. There is considerable disagreement about using the term to refer to children who have not yet developed communication skills.

2. Attempts have been made to specify particular aphasic disabilities. *Sensory aphasia* or *receptive aphasia* refers to the loss of the power to understand spoken words, signs, gestures, or print. *Expressive aphasia* or *motor aphasia* means loss of the ability to speak or even communicate to others through gestures.

3. *Alexia* is loss of the ability to read, sometimes called *word blindness*. *Dyslexia* is a mild degree of alexia; this term is commonly applied to a child's difficulty in learning to read.

4. The loss of arithmetical ability is called *acalculia*. At a lower level, the disability to learn numbers and number relationships is referred to as *dyscalculia*.

5. An inability to recognize sensory impressions visually, auditorily, or tactually is referred to as *agnosia*. A child who is unable to learn to understand words spoken to him, even though he can hear, is said to have *auditory agnosia*. One who is unable to learn to recognize objects or pictures is said to have *visual agnosia*.

6. The inability to learn to write has been called *agraphia*. A child who has this condition can copy but cannot write spontaneously. The term *dysgraphia* is applied to a mild degree of agraphia.

7. *Apraxia* is the inability to carry out voluntary movements or purposeful acts. The inability to speak is sometimes considered apraxia, but the word is usually used with reference to purposeful motor or manual gestures. In these cases the motor function is intact.

While the medical specialist is concerned with the relation between the communication disorders and the location of the cerebral dysfunction in children, the special educator is concerned primarily with the assessment of the behavioral symptoms and with special methods of ameliorating the disability. Since in many cases it is difficult to determine whether or not there is a cerebral dysfunction except by inference from the behavior, the educator is interested chiefly in the behavior deficits rather than in the location or extent of brain damage. Knowing whether a reading disability stems from lack of development of or injury to the angular gyrus, or some other area, does not, in most instances, alter the remedial procedure. The latter is dependent upon the behavioral symptoms, not the neurological findings.

Procedures in Diagnosing Severe Reading Disabilities (Dyslexia)

A remedial reading diagnostician attempts to (1) determine the capacity or potentiality of the child for reading, (2) determine the discrepancy between this capacity and the child's achievement in reading, (3) analyze the process of reading and detect specific symptoms of poor reading, (4) determine as fully as possible, on the basis of the related disabilities present, why the child has failed to learn to read, and (5) recommend remedial procedures which will remove the symptoms of poor reading and thereby increase the reading level. The procedures of diagnosis and remediation will be illustrated by the case study of William.

1. *Determining reading potential or capacity.* William, age 11–2, was referred for examination because he had been unable to learn to read although he had attended school for over five years. To determine his capacity for reading and the possibility of mental retardation as a cause of his disability, a Stanford-Binet examination was administered. His mental age was found to be 11–6, as shown in Figure 22. Since reading

FIGURE 22

Profile of a Case of Reading Disability

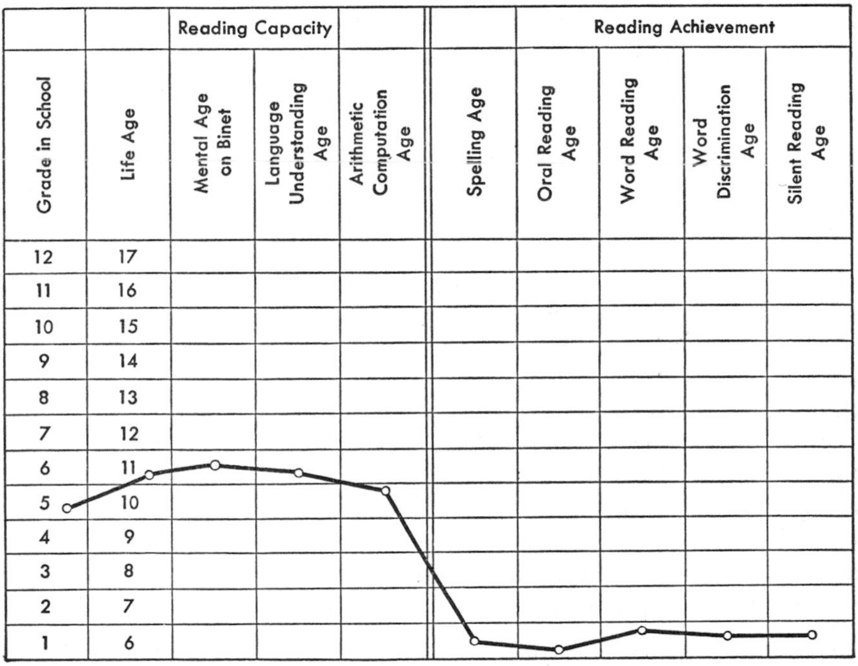

Grade in School	Life Age	Reading Capacity			Spelling Age	Reading Achievement			
		Mental Age on Binet	Language Understanding Age	Arithmetic Computation Age		Oral Reading Age	Word Reading Age	Word Discrimination Age	Silent Reading Age
12	17								
11	16								
10	15								
9	14								
8	13								
7	12								
6	11								
5	10								
4	9								
3	8								
2	7								
1	6								

capacity is also related to verbal understanding, he was given the Peabody Picture Vocabulary Test, which tests the understanding of spoken words. On the Peabody his vocabulary age was 11–3. Since arithmetic computation ability, however, does not require reading, he was given a standardized arithmetic computation test, on which he rated at high fifth-grade level with an arithmetic age of 10–10. It would appear from these three measures that on verbal intelligence, on vocabulary, and on arithmetic computation William has been developing at an average rate. He is not mentally retarded and is able to learn a subject like arithmetic in school as other children do.

2. *Determining reading level.* The next step in the diagnosis was to determine William's reading level. In addition to a spelling test, four reading tests were administered: oral reading, word reading, a test of word discrimination, and a silent reading test, on all of which he scored below the beginning second-grade level. Since according to his life age and reading capacity he should be reading at the sixth-grade level, William is considered four years retarded in reading. The observations of the examiner and the report of the teacher confirmed the test results. The latter reported that he appears intelligent in some ways, can perform as well as other children in arithmetic and other subjects not related to reading, but does not seem to be able to read or spell.

3. *Determining symptoms of faulty reading.* The next step in the diagnosis is to observe and analyze the process by which William tries to read. How does he attack words? What does he do with unknown words? What kinds of errors does he make when he attempts to read new words? To answer these questions several analyses were made, including an analysis of errors in reading. Figure 23 shows the most frequent errors made by William as he read.[31] It will be noted that his excessive errors occurred with vowels, consonants, addition of sounds, and omission of sounds. He did not make an excess of reversal errors or of substitutions. Not shown in the error profile is the fact that he tried to recognize new words by spelling the individual letters and not by sight recognition. Since the spelling method of teaching word recognition is not taught in school, we can infer that this was *his* method of learning to read because he could not recognize whole words by sight.

4. *Analysis of correlated factors.* The next step in the diagnosis was to find out why he had not learned sight words, why he made excessive errors in vowels, consonants, addition and omission of sounds, and why he had resorted to a spelling method of word recognition. The medical and social history and certain analytical tests gave some clues: (a) He was diagnosed as having mild right hemiplegic spastic cerebral palsy; the

[31] Marion Monroe, *Children Who Cannot Read* (Chicago: University of Chicago Press, 1932).

FIGURE 23

Profile of Errors in Reading

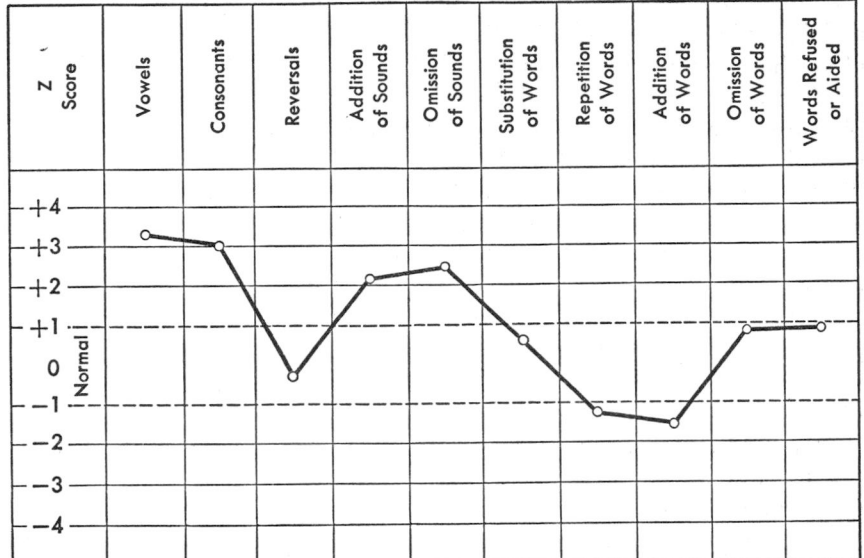

degree of spasticity was so mild that it was not detected by casual observation. (b) There were no visual or hearing defects. (c) He was right handed. (d) On a sound blending test he was able to fuse auditory sounds into words quite adequately. (e) On a test of visual memory of a sequence of letters or forms he was very inferior, indicating a deficiency in visualization ability.

The diagnostic inference from these data was that because of a cerebral dysfunction William has a deficiency in visualization ability as shown in (e) above and consequently is unable to learn words as wholes. That is probably why he resorted, through trial and error, to spelling the letters in a word, using his sound blending ability to recognize some words. But this system was not efficient because spelling the letters c-a-t would blend into "sate," and spelling b-i-t would sound to him like "bite."

William presented the kind of disability which some would label "dyslexia" or "word blindness."

The facts derived by these four steps in analyzing the reading behavior indicate that (a) William can be considered a case of learning disability since he is four years retarded in reading achievement below his reading capacity; (b) his common errors in reading are vowel and consonant errors and omissions and additions of sounds; (c) these errors appear related to his spelling method of word recognition; and (d) these factors are probably related to a visual-sequence memory deficiency (visualization deficiency) possibly due to cerebral dysfunction.

5. *Recommended remediation.* Since William can learn isolated letters and has adequate sound blending ability, a systematic phonic method of teaching reading was recommended, one which utilizes his abilities to "build in" gradually a visual sound-word recognition method. Such a phonic system has been organized by Hegge, Kirk, and Kirk.[32] Very possibly the case reported by Flesch and taught by this phonic method illustrates just such a learning disability.[33] Flesch did not relate possible cerebral dysfunction in some children to their inability to respond to ordinary instruction by the "whole-word" method, in which case they may indeed require an elemental method if they are to learn to read. This does not mean, however, that all children need a systematic elemental phonic approach.

Procedures for Diagnosing Psycholinguistic Disorders

The child with a cerebral dysfunction, with or without cerebral palsy, can have many kinds of distortions in perception, expression, or symbolic thinking. Strauss and Lehtinen have stressed the diagnosis of perceptual disturbance, thinking disorders, and behavior disorders in brain-injured children for the purpose of designing remedial procedures for correction or amelioration of these disabilities.[34] Their procedures of examination are qualitative in nature, requiring considerable clinical insight and experience on the part of the examiner.

Kirk and McCarthy have devised a quantitative test of psycholinguistic abilities for children whose ages range between 2 and 9.[35] It attempts to measure the level of development of the child in nine different psycholinguistic abilities and to pinpoint the areas of weakness.

The general idea of the test is to determine which functions have developed and which are defective. For example, a child may be able to understand what is spoken to him but be unable to speak. That is, he decodes or interprets what is heard but cannot encode or express himself in words. From the examination, we would say he has normal auditory decoding ability but a deficiency in vocal encoding. Sometimes a child can understand what he hears but cannot interpret what he sees. In this case we can say that he has auditory decoding ability but a deficiency

[32] T. G. Hegge, S. A. Kirk, and W. D. Kirk, *Remedial Reading Drills* (Ann Arbor, Mich.: George Wahr Publishing Company, 1940).

[33] Rudolf Flesch, *Why Johnny Can't Read* (New York: Harper & Brothers, 1955).

[34] Strauss and Lehtinen, *op. cit.*

[35] Samuel A. Kirk and James J. McCarthy, "The Illinois Test of Psycholinguistic Abilities — An Approach to Differential Diagnosis," *American Journal of Mental Deficiency,* 66 (November, 1961), 399–412.

in visual decoding, or visual perception. Likewise the child may be unable to express himself in words but able to express himself in gestures, where we say he has motor encoding ability but a deficiency in vocal encoding. The nine tests which have thus far been developed attempt to determine relative abilities and disabilities in children so that remedial instruction can be programmed according to specific needs. To illustrate this procedure, the nine tests will be defined, and a case study with its profile will be presented.

The Auditory Decoding Test determines how well the child understands spoken language.

The Visual Decoding Test determines how well the child understands the significance of pictured items.

The Auditory-Vocal Association Test determines how well a child can associate elements of spoken language and respond vocally with the correct answer.

The Visual-Motor Association Test determines how well the child can associate objects or pictures which belong together, such as a sock to a shoe instead of other objects. No aural ability or oral response is required.

The Vocal Encoding Test determines how well a child can express himself vocally about objects which he sees and holds.

The Motor Encoding Test determines how well a child can express himself by gestures without vocal response.

The Auditory-Vocal Automatic Test measures how well the child has learned the elementary grammatical constructions of language.

The Auditory-Vocal Sequential Test assesses the child's auditory memory for digits.

The Visual-Motor Sequential Test assesses the child's sequential visual memory.

As in the diagnostic procedures in reading, the first step in diagnosing a psycholinguistic disability is to assess the child's general intellectual ability. The second step is to assess his psycholinguistic abilities and to profile the results. The third step is to organize remedial procedures for the amelioration of the major deficits. An illustration of this type of diagnosis is presented in Figure 24.

McCarthy and Kirk report this case and the interpretation of the profile as follows:

> Case 2, M. W., was referred for examination because of the inability of the school to understand his lack of progress. M. W. entered school at the age of six. He made no progress in school because of his apparent inability to understand the teacher. It was believed that he had a severe hearing loss and he was placed in a class for hard-of-hearing children. After a year in this class, it was discovered through his speech and audio-

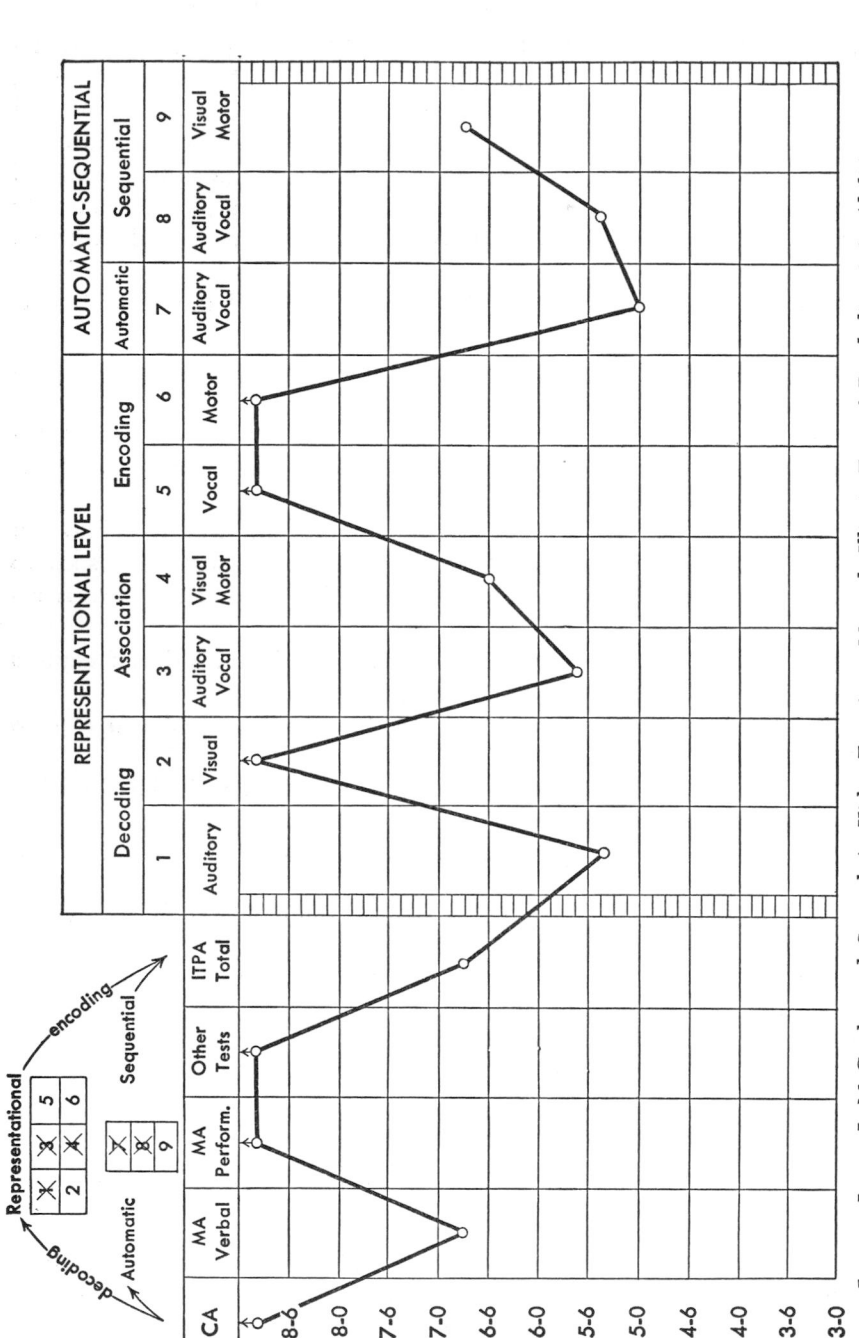

Source: James J. McCarthy and Samuel A. Kirk. *Examiners Manual, Illinois Test of Psycholinguistic Abilities* (Urbana: Institute for Research on Exceptional Children, University of Illinois, experimental edition, 1961).

metric tests that he did not have a hearing loss. He was returned to the regular grades and remained in the second grade until the age of nine. At this time the teacher reported that he was unable to learn and that he seemed unable to understand directions.

Intelligence tests resulted in an IQ of 66 on the WISC verbal and 73 on the Binet, although he was within the normal range on performance tests. On the basis of his lack of academic progress in class and the psychometric tests, he was placed in a class for the educable mentally retarded.

At age 10–1 the boy was again examined with various psychometric tests including the test battery of the ITPA. . . . On verbal tests (the Binet and WISC Verbal) M. W. is in the category of mental retardation, but on performance tests (the WISC Performance and the Ontario School Ability Examination), he is in the normal range.

On the profile of psycholinguistic abilities, the assets and deficits of this boy appear in a clearer focus. He scored above the norms on visual decoding at the representational level, and was relatively superior in both vocal and motor encoding.

Although several examiners had suggested that this boy's responses approached those of a "sensory aphasic," or "aphasoid" child, no examiner was willing to make such a diagnosis because of M. W.'s vocal encoding ability. The profile, however, shows the various deficits in the boy and helps to explain why he was unable to respond to the instruction in the classroom. Specifically, this boy's major deficits . . . may be explained further as follows:

1. The lowest point on the profile is in the automatic-sequential level in the auditory-vocal channel. The auditory-vocal automatic deficit (Test 7) means that he has not learned such auditory-vocal responses even after years of hearing them used daily. We know that this deficit is not the result of a deficit in vocal encoding since he scored relatively high in this area. We also found that he has little or no ability in auditory fusion, since he was unable to blend two sounds, like "sh-oe," presented auditorily.

2. Auditory memory at the sequential level was also deficient. He is unable to reproduce a sequence of auditory stimuli such as digit repetition. In memory of discrete visual forms, he was superior to auditory-vocal sequential memory.

3. Another major deficit is in auditory decoding. Here he is unable to interpret adequately, words and sentences presented auditorily. These results conformed to the teachers' description of the boy as unable to understand directions.

4. M. W. shows deficiencies in association, in both the auditory-vocal and visual-motor channels.

The assets of this boy, together with the deficits shown in the profile, now give us clues to a training program which were not forthcoming from the series of verbal and performance psychometric tests given previously. Programmed instruction for this boy can follow a pattern of instruction which will utilize the assets to develop the deficits. These may be described briefly as follows:

1. The superiority in visual decoding and visual sequencing indicate, from the few similar cases observed, that this boy will probably learn to read by the "look-and-say" method of teaching reading, i.e., an emphasis on the visual approach. Interestingly, he has learned word recognition by the "whole" method and can read at about the low first grade level. He has no ability to sound words or to recognize unknown words. But he has acquired a limited sight vocabulary. It is possible that this kind of profile could tell us to emphasize the sight method of teaching reading, while an opposite profile, with basic deficiencies in the visual decoding and visual-motor sequencing, would require phonic training. . . .

2. Two programs of instruction for the training of deficits are suggested from the diagnoisis. The first is to organize a program of instruction for both auditory decoding and auditory-vocal association. Such a program can utilize his visual decoding ability through such tasks as (a) showing him a picture which he can decode visually, then (b) asking him to tell which man in the picture is the biggest, or tallest, or is performing a certain task. In this way he will have a visual clue to aid him in auditory decoding and in auditory-vocal association. The second area of instruction should include training in the auditory memory of non-meaningful materials. Whether such deficits can be ameliorated by specific training is the subject of present on-going research in the training of psycholinguistic abilities.[36]

Procedures for Diagnosing Spelling, Writing, and Arithmetic Disabilities

Similar procedures are used for the disabilities of spelling, writing, and arithmetic, namely, (1) determining general capacity for learning, (2) obtaining the degree of discrepancy in development between capacity and the functions under study, (3) analyzing the process by which the child attempts to achieve in his areas of deficiency, (4) evolving hypotheses about the major deficiencies, and (5) programming remedial instruction for the correction or amelioration of the disorder.

Discussion

The concept of learning disabilities has a restricted use here. It does not refer to a deaf child or a blind child whose learning difficulty stems from a peripheral handicap which obstructs learning. It does not refer to most mentally retarded children since the discrepancy between their ability and their achievement is not great. It is used, instead, to refer to a group of exceptional children who do not fit other categories but whose

---

[36] James J. McCarthy and Samuel A. Kirk, *Examiners Manual, Illinois Test of Psycholinguistic Abilities* (Urbana: Institute for Research on Exceptional Children, University of Illinois, experimental edition, 1961), pp. 10–13.

retardation results from an exceptionality within the child himself.

The fact that cerebral dysfunction cannot be observed like blindness, deafness, or mental retardation, and in some cases cannot be readily identified even with modern neurological techniques, is no reason why the child should be neglected. The advisable procedure is to rely on the behavioral symptoms, as illustrated earlier with language and reading disabilities, and to attempt to remedy the deficits through appropriate remedial methods. The major difficulty with this concept is in the differentiation between educational retardation caused by poor instruction, inadequate educational opportunities, or lack of interest and educational retardation caused by factors within the child, such as cerebral dysfunction, which inhibit his ability to learn under ordinary circumstances.

Summary

1. Cerebral palsy is a nueromotor handicap resulting from cerebral dysfunction and in many instances is associated with other handicaps — in vision, hearing, mental retardation — and with learning disabilities in speech, language, reading, writing, spelling, arithmetic, and other school subjects.

2. To evaluate a cerebral-palsied child one must know (a) the type of cerebral palsy — spastic, athetoid, ataxic, tremor, or rigidity; (b) the degree of physical handicap — mild, moderate, or severe; (c) the intellectual level; and (d) associated handicaps in sensory functions, speech, and learning disabilities.

3. Because of the multiple handicaps in cerebral palsy, programs of education and habilitation require a team approach by members of various professions, including medicine, physical and occupational therapy, speech correction, psychology, social work, recreation, and education.

4. Educational programs for the cerebral palsied vary according to level of intellectual ability, degree of physical handicap, and associated learning disability. They include custodial care in institutions for the totally dependent and the trainable mentally retarded cerebral palsied, home instruction for those with adequate learning ability but with severe physical handicaps, hospital schools, clinic schools, sheltered care, special schools and classes, regular grades for the intellectually normal cerebral-palsied child with mild physical handicaps, and itinerant teachers for those with learning disabilities.

5. Because of the neuromuscular handicap and associated management problems, education and habilitation should begin as early as possible in the home and continue into nursery schools and kindergartens and through elementary and secondary schools.

6. Learning disabilities in speech, language, reading, writing, spelling,

arithmetic, and other school subjects which result from cerebral dysfunctions are the subject of a developing field of scientific pedagogy. Methods of differential diagnosis have been developed to assist teachers in programming instructional procedures for these deficits in children.

DISCUSSION QUESTIONS

1. Suggest alternative titles for this chapter. Give reasons for your selection.

2. In describing a cerebral-palsied child, it is customary to describe him in three dimensions, as for example "spastic, right monoplegia, moderate degree." List all the combinations you can think of in such descriptions for cerebral-palsied children.

3. The statement by Illingworth on pages 250–251 presents correlated factors found in cerebral-palsied children as evidence of causative agents. Does this evidence necessarily suggest a genetic factor or might there be nongenetic factors which result in various related anomalies?

4. In a population of 1000 cerebral-palsied children, how many of them would be mentally retarded? How many speech defectives? How many with vision problems, hearing problems?

5. In a community seventy children have been diagnosed as cerebral palsied. The children range in age from five to fourteen. Of these seventy children, twenty-five are found to require hospital and institutional care. The remainder are suitable for educational programs in the local school system. Outline the educational organization for the school system, and indicate the special emphasis in educational and medical habilitation for each grouping.

6. The neurological terms of aphasia, alexia, agraphia, and so forth originated and are used primarily in reference to adults who have lost an ability once acquired. If we do not use these terms with children with developmental disabilities, what substitute educational terminology can be used to describe the learning disabilities?

7. Give all the reasons you can think of for each of the five steps in diagnosing a case of severe reading disability as described in your text.

8. What are the major similarities between the diagnostic procedures for cases of reading and psycholinguistic disabilities?

SELECTED REFERENCES

Bender, Lauretta. *Psychopathology of Children with Organic Brain Disorders.* Springfield, Ill.: Charles C. Thomas, 1956.

Cardwell, Viola E. *Cerebral Palsy: Advances in Understanding and Care.* New York: Association for the Aid of Crippled Children, 1956.

Crothers, Bronson, and Richmond S. Paine. *The Natural History of Cerebral Palsy.* Cambridge: Harvard University Press, 1959.

Cruickshank, William M., and George M. Raus, eds. *Cerebral Palsy: Its Individual and Community Problems.* Syracuse, N.Y.: Syracuse University Press, 1955.

Deaver, George. "Cerebral Palsy: Methods of Evaluation and Treatment," *Rehabilitation Monograph IX.* New York: Institute of Physical Medicine and Rehabilitation, 1955.

Denhoff, Eric, and Isabel Robinault. *Cerebral Palsy and Related Disorders: A Developmental Approach to Dysfunction.* New York: McGraw-Hill Book Company, 1960.

Fouracre, Maurice, ed. *Realistic Educational Planning for Children with Cerebral Palsy.* Pamphlet 1, 1951; Pamphlet 2, "Pre-Elementary School Level," 1952; Pamphlet 3, "Elementary School Level," 1952; Pamphlet 4, "Post-Elementary Level," 1953; Pamphlet 5, "Psychological Evaluation," 1953; Pamphlet 6, "Guidance and Counseling," 1953. New York: United Cerebral Palsy Associations.

Gore, Beatrice S., and Stoddard Lane. *Teaching the Cerebral Palsied Child.* Sacramento: California State Department of Education, 1954.

Hopkins, T. W., H. V. Bice, and Kathryn C. Colton. *Evaluation and Education of the Cerebral Palsied Child.* Washington: International Council for Exceptional Children, 1954.

Illingworth, R. S., ed. *Recent Advances in Cerebral Palsy.* London: J. & A. Churchill, Ltd., 1958.

Michell, J. T., ed. *Proceedings of the Third Medical and Educational Conference of the Australian Cerebral Palsy Association.* Perth, Western Australia: Carroll's Pty., Ltd., 1957.

Schonell, F. Eleanor. *Educating Spastic Children.* London: Oliver and Boyd, 1956.

Stevens, Godfrey D., and Jack W. Birch. *Guidelines for the Future: Cerebral Palsy.* New York: United Cerebral Palsy Associations, 1959.

Strauss, Alfred A., and Laura E. Lehtinen. *Psychopathology and Education of the Brain-Injured Child.* New York: Grune and Stratton. 1947.

Taylor, Edith M. *Psychological Appraisal of Children with Cerebral Defects.* Cambridge: Harvard University Press, 1959.

West, Jessie. *Congenital Malformation and Birth Injury, A Handbook of Nursing.* New York: Association for the Aid of Crippled Children, 1954.

II

Orthopedic and
Special Health Problems

In addition to the cerebral palsied there are some children who are crippled, deformed, or otherwise physically handicapped, and still others who have health problems which interfere with their normal functioning in a regular classroom. More than the deaf or blind, these children represent a heterogeneous group of disabilities, each requiring a special adaptation of physical facilities, plant modification, and special aids and procedures in instruction.

Mackie distributed a questionnaire to schools and hospitals for crippled children throughout the United States and Hawaii in 1939–1942.[1] Of the 16,696 children in the study, 14,714, or 82.1 per cent, had physical disabilities. Of these, 55 per cent resulted from cerebral palsy or infectious diseases such as poliomyelitis (cerebral palsy, 17.7 per cent; polio, 21 per cent; other infectious diseases, 16.3 per cent). An earlier study in Wisconsin in 1928 found 32 per cent crippled from polio and 14½ per cent from cerebral palsy.[2]

[1] Romaine P. Mackie, *Crippled Children in American Education* (New York: Bureau of Publications, Teachers College, Columbia University, 1945).

[2] Marguerite M. Lisan, *Care and Education of Crippled Children and Disabled Adults,* Bulletin No. 1 (Madison, Wis.: State Department of Public Instruction, July, 1928).

More recent data compiled from the Chicago schools in 1954 are presented in Figure 25. Here, it will be noticed, there is a much higher proportion of cerebral palsy, although cases of cerebral palsy and of polio combined still form over half of the enrollment in classes for the crippled.

FIGURE 25

Reasons for Placement in Special School

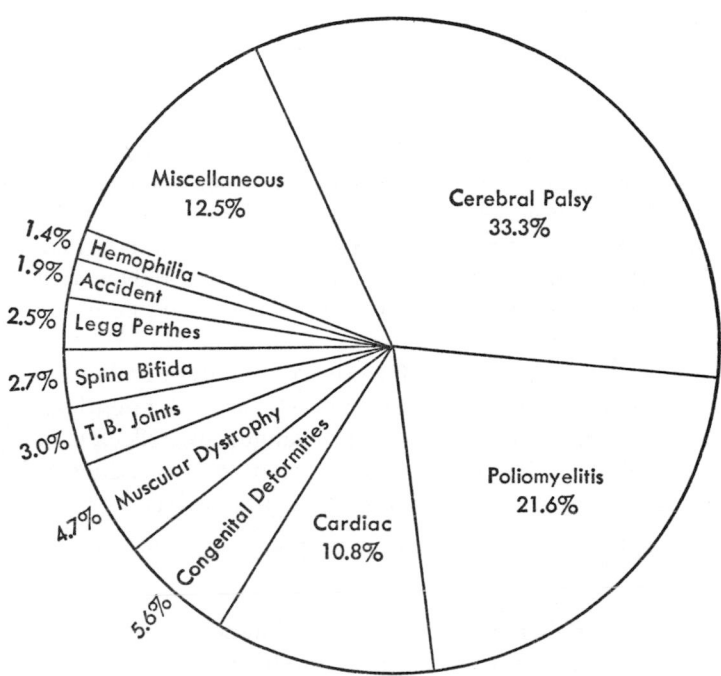

Source: *The Needs of Physically Handicapped Children* (Chicago: Chicago Board of Education, April 1, 1954), p. 14.

The higher number of cerebral-palsied children in these classes probably reflects not greater prevalence of this condition but greater efforts to enroll cerebral-palsied children in schools for the crippled. This campaign was probably a result of the increased interest and promotion on the part of the United Cerebral Palsy Associations and the National Society for Crippled Children and Adults.

These children, whose physical needs require some modifications and adaptations of school practice, have been classified into two broad categories, (a) crippled or orthopedically handicapped children and (b) children with special health problems.

277

The Crippled Child

The crippled child is one who has an orthopedic impairment interfering with the normal functions of the bones, joints, or muscles to such an extent that special arrangements must be made by the school. Included in the category of the crippled are (1) children who are born with handicaps (congenital anomalies) such as dislocated hips or joints, clubfeet, spina bifida (a congenital anomaly affecting the spinal cord), and other conditions, and (2) children who acquire a crippling condition through accidents or through infection, such as poliomyelitis (infantile paralysis), tuberculosis of the bones or joints, and so forth.

The prevention and treatment of crippling in children has been and is primarily a medical problem. But since children who already are crippled require education, and since many conditions cannot be prevented or cured, it has been necessary to organize special educational programs. According to Solenberger, the first public school for crippled children in the United States was organized in Chicago in 1899 and opened in 1900.[3] Similar classes were opened in New York in 1906, in Detroit and Cleveland in 1910, and in Philadelphia and Baltimore in 1913.

The type of program suitable for crippled children is dependent upon the type of children requiring special educational attention. As was pointed out earlier, social and medical changes are reflected in changes in the kind of crippling problem most frequently needing help. The following conditions are common in varying proportions.

Cerebral Palsy. Cerebral palsy was discussed in the preceding chapter.

Poliomyelitis. Poliomyelitis, known as infantile paralysis, accounted for the largest single enrollment of children in schools for the crippled in 1939–1942, prior to the greater influx of cerebral-palsied children. This contagious disease is caused by a virus which in some cases attacks the gray matter of the spinal cord and paralyzes the individual. In some communities epidemics of poliomyelitis have required the expansion or organization of programs for crippled children.

There is now hope that poliomyelitis will disappear and that within the next twenty years few, if any, children will be crippled by it. This hope is based on discovery of the Salk vaccine, which as early as 1956 had cut the incidence of paralytic polio in the United States by one-half.[4]

[3] Edith Reeves Solenberger, *Public School Classes for Crippled Children*, U.S. Department of the Interior, Bulletin No. 10 (Washington: Government Printing Office, 1918).

[4] *1957 Britannica Book of the Year* (Chicago: Encyclopaedia Britannica, Inc., 1957), p. 619.

A live polio vaccine in pill form has recently been sanctioned by the U.S. Public Health Service. Although easier to administer than the Salk vaccine, which requires a series of injections, this oral vaccine at present guards against only one rather than four types of polio. These measures may eventually make poliomyelitis as infrequent as diphtheria and smallpox have become owing to injections and vaccinations.

Other Infectious Diseases. Tuberculosis of the bone, osteomyelitis, and arthritis are examples of other infectious diseases having crippling effects which require special programs. Here, too, much medical progress has been made in remediation.

Congenital Anomalies. Children are sometimes born with defects of nerves, muscles, or bones, the result either of inheritance or of a defect in development during the prenatal period. Spina bifida is a condition in which the bony elements of the spine have not made a complete closure, so that some of the nerves protrude. It commonly involves the lower part of the vertebral column. In many cases the child lacks bowel and bladder control. Other congenital defects include clubfeet or clubbed hands, the absence of an arm or arms, or defects in the legs, neck, or hips.

Traumatic Conditions. Accidents such as burns, fractures, and amputations of the legs or arms mean that children must often spend long convalescent periods in hospitals or at home. Many conditions resulting from accidents are temporary, and special instruction in the home or hospital is offered until the child is able to return to his regular school.

Other Crippling Conditions. A small proportion of children are classified as having miscellaneous conditions: defective posture, such as lordosis (curvature of the spine), wry neck, muscular dystrophy (a progressive deterioration of the muscles), and other deforming or crippling conditions.

Special Health Problems

Children with special health problems are those whose weakened physical condition renders them relatively inactive or requires special health precautions in school. Children who have cardiac (heart) anomalies, tuberculosis, anemia, epilepsy, and other abnormal physiological conditions, and those who are undernourished have been termed "delicate children" or "children with low vitality."

Epilepsy. Epileptic children logically could have been discussed in the chapter on cerebral palsy since epilepsy is a cerebral dysfunction.

They are discussed here because they require medication and management rather than physical rehabilitation.

Epilepsy has been a frightening condition because of the nature of the seizures, which appear quite disturbing to others and particularly to children in school. Not all seizures are of a severe type, however. Actually four types of epilepsy have been identified. The best-known is the *grand mal* type, the true convulsion in which the individual falls and loses consciousness. In *petit mal* the individual may lose consciousness only momentarily. The eyes stare and the eyelids twitch, but there is no convulsion of the body. In *psychomotor epilepsy* one may have short periods of amnesia. He may stare, mumble, or drop things. *Jacksonian epilepsy* is a convulsion of one side of the body, beginning at the foot and working up one arm.

Schools for epileptic children were originally organized because educators felt that a regular teacher could not cope with major convulsions in a classroom and that these children needed attention in a special class or special school. Within the last two decades, however, various anticonvulsant drugs have been successful in greatly controlling seizures without making the child sleepy or sluggish. This advance in medicine has made it possible to retain many epileptic children in the regular grades if they are of average intelligence and have no other disabilities. The necessity for special schools and classes or special education for the epileptic is diminishing.

It should be remembered that convulsions may occur in conjunction with other handicaps. For example, convulsions are associated with cerebral palsy and are frequent among the brain-damaged and severe mental defectives. Special educational provisions for epileptic children who have other handicaps are still necessary.

Cardiac Conditions. Children with heart conditions constitute 10 to 15 per cent of enrollees in special schools for the crippled. Although these children are not crippled in an orthopedic sense, they are thought of as having crippled hearts and as requiring special provisions in a school.

Some children are born with congenital heart conditions. Others acquire the condition, principally from an attack of rheumatic fever, which most often strikes children of school age and sometimes permanently affects the heart.

Most children with heart conditions are able to attend the regular school as long as the teacher is aware of the condition and is able to follow the physician's recommendations in controlling the activity of the child. If the child is confined to the home for certain periods, a home teacher is provided.

Tuberculosis. Children with tuberculosis have been confined to sanatoriums or hospitals during the active stages, and education has been furnished them in these residential centers. With advances in the medical treatment of tuberculosis and the efforts of the National Tuberculosis and Health Association this disease is gradually coming under control. The number of children with tuberculosis in sanatoriums and special schools is decreasing while those who have contracted the disease can now be treated early and effectively in short periods of time and returned to the regular grades. It is anticipated that the need for special education for tubercular children will diminish further.

Other Special Health Conditions. Other health conditions requiring certain precautions in school and at home include *diabetes*, which requires control of diet; *allergies*, which may require control of temperature, atmospheric conditions, and/or diet; *malnutrition*, including overweight and underweight, and similar conditions. Children so affected do not have more learning disabilities than normal, nor do they require different curriculums or special methods of instruction since they learn like other children. Organization of schools and classes for them is primarily to facilitate health and to adapt instruction to reduced strength, energy, or motivation and to personality factors. The large majority of such children can be enrolled in the regular grades.

Special Educational Organizations

Organized programs for children with crippling conditions and special health problems vary with the community and with the type and degree of handicap.

Classes for Crippled Children

Mackie has classified the various types of educational organizations into nine groups, as follows:[5]

Type I. School for Crippled. This type of school is usually only for crippled children but in some instances also includes cardiac children.

Type II. School for Various Types of Handicapped. This school enrolls all sorts of physically handicapped children including those with hearing and vision defects.

Type III. Center for Crippled Children in School for Normal Children. Consisting of one or more classes for crippled children in a school for normal children, such a center is sometimes for crippled children only

[5] Mackie, *op. cit.*, pp. 13–14.

and sometimes for crippled children and other types of handicapped children.

Type IV. Single Multigrade Class for Crippled Children in School for Normal Children. A single class but made up of many grades, as in the old-fashioned country school, is often found in smaller communities where there are only a few crippled children in the school system, necessitating a wide age range of crippled children in each class.

Type V. Residential Institution Class. Children who are chronic cases and who require long-time general care are enrolled in residential institution classes.

Type VI. Convalescent Home Class. Children are assigned to convalescent homes after serious illness or during an intermediate period between hospital care and return to the home. The classes in these centers continue the education of the children while they are convalescing.

Type VII. Hospital Class. Education in hospitals consists of bedside teaching as well as small-group instruction.

Type VIII. Sanatorium Class. Sanatorium classes are usually for children with bone and joint tuberculosis who are confined to sanatoriums.

Type IX. Home Instruction. Teachers are assigned to homes of children who are unable to attend regular classes or classes for the physically handicapped. This is an interim program and continues until the child is able to return to school.

Special Classes for Special Health Problems

In addition to classes for crippled children, classes have been established for children with special health problems (sometimes called "delicate children," or children with "low vitality") providing programs for the improvement of their health, such as rest periods, varying degrees of activity, and diet where necessary, not common in regular grades.

It should be pointed out that enrollment in these special classes has not increased over the years as it has for some other types of exceptional children. From Table II in Chapter 1 it can be noted that enrollment in classes for special health problems was higher in 1932 and 1940 (24,020 and 27,291, respectively) than it has been since these dates. In spite of the increase in population, the enrollment in classes for special health problems in 1958 was 21,714, a considerable decrease from the enrollment of 1932–1940. This decrease is due to advances in medical treatment as well as to a changing philosophy which allows many of these children to get the special health education and care they need while they attend the regular grades.

Special Educational Procedures

The reader will surmise from the foregoing discussion that the education of crippled children (excluding those with cerebral palsy) and children with special health problems is not as "special" from the school's point of view as is the education of other types of exceptional children. The provisions which have to be made are for physical, medical, and health reasons, rather than for the promotion of academic accomplishments. This fact is readily understandable when we consider that a child who has been crippled by poliomyelitis is not necessarily affected in the way he learns to read or write or study history. He may have psychological and emotional hurdles to clear, but the learning process is the same in him as in children who are not crippled. The adjustments necessary are physical and emotional rather than educational. If he is unable to hold his book or to write because of the physical handicap, it becomes necessary to develop devices which will facilitate his holding a book or communicating on paper. In other words, the "special" part of the school becomes an adaptation of the physical surroundings for the facilitation of learning, rather than the devising of special methods of teaching, such as braille for the blind.

Special Adaptations and Modifications

Educational programs in special schools and special classes can justify themselves only when the necessary adaptations and modifications cannot be accomplished in the regular grades. Because of the heterogeneity of crippling conditions it is difficult to describe facilities for all of the children. One child may be crippled in one arm, another in both arms but not in the legs, and another in both legs but not in the arms. One is mobile in the classroom, another is mobile on crutches, and still another is confined to a wheel chair. Some of the conditions are of long standing; others may be of short duration. With these differences in physical abilities in mind it becomes obvious that we can consider here only the more general types of modification.

School Housing. Some school buildings with slippery floors, swinging doors, easily overturned equipment, stairways to maneuver, and other features which are taken in stride by the vigorous nonhandicapped child are not suitable for crippled children. If a regular school is to enroll crippled children in either regular or special classes, or if a special school is designed, it will be necessary to make adjustments in the physical plant for them. Ramps, elevators, sturdy equipment, hand rails, wide hallways, and spacious classrooms are designed to encourage the child to be as independent as possible and to promote freedom of movement and physical activity. In addition, lavatories should be readily available and equipped with hand rails and other aids to facilitate independence. In new schools or remodeled older ones doors should be wide enough for wheel chairs, floors should be covered with rubber tile, and there should be sufficient storage space for wheeled cubicles and wheel chairs.

Transportation. The transportation phase of the program for crippled children and those with health problems is expensive. Most of these children will require transportation to and from school, and being scattered in many areas of the city, they will have to be transported for some distance. This means providing facilities for carrying some of the children into the bus and arranging their seating for comfort, especially if they have severe handicaps.

Special Equipment. In most of the schools for crippled children special rooms for physical therapy and occupational therapy are equipped with necessary materials used in the treatment of muscle disabilities and in improving motor coordination. Special chairs and cut-out tables which will support a child as he sits or stands are common classroom equipment. Sometimes such equipment has to be made to specifications for a particular child if the physician in charge recommends special supports in his chair or table.

In addition to the modifications necessary in the gross physical environment, the teacher utilizes numerous aids and devices for instructional use. All of these pieces of equipment have special purposes: book racks for children who cannot hold books, ceiling projectors for children in bed in hospitals or at home, electric typewriters with remote control devices for children in bed, cots for special rest periods, and so on. What is actually needed in a particular special class depends upon the children in the class. The child who has to have support as he stands needs a standing table. The child who cannot use his hands to turn pages needs an automatic page turner. The child who can barely use his fingers to type needs an electric typewriter. The child who cannot follow a line or hold a pencil firmly needs a pencil holder or needs guides in writing. Special equipment is usually obtained only when there is a specific requirement for it since it is just an aid and has to be selected on an individual rather than a group basis.

Medical Supervision

Children are assigned to schools and classes for the crippled and for special health supervision on the basis of medical recommendations. The school authorities are responsible for the total program of the child, which includes not only the classroom instruction but also the child's health program. If the physician has recommended the child for a special class he has specifically prescribed that the child is to have rest periods and not become fatigued, or that his diet is to be controlled according to his physical needs, or that a particular postural aid is to be used to correct certain deformities. A teacher organizes her program with health and physical requirements in mind, since it is for health and physical reasons that the child has been placed in that particular class.

Individualized Instruction

Because of the heterogenous nature of the group of children in these special classes, and because of the wide range of adaptations necessary for varying abilities and achievements, much of the work is individualized. This situation, however, should not exclude group instruction for certain activities. For example, many of the children have limited firsthand experiences about their community or about the world. Secondary experiences are therefore necessary, especially through the use of visual aids, and particularly appropriate educational films and television. Carefully planned trips to centers of interest are used in many classes for crippled children.

The attitude of the teacher in these classes toward each child's personality and adjustment is of utmost importance. She must not only understand the physical problems and their requirements but also be an expert in motivating the child who is depressed and withdrawn, handling the tantrums which sometimes follow frustration, and in general promoting the personal and emotional adjustment of these children.

Personal and Social Adjustment

In working with the crippled, one of the most difficult tasks is personality adjustment. It is heartwarming to see a child crippled in body but with a friendly, cheerful disposition and a zest for doing the things which he can do. Many of these children have found a good adjustment to their way of life and a means of adapting to what could be great frustration.

On the other hand, the group as a whole shows a greater tendency toward a personalized, introspective view of life with concern over the effect of the disability.[6] Closely related to this are the findings of

[6] W. M. Cruickshank, "A Study of the Relation of Physical Disability to Social Adjustment," *American Journal of Occupational Therapy*, 6 (1952), 100–109.

Cruickshank and his associates, which indicate that many crippled children have difficulty facing social situations and situations which may imply guilt or personal inadequacy.[7]

The Cruickshank studies utilized projective techniques in determining handicapped children's attitudes as compared to those of nonhandicapped children. Other studies utilizing objective techniques produced conflicting results, some showing little difference in the crippled children's adjustment and some showing more unsatisfactory adjustment among the crippled.

As Kammerer points out, the prevailing opinion in the literature (usually without experimental evidence) "is that crippling, because it interferes with the child's intellectual, emotional, and social development, inevitably leads to a 'crippled' or disordered personality."[8] Yet his study, which compared fifty cases of scoliosis and thirty cases of osteomyelitis with norms for normal children, did not support this view. The ratings of personality traits led him to conclude, "There is no evidence that a 'crippled personality' inevitably results from physical defects."[9] Where personality problems occur they seem to be "dependent upon the number and severity of the problems confronting the crippled child."

Barker and his associates have surveyed the studies on the adjustment of physically handicapped individuals.[10] Many of the investigations were carried out on adults but some included children. From these studies on crippled children there appears to be some evidence for the following generalizations:

1. Many of the studies failed to find a clear difference with the methods used between crippled children and noncrippled children. Some, however, found that physically disabled children, more frequently than normal children, exhibit behavior which is commonly termed maladjusted. It should be remembered that even in those studies which found greater maladjustment among the crippled 35 to 45 per cent of the physically handicapped children were just as well adjusted as physically nonhandicapped children. We can conclude that, in addition to crippling, there are other variables operative which could cause maladjustment.

[7] D. C. Broida, C. E. Izard, and W. M. Cruickshank, "Thematic Apperception Reactions of Crippled Children," *Journal of Clinical Psychology*, 6 (1950), 243–248. C. Smock and W. M. Cruickshank, "Responses of Handicapped and Normal Children to the Rosenzweig P-F Study," *Quarterly Journal of Child Behavior*, 4 (1952), 156–164. W. M. Cruickshank, "The Relation of Physical Disability to Fear and Guilt Feelings," *Child Development*, 20 (December, 1951), 291–298.

[8] Robert C. Kammerer, "An Exploratory Psychological Study of Crippled Children," *Psychological Record*, 4 (1940), 47.

[9] *Ibid.*, p. 98.

[10] Roger G. Barker, Beatrice A. Wright, Lee Meyerson, and Mollie R. Gonick, *Adjustment to Physical Handicap and Illness: A Survey of the Social Psychology of Physique and Disability*, Bulletin No. 55, rev. (New York: Social Science Research Council, 1953).

2. The kinds of maladjusted behavior exhibited were not necessarily peculiar to the physically handicapped. Any type of maladjustment found among the physically handicapped was also found among the non-handicapped. If anything, there is probably more withdrawing behavior than aggressive behavior, a little more timidity, and a little more self-consciousness among the handicapped than among the nonhandi-capped.

3. There did not seem to be much evidence of a relationship between the kind of physical handicap and the kind of maladjustment. The same kind of physical handicap results in varying types of maladjustment, and different kinds of physically handicapped individuals can be found with the same maladjustment.

4. The person with a long history of physical handicap has a greater amount of maladjustment than the person with a short history of physical handicap. At the adolescent-adult level, personalities are fairly well formed. A physically disabling condition incurred at that age probably does not change the personality to any great extent.

5. The attitudes of the parents toward their crippled children, whether rejecting or overprotecting, tend to be more extreme than their attitudes toward normal children. They usually overprotect more than reject and are inclined to press for greater accomplishments.

In general the studies have not revealed important factors in adjust-ment and maladjustment of crippled children. The problems of adjust-ment faced by the crippled and those faced by the noncrippled differ more in quantity than in quality, for both have barriers to physical ac-complishment and both must learn to establish goals within their ability to achieve. The greater restriction to their activity and the lowered frustration tolerance of the handicapped, however, make necessary more careful control of the environment and greater help in making the psychological and emotional adjustments necessary.

On the basis of case studies and comparative studies available, one can speculate on some of the factors involved.

Motivation

Like the nonhandicapped, the crippled have certain hopes and aspira-tions which determine the direction of their drives. Their basic needs are much the same as a normal child's, but their means of satisfying them must be different. They sometimes require help in finding realistic ways to attain certain satisfactions which are within their ability. It is the gap between their ability to perform and their aspirations which creates tension, frustration, unhappiness, and unfortunate compensatory behavior.

It might be well to outline a few examples of basic needs which both crippled and noncrippled experience.

Affection and Recognition. To be recognized as a worthwhile individual is one of the most universal desires of mankind. Whatever his age, station, or condition, an individual seeks approval from others. Because society has placed a premium on physical beauty, strength, and ability, it is easy for a crippled child to devaluate himself because he does not have these qualities. He sometimes needs help in realizing that while he lacks these qualities he has others which also are of value. The fact that he is inferior in some ways does not make him inferior as a person. He may need more than the usual assurance, in word or deed, that he is loved for himself as a unique individual.

Self-Realization. The need to overcome obstacles, to do something well, to gain self-esteem is also very strong in our culture. Steering a crippled child's efforts in a direction where he can succeed and giving him a feeling of accomplishment may help him to satisfy this motive of self-realization.

A person's body is something he can never get away from, and quite understandably a child's concept of his *self* is greatly influenced by the concept he has of his body: his *body image.* Thus, if there is shame or disgust or fear in his attitude toward his body, this same attitude is likely to attach itself to his concept of himself as a person. He often needs help and guidance in integrating a physical disability into a healthy self-concept.

Security. There are many kinds of security — physical security, emotional security, social security. A crippling condition may make a child vulnerable in any of these areas. Physically he has many obstacles and threatening situations; emotionally he may be subject to doubts about himself and his abilities; socially he has to compete in limited areas for recognition and approval and is often uncertain as to how others may react to him.

Because of the child's inability to gain a normal feeling of security, and because often he has been overprotected at home, there is a tendency for him to rely on the protectiveness of other people and to prolong his dependency. This reaction is a normal consequence of the striving for a feeling of security. Educational efforts at home and at school should be directed toward substituting more mature and desirable ways of gaining security. Even though one cannot gain physical independence, he can do much to approximate independence, since after all, the feeling of security is a psychological phenomenon rather than purely a physical one.

Frustration

Although the crippled child has the same needs as other children, his means of satisfying them are more limited. In addition, secondary needs and means of satisfying the more basic motives are developed by the values and aspirations of the culture in which a child finds himself. Whereas the nonhandicapped child experiences many obstacles in his environment which thwart or frustrate the fulfillment of his strivings, the crippled child has two types of obstacles: (1) the usual ones within the environment which are faced by all children, and (2) the crippling condition which poses difficulties over and above those faced by other children. It is sometimes said that crippled children have a low frustration tolerance, but the opposite may actually be the case. When frustration appears, it may not be that the limen of frustration was low but rather that the frustrating stimuli were very high.

The primitive response to frustration is physical aggression, but children learn from the cradle up that aggression will not be tolerated by others. Thus the child learns to substitute other types of response — some better, some worse — by which to relieve the tension caused by frustration. The problem of frustration will be discussed in greater detail in Chapter 13. It is sufficient here to recognize that frustration is the result of a discrepancy between the goals set by the child or by society and his ability to achieve those goals. When such a discrepancy creates frustration, a crippled child (like anyone else) may respond in one or several of the following ways:

1. He may allow his frustration to make him *aggressive,* if not physically, then verbally.

2. He may *blame other people.*

3. He may *repress his desires* and superficially accept the situation without efforts at other forms of adjustment.

4. He may *withdraw into fantasy.*

5. He may react against the original goal and say it is not worth achieving, degrading others who achieve it (*reaction formation*).

6. He may *regress* into less mature modes of behavior, demanding more help from others.

7. He may *compensate* for his disability by finding an alternate interest which will satisfy the same motives.

Compensation

Compensating for one deficiency by exaggerating abilities in another area often provides much needed satisfactions. Most of us compensate in some direction or other, but we have a wider range of abilities and activities on which to draw. Once these children achieve success, they usually become more objective toward their physical handicaps and are willing to accept them. If they cannot achieve in any area, they do not obtain the satisfaction needed for adjustment.

There has been a tendency to feel that crippled children can compensate for their handicaps by high academic achievement. A number of men who had physical defects did become mental giants, but some parents and schools have pushed children too hard in this area. Not all children can achieve in intellectual pursuits. Perhaps this is not the direction of compensation for them. Some may gain satisfaction from social and personal achievement, others in aesthetics. All that can be said in this respect is that attempts should be made to determine the areas in which these children can really achieve to their own satisfaction.

Importance of the Home Contacts

In studying crippled children an analysis of the home must be made. It is difficult for a parent to accept a handicapped child, especially at the time the handicap is first discovered. This is a major trauma for parents. Should they institutionalize the child or keep him at home? How will the other children in the family be affected? What goes on in the minds of parents and in their dreams is not known. Teachers sometimes see just the end result, the oversolicitation or apparent rejection by the parents. An educational program cannot be organized without taking into consideration what has happened to both child and parents during the child's infancy and early childhood. That is the important age for socialization, for the factors of personal security, self-concept, and a feeling of belonging are important in adjustment. If a child has good personal security and stability during the first seven years of life, he can accept many frustrations.

Pupils cannot all be treated alike in school. If the child has been rejected and is insecure, the teacher must compensate for the home and give him additional attention. If the child has had too much attention at home and has security but no independence, the teacher must use "scientific neglect," which is neglect according to a plan and not based on feelings and emotions.

The Role of the School

Can a child develop better adjustment in a school for crippled children or is it better for him to be in classes for normal children when possible? Little evidence for either point of view is forthcoming. The consensus of opinion, however, is that he should be placed with normal children unless other factors counterindicate such placement.

Force, studying the social acceptance and social relationship of physically handicapped children who were educated in classes for normal children, found that the orthopedically handicapped children were chosen fewer times as playmates, friends, and workmates than other children.[11] This finding, however, although showing lack of popularity of crippled children in regular grades, does not necessarily indicate that they would be better accepted if they were in a special class for crippled children.

Naturally, crippled children in a class for normal children face certain kinds of frustration which do not exist in a special class. They cannot play like other children and with other children in games requiring mobility such as football or baseball. In a special class, games and activities are designed for children with little mobility; hence the problem does not appear. It is likely that the most realistic program for crippled children will be a combination of (1) association with other children with handicaps for the purpose of giving them insight into the problems and achievements of the handicapped and a sense of belongingness to one group, and (2) association with nonhandicapped children so that they will learn about the activities of normal children. When this group becomes too frustrating, they can identify with the handicapped for their own security. When they attain security and some independence, they can then tolerate the problems which arise when they are with nonhandicapped children. Both environments are probably more desirable than either one alone.

Summary

1. Crippled children are those who have orthopedic impairments which interfere with the normal functioning of the bones, muscles, or joints. Children with special health problems are those who, because of some health condition, are relatively inactive and require unusual health precautions in school.

2. Special educational provisions are made for these children in hospital classes, convalescent home classes, sanatoriums, residential schools, and in their own homes as well as in day classes in special buildings, in centers or units in the regular schools, and in single multigrade classes.

3. The educational adaptations are similar to the physical adaptations and treatment required for cerebral-palsied children with emphasis on changing the physical environment in such a way as to facilitate the educational program.

4. Crippled children experience the same needs for recognition, security, and self-esteem as do normal children but often have to have guid-

---

[11] Dewey G. Force, Jr., *"Social Status of Physically Handicapped Children," Journal of Exceptional Children,* 23 (December, 1956), 104–107, 132.

ance in adjusting to their handicap and finding compensatory satisfactions.

DISCUSSION QUESTIONS

1. Figure 25 shows the percentage of various physically handicapped children in the Chicago schools in 1954. Considering the preventive measures which have been discovered since, what will this chart probably look like in 1970?

2. Special classes for children with health problems, unlike those for children with other handicapping conditions, are either decreasing or at least not increasing. Explain why this trend is now becoming evident.

3. List all the factors which you consider "special" in the special education of crippled children and children with health problems.

4. From your knowledge of personality theory, what do you think might be the difference in personality adjustment problems between a child who becomes crippled at age twelve and one who was born with a crippled condition?

5. What advice would you give parents who have a four-year-old crippled child (the crippling a result of poliomyelitis)?

SELECTED REFERENCES

Barker, Roger G., Beatrice A. Wright, Lee Meyerson, and Mollie R. Gonick. *Adjustment to Physical Handicap and Illness: A Survey of the Social Psychology of Physique and Disability.* Bulletin No. 55, rev. New York: Social Science Research Council, 1953.

Garrett, James F., ed. *Psychological Aspects of Physical Disability.* Federal Security Agency, Office of Vocational Rehabilitation. Washington: Government Printing Office, 1952.

Health Supervision of Young Children. New York: American Public Health Association, 1955.

Mackie, Romaine P. *Crippled Children in School.* Federal Security Agency, Office of Education, Bulletin No. 5. Washington: Government Printing Office, 1948.

Mackie, Romaine P. *School Housing for Physically Handicapped Children.* Federal Security Agency, Office of Education, Bulletin No. 17. Washington: Government Printing Office, 1951.

Mackie, Romaine P., and Margaret Fitzgerald. *School in the Hospital.* Federal Security Agency, Office of Education, Bulletin No. 3. Washington: Government Printing Office, 1949.

Open Air Classes and the Care of Below Par Children. New York: Board of Education of the City of New York, 1941.

Services for Handicapped Children. New York: American Public Health Association, 1955.

Wright, Beatrice. *Physical Disability — A Psychological Approach.* New York: Harper & Brothers, 1960.

Wrightstone, J. Wayne, Joseph Justman, and Sue Moskowitz, eds. *Studies of Children with Physical Handicaps: II. The Child With Orthopedic Limitations.* Publication No. 33. New York: Board of Education of the City of New York, June, 1954.

12

Speech-Handicapped Children

Speech involves more than the ability to pronounce sounds. It calls for assimilation of sounds into words, then combination of words into units to make a meaningful whole. Thus speech becomes the tool which assists in developing a formalized language. It is the result of visual, auditory, kinesthetic, and perceptual experiences and its aim is to convey some constellation of ideas to a listener. Its lack has been mentioned earlier as a problem in mental retardation, auditory handicaps, and cerebral palsy. But speech defects are found also in all other groups of children — the handicapped, the gifted, and otherwise normal children.

In the development of speech and language in children, organic factors (such as hearing loss and cerebral dysfunction) and functional factors (environment and emotions) may produce defects, and it is with these that we are concerned in this chapter.

Definition of Defective Speech

What is defective speech? It is generally accepted that any speech which deviates from the average so far as to draw unfavorable attention to the speaker, whether through unpleasant sound, inappropriateness to the age level, or lack of intelligibility, may be classified as defective. The 5-year-old, for example, who says "wittle" for "little" is accepted without consternation, but the male adult of 21 who says "wittle" might attract unfavorable attention. When speech shows such a deficiency its user is in need of speech correction. To be normal, speech should be pleasant, should be audible, should be intelligible, and should not have any undesirable concomitants, such as grimaces, smacking of lips, or tongue protrusion.

Speech adequacy, of course, may vary to some extent in different locales. The southern drawl, the eastern twang, and the midwestern nasality might be considered unpleasant in other areas, but the persons living in these environs would not be thought subjects for clinical investigation or speech correction. Even the student from another country should not necessarily try to completely eradicate his intonations and sound difficulties. He can be assisted in acquiring an approximation of the English sounds, but perfecting them is unrealistic.

Relation of Speech Defects to Other Disabilities

In the previous discussion of learning disabilities, pages 262–274, it was pointed out that disabilities in the communication processes may be in speech, language, reading, writing, or spelling. Sometimes a learning disability in one area is correlated with retardation in other areas; in other cases the learning disability is specific to one area only. Of interest to investigators has been the question of the relation of a speech defect to other facets of development.

Since the child with defective speech may be found in any group of exceptional or otherwise normal children, he may have a high or a low IQ; he may be severely handicapped in motor skills or have good coordination; he may hear exceptionally well or be hard of hearing; he may be well adjusted emotionally and socially or emotionally disturbed; he may have normal vision or he may be blind; he may have a well-built body or suffer from multiple physical handicaps; he may be energetic or lazy; he may come from a professional home or from a laborer's home. However, speech difficulties are encountered most frequently in the cerebral palsied, deaf and hard of hearing, and mentally retarded. In addition, children who are not exceptional in any other characteristic sometimes have speech difficulties as the sole deficiency in their development, as represented in Chapter 1, Figure 5.

A direct relationship between speech defects and lack of educational achievement has not been clearly established. In a review of the literature dealing with speech and reading difficulties, Artley concluded that there appeared to be a relationship between speech difficulties and reading deficiencies but no agreement as to the extent of this relationship. On the whole, studies indicated that speech defects might be the "cause of reading defects, the result of reading defects, or the two may exist as a result of some common factor."[1] Jackson, studying various differences between 300 advanced readers and 300 retarded readers in Grades 2 through 4, found 23 per cent of the retarded readers had speech defects in comparison with 10 per cent within the advanced group.[2] Monroe found that among 415 reading defectives 27 per cent had speech defects, compared to 8 per cent of a control group of 101 normal readers.[3] Robinson found, however, that when speech difficulties which appeared to be caused by retarded reading were removed, the reading did not improve.[4]

Weaver, Furbee, and Everhart believe that research has not found an underlying variable which can account for both adequate speech and reading.[5] They feel, however, that if there is a causal relationship between poor speech and poor reading it could be accounted for in one of the following ways:

1. Poor speech habits may generalize to silent reading.

2. The reader, intent on his speech, may ignore the meaning.

3. Speech defects may interfere with rate and phrasing.

4. Articulatory disorders may result in misunderstanding of words.

5. Speech defects may cause reading to be unpleasant and result in less practice.

Development of Speech

The development of speech may be common knowledge for classroom teachers and parents. At least they may be able to evaluate roughly the progress of the child's oral communicative ability. At this point it might be of value to review the stages of speech and language development.

The child is born with respiratory and vegetative mechanisms which are adapted to the production of speech. The first weak wail at the time of birth announces that respiration has gained a foothold, that oxygen

[1] A. S. Artley, "A Study of Certain Factors Presumed to Be Associated with Reading and Speech Difficulties," *Journal of Speech and Hearing Disorders,* 13 (December, 1948), 359.

[2] J. A. Jackson, "A Survey of Psychological, Social and Environmental Differences Between Advanced and Retarded Readers," *Journal of Genetic Psychology,* 65 (September, 1944), 113–131.

[3] Marion Monroe, *Children Who Cannot Read* (Chicago: University of Chicago Press, 1932).

[4] Helen Robinson, *Why Pupils Fail in Reading* (Chicago: University of Chicago Press, 1946).

[5] C. H. Weaver, Catherine Furbee, and R. W. Everhart, "Articulatory Competence and Reading Readiness," *Journal of Speech and Hearing Research,* 3 (June, 1960), 174–180.

has rushed into the oral cavity, down the pharynx, into the larynx, thence to the bronchial tubes, bronchioles, and air sacs of the lungs, its final destination. This flow of incoming air has been induced by the contraction of the diaphragm and the intercostal muscles of the chest, which produces a vacuum in the lungs so that oxygen can be pulled into the tiny body. Then with responding precision the air stream, heavily loaded with carbon dioxide, is pushed back up the same pathway, but as it passes the vocal cords housed in the larynx, stimuli may set up vibrations so that a sound will be produced or phonated. *This is the birth cry.*

During the next several weeks, the wail becomes stronger, louder, more persistent. During the next several months the infant begins to coo and make throaty noises. By about the fourth month he is experimenting with the noises which are formed by the lips and tongue. In this experimental period he learns to manipulate his tongue and lips and his throat and voice. He babbles to himself and makes many chance sounds. He hears his own sounds and often repeats them as he plays with his newfound voice and voice mechanism. *This is the babbling period.*

The babbling continues into a *period of imitation,* in which the infant begins to repeat sounds from his environment. Often his sounds are repeated by those standing near. The give-and-take of sounds he hears and sounds he makes stimulates further speech activity. The feel of his tongue, lips, and throat, the sounds he makes and hears, the association of other people's voices with lip and facial movements all play a part in the development of speech. During the period of imitation he is still experimenting and learning to make an increasing variety of sounds and by six months he has quite a repertoire. The child profits from the presence of a listener and responder. If left safely cloistered day after day in a bedroom, closed in by a gate and with no visitors to return his speech efforts, he may become a nontalker.

By 9 months of age, if speech is developing according to the normal schedule, the baby is combining syllables, is imitating sounds he hears, and is paying attention to his own name and to "no, no." By 12 months he can imitate a few familiar words. Now he is beginning to attach meaning to some of the things he hears and the sounds he makes. This is *the period of meaningful speech,* which continues into adulthood. By 18 months of age he uses from five to twenty single words, usually names of people, things, or activities; he chatters in a jargon all his own; he understands some expressions, such as "Give me the doll," and "Get the ball."

If normal progress continues and the climate is encouraging, the child is combining two and three words by 2 years of age and using short sentences by the time he is 3, when he can relay an idea or express feeliags, desires, and problems verbally. By this time he is beginning to use past tense and plurals (although not always correctly), prepositions and pronouns (referring to himself as "I"), and he can often report his last name, his sex, the street he lives on, and can repeat a few rhymes.

During these first three years the influence of the environment is very significant. Speech does not develop in a vacuum, as is exemplified by the fact that a congenitally deaf child does not learn to talk. Less extreme deprivation produces less marked retardation. A good example of the influence of environment is the differential speech development of twin boys, A, who was physically normal, and B, who was crippled by clubfeet. The twins had been separated as infants, B spending 80 per cent of his life in an army hospital while A grew up at home. At the age of 3½, B, in braces, was brought to a speech clinic. He had no speech except some grunts and many gestures. He could work the most intricate puzzles and knew how to get what he wanted without tantrums and with a winning smile. He was also perceptive, lively, and active in spite of his braces. A, his brother, could not work the simplest puzzle, was quiet, had normal speech and an average mentality. Probably the differences could be explained by the environment. The hospital attendants had found it easy to give B puzzles to keep him quiet and difficult to take the time to stimulate him for speech during the speech readiness period, whereas A was reared in an average speech environment. B, however, made excellent progress in speech during six months of speech re-education.

Articulation may sound infantile for some time, even after the child goes to school. In fact, the 7-year-old may still be trying to master the sounds r and s. This rate of maturation is not abnormal. Poole has found the approximate age level for sounds to be as follows: at 3½ years, b, p, m, w, h; at 4½ years, d, t, n, k, ng, y; at 5½ years, f; at 6½ years, v, th (voiced), zh, sh; at 7½ years, s, z, r, th (voiceless), wh.[6]

Somewhere along the line, a minimum of 5 per cent of the future school population will not reach the efficiency in speech which is considered normal or adequate for the age level. Some children will not be talking at 4 and 5 years, some will start to speak normally but because of some trauma will stop talking, some will develop their own lingo (prevalent among twin members, who devise their own code, called idiopathic speech), some will have difficulty with sounds for a number of reasons, some will stutter, some will have unintelligible speech, some will show laryngeal nodes due to crying and yelling, and a few will even have a laryngeal web. Although a speech impairment is associated often with a physical of psychological disorder or as one of multiple handicaps,

[6] Irene Poole, "Genetic Development of Articulation of Consonant Sounds in Speech," *Elementary English Review*, 2 (June, 1934), 159–161.

there is a preponderance, as far as percentage is concerned, of speech difficulties with the outgoing, normally participating child. If the speech difficulty exists as a single handicap, it may vary from one which gives a slight degree of annoyance to one which promotes frustrating experiences, causing withdrawal from speech attempts and insecurity in social experiences.

Identification and Diagnosis

In many school systems the procedure in establishing a speech correction program follows three stages: (1) screening children in the grades to identify those requiring further diagnosis, (2) diagnosing those selected from the initial screening tests, and (3) choosing those children who require and can benefit from speech correction.

Screening Procedures

Preparatory to diagnostic testing, the speech correctionist will screen certain grades each year, depending on the routine established within the school system. Those who indicate some speech deficiency — articulatory, vocal, rhythmical, linguistic — are called back at a later time for diagnostic testing. In screening, most speech correctionists use a picture type of test, such as the Clark Picture Inventory,[7] the Boston University Speech Sound Discrimination Picture Test,[8] the Ammons and Ammons Full Range Picture Vocabulary Test,[9] the Peabody Picture Vocabulary Test,[10] and the Bryngelson-Glaspey Speech Improvement Cards.[11] Some use their own picture test cards for convenience, even though they have not been validated. The Templin-Darley Screening and Diagnostic Tests of Articulation provide a total of 176 items, 50 of which may be used for screening purposes.[12] Previous research by Templin on the development of articulation in children provides test items and norms.[13] In addition to the validated test material, objects are sometimes used to stimulate conversation for identification of other than articulatory disorders.

[7] *Clark Picture Inventory* (Boston: Communication Foundations, Ltd.).
[8] *Boston University Speech Sound Discrimination Picture Test* (Boston: Boston University).
[9] R. B. Ammons and H. S. Ammons, *The Full Range Picture Vocabulary Test* (New Orleans: R. B. Ammons, 1948).
[10] *Peabody Picture Vocabulary Test* (Minneapolis: Minnesota Test Bureau).
[11] *Bryngelson-Glaspey Speech Improvement Cards* (Chicago: Scott, Foresman and Company).
[12] *Templin-Darley Screening and Diagnostic Tests of Articulation* (Iowa City: Bureau of Educational Research and Service, Extension Division, University of Iowa.)
[13] Mildred Templin, "Speech Development in the Young Child," *Journal of Speech and Hearing Disorders,* 17 (September, 1952), 280–285.

Diagnosis

Children who are referred by teachers or parents for speech correction and those who have been identified through the screening procedure require a diagnosis of their specific problems before correction can be started. The procedure in the diagnosis includes steps similar to those described in Chapter 10 under "Learning Disabilities." These include the following:

Intellectual Assessment. The first assessment to be made of a child with a speech defect is his intellectual development. In some cases psychological tests of a performance (nonverbal) type are administered, in order to determine whether the child's delay in speech or the articulatory defects are due to severe mental retardation. Inasmuch as many children referred for speech correction have a history and a record of normal intellectual development, psychometric evaluations may not be necessary in such cases.

Diagnosis of Defect. A speech correctionist attempts to ascertain the defect or defects by (1) obtaining spontaneous vocal responses from the child by showing him pictures to be named, (2) asking the child to repeat after the examiner certain words which will identify the articulation defect, and (3) asking the child to repeat sounds in nonsense formation. Each of these procedures — spontaneous speech, imitation, or nonsense syllable routine — has its place in helping the correctionist determine the type of speech defect. From this initial assessment he obtains clues to further diagnosis and recommendations for remediation.

Determining Causal Factors and Associated Defects. If a child has delayed speech or a defect in articulation, voice, or rhythm, the next question is, Why? What factors are responsible for or associated with this difficulty? In the examination, the speech diagnostician will assess critically tongue movements and position, alignment and irregularities of teeth, occlusion of jaws, and palate intactness to note their role, if any, in causing the defect. He will survey the home environment to find whether or not factors there may be responsible for the defect. He will consider organic possibilities, including hearing impairment, cleft palate, or cerebral dysfunction. The symptoms or syndromes observed will indicate the necessity for referral to other specialists, such as audiologists or neurologists, for further diagnosis.

Ordinarily, the initial diagnosis suggests the initial remedial procedures. Diagnosis, however, is an ongoing procedure since many aspects of the child's difficulty will come to light during the process of remediation. The major purpose of the diagnosis is to assess the special defects and so lead to a program for correction. The speech correction lessons which follow will depend in each case on the diagnosis of speech defect, the severity of the defect, and the motivational factors involved.

Classification and Prevalence of Speech Disorders

The classifications of speech disorders are various, depending to some extent on whether the category is to be used in a public school system, a clinical organization within a hospital, or a speech and hearing clinic. Thus far no one has been successful in finding a classification in which the terminology is consistently logical — that is, one which is arranged totally according to etiology or one which indicates only the phenomenology or description of the speech deficiency.

Categories of Speech Disorders

In most texts on speech disorders the grouping of speech defects has been narrowed for practical rather than logical reasons to include (1) disorders of articulation, (2) disorders of voice, (3) stuttering, (4) retarded speech development, (5) cleft palate, (6) cerebral palsy, (7) impaired hearing, and (8) aphasia. This type of grouping may give the impression that there is a speech disorder called "cerebral palsy" or "cleft palate speech" or "mentally retarded speech." Although this terminology is used by the speech correctionist, the practice is unfortunate. Some who have cerebral palsy may have adequate speech, some no speech. The lack of speech may be due to mental retardation, to hearing impairment, to congenital aphasia, or to the cerebral dysfunction which caused the neuromuscular handicap. It is more accurate to speak of a speech disorder *associated with* hearing loss, cleft palate, mental retardation, or cerebral palsy rather than designating the speech defect as a distinct characteristic of another handicap.

West, Ansberry, and Carr have established categories of speech defects which they admit are still "miscellaneous, illogical and overlapping."[14] Since they do not include in their list the functional articulatory group, which is so prevalent in the schools, a modified list, as given below, may prove more valuable to the speech diagnostician:

Misarticulation (articulation defects with functional origin). Dyslalia (articulation difficulties due to structural anomalies such as in cleft palate) and alalia (no articulation).
Dysarthria (articulation disorders due to cerebral dysfunction, such as in cerebral palsy).

[14] R. West, M. Ansberry, and Anna Carr, *The Rehabilitation of Speech* (New York: Harper & Brothers, 1957), p. 13.

Dysphonia (voice disturbances, including faulty phonation or resonation and pitch deviations) and aphonia (no voice).

Dysrhythmia (vocal timing disturbances, as in stuttering).

Aphasia (symbolization and comprehension disorders due to cerebral dysfunction) and dysphasia (disturbance of language).

Dyslogia (linguistic disturbances, as in mental retardation).

Defects due to auditory difficulties (articulation and voice disturbances, as in impaired hearing).

Surveys

Two contrasting surveys made within the last ten years are interesting for general comparison of prevalence and for classifications. The Mid-century White House Conference report on "Speech Disorders and Speech Correction," basing its data on an assumed total population of 40,000,000 children between the ages of 5 and 21 years, estimated that 5 per cent are handicapped by speech difficulties. The committee reports, however, that the figures are the "lowest defensible estimates" and "leave out of account an estimated additional five per cent, or 2,000,000, children who have relatively minor speech and voice defects, unimportant for most practical purposes but serious in their effects on personal and social adjustment in some cases, and obviously significant for children destined for fields of work, such as teaching, requiring good speech."[15] Statistics on prevalence in each of the categories of speech defects are listed in Table IX.

The second study was sponsored by the American Speech and Hearing Association committee to study the facilities and organization of public school speech and hearing services in the United States.[16] In an effort to find the prevalence of various speech disorders in the speech correctionist's case load, the classification of disorders presented in Table X was sent to speech correctionists in five geographic areas. Data were tabulated according to the percentage of defects found within the speech-handicapped group.

Inasmuch as most school systems probably are using a classification similar to one of the last two, it may prove helpful to follow the briefer list (White House Conference) in this chapter, noting that mental retardation and aphasia will be classified under delayed speech, and bilingualism will be considered an articulatory defect. *A functional speech defect* is usually one which is due to inadequate learning, perseveration,

[15] Midcentury White House Conference, "Speech Disorders and Speech Correction," *Journal of Speech and Hearing Disorders,* 17 (June, 1952), 129–137.

[16] American Speech and Hearing Association, "Public School Speech and Hearing Services," *Journal of Speech and Hearing Disorders, Monograph Supplement 8* (Danville, Ill.: Interstate Printers and Publishers, Inc., 1961).

TABLE IX

Estimate of Incidence of Speech Defects Among Children in the United States Between the Ages of 5 and 21 Years, Based on an Assumed Total Population of 40,000,000[a]

(Gross estimates for all age levels, based on an assumed total population of 150,000,000, and on the same percentages, are also shown.)

Type of Defect	Ages 5–21 Years		All Ages
	Per Cent	Number	Number
Functional articulatory	3.0	1,200,000	4,500,000
Stuttering	.7	280,000	1,050,000
Voice	.2	80,000	300,000
Cleft palate speech	.1	40,000	150,000
Cerebral palsy speech	.2	80,000	300,000
Retarded speech development	.3	120,000	450,000
Impaired hearing (with speech defect)	.5	200,000	750,000
Total	5.0	2,000,000	7,500,000

[a] American Speech and Hearing Association, Committee on the Midcentury White House Conference, "Speech Disorders and Speech Correction," *Journal of Speech and Hearing Disorders,* 17 (June, 1952), 130.

TABLE X

Percentage of Defects in Speech-Handicapped Groups in Public Schools

Articulation	81.0%
Stuttering	6.5%
Delayed speech	4.5%
Hard of hearing	2.5%
Voice problems	2.3%
Cleft palate	1.5%
Cerebral palsy	1.0%
Bilingual Mentally retarded Aphasia	0.7%

Source: American Speech and Hearing Association, "Public School and Hearing Services," *Journal of Speech and Hearing Disorders, Monograph Supplement 8* (Danville, Ill.: Interstate Printers and Publishers, Inc., 1961), p. 38.

or imitative habits resulting from environment, emotional factors, or auditory discrimination. An *organic speech defect* is one associated with structural malformations or neurological dysfunctions.

One of the major difficulties in classification of speech disorders is the overlapping of categories. Articulatory defects, in which the formation, blending, and enunciation of sounds for intelligibility are involved, may be present without an associated handicap. They occur also in cerebral palsy, in mental retardation, in cleft palate disorders, and with other associated handicaps. Deviations of the vocal aspect of speech (which involves the phonation of speech sounds, as well as their intensity, resonance, and pitch) occur in hearing-impaired children, the cerebral palsied, and others. With these overlapping defects in mind, the subsequent discussions will be organized around (1) articulatory disorders, (2) vocal disorders, (3) stuttering, (4) delayed speech, (5) speech defects associated with hearing impairments, (6) speech defects associated with cleft palate, and (7) speech defects associated with cerebral palsy.

Articulatory Disorders

Articulatory disorders are those deviations which involve substitutions, omissions, distortions, and additions of sounds. These difficulties may occur as the articulators (tongue, teeth, lips, palates, jaws) modify the flow of air from the larynx by changing their positions and contacts. Learning to direct the air flow and to make rapid shifts in the position of the articulators in order to emit intelligible sounds and sound sequences is largely imitative and associative, utilizing visual perception, kinesthetic awareness, memory, and auditory discrimination.

Articulatory Mechanism

The articulatory mechanism is part of an intricate speaking system, any part of which may show abnormalities of structure or function. It includes (1) a breathing apparatus to assist in the production, formation, and direction of sounds through various resonating cavities; (2) two vocal cords housed in the larynx to vibrate for the phonation of sounds; (3) an auditory mechanism for discrimination between sounds; (4) an intact brain and nervous system for reception and perception of sounds; (5) swallowing musculature, involving tongue and pharynx; and (6) oral mechanism, including tongue, lips, teeth, palates, and jaws, which can be utilized in modifying the sounds coming from the larynx.

Malfunctioning of any of these parts may cause speech difficulty. In the mouth alone, for example, there are many parts which have to function properly. But it should be noted that many persons have malocclusions of the teeth, dental omissions, lazy tongues, high and narrow hard palates, and various other structural malformations and still have good speech. Even with these deviations, adjustments are possible without any particular effort for many persons and exceedingly difficult for others. Often there are misarticulations with no apparent structural defect. These disorders of functional origin have been attributed to varied influences, including impoverished environment, infantile perseveration, bilingualism, emotional problems, slow maturation, and overindulgence in the home. There are times when the diagnostic finger apparently cannot be pointed at any maladjustment, lack of experience, or retardation. All one can do is treat the symptoms of the disorder directly.

Symptoms of Articulatory Defects

The most common speech errors found with articulatory defects have been classified as (1) substitutions, (2) omissions, (3) distortions, and (4) additions of sounds.

Typical *substitutions* are *w* for *r*, as in "wight" for "right"; or *w* for *l*, as in "yewo" for "yellow"; or *th* for *s*, as in "yeth" for "yes." This type of error is commonly found among young children with immature speech. Sometimes a sound like *p* is substituted for almost every plosive sound, as *t* or *k*, or for the fricative *f*, as "I peel punny." The substitution may not always be consistent, for a child sometimes will substitute for a sound which he is capable of pronouncing perfectly and which he sometimes uses easily. Often the position of the letter in the word determines whether he substitutes or not, as at the beginning (initial position) of a word, in the middle (medial position), or at the end (final position).

Omissions, when extensive, may make a child's speech nearly unintelligible. The consonants are most likely to be dropped from the endings of words, though they may be dropped from the beginning or the middle, and sometimes from all three positions. Occasionally there is a stoppage of air (a glottal stop) between the vowels of successive syllables which substitutes for a consonant.

Distortions show an attempt to approximate the correct sound. Among older children they are relatively more frequent than omissions or substitutions. Whereas a younger child will omit a sound or substitute another, an older child may try to imitate the proper sound but produce a distortion. A distorted *s* sound can have many near approaches to the correct sound, as the sibilant *s* (whistling), the lateral *s* (air emitted at side of tongue), and the dental *s* (tongue thrust against teeth), all of which can be corrected by the modification of the air stream and shift in oral pressures and positions. Studies have shown that distortions (except for the lateral *s*) are more readily corrected than substitutions and that omissions are the most difficult to correct.

Additions are found in unintelligible speech or jargon, such as in the codes which siblings, especially twin members, have established, and in the speech of deaf children, who may say "sumber" for "summer" or add a vowel between other syllables, as "on-a the table."

In the broadest sense, articulatory difficulties may permeate every kind of speech deviation. Sometimes they exist alone or are associated with a concomitant dysfunction as stuttering. Sometimes they occur as one of several speech handicapping factors, as in cerebral palsy, where vocal factors such as timing, pitch, and quality merge into the articulatory defects.

Speech Correction for Articulatory Disorders

Speech correctionists, assigned to schools for the purpose of correcting various types of speech defects in children, find that about 80 to 85 per cent of their cases display articulatory deviations. This type of defect is particularly common in young children. The correctionist is therefore not unduly perturbed by the kindergarten child who is still unable to make the *r* or *s* or *th* sound. Maturation will probably take care of his speech development with a little help from the wise teacher. Since the correctionist cannot spread his time to help every minor need, he must choose the children most in need of help. Unless the young child shows extreme difficulties, the correctionist usually gives time and nature a chance to work, rather than filling his schedule with cases not actually requiring immediate attention.

The children selected for speech correction are scheduled either for individual lessons or for group lessons. If the child is given individual lessons he meets with the correctionist at least twice a week. The cooperation of the teacher and the parent is solicited in this matter in order to transfer the practice in individual lessons to the home and school situations.

Group speech correction is utilized very successfully by many correctionists to save time and also to stimulate speech and interest. A developmental speech group for the early grade pupils offers the correctionist one of the best opportunities for further studying the children's reactions, interests, and amount of language employed, as well as their adjustment among peers. Backus and Beasley advocate group work through conversational experiences, grouping children with all types of disorders together, but this type of teaching requires great skill and ingenuity.[17]

In kindergarten and first and second grades speech improvement services from the classroom teacher will help every child toward more articu-

[17] Ollie Backus and Jane Beasley, *Speech Therapy with Children* (Boston: Houghton Mifflin Company, 1951).

late speech without pointing up those who appear to be different. The speech correctionist supervises this type of program, providing the teacher with material and routine procedures. Usually the correctionist takes over once a week and the teacher is responsible for the sessions twice a week.

Bilingual students will profit from group activity rather than from individual work, but the group must include some who are not bilingual. They need help in listening to others, in identifying objects, and in speaking accurately in situational experiences.

Vocal Disorders

Vocal disorders, not as common as articulatory disorders, appear mainly in connection with (1) vocal quality, (2) vocal pitch, and (3) vocal intensity. Instead of speaking of the *formation* of sounds, one is concerned with the *production* of sound in the larynx, with the amplification of that sound in the various resonating cavities, with the pitch level and intonation pattern of sound sequences, and with the loudness or softness of vocal production. Ideally, there should be a clear tone from the vibrating vocal cords, a resonated tone which will give a pleasant quality, a well-pitched tone which is not too high for the boys and not too low for the girls, and a tone which can be heard without undue straining. One hopes, too, for an inflectional speech pattern which will give meaning to what is said, rather than a monotone, often assumed by adolescents.

Vocal Quality

The more common defects in vocal quality are found in (1) phonation or the production of sounds and (2) resonance.

Phonation. The phonation or production of sound, originating in the larynx, sometimes exhibits a breathiness, hoarseness, or huskiness, caused by failure of the vocal cords to approximate properly in order to produce the correct vibrations in the air flow. If vocalization is impeded by small benign growths, called variously nodules, nodes, or contact ulcers, or by irregularity or paralysis of one of the cords, then too much air will escape and predominate over phonation, resulting in breathiness or huskiness. In every school after an intensive basketball or football schedule, with its accompanying yelling and tension, many children will speak with hoarse and husky voices, sometimes with a whisper (aspirate quality), and sometimes with no voice at all, owing to inflammation of the laryngeal tissue and the vocal cords. If a child continues with vocal abuse on the playground, he may develop nodes on the vocal cords, which can be removed by surgical procedure or corrected by careful use of the voice. Children have been known to acquire contact ulcers at an early age from excessive crying. Abnormal growths can appear also without misuse and may affect breathing to a marked degree unless there is laryngeal attention.

Resonance. Resonance depends upon the balance of amplification in the various cavities used for this purpose — the oral cavity, the nasal cavity, the pharyngeal cavity (back of throat), and the laryngeal cavity (the phonation area). This balance of resonance is affected by the size of the cavities and the person's ability to direct amplification if he so chooses.

Two types of difficulty are common — hypernasal speech and denasal speech. In *hypernasal speech* too much resonance occurs in the nasal cavity, so that the voice has a nasal twangy quality. This occurs often in postbulbar poliomyelitis, owing to partial or complete paralysis of the soft palate. The same condition sometimes accompanies cerebral palsy. In a child with cleft palate the abnormal structure of the mouth and nose provides an open passageway into the nasal cavity and results in hypernasality. Injury to the palate, caused by accidents such as running a stick through the palate, may also cause hypernasal speech. One is not too concerned with the typical nasal (twangy) quality of children's voices because it appears to go with the high vocal pitch and the bodily tension involved in growing and maturing. Sometimes, however, it is imitated from one of the parents, and if not corrected the unpleasant habit may persist through life.

In contrast, *denasal speech* results from inability to direct the air stream into the nasal cavity for the sounds usually resonated there, *m, n,* and *ng.* When the air stream is blocked by adenoidal tissue or by tissue swollen by allergy or a severe cold, *b* will be substituted for *m, d* for *n, g* for *ng.* The difference in the production lies in the direction of the air stream. The nasal continuants *m, n,* and *ng* are produced by "humming" into the nasal cavity. The plosives *b, d,* and *g* are produced by the blockage of the air stream which is directed by the articulators into the oral cavity. Instead of "Come to see me soon," we hear "Cub to see be sood," and instead of "Spring has come," it is "Sprig has cub." If the correctionist suspects excessive adenoidal growth, he will make a medical referral with the hope that an adenoidectomy will clear the speech before he checks again to find out if speech correction is necessary.

Vocal Pitch

Generally, pitch disturbances can be corrected when the child is older. Because the growing larynx develops at times faster than the rest of the body, pitch may remain at a high-key level into adolescence. Usually one expects a natural voice change, but there are instances of voice breaks and falsetto voice which should be corrected by the time a boy starts high school or shortly thereafter. He wants to assume the vocal virility which comes with maleness and near-adulthood. Unless there is a glandular disturbance, the speech correctionist will have no difficulty in finding his optimum pitch (pitch which is most natural for his vocal mechanism to assume) and teaching him to employ it.

Sometimes a youngster has difficulty with pitch because of a rapid or irregular growth pattern. One 11-year-old boy who had this type of pitch instability insisted that he *could not* sing, while the principal insisted that he *could* sing if he wanted to. The boy refused to go to singing class and was ready to be expelled for disciplinary reasons, when a laryngologist convinced the school officials that the boy could not and indeed should not sing. He was freed from further singing efforts until he could manage his rapidly growing larynx. Eventually his height and bodily structure caught up with the larynx and he could sing again.

Vocal Intensity

Intensity of voice means its loudness and softness, the emphasis and stress used to give meaning. There may be many loud voices, especially among children seeking attention or among boys who cannot control the vocal power which comes from laryngeal growth. There may be many soft voices among children who are immature and insecure. If the speech correctionist has time to help these youngsters, it will be time well spent because of their need for adjustment to their peers.

Speech Correction for Vocal Disorders

Retraining voices is a special form of speech correction, not necessarily related to the correction of articulation disorders. Many training centers spend so much time on articulatory disorders that the vocal aspect is sometimes neglected. The ear must be trained to be sensitive to these vocal differences, and such discrimination takes more skill and time than is necessary to learn how to teach the production of sounds.

With the child too many other items appear to be important, so a nasal voice, a high-pitched voice, or a monotone is passed by as one of the nonessentials. Often growth will solve the problem. If it does not, the speech correctionist will have to deal with this problem later. It is necessary to assist the child in training his ear so that he can hear how his voice sounds. In these cases listening is the password to success. It includes listening to others, listening to his own voice by means of a tape recorder, listening to television shows for identification of different kinds of voices, listening to one's peers, to one's parents, to one's teachers, and to others who can set a good example.

Stuttering

Stuttering is generally considered a disorder of rhythm. Actually, everyone has a different speech rhythm, different timing of speech, different degrees of fluency, and observable hesitations and breaks in speech. It is only when the rhythm appears out of control that one becomes concerned with the phenomenon of stuttering.

Theories of Stuttering

From a theoretical point of view, stuttering has been an enigma to speech pathologists, psychologists, psychiatrists, neurophysiologists, and others for many years. Experts have yet to discover a syndrome or symptom which reveals a cause acceptable to everyone. West has established a ten-fact yardstick listing factors which must be accounted for by an adequate theory of stuttering.[18] These may be summarized as follows:

1. Stuttering is a phenomenon of childhood.

2. Stuttering is more prevalent among males than females (ratio between 3:1 and 8:1).

3. Stuttering runs in families.[19, 20]

4. Stuttering is found in association with left-handedness.[20]

5. Stuttering is found in association with twinning.[21]

6. Stuttering is associated with late acquisition of speech and perseveration.[22]

7. Stuttering is rarely episodic.

8. Stuttering is a convulsive phenomenon.

9. Stuttering is psychosocially reflexive.

10. Stutterers show basic physiological differences from nonstutterers: in susceptibility to allergies, age of regularization of the heartbeat, blood-sugar ratings.[23]

---

[18] R. West, "An Agnostic's Speculations About Stuttering," in *Stuttering: A Symposium*, Jon Eisenson, ed. (New York: Harper & Brothers, 1958), pp. 169–222.

[19] Severina E. Nelson, "The Role of Heredity in Stuttering," *Journal of Pediatrics*, 14 (1939), 3–15.

[20] R. West, Severina E. Nelson, and Mildred F. Berry, "The Heredity of Stuttering," *Quarterly Journal of Speech*, 25 (February, 1939), 23–30.

[21] Mildred F. Berry, "Twinning in Stutterring Families," *Human Biology*, 9 (September, 1937), 329–346.

[22] Adapted from Jon Eisenson, "A Perseverative Theory of Stuttering," in Eisenson, ed., *op. cit.*, pp. 223–275.

[23] G. A. Kopp, "Metabolic Studies of Stutterers," *Speech Monographs*, No. 7 (Bloomington, Ind.: Speech Association of America, 1934).

West claims that in the field of stuttering he belongs to the ranks of the agnostics and feels that no one really knows the basic etiology of stuttering. In his view, however, "stuttering is primarily an epileptic disorder that manifests itself in dys-synergies of the neuromotor mechanism for oral language. Its spasms are precipitated by social anxieties involved in communication by oral language."[24]

Theories which explain the stuttering phenomena are numerous but can be categorized into two major groups: (1) organic theories and (2) behavioral (psychological or sociological) theories.

Organic Theories. The theory of cerebral dominance, proposed in 1931 by Lee Edward Travis,[25] has had its advocates in the past. This theory has it that stuttering is the result of lack of cerebral dominance. In most individuals one cerebral hemisphere of the brain controls the flow of speech, while the other hemisphere remains subordinate. Lacking cerebral dominance, so that neither hemisphere takes the lead role or there is an alternation of roles, the individual stutters. For some years, Travis and his colleagues based their research on the neurological theory that cerebral dominance played an important part in causing the stuttering phenomena. If handedness was shifted to the right in one who was neurologically inclined to be left handed, confusion in the production of speech resulted. Research evidence, however, did not substantiate the theory and at present it has few advocates.

There are a number of neurophysiological theories of stuttering, all pointing to some difficulty in the neural flow, which in turn causes incoordination, hesitation, and repetition in the muscular activity of speech.

Eisenson indicates that from 55 to 60 per cent of the stutterers are constitutionally predisposed to stuttering on the basis of perseveration (persistent effect of the "no-longer-present" stimulating situation).[26] In this case the etiology is in the neurological makeup of the speaker: peculiarities of cortical development, possible competition between cortical centers for control of language function, neurological damage before, during, or after birth, and usually before language control normally is established. These are the organic stutterers. Eisenson admits, however, that there may be another group, the nonorganic stutterers, who have traits of ambivalence, overgeneralization, or repression, but he adds that these same factors may be present for children who do not become stutterers.

Psychological Theories Some theories dealing with psychoanalytic

[24] West, *op. cit.*, p. 197.
[25] L. E. Travis, *Speech Pathology* (New York: Appleton, 1931).
[26] Eisenson, ed., *op. cit.*

concepts and learning theory have been proposed to explain stuttering. These include the following.

Johnson's "diagnosogenic" theory states that parents, failing to realize that the very young child is passing through a normal stage of language learning, diagnose the child's normal repetitions and hesitations as stuttering, a label which becomes a stigma, adding fear to anxiety.[27] Then, when the parental responses show concern or are not understanding, the child hastens to get the words out before he is reproved, thus continuing the cycle of fear–anxiety–nonfluency. The stuttering of the child, then, is initially something in the mind of the parent. Eventually the child will experience "anticipatory, apprehensive, hypertonic, avoidance reactions"[28] in speech situations, which is another way of saying the child anticipates stuttering, dreads it, becomes tense in trying to avoid it, and so stutters.

Most of the psychological theories which have been proposed relate stuttering to an emotional factor which has developed through past experiences. Among these is Sheehan's conflict theory of stuttering.[29] He explains the blocks in stuttering as an equilibrium of approach-avoidance tendencies. Speech is demanded by society and the individual pays a penalty for both speaking and not speaking. Sheehan considers stuttering a neurotic symptom.

Van Riper believes that stuttering probably has a multiple origin.[30] The stutterer may have a constitutional predisposition, he may show emotional conflict, and he may come from a background of low frustration tolerance. He may have poorly timed coordinations, or his stuttering may be caused by parental labeling, as explained by Johnson. In other words, the search for one theory to explain all stuttering seems to be futile. It is possible that there are many causes for stuttering.

The Management of Stuttering

As indicated earlier, the main concern of many — the practical concern — is to be able to eliminate stuttering or to decrease its effect. In general there have been two approaches to the amelioration of stuttering, (1) symptomatic treatment and (2) psychotherapy.

Symptomatic Treatment. When a stutterer seeks help he does not seek a removal of the cause but a removal of the symptom itself. He wants to

[27] W. Johnson, "A Study of the Onset and Development of Stuttering," *Journal of Speech Disorders,* 7 (September, 1942), 251–257.

[28] W. Johnson, *Speech Handicapped School Children* (New York: Harper & Brothers, 1956), p. 217.

[29] J. G. Sheehan, "Conflict Theory of Stuttering," in Eisenson, ed., *op. cit.,* pp. 123–166.

[30] C. Van Riper, *Speech Correction* (New York: Prentice-Hall, Inc., 1954), pp. 343–350.

stop stuttering and speak fluently, without hesitations, blocks, and repetitions. Van Riper states:

> . . . When a stutterer presents himself for treatment, he has already experienced a large variety of symptomatic techniques which have failed to give more than temporary relief. . . . He has swung his arm, varied his rate of speech, yelled or whispered, used his will power, tried to relax, chanted in unison, and employed many other equally superficial efforts to avoid the occurrence of his stuttering symptoms.[31]

Explaining symptomatic treatment, Van Riper asserts that there are two kinds. The first tries to teach stutterers to talk without stuttering, and the second teaches them to stutter in a manner which is tolerable to themselves and to others. The first method attempts to teach the individual to inhibit stuttering, while the second teaches the individual to exhibit controlled stuttering. In the first, the techniques of breath-chewing, rate-controlled speech, phrasing, repeating what is said, chanting in unison, and so forth, may all serve as distraction devices, since they focus the attention of the stutterer on the technique being used. In the second, the individual is taught step by step to articulate and gradually develop fluency.

Psychotherapy. A different approach to treatment is the offshoot of psychoanalysis. Speech pathologists have recommended psychotherapy of varying degrees of intensity, from the mild mental hygiene approach to nondirective counseling and psychoanalysis. It is assumed that stuttering is a symptom of neurotic behavior and that psychotherapy is the major treatment technique for reducing neuroticism.

In outlining techniques for the prevention and control of stuttering, Van Riper has recommended indirect measures for the child in the early stages of stuttering (primary stuttering), before the problem has become ingrained and tension-producing.[32] These include: (1) attempting to remove speech conflicts; (2) keeping the child in good physical condition; (3) attempting to provide a pleasant, relaxed home situation; (4) inhibiting any emotional reaction to the child's stuttering blocks; (5) providing favorable speech conditions in the school and on the playground; (6) providing as many ideal speech situations as possible; (7) determining and utilizing hand preference; (8) attempting to utilize the child's personality assets and minimize his liabilities; and (9) acknowledging his hesitations but not giving the impression that they are abnormal.

[31] C. Van Riper, "Symptomatic Therapy for Stuttering," in *Handbook of Speech Pathology*, L. E. Travis, ed. (New York: Appleton-Century-Crofts, Inc., 1957), p. 878.

[32] Van Riper, *Speech Correction*, pp. 354–359.

For those stutterers who have developed fear and avoidance reactions (secondary stuttering), Van Riper recommends attacking the problem more directly. "The method for treating the secondary stutterer . . . points its therapy at the following goals: (1) Decrease the practices that reinforce the strength of the stuttering reaction. (2) Help the stutterer solve as many of his emotional conflicts as possible and change, if we can, the environmental conditions which tend to keep him a fundamentally hesitant person. (3) Decrease the fears and malattitudes by teaching the stutterer to admit and accept his stuttering as a temporary problem which must be faced and conquered. (4) Modify and lessen the severity of the stuttering blocks by eliminating the secondary symptoms of stuttering. (5) Teach the stutterer not to avoid fears or blocks, but to use them in learning how to stutter in an easy, effortless fashion, with a minimum of interruption or abnormality."[33] Van Riper has also conducted experiments with various procedures for alleviation of stuttering over a period extending from 1936 to 1957.[34] His techniques included desensitization; tolerance of stuttering pattern, frustration and abnormality; anxiety reduction; nonreinforcement; ego building; voluntary control; self-understanding; fluent nonabnormal stuttering; and negative practice. He concluded,

> And so we come to the end of more than 20 years of exploration, wondering how much we have actually accomplished, knowing how much more needs to be done and realizing that this therapist will not be able to do it. The will-o'-the wisp still dances out of reach but its spoor appears to be hot, as it often has appeared. It is good to grow old on the trail. Good hunting![35]

Delayed Speech

Some children do not develop speech according to their age level, or they develop only a partial understanding of language or vocal expression. This lack or retardation in speech development has been classified as delayed speech. Some of the causes of delayed speech have been discussed in previous chapters and include hearing loss, mental retardation, emotional disturbances, environmental deprivation, cerebral dysfunction, glandular irregularities, and the intangible "congenital aphasia." Pinning down the cause of delayed speech sometimes requires diagnostic services from a number of professions. The neurologist, for ex-

[33] *Ibid.*, p. 414.
[34] C. Van Riper, "Experiments in Stuttering Therapy," in Eisenson, ed., *op cit.*, pp. 275–390.
[35] *Ibid.*, p. 390.

ample, looks for evidence of cerebral dysfunction, while the clinical psychologist attempts to rule out mental retardation. The audiologist is responsible for determining hearing acuity, and the social worker, psychiatrist, or psychologist tries to find factors in the home or in the emotional stability of the child which have a bearing on delayed speech.

Delayed speech due to mental retardation and delayed speech due to hearing loss have already been discussed. An objective method of evaluation of psycholinguistic disorders relating to the aphasias has also been discussed, on pages 268–272. The procedures described for diagnosis, classification, and remediation of delayed development in psycholinguistic processes, including delayed speech, are necessary in view of disagreements in discussions on congenital aphasia. Gens and Bibey state, "It is difficult to make a diagnosis of aphasia in a child who does not present definite neurological symptoms. A significant number of exogenous children present no accompanying motor or paralyzing involvements. In many cases, neurological examinations do not produce supportive evidence of neuropathologies."[36] The authors conclude, after citing their success with an aphasoid child, that in those "whose psychological tests show a near-normal performance intelligence in contrast with severely limited verbal abilities, a diagnosis of congenital aphasia seems justified."[37] Since the term "aphasia" implies the loss of learned speech, however, some doubt the wisdom of calling a child who has never experienced verbal symbolization an aphasic.

Myklebust differentiates among the receptive aphasic, psychic deaf, mentally deficient, and peripherally deaf, according to patterns which he has established.[38] Bender, among those skeptical concerning the label "congenital aphasia," suggests that a diagnosis of schizophrenic autism would be more advisable and correct.[39] Wood defines differences according to the disturbances of symbolic language formulation.[40] For example, she states that the mentally deficient child shows a retarded symbolic level, but this is not his only area of deficiency. The deaf child, on the other hand, does not develop speech because he is unable to hear; he may, however, have symbolic language which does not require sound. The emotionally disturbed child may reject sound, but his problem is not one of primary disturbance or symbolic formulation.

---

[36] G. Gens and M. Lois Bibey, "Congenital Aphasia," *Journal of Speech and Hearing Disorders,* 17 (March, 1952), 32–38.

[37] *Ibid.,* p. 38.

[38] H. R. Myklebust, *Auditory Disorders in Children* (New York: Grune and Stratton, 1954).

[39] Lauretta Bender, "Psychiatric Aspects," in *Symposium on the Concept of Congenital Aphasia from the Standpoint of Dynamic Differential Diagnosis* (Washington: American Speech and Hearing Association, 1958), pp. 15–20.

[40] Nancy E. Wood, *Language Disorders in Children* (Chicago: National Society for Crippled Children and Adults, 1959).

Hannigan,[41] Myklebust, and Wood are in general agreement about the behavior of the "congenitally aphasic" child. Hannigan's report will offer the typical picture. Her study over a period of seven years included twenty children showing aphasoid reaction with cerebral palsy (athetoid type). Their age range was from 2 to 9 years. Seventeen of the children were diagnosed as expressive-receptive (difficulty in speaking and understanding language). When she first started to work with them, their vocalizations ranged from high-pitched squeals or grunts to a vocabulary of approximately fifteen words, with phrases used inconsistently but appropriately. Their behavior was highly distractible, uninhibited, and perseverating, and their attitude was self-sufficient and independent. Although they were conscious of situational cues, they appeared to get along very well without too many cues.

Hannigan's pattern of remediation follows the typical procedures of teaching the child to listen, having him name objects and animals, having him identify animals by the calls and cries they make, as *moo-o-o* for the cow, and having him match the spoken word with pictures.

In view of the confusion which has arisen about the different meanings of the word "aphasia" with children, and the vague procedures used in remediation, the present author prefers to deal with behavior manifestations of learning disabilities as explained on pages 268–272. The terms "delayed speech" and "aphasia" are not necessary in this formulation. Instead, the evaluation of the child will deal with a learning disability as related to *auditory decoding* or *vocal encoding* or one or more of the nine learning disabilities which have been isolated. This method of attack on the problem of perception, speech, and language can lead to specific programs of remediation.

Such an approach can also be applied to delayed speech in the mentally retarded, and as a method of differentiation between the child who is retarded in all psycholinguistic abilities and the child with the same IQ who is severely retarded in some areas of language but is near normal in other areas.

Speech Defects Associated with Hearing Impairment

As indicated in Chapters 6 and 7, another type of delayed or inadequate speech which has an organic origin is that associated with hearing loss. In many school systems, the school speech correctionist is responsible for the hearing tests of his speech cases. If a hearing loss is apparent,

[41] Helen Hannigan, "Rh Child: Deaf or 'Aphasic'? Language and Behavior Problems of the Rh Aphasic Child," *Journal of Speech and Hearing Disorders*, 21 (December, 1956), 413–417.

then referral is made to the otologist through the school nurse. Hearing aids will be selected according to the prescription of the otologist and may be fitted by the audiologist or by the speech correctionist if he is trained for this procedure.

Studies agree that there is a relationship between articulatory difficulties and hearing loss. Mase found that hearing loss is more prevalent among those having articulation difficulties than among those with normal articulation.[42] Utley discovered that a 512-frequency loss appeared to be causal to a lack of consonant discrimination.[43] In hearing impairment, speech will exhibit various deficiencies, depending on the severity and the kind of loss. In a sensory-neural loss there may be omissions and distortions of sounds in the high-frequency range (such as the fricative), omissions and indistinctness of word endings, and poor discrimination between voiced and voiceless sounds. In addition, intonations will lack intensity and stress, and the articulatory errors will be more severe and more difficult to eradicate. The person with a conductive loss, however, will hear his own speech through bone conduction and as a result will have fewer and less severe articulatory errors. Children with this type of loss will be able to improve more readily and the correction will be more permanent.

Speech Correction for Children with Hearing Losses

Corrective procedures for the hard-of-hearing child will follow general procedures used for articulatory errors which are functional in origin. In addition, amplification and speech reading (lip reading) will be employed, more intensive auditory training will be necessary, and motokinesthetic stimulation will prove valuable. Matching the child's word or sound with the correctionist's via the tape recorder is helpful.

The significance of the auditory memory span has become debatable in speech circles. Van Riper and Irwin are of the opinion that the time interval, or delay, and the inconsistency of sound production may be the cause of the inability to recall what has been heard auditorily.[44] At any rate, stimulating recall through auditory, visual, and kinesthetic cues is part of the speech correctionist's program for those who are hard of hearing. Procedures will be varied depending on the difficulties of each child.

In addition to the articulatory aspect of the hearing problem, there is a vocal difficulty. The child may speak softly as well as indistinctly, espe-

---

[42] D. J. Mase, "Etiology of Articulatory Speech Defects," *Teachers College Contributions to Education,* 1946, p. 921.

[43] Jean Utley, "The Relationship Between Speech Sounds, Discrimination and Percentage of Hearing Loss," *Journal of Speech Disorders,* 9 (June, 1944), 103–112.

[44] C. Van Riper and J. V. Irwin, *Voice and Articulation* (New York: Prentice-Hall, Inc., 1958), pp. 26–29.

cially if he has a conductive loss. He may pitch his voice high, with accompanying intonations which reflect a monotonous, plaintive pattern, if he is severely hard of hearing. Indicating high and low pitch on a piano, diagramming on the blackboard to show "up and down," and hitting blocks together to indicate loudness and softness are useful devices to secure varied inflections, lower pitch, and greater flexibility in stress.

The speech development of deaf children and the methods used in teaching speech to the deaf have been discussed in Chapter 7.

Speech Defects Associated with Cleft Palate

The congenital anomaly of cleft palate and lip in the newborn infant is traumatic to the parents because of the cosmetic appearance of the infant. It is important to inform the parents of the skillful plastic surgery and the orthodontic and prosthodontic wonders which can obliterate or ameliorate most of the deformity. As the child grows older, they find that the speech disturbances are as handicapping to the child as is the facial appearance.

The speech disorder with cleft palate and lip is due not to cerebral dysfunction but to structural deficiencies caused by the embryonal failure of the bone and tissue of the palates to fuse during the second and third months of pregnancy. If at this time development is arrested so that fusion does not take place, the child will be born with a cleft in the roof of the mouth and sometimes in the lip. Research has not found the cause of this failure to fuse, but probably Stark's study with nine human embryos showing clefts is the most authentic at this time.[45] His research indicates that development is arrested because of mesoderm deficiency. Holdsworth postulates that embryonic circulation could show a deficiency at the period of arrestment, because the "cardiovascular system develops (during the second month) to replace simple fluid permeation as a form of circulation."[46] Consequently, "defective development at the periphery of adjoining processes" would interfere with fusion and, once the appointed time had passed, growth would increase the gap so created. A number of studies have indicated that cleft palate and lip may be hereditary but do not explain what factor or combination of factors in the germ plasm may be causing the difficulty. The classic study of Fogh-Anderson reveals that inheritance is more likely to be

[45] R. B. Stark, "The Pathogenesis of Harelip and Cleft Palate," *Plastic and Reconstructive Surgery*, 13 (1954), 20–39.

[46] W. G. Holdsworth, *Cleft Lip and Palate* (New York: Grune and Stratton, 1951), p. 17.

associated with the cleft palate and lip combination than with the isolated cleft palate.[47] Other suggestions concerning cause include malnutrition of the mother, endocrine deficiency, and lack of oxygen supply.

Types of Clefts

Clefts are varied in type and extent of facial structure involved. Generally they fall into these broad classifications: (1) cleft of lip tissue, which may be medial, unilateral, or bilateral and may extend into either nostril or both; (2) cleft of the lip and hard palate, which may extend partially into the soft palate; (3) cleft of the soft palate alone; (4) cleft of the uvula, producing a bifid condition which is not serious for speech production if the soft palate is sufficient in length and activity; and (5) submucous cleft of the palate, which externally shows no cleft. Because growth occurs medially and is completed dorsally, the last part to be closed will be the soft palate, including its appendage, the uvula.

Associated defects which may occur with this condition are: dental irregularities in alignment; supernumerary teeth; a tongue too large and rigid; misplaced tooth buds because of surgery; respiratory infection affecting the middle ear, causing otitis media and possible hearing impairment; and other anomalies such as webfingers, missing ear, hypertelorism, and clubfoot.

Incidence of Cleft Palate and/or Lip

The incidence of cleft palate and/or lip varies in different locales but there is an accepted ratio of one in every 750 live births. In Denmark, Fogh-Andersen found one-fourth of the cleft palate population had cleft palate only, one-fourth had cleft lip only, and one-half had cleft lip and palate.[48] He also noted that if the cleft is unilateral it occurs more frequently on the left side, that males show the cleft lip and palate combination more frequently than females (who show more frequently only the cleft palate), and that cleft lip and palate occurs more frequently in later birth ranks. The American Public Health Association reported that in 1952 an estimated 64,000 children under 18 years of age in the United States had some form of facial cleft.[49]

Surgical Habilitation

In the past, speech case histories were loaded with information about the surgical procedures for the cleft palate child. They reported children

[47] P. Fogh-Anderson, *Inheritance of Harelip and Cleft Palate* (Copenhagen: Nyt Nordisk Forlag, Arnold Busck, 1942).

[48] *Ibid.*

[49] *Services for Children with Cleft Lip and Cleft Palate* (New York: American Public Health Association, 1955), p. 12.

or adults showing irregular lip scars, taut nostrils, and underdeveloped maxilla even after as many as twelve operations. Some of these cases responded to speech correction if the soft palate was proficient in movement toward the pharyngeal wall and sufficient in tissue so that an approximation could be made with the superior pharyngeal constrictor muscle at a point called Passavant's cushion. When this competency was not found, no amount of intensive speech correction appeared to alleviate the speech defect.

Since 1945 surgical procedures have changed from the goal of closing the cleft for vegetative purposes to that of speech adequacy. This shift in philosophy was due no doubt to the activity of the American Association for Cleft Palate Rehabilitation, which brought together pediatricians, surgeons, orthodontists, prosthodontists, psychologists, and speech pathologists to discuss the problem, not of vegetation, but of improving speech. The change in emphasis was so great that many of the medical profession began speaking of "speech aids" rather than of prosthetic devices.

It is no longer necessary for parents to be harassed by the specter of gross deformity and severely distorted, nasal speech in their child. At present there are many hospitals where a professional team, working together, decide on the time for surgery according to each child's cephalic growth.[50] Through adequate surgery and skin graftings at the appropriate growth stages the physical and cosmetic deformities can be obliterated. The procedure gives the speech correctionist a more pliable and competent mechanism for speech production.

Speech Problems Associated with Cleft Palate and Lip

The number of persons with cleft palate and lip deformity having no speech deviations is small. Occasionally, however, one will find some who have had sufficient tissue to obtain excellent surgical results, and consequently adequate speech. Others have worked conscientiously with their speech problem to produce speech without a flaw. In most children with cleft palate and lip the speech is so defective that they are often judged mentally retarded by laymen.

In normal speech the air is directed mainly through the oral cavity on all sounds except the nasal continuants, *m, n,* and *ng.* In the child with cleft palate, the muscular tissue which makes up the soft palate may be insufficient to allow a closure between the oral cavity and the nasal cavity (called velar-pharyngeal insufficiency). The air stream coming up from the larynx is therefore directed through the nose instead of the mouth. This produces a nasal quality and many defects of articu-

[50] Pediatric Clinics of North America, *The Child's Mouth* (Philadelphia: W. B. Saunders Company, 1956), pp. 995–1071.

lation. The plosive sounds, such as *p, t, k,* cannot be made because the necessary pressure in the mouth cannot be built up. A glottal stop is substituted for *l* and *t,* and sounds like *f, v, s,* and *z* cannot be channeled through the mouth. Many of these sounds approach "snorts" rather than their proper sound. *M, n,* and *ng* are usually the only consonants adequately made.

If surgery has permitted some flexibility in the tissue, then the first objective in speech correction is to relieve the tautness of the whole speech effort by alleviating tension in the jaw, pharynx, tongue, and larynx, and by making the person realize that he is starting to learn how to use a new speaking mechanism.

The speech correctionist often refers the child back to the surgeon for further examination of tissue and scars and for the possibility of a prosthetic device which will partially fill the opening and assist in the speech habilitation process. Subtelny has offered valuable advice in suggesting that the adenoidal tissue should not be removed in the child with this difficulty because the point of velar contact in a child is at the posterior location of the adenoids and not at Passavant's cushion, which is inferior in position.[51] Thus, approximation is aided by the bulge provided by the adenoidal tissue. One should add that a prosthesis is an excellent aid for good speech and also for cosmetic appearance, especially if teeth are missing or the maxilla is recessive. The tape recorder serves as an aid for listening and training in discrimination.

Speech Disorders Associated with Cerebral Palsy

Denhoff and Robinault's thesis points up the chief departure in therapy for cerebral-palsied children by asserting, "The neuromotor disturbances may appear to be the most important component to overcome, but in the long run, the associated visual, hearing, speech, perceptual, behavioral, and emotional handicaps can affect the ultimate development more than does the motor status."[52]

In contrast to the typical functional articulation case, the child with cerebral palsy may show a number of defects in almost every aspect of speech. He may have perfect speech or no speech. He may have speech which varies from jargon to a fairly intelligible effort. He may stutter, and he may have articulatory defects which are not associated with the brain lesion. In a study of fifty cases of cerebral-palsied children, Wolfe

[51] J. D. Subtelny, "The Significance of Adenoid Tissue on the Velopharyngeal Function," *Plastic and Reconstructive Surgery,* 17 (1956), 255.
[52] E. Denhoff and Isabel Robinault, *Cerebral Palsy and Related Disorders* (New York: McGraw-Hill Book Company, 1960), p. 27.

found that 30 per cent had normal articulation while 70 per cent had inadequate articulation.[53] Of the group of 70 per cent with articulation disorders, 40 per cent showed causal relationships to the condition of cerebral palsy, in 4 per cent the defects were due to other organic factors, and in 26 per cent the causes were functional.

Although some authorities define dysarthria as disturbed articulation resulting from a lesion of the central nervous system, the speech syndrome appears to be more complex. The articulatory difficulties are changed in character by disturbances of the respiratory and phonatory musculature and the resonating mechanism. In this particular condition, one cannot treat the malfunctioning of the various organs used for production and amplification of sound as a defect discrete from the articulation of sounds.

Respiratory and Rhythmical Involvements

The respiratory mechanism may fail to produce coordinated breathing patterns, thus hindering the air flow for sound production. The children affected sometimes have reversal patterns of breathing. They may acquire the habit of attempting to talk on inhalation or on residual air rather than on exhalation. In the presence of this respiratory failure speech will exhibit weak vocalization, breathiness, or aspirate quality. Furthermore, since the timing aspect for easy, rhythmical responses is affected by the respiratory deviations, the pattern of speech becomes scanning, spasmodic, staccato, or explosive, depending on the kind of control the child tries to employ.

Vocal Involvements

Phonatory disturbances due to adductor constriction of the vocal cords and abnormal tension present as serious a problem as do respiratory and lingual difficulties. This involvement will be revealed either spasmodically or continuously in unusual inflections and fluctuating pitch patterns or in monotone.

Resonance, which gives the voice a pleasant timbre or quality if well balanced, will be affected by a number of anomalies including ineffective direction of air flow, hypertonicity, or paralysis of the pharyngeal musculature (the pharyngeal cavity, which extends posteriorly from the nasal port down the back of the throat to the larynx, is an important resonator), velar-pharyngeal insufficiency (discussed under cleft palate), incorrect tongue positions (especially the humped-up position posteriorly, which will interfere with resonance balance and distinctness), and high narrow palate, which does not always permit good tongue placement.

[53] W. G. Wolfe, "A Comprehensive Evaluation of Fifty Cases of Cerebral Palsy," *Journal of Speech and Hearing Disorders*, 15 (September, 1950), 234–251.

These deviations will produce nasal, weak, and aspirate sounds resulting in poor vocalization.

Articulatory Involvements

Oral examination may reveal many structural differences and involvements which can account for misarticulation. These involvements, depending on how many of the articulators fail in the coordinating process, may result in labored articulation, often accompanied by drooling, inadequate assimilation of sounds, indistinctness and lack of intelligibility due to slurring of sounds as well as omissions, distortions, and substitutions.

Consequently, one will hear in the speech associated with cerebral palsy a lack of fine discrimination and often unintelligible articulation. These defects result from fluctuating patterns of intensity, timing, pitch, and phonation. Furthermore, this uncontrolled speech pattern responds readily to the influences of the environment, even though it may be kept within bounds in the clinic or school. One is inclined to agree with Peacher, who states, "Actually the motor basis of speech is dependent upon the coordination of the above basic mechanisms (articulatory, phonatory, resonating, respiratory) in order to effect a smoothly working system, even though the higher functional levels of integrative behavior inevitably affect these performances."[54]

Speech Characteristics of Cerebral-Palsied Children

In Chapter 10 five different types of cerebral palsy were explained. The most common, however, and those which include major speech defects are the spastic, athetoid, and ataxic. Generalizations can be made on the speech characteristics of these three types which are dealt with by the speech correctionist:

1. The speech of the spastic will show greater articulatory deviations than the speech of the other types. Speech will be labored and indistinct. and sounds will be omitted, slurred, or distorted, especially consonant blends like *sk* or *tsh*. Pitch changes will be uncontrolled and abrupt rather than gradual and continuous. Vocal quality may be husky, guttural, and tense and may show hypernasality of vowels. Saliva is likely to be excessive in sound formation.

2. The speech of the athetoid usually is slurring in rhythm and constantly changing in pitch, inflection, effort, and emphasis, not unlike the postural balance. Sounds are distorted inconsistently because of the continuous involuntary movements. The voice may be lacking in force owing to respiratory disturbances and excessive movement. It may be

[54] W. G. Peacher, "The Etiology and Differential Diagnosis of Dysarthria," *Journal of Speech and Hearing Disorders*, 15 (September, 1950), 252.

unintelligible because of the irregular movements to which the speech musculature is subjected. If there is an effort at voluntary control, the resulting coordination is much like that of the spastic; hence the term *tension athetoid.*

3. The ataxic will talk with the same rhythm shown in his walk and bodily movements. He may give the impressions that he is walking on stilts or as if he were a mechanical doll which has been wound up for motor performance. His speech sounds mechanically motivated also, for it exhibits spasmodic breaks and pauses rather than the slurring and scanning rhythm. At times his speech seems to fade away as if the mechanism needs to be wound up again. Assimilation of sounds and intonational patterns appear to be most difficult.

Speech Correction for the Cerebral-Palsied Child

The correction of speech impairments in the cerebral-palsied child does not differ greatly from that for other children. There are six major areas requiring attention.

1. Because of the cerebral-palsied child's physical difficulties in walking, chewing, and swallowing, the parents tend to overprotect or do too much for him. Sometimes the speech is delayed or inadequate, partly because the parents do not give him the opportunity to try to exercise his vocal musculature. When this situation prevails it is necessary to solicit the cooperation of the parents and to motivate speech through experience and exercise.

2. Sometimes the speech correctionist must alleviate as soon as possible the stigmata generally associated with cerebral palsy such as drooling and the protruded tongue hanging from an open mouth. The child should be taught to swallow acceptably, to close the mouth and enclose the tongue in its habitat. Again the cooperation of the parents is required since they are in daily or hourly contact with the child. Conscientious parents will remind him to swallow continuously and so prevent drooling.

3. The use of mirrors in speech correction is sometimes thought to create greater muscular tension when the child sees his own reactions. It is considered by some an unacceptable technique. Others feel that if the child is readied for what he sees in the mirror he will learn to live with his handicap and profit from the use of a mirror. He can thus be prepared for control in speech as well as for social living.

4. Language is aided by exploration, experience, and the need for verbal expression. The severely palsied child is restricted in movement and does not have normal opportunities to explore his environment. He needs experiences in motor activities. Since speech is a motor activity it is necessary to use what speech specialists call a multiple-sense modality

approach: the use of auditory, visual, and kinesthetic senses in the production of speech. At times speech correction is conducted in collaboration with physiotherapy.

5. Children do not speak unless they are motivated to speak. One of the problems with cerebral-palsied children is how to create a need in them for improving their speech. Their own efforts in exercises to correct inappropriate tongue and jaw movements or breathing require concentrated attention on their part. How to supply the necessary motivation is one of the major concerns of a speech correctionist.

6. Finally, it will be necessary for a speech correctionist to help the child manage his tongue movements, control the synergic movements of swallowing, control facial musculature (grimaces, tics) and muscles of breathing, and control inflection and intonations of voice.

Public School Speech Correction Programs

Speech correction is conducted in hospitals and clinics, through private practice, and in schools. The largest number of speech correctionists are employed in public school systems and university clinics and the largest number of children are being served in schools. The most recent survey of speech and hearing services in public schools was made by the Research Committee of the American Speech and Hearing Association.[55] Some of the results of this survey are summarized below:

1. *Titles.* Persons who render special remedial services to speech-handicapped children are called variously: speech therapists, speech and hearing therapists, or speech correctionists. The survey indicated that 56 per cent employ the title "therapist" while 26 per cent use the title "correctionist." In the midwest, 40 per cent were called speech correctionists. Many of the personnel themselves prefer the apparently prestige term "therapist" to "speech correction teacher."

2. *Personnel.* As a group, speech correctionists employed by schools fit the following description: (a) They are under 35 years of age (60 per cent), (b) three-fourths are women, (c) the majority receive between $4000 and $5500 a year in salary, (d) 42 per cent have been classroom teachers, and (e) 40 per cent hold the master's degree and 75 per cent have had graduate work beyond the bachelor's degree.

3. *State certification.* Thirty-two states have state certification requirements for speech correctionists equivalent to those for basic certification in the American Speech and Hearing Association. About one-half of the speech correctionists in schools hold state certificates.

[55] American Speech and Hearing Association, "Public School Speech and Hearing Services," *Journal of Speech and Hearing Disorders, Monograph Supplement 8* (Danville, Ill.: Interstate Printers and Publishers, Inc., 1961).

4. *Duties.* The major duty of a speech correctionist is to offer remedial speech to speech-handicapped children. Some correctionists, however, reported additional duties, such as (a) regular hearing therapy (35 per cent) and occasional hearing therapy (35 per cent), (b) regular hearing testing (20 per cent) and occasional hearing testing (35 per cent), and (c) psychological testing (2 per cent).

5. *Case load.* The average annual case load was 130 children, with 111 seen weekly. Of the latter group, 10 are seen individually and 101 are seen in groups of four or five usually twice a week, and in some cases once a week. The case load is sometimes limited by state or local regulations and sometimes left to the discretion of the speech correctionist.

6. *Selection of Children.* The selection of children for speech correction is left largely to the discretion of the speech correctionist. The general policies of selection, however, are made by state regulations and by the local administrator of speech services.

7. *Grade levels of children.* The concentration of speech correction services is in the kindergarten, first, and second grades, where 75 per cent of the services are found. Another 18 per cent of the services are found in Grades 3 and 4. The remaining 6 per cent of cases are scattered from Grade 5 through Grade 12.

8. *Number of schools served.* About one-half of the speech correctionists served three to six schools, and about 30 per cent served children in more than six schools.

9. *Financing program.* Ninety per cent of the regions surveyed indicated that they were partially or totally reimbursed for the speech correction program by the state. Seven per cent reported no reimbursement, and 3 per cent gave no response.

10. *Research.* Considerable research is needed to solve many of the persistent problems in public school speech correction. Included among these are "(a) the collection of longitudinal normative data on speech, (b) comparative studies of program organization (with special attention to the frequency, duration, and intensity of therapy), and (c) comparative studies of the use of different remedial procedures with children of various ages presenting different speech, voice, and language problems."[56]

Summary

1. Speech is considered defective when its deviation from average speech draws unfavorable attention to the speaker.

2. Approximately 5 per cent of school children exhibit deviations in speech requiring correction.

[56] *Ibid.*, p. 131.

3. Speech defects are the result of (a) organic factors, such as hearing losses, cleft palate, and cerebral dysfunction, and (b) environmental and emotional factors.

4. Speech defects are classified into (a) articulatory disorders, (b) vocal disorders, (c) stuttering, (d) delayed speech, (e) speech disorders associated with hearing impairment, cleft palate, or cerebral palsy.

5. Approximately 80 per cent of speech cases in school display functional articulation disorders.

6. Schools employ the largest number of speech correctionists and serve the largest number of children.

7. In general, speech correction in public schools serves young children. Over three-fourths of the case load of speech correctionists is in the kindergarten and first and second grades.

DISCUSSION QUESTIONS

1. Although marked speech defects, such as are found in children with cleft palate or cerebral palsy, are readily recognized, minor speech defects are less easily detected. How can one establish the prevalence of minor speech defects in otherwise normal children when normal speech is relative to environmental and other factors?

2. If you were asked to identify speech-defective children in a public school system, what procedures would you use, assuming you had the technical skill and knowledge to conduct the examinations?

3. How is it possible to classify speech defects as in Table IX when there is such overlapping between one defect and another?

4. How can we reconcile the following conflicts in speech correction: (a) the practice of beginning speech correction at an early age to avoid fixation of the habit, which makes correction more difficult at a later age, and (b) the fact that many young children have speech defects at ages five, six, and seven, but overcome them without correction through normal maturation and experience?

5. What can a teacher do in a classroom to help children develop relatively proper vocal quality, pitch, and intensity?

6. Since theories of stuttering vary so widely, how can one determine treatment methods?

7. How can one differentiate between the different causes for delayed speech? Discuss the procedures that can be used for such a differential diagnosis.

8. Is the classification "functional and organic" a useful one? How does this classification clarify issues, and in what ways does it confuse them?

9. What should be the relationship between the classroom teacher and the speech correctionist? Whose responsibility is it to take the lead in co-operation?

10. Should one who does speech correction in schools be called a "speech correctionist" or a "speech therapist"?

Selected References

American Speech and Hearing Association. "Public School Speech and Hearing Services," *Journal of Speech and Hearing Disorders, Monograph Supplement 8.* Danville, Ill.: Interstate Printers and Publishers, Inc., 1961.

Backus, O. L., and J. Beasley. *Speech Therapy with Children.* Boston: Houghton Mifflin Company, 1951.

Barrows, S., and A. Pierce. *The Voice: How to Use It.* Boston: Expression Company, rev. ed., 1942.

Berry, M. F., and J. Eisenson. *Speech Disorders; Principles and Practices of Therapy.* New York: Appleton-Century-Crofts, Inc., 1956.

Black, M., and S. E. Nelson, eds. *The Illinois Plan for Special Education of Exceptional Children: Speech Correction in High Schools.* Springfield, Ill.: State Office of Public Instruction, 1960.

Bluemel, C. S. *The Riddle of Stuttering.* Danville, Ill.: Interstate Printers and Publishers, Inc., 1957.

Brodnitz, F. S. *Vocal Rehabilitation.* Rochester, Minn.: American Academy of Ophthalmology and Otolaryngology, 1959.

Carrell, J. A., and W. R. Tiffany. *Phonetics: Theory and Application to Speech Improvement.* New York: McGraw-Hill Book Company, 1960.

Cypreansen, L., J. H. Wiley, and L. T. Lasse. *Speech Development, Improvement, and Correction.* New York: Ronald Press Company, 1959.

Eisenson, J., ed. *Stuttering; A Symposium.* New York: Harper & Brothers, 1958.

Eisenson, J., and M. Ogilvie. *Speech Correction in the Schools.* New York: The Macmillan Company, 1957.

Fairbanks, G. *Voice and Articulation Drillbook.* New York: Harper & Brothers, 2nd ed., 1960.

Greene, M. *The Voice and Its Disorders.* New York: The Macmillan Company, 1957.

Hahn, E. F. *Stuttering: Significant Theories and Therapies.* Stanford, Calif.: Stanford University Press, 2nd ed., 1956.

Hahn, E. F., D. E. Hargis, C. W. Lomas, and D. Vandraegen. *Basic Voice Training for Speech*. New York: McGraw-Hill Book Company, 1952.

Heltman, H. J. *First Aids for Stutterers*. Boston: Expression Company, 1943.

Holdsworth, W. G. *Cleft Lip and Palate*. New York: Grune and Stratton, 1951.

Johnson, W. *Toward Understanding Stuttering*. Chicago: National Society for Crippled Children and Adults, 1958.

Johnson, W., S. Brown, J. F. Curtis, C. W. Edney, and J. Keaster. *Speech Handicapped School Children*. New York: Harper & Brothers, rev. ed., 1956.

Myklebust, H. R. *Auditory Disorders in Children*. New York: Grune and Stratton, 1954.

Pronovost, W. *The Teaching of Speaking and Listening in the Eelementary School*. New York: Longmans, Green and Company, 1959.

Travis, L. E., ed. *Handbook of Speech Pathology*. New York: Appleton-Century-Crofts, Inc., 1957.

Van Riper, C. *Speech Correction: Principles and Methods*. New York: Prentice-Hall, Inc., 3rd ed., 1954.

Van Riper, C. *Stuttering*. Chicago: National Society for Crippled Children and Adults, 1958.

Van Riper, C., and J. V. Irwin. *Voice and Articulation*. Englewood Cliffs, N.J.: Prentice-Hall, Inc., 1958.

West, R., W. M. Ansberry, and A. V. Carr. *The Rehabilitation of Speech*. New York: Harper & Brothers, rev. ed., 1957.

Westlake, H. *A System for Developing Speech with Cerebral Palsied Children*. Chicago: National Society for Crippled Children and Adults, 1951.

13

Behavior Deviations in Children

One can define behavior deviations in terms of the dynamics of personality or in terms of conduct which has an impact on the individual or on other people. Thus, for the purpose of this chapter, *a behavior deviation is that behavior of a child which (1) has a detrimental effect on his development and adjustment and/or (2) interferes with the lives of other people.* A child who is extremely withdrawn and does not relate to other people, who does not seem to respond to his environment (even though he is average in intelligence), is one whose behavior is interfering with his own growth process. Such children have been termed "withdrawn," "introverted," "autistic," or "schizophrenic." A child who behaves in such a way that he has repeated conflicts with his siblings, parents, classmates, teachers, and community is interfering with the lives of other people. Parents call him a "bad boy." Teachers call him "incorrigible." Social workers say he is "socially maladjusted." Psychiatrists and psychologists may say he is "emotionally disturbed." And if he comes in conflict with the law, the judge calls him "delinquent." Behavior deviations in children may be actions which retard social and emotional and sometimes educational growth, or they may be actions which are detrimental to other people.

The major difficulty in delineating behavior deviations is inherent in the use of certain terms and concepts and appears to be related to (1) the kind of deviation under discussion, (2) the degree of deviation, (3) the situation in which the deviation occurs, and (4) the individual who concludes that a deviation exists. A simple example may be a good illustration of the multidimensional nature of behavior deviations. Here is a boy eating candy. Many will state, "There is nothing wrong or abnormal about a boy eating candy," and, "Most boys eat candy; hence it is a normal activity." But a child who ate candy he took from a shelf in a store and did not pay for would be considered to have been stealing. A child who ate candy in a classroom when the teacher specifically prohibited eating candy in class would be thought disobedient. A child who ate candy when he was aware that since he had diabetes eating candy would make him sick might be considered compulsive or masochistic. Furthermore, the mother of the child who took candy from the store shelf might think his behavior, not deviant, but an innocent response, since he had been used to helping himself to candy when he saw it. The storekeeper, on the other hand, would undoubtedly call it stealing, which is a form of delinquency.

The area of behavior deviations is of interest to many professions: social work, psychology, psychiatry, sociology, neurology, education, and related disciplines. Education deals with the majority of deviant children, generally those with minor deviations. Psychiatry, on the other hand, deals with the more extreme forms of emotional deviations, the neuroses and psychoses, while the courts deal with extreme social deviations. The general discussion of this chapter will center on those deviations with which the school is primarily concerned — emotional maladjustment and social maladjustment.

Although social maladjustment and emotional disturbance in children are not necessarily synonymous, there is considerable overlap between them. Social maladjustment refers to behavior of children which is not "within the range of the 'culturally permissible,' either at home, in the school, or in the community."[1] These children are unmanageable in the home, causing difficulties for the parents and siblings. They are generally problems in school, retarded in educational achievements, destructive, quarrelsome, and often socially immature. In the community they may seek undesirable companions or be isolates. Delinquents are a subgroup of the socially maladjusted, "delinquent" being a legal term and referring primarily to children who have come in conflict with the law.

The term "emotionally disturbed children" refers to those who have inner tensions and show anxiety, neuroticism, or psychotic behavior. The behavior of many emotionally disturbed children is also considered so-

---

[1] Romaine P. Mackie, William C. Kvaraceus, and Harold M. Williams, *Teachers of Children Who Are Socially and Emotionally Maladjusted*, U.S. Office of Education (Washington: Government Printing Office, 1957).

cial maladjustment. The isolate, or withdrawn child, may be considered emotionally disturbed but not necessarily socially maladjusted since his behavior or lack of it does not conflict with the lives of others.

The differentiation between social maladjustment, emotional disturbance, and delinquency is a difficult one to make since the dynamics of behavior in all three categories may be the same. Some children who are emotionally disturbed may, through conflict with parents and siblings at home and with classmates and teachers in school, be considered socially maladjusted. The maladjustment may lead to aggressive behavior, stealing, or destruction of property and cause conflict with the law. Such a child may become legally a delinquent. On the other hand, a socially maladjusted child who does not behave within the "culturally permissible" range need not be either emotionally disturbed or delinquent.

Some Bases for Behavior Deviations

To adjust situations or to organize programs for the prevention or remediation of behavior deviations, it is necessary to view some factors which contribute to behavior problems, incorrigibility, delinquency, social maladjustment, or emotional disorders. Three general factors which appear to be related to behavior deviations in children will be discussed, namely, (1) psychological factors, (2) psychosocial factors, and (3) physiological factors.

Psychological Factors in Behavior Deviations

In a physiological laboratory in Russia, Pavlov and his colleagues were studying the conditioned response in dogs.[2] In one experiment Krestovnikova presented a dog simultaneously with meat powder and the visual stimulus of a circle. The dog, who was placed in a harness to keep him in a stationary position, salivated normally at the presentation of the meat powder. By repeated presentations of the meat powder (which elicited the salivary response) with the circle, the dog learned or was conditioned to salivate to the circle without the unconditioned stimulus of meat powder. Krestovnikova also presented the dog with the visual stimulus of an ellipse without the meat powder, to which situation the dog did not salivate. Thus the dog could evidently discriminate between a circle and an ellipse, salivating when the circle was presented and not salivating when the ellipse was presented. Krestovnikova then decreased the proportions of the ellipse on successive presentations from a ratio of two to one to a ratio of three to two, then four to three, and

[2] I. P. Pavlov, *Lectures on Conditioned Reflexes,* translated by W. H. Gantt (New York: International Publishers Company, 1928).

so on until she was presenting a circle and an ellipse with a ratio of eight to seven. At this point the dog continued to salivate to the circle and to give no response to the ellipse.

When the dog was presented with a circle and an ellipse with a ratio of nine to eight he is reported to have "broken down." He salivated to any visual stimulus connected with the experiment — the circle, the ellipse, and other visual stimuli incidental to the situation. In addition, his behavior in the laboratory changed. He squealed, struggled, bit at the harness, and when released from the harness barked violently. He was later tested on the simpler visual discrimination between a circle and an ellipse (with a ratio of two to three) but was now unable to make the discriminations which were at one time part of his habit repertoire. The benefit of training was now lost. The dog was showing deviant behavior. Pavlov termed this behavior *experimental neurosis.*

The experiment by Krestovnikova has been repeated by other experimenters on dogs and other animals (pigs, sheep, and cats) with similar results.[3] The stress and strain placed on the discriminative capacities of the animals produced deviating behavior and caused the animals to lose some of the habits which had once been established. Similar results were obtained with a 6-year-old boy by Panferov, another worker in Pavlov's laboratory. This child was first trained to give a motor response to a metronome beat of 144 beats per minute. Differential responses were required for metronome beats of 144 and 92, wherein the boy responded positively to the 144 beats per minute and inhibited his response to the metronome beat of 92 beats per minute. Panferov then increased the slower metronome beat from 92 to 100, then to 120. At this point the child began to show some emotional tensions and disliked going to the laboratory. The experimenter then increased the beat to 132 (holding the other metronome beat at 144) and at this point the child "broke down." It is reported that he became disobedient, excited, closed his eyes, and even went to sleep when presented with the experimental situation. When Panferov presented him with metronome beats of 144 and 120, a differentiation which he had previously made, it was found that the boy had lost the earlier ability to respond. Pavlov considered this an experimental neurosis induced by the strain posed by the experimental situation. A retraining period was then introduced with a discrimination task of 144 and 92 beats, which the boy relearned. The difficulty of discrimination was again increased until it reached 144 and 120 metronome beats a minute. He now made these discriminations without out-

[3] Ernest R. Hilgard and Donald G. Marquis, *Conditioning and Learning* (New York: D. Appleton-Century Company, 1940), chap. 12. N. R. F. Maier, *Frustration: The Study of Behavior Without a Goal* (New York: McGraw-Hill Book Company, 1949).

ward signs of emotionality. He no longer exhibited the deviant behavior of disobedience, going to sleep, or refusal to cooperate.

Maier has conducted a series of experiments with animals and humans from which, together with the experiments of others, he has extended the concepts of Pavlov into the field of behavior deviations resulting from frustration.[4] His experiments deal primarily with the relation of frustration to abnormal fixation. This deviation of fixation, together with aggression, regression, and resignation, all of which have been attributed to frustration, will be described below.

Abnormal Fixation. In experiments with animals, Maier presented rats with no-solution problems, using a Lashley jumping apparatus in which, under ordinary learning situations, the rat would learn to jump off a stand to a black or white card. One of the cards would be locked in position, the other unlocked and easily pushed over. When the rat jumped to the unlocked card it fell and he obtained food. Under normal conditions the rat learned to jump at the appropriate card as the cards were irregularly alternated. The rat thus was able to choose consistently the card which was unlocked, whether it was on the right of the screen or the left. In the frustration experiments the symbols, black and white, were alternated in such a way that learning was impossible, for the white card was locked some of the times and the black at other times. In these experiments, the rat often developed a position stereotype. He began to jump always to the right or always to the left. Some rats developed a stereotype of jumping to the same symbol in spite of lack of reward. Maier termed these responses *abnormal fixations.*

Maier also tried to break the stereotyped or fixated behavior by presenting the rat with a solvable problem. He could not remove the abnormal fixation, however, until he guided the rat manually to the correct solution. According to Maier, guidance served as the therapy for the removal of abnormal fixations.

Maier reports similar experiments with humans. In a no-solution frustration problem with college students, fixations also occurred:

> Human subjects were similarly caused to develop a degree of rigidity to change. This rigidity in behavior was measured by a greatly retarded ability to learn in a situation that previously had been frustrating. Thus after frustration human beings have difficulty in learning simple discrimination problems.[5]

Maier distinguishes between habits and abnormal fixations caused by frustration. He feels that the various forms of compulsions, ritualistic

[4] Maier, *op. cit.*
[5] *Ibid.*, p. 82.

acts, obsessions, phobias, irrational behavior, and stubbornness can be explained by abnormal fixations and cites other studies with humans to support his contention.

Aggression. Dollard, Doob, Miller, Mowrer, and Sears postulated the well-known frustration-aggression hypothesis.[6] They explain that when goal-directed behavior meets interference the individual is frustrated, and this frustration leads to aggression — striking, fighting, abusive language, and anger. In most instances the aggression reduces the tension aroused by the frustration and no permanent personality changes occur. In children, aggression takes the form of hostility and destructiveness. Play therapy is an attempt to allow the child to express his aggressions in a controlled situation.

Regression. Barker, Dembo, and Lewin demonstrated with young children that frustration can lead to regression, defined as returning to an earlier form of behavior.[7] In their experiment they allowed children to play with toys, then restricted them to one part of the room with only some of the toys. The children could see the toys in the other part of the room but were prevented by a wire screen from obtaining them. According to the authors some of the children showed aggression, but the majority regressed one and one-half years in their play activities. This was interpreted as regression to earlier forms of play caused by frustration. It is possible that dependence on the mother, whining, excessive crying, infantile speech, and nonconstructive play are examples of regressive behavior caused by frustration.

Resignation. Maier cites resignation as another reaction to frustration. This behavior deviation seems to be a loss of motivation and inability to respond constructively following repeated frustration. It is characterized by a *lack* of overt behavior rather than a positive action such as aggression, regression, or fixation. It is one way of avoiding further frustration, since frustration is marked by a discrepancy between the goal and the ability to attain it. Research is lacking in this field, but resignation has been cited as a reaction to prolonged unemployment[8] and to persecution under the Nazis.[9]

In attempting to explain the different reactions to frustration, Maier

[6] J. Dollard, L. W. Doob, N. E. Miller, H. O. Mowrer, and R. R. Sears, *Frustration and Aggression* (New Haven: Yale University Press, 1939).

[7] R. Barker, T. Dembo, and K. Lewin, *Frustration and Regression: An Experiment with Young Children* (Iowa City: University of Iowa Press, 1941).

[8] P. Eisenberg and P. F. Lazarsfeld, "The Psychological Effects of Unemployment," *Psychological Bulletin*, 35 (1938), 358–390.

[9] G. W. Allport, J. S. Bruner, and E. M. Jandorf, "Personality Under Social Catastrophe: Ninety Life-Histories of the Nazi Revolution," *Character and Personality*, 10 (1941), 1–22.

states that aggression occurs in a situation in which behavior is not restricted by barriers — or in other words, in a free situation where variable behavior is permissible.[10] Regression, likewise, occurs in similar situations and at times alternates with aggression, i.e., fighting and then crying. Fixations and resignations occur in frustrating situations which are restrictive and persistent. Maier speculates that "Perhaps psychoneurosis and resignation represent final stages of frustration, and aggression, regression, and fixation are the more preliminary or intermediate conditions."[11]

The Concept of Discrepancy. Although experimentation with humans under controlled frustrating situations is not always practical, there are, as has been indicated, many analogies from everyday life and human experimentation in which the behavior deviations and problems of children can be explained as responses to frustration. When children or adults are placed in situations in which their capacities are strained or in which they are unable to satisfy their motives and drives, behavior deviations of aggression, regression, compulsive behavior, fixations, resignations, or other out-of-the-ordinary or abnormal reactions may result. When children are unable to choose between one of two courses of action (the proverbial donkey between two bales of hay), or when the courses of action do not reduce their tensions, they react in an emotional way — by temper tantrums, fighting, sulking, regressing, and other bizarre types of behavior. These situations lead to the statement that *behavior problems are the outcome of frustration resulting from the discrepancy between the child's capacity to behave and the requirements of the environment.*

The concept of a discrepancy between the child's ability to perform and some of the requirements of the home or the school may be applicable to the situations in experiments with animals and those cited with humans. In some cases where the child is forced to attempt a task which he cannot perform he becomes tense and excited and may get angry at objects or people. Or he resorts to irrational or silly maneuvers. In many situations he escapes the requirement. For example, truancy from school is more prevalent among slow learners and among the educationally retarded than among those who are succeeding in school. Although other factors operate in truancy, when the home and school require of the child certain achievements which he cannot accomplish he tends to run away from the situation or become aggressive and hostile. An account of a behavior deviation in a retarded child who also had a learning disability will illustrate what is meant.

[10] Maier, *op. cit.*
[11] *Ibid.,* pp. 114–115.

A teacher reported that Roy — a fourteen-year-old subnormal boy — was creating a disturbance in class. When asked to report her observations, she noted that while he was drawing or doing his arithmetic he was perfectly satisfied. But when she asked him to read or to do something related to reading, he exhibited bizarre behavior. He would hold the book in his hand, pretend to read by telling a good story, but without actually reading one word. When she suggested that he was bluffing, Roy had a temper-tantrum. To avoid this performance in class the teacher permitted him to continue bluffing.

An analysis of Roy's difficulties suggested that because of his subnormal intelligence (IQ of 70) his discriminative capacity in reading had been taxed during his earlier years in school. He had not had the ability then to learn to read and yet the school insisted that he learn. He had been passed from grade to grade because his teachers wished to be rid of him.

At the time of this study Roy had a mental age of nine or ten years. He had the ability to learn to read, yet he had failed to do so. The only explanation found was that he had become too disintegrated to learn, or in other words, his "reading neurosis" was inhibiting his chances for learning. His condition was similar to that of Krestovnikova's dog and to Panferov's boy, who were unable to make differential responses which had once been established.

In "re-integrading" Roy it was necessary to use such simple material that success would be certain. As in the laboratory situations described above, the conditioning was to be carried on at a level below that at which he could have at one time responded readily. This, of course, would have necessitated using primers and baby books. For this reason all books were discarded and in their place simple materials only remotely connected with reading were used. The approach to the ordinary reading situation was made gradually and not until it was certain that he would be successful. In about three months Roy returned to the classroom, read books, and did his work enthustically. The teacher reported that he was making an excellent adjustment, with no more disturbance, no more evasive behavior, and no more temper-tantrums in the classroom.[12]

Many examples of situations can be given wherein the child becomes frustrated because he is unable to perform as required by parents and teachers. In one instructional period the author noticed that when a teacher was quizzing a child, first with a problem he could answer, then with a little harder one, until the question became so difficult that the child was unable to find a solution, he diverted his own attention and

[12] Reprinted by permission of the Association for Childhood Education International, 3615 Wisconsin Avenue, N.W., Washington 16, D.C. Excerpt from "Integrating Personality," by Samuel A. Kirk. From *Childhood Education*, April, 1938, Vol. 14, No. 8, 357.

the attention of the teacher by saying, "Oh, teacher, you have a pretty dress on today." This response was not a neurosis or a breakdown, but when the situation persists and the child is repeatedly taxed beyond his capacity, he may become more aggressive, or he may regress to more immature behavior. Many parents are overly ambitious for their children's progress in school. They are not satisfied with average or even above-average progress. They want their children to be top students in class even though the children do not have the capacity. Persistence in this attitude develops in the children various forms of deviant behavior. They may rebel against school and do less well than they would have otherwise, or they may withdraw from efforts to succeed.

Psychosocial Factors in Behavior Deviations

Not all behavior deviations arise from frustrations in an immediate situation or from the discrepancy between the child's capacity to behave and the requirements of the environment. Other factors include (1) early home experiences and (2) the social and economic aspects of the child's environment.

The psychoanalytic school initiated by Sigmund Freud has attempted to explain behavior deviations by the experiences of children at an early age. According to psychoanalytical theory certain unpleasant early experiences may become repressed in the unconscious but continue to determine behavior and deviations in behavior. Deviations would be explained in these terms instead of the more behavioristic terms of Pavlov, Maier, and others discussed earlier.

The influence of early home experience has been studied by numerous investigators. Many factors within the home, especially relations with the mother, father, and siblings, have been associated with behavior deviations. Some studies of this nature will be reviewed here to point up the connection between early home factors and maladjustment.

Hewitt and Jenkins analyzed 500 cases of maladjusted children referred to child guidance clinics and by means of correlations attempted to relate (1) a particular type of maladjustment in a child with (2) the specific home situation in which this pattern of behavior was developed.[13] They identified three major patterns of maladjustment which seemed to be associated with three different home situations.

1. One category included *unsocialized aggressive children,* children who defied all authority, were hostile toward authority figures (policemen, teachers, and so forth), were cruel, malicious, and assaultive, and had inadequate guilt feelings. They were jealous, deceitful, and blameful of others. In a sense they operated aggressively in isolation. Children

[13] L. E. Hewitt and R. L. Jenkins, *Fundamental Patterns of Maladjustment: The Dynamics of Their Origin* (Springfield: State of Illinois, 1945).

of this type came from broken homes where they received no love and attention. Many were illegitimate or the products of forced marriages. They were unwanted by their mothers in infancy. It appeared that they had developed little attachment for anyone, and their acts, particularly their delinquent acts, were hostile, aggressive, and hateful. It is presumed that these children had no opportunity at an early age to form positive interpersonal attachments, especially with their mothers. In psychoanalytic terms, they did not develop a superego or conscience.

2. Another group of children was categorized as *socialized aggressive*. Although they were also aggressive and hostile to authority figures, they were socialized within their peer groups, usually the gang or companions in misdemeanor and crime. This group defied authority but at the same time showed attachment and loyalty (socialization) to their companions and the gang. Activities consisted of stealing with others, truancy from school, desertion of home, and gang doings. These maladjusted children also came from incompatible and broken homes, but in contrast to the unsocialized aggressive child they had some security with their mother in early infancy and childhood even though at a later age they were rejected. The assumption is that they formed some socialized attitudes in early infancy which caused them to be loyal to some group such as the gang, even though their behavior was hostile toward authority.

3. Maladjusted children in a third group were categorized as *overinhibited*. These children were shy, timid, withdrawing, seclusive, sensitive, and submissive. They tended to lack close friendships, were overdependant and easily depressed, and had frequent physical complaints. This type of child usually came from a family of a higher economic level which tended to overprotect the child while sometimes rejecting him. His home atmosphere was likely to be restrictive.

Hewitt and Jenkins found a positive relationship between each of these three types and a corresponding child-rearing situation, but low or no correlation with other situations. The unsocialized aggressive syndrome correlated .48 with a rejecting situation; the socialized delinquent, .63 with negligence and exposure to delinquent behavior; the overinhibited, .52 with restriction and physical deficiency situations. It should be pointed out, however, that about two-thirds of the original group of children could not be clearly classified in any of the three groups.

Many studies have shown that child-rearing methods featuring inconsistent discipline and rejection or hostility on the part of parents are positively correlated with social maladjustments. These same factors are thought to be related to many forms of emotional maladjustment. In relation to delinquency, for example, Bandura and Walters found that certain child-training factors and family interrelationships differentiated a group of aggressive boys who had come into conflict with school authorities or county probation authorities from a group of high school boys not in such conflict.[14] They found that parent attitudes rejecting dependence, encouraging aggressiveness outside the home, and placing fewer demands for obedience, responsibility, and school achievement were significant. There was also less affection shown between father and mother and between parents and the boy.

An investigation which highlights the interplay of sociological factors with those of family life is that done by McCord and McCord.[15] Many aspects of home life and environmental influences were examined. Of significance was the frequency with which delinquency was associated with lax or erratic discipline which was punitive in nature, membership in gangs, and quarrelsome and neglecting home life. Certain constellations of factors seemed to indicate higher relationships than did single factors — for example, a quarrelsome home plus lax discipline, or a neglecting mother who provided a deviant role model and whose discipline was erratic and primitive.

One of the early efforts to evaluate the influences of home and family was published in 1936 by Healy and Bronner.[16] Although the authors did not always define and pinpoint the factors they were studying, they concluded that children show delinquent behavior because of the frustrations they suffer at the hands of their families. They found, for example, that 91 per cent of the delinquents (compared to 13 per cent of the nondelinquent siblings) showed unhappiness, discontent, or emotional disturbance over the conditions of their lives.

Over and above the effect of family and home, there are other influences from the community at large which help determine the course of a child's social and emotional development. Much of the conflict with the law which arises in lower-class urban areas is complicated by community factors as well as family influences.

The classic studies of Shaw and his colleagues indicated that in Chicago delinquency areas were identifiable.[17] The highest rates were in the inner zone (the business area), the next highest in the bordering slum areas, and the next in the workingman's area. The lowest rates were in the outer zones of the city. It is in the high-delinquency areas that the criminal tradition is handed down from one generation to the

---

[14] Albert Bandura and Richard H. Walters, *Adolescent Aggression* (New York: Ronald Press Company, 1959).

[15] W. McCord and Joan McCord, *Origins of Crime: A New Evaluation of the Cambridge-Somerville Youth Study* (New York: Columbia University Press, 1959).

[16] W. Healy and Augusta F. Bronner, *New Light on Delinquency and Its Treatment* (New Haven: Yale University Press, 1936).

[17] Clifford R. Shaw and H. D. McKay, *Juvenile Delinquency and Urban Areas* (Chicago: University of Chicago Press, 1942).

next through what is known as "cultural transmission." In studies of other factors, Macoby, Johnson, and Church found that in areas of high delinquency the community was heterogeneous in religious beliefs and ethnic background and that there was greater impersonality among the neighbors.[18]

It is now rather widely accepted that we do not have a classless society in this country. Many sociologists believe that the social values of lower-class culture are an inversion of middle-class standards and derive from the disadvantageous position in which the members of the lower class find themselves. Cohen has dwelt at length on a delinquent subculture characterized by elements of nonutility, negativism, and maliciousness, which he postulates is a reaction against middle-class standards by a lower-class group placed in a disadvantageous position because of their social status.[19]

> This . . . may require a certain measure of reaction-formation, going beyond indifference to active hostility and contempt for all those who do not share his subculture. . . . [Our view] holds that the problems of adjustment to which the delinquent subculture is a response are determined, in part, by those very values which respectable society holds most valid.[20]

A somewhat different point of view is held by Miller, a cultural anthropologist, who believes that social class status is now superseding the ethnic differences prevalent during surges of immigration to this country and that we do have a growing and distinct "lower class" with a hard core of some 15 per cent of the population and probably twice that many influenced to a lesser degree by the mores of that group.[21] Miller uses the term "lower class" in a descriptive sense rather than as a negative evaluation.

> To discriminate *between* important subsegments of our society is not to discriminate *against* them. . . . [Lower-class culture is] a cultural system in its own right, with an integrity of its own, with a characteristic set of practices, focal concerns, and ways of behaving that are meaningfully and systematically related to one another rather than to corresponding features of middle-class culture.[22]

[18] Eleanor E. Macoby, J. P. Johnson, and R. M. Church, "Community Integration and the Social Control of Juvenile Delinquency," *Journal of Social Issues,* 14 (1958), 38–51.

[19] Albert K. Cohen, *Delinquent Boys: The Culture of the Gang* (Glencoe, Ill.: The Free Press, 1955).

[20] *Ibid.,* pp. 136–137.

[21] Walter B. Miller, "Lower-Class Culture as a Generating Milieu of Gang Delinquency," *Journal of Social Issues,* 14 (1958).

[22] Walter B. Miller, "Implications of Urban Lower-Class Culture for Social Work," *Social Service Review,* 33 (September, 1959), 222–223.

"Lower-class" concerns center on immediate problems. Goods are to be used, money is to be spent, and life is to be lived. The focal concerns of this group, according to Miller, are: trouble, toughness, smartness, excitement, fate, and autonomy.[23] It should be pointed out that these concerns of "getting into trouble," "staying out of trouble," being masculine and strong and able to endure pain and fatigue, outsmarting others, being one's own boss, and so forth, rather than the economic factor of being rich or poor are what differentiate this group. In some ways, the "beatnik" element is an intellectual, "middle-class" counterpart of the "lower-class" subculture. The "lower class" can be further subdivided into lesser subcultures, one of which is the delinquent gang.

Reiss and Rhodes have commented on the relationships of social status, structure of the community, and cultural tradition:

> There is no simple relationship between ascribed social status and delinquency. Both the status structure of the residential community and the extent to which delinquency is a function of a cultural tradition in a residential community affect the delinquency life-chances of a boy at each ascribed social class level. The largest proportion of delinquents for any status group comes from the more homogeneous status areas for that group, while the delinquency life-chances of boys in any status group tend to be greatest in the lower status areas and in high delinquency rate areas. Evidence presented in the paper for types of conforming and deviating boys lends support to the conclusions that (1) there is more frequent and serious delinquent deviation in the lower than in the middle stratum when self-reports of delinquent deviation are examined, (2) that the career oriented delinquent is found only among lower class boys, (3) that the major type of lower status boy is a conforming non-achiever while the conforming achiever is the major type in the middle class, (4) that conformers are more likely to be isolates than are non-conformers, and (5) that peer-oriented delinquency is the most common form of delinquent organization at both lower and middle status levels.[24]

The factors in the home and the community which influence social and emotional maladjustment in children are reflected in the school — the community agency which deals with all children. Teachers must understand these influences if they are to handle effectively children whose maladjustments stem largely from these out-of-school factors. Although the social and cultural forces in a society are beyond the control of a school, the school can contribute to the home and the community through

23 Cf. Miller, "Lower-Class Culture as a Generating Milieu of Gang Delinquency," pp. 6–17.
24 Albert J. Reiss, Jr., and Albert L. Rhodes, "The Distribution of Juvenile Delinquency in the Social Class Structure," *American Sociological Review*, 26 (1961), 720.

the activities of children. It is this role that the school must play to ameliorate or compensate for the detrimental influences of the home and community on the mental health of children.

The Role of Physiological Factors in Behavior Deviations

Neither psychological factors nor psychosocial factors explain all forms of behavior deviations. Brain damage is considered by many to be another cause. There is probably no question about the role of cerebral dysfunctions in some cases of behavior deviations. In addition to brain dysfunction, many physiological conditions may exist which are not detected and corrected. One such case which came to the author's attention is described below. It also illustrates how special theories may sometimes divert the attention of clinicians from the real bases of behavior.

The case is one of a 12-year-old boy who caused extreme difficulties in school. He seemed to behave fairly well early in the morning, but before noon created all sorts of disturbances within the classroom. Upon returning from the lunch period he behaved for an hour or two and then began to pant, run around the classroom, fight with the children, and at times attempted to jump out of the window. One psychiatrist diagnosed him as a psychopathic personality. Another, more psychoanalytically inclined, ascribed his behavior to a traumatic experience which he had had in early childhood. A third felt that there might have been a brain injury as a result of encephalitis.

As far as the teachers were concerned, they were unable to do anything about his psychopathic personality, his neurotic personality, or the possible postencephalitis. This behavior continued for many years until the child was sent to an institution because the school could no longer handle him within a classroom situation.

In the institution the same behavior pattern persisted. Teachers would accept him in class for a week or two and then state that they could not manage the class with such a child as a member. Teacher after teacher tried her hand at controlling him but to no avail.

After a conference it was suggested to the teacher that when the boy began to misbehave in school she should call in the psychiatric social worker. The latter walked with him around the block, gave him a piece of candy, discussed his problems with him, calmed him down, and returned him to the classroom. This routine usually occurred once in the morning and once in the afternoon.

At a later staff conference, no one seemed able to identify the factor which produced the abnormal behavior or the factors which diminished it. The staff speculated about many things, including identification with the social worker. A pediatrician at the conference, referring to the series of medical diagnoses made on this boy, discovered that the boy had never had a blood sugar test. He hypothesized that the piece of candy which the social worker always gave him might have had some relation to decreasing his hyperactive behavior.

A subsequent examination revealed that the boy had hypoglycemia, a condition causing a deficiency in blood sugar. The treatment prescribed was to give him a glass of milk with sugar in it about ten o'clock in the morning, at two o'clock in the afternoon, and again in the evening. From that day on the boy became a model child and learned in school at a much more rapid rate. This boy's behavior deviation was apparently an attempt on his part to reduce the tension or suffocation his body was experiencing when the blood sugar was used up.

Cases such as this emphasize the fact that when children are causing difficulties in school the role of physiological factors should not be overlooked. Irritability caused by incipient rheumatic fever or glandular disturbances such as hyperthyroidism may be the basis of maladjustment in school and apparent emotional disturbance. Many children displaying such symptoms have had cursory examinations, but conditions like the one described are not always easily detected.

We have heard a great deal about the term "psychosomatic disturbances," meaning the effect of the mind on the body. Because of considerable discussion and literature from psychoanalysis we tend sometimes to forget that there is also a somatopsychological factor, that is, the effect of the body on the mind and the emotions. This case is a good example of a somatopsychological disturbance.

Emotionally Disturbed Children

As indicated earlier, the term "behavior deviations" takes in a wide range of problems, including emotional disturbance and social maladjustment. The category of emotional disturbance can include the socially maladjusted, but it does not follow that all socially maladjusted children are emotionally disturbed. In describing emotional disturbance, the major focus will be on (1) signs of emotional disturbance among school children and (2) the prevalence of the condition in school.

Recognizing Signs of Emotional Disturbance

From a psychological point of view children who are emotionally disturbed have certain inner tensions which create anxiety, frustration, fears, and impulsive behavior. The emotional disturbance is the anxiety, worry, or generalized fear within the child, and this in turn may make him behave in a somewhat ineffectual manner in a school situation. His behavior may then lead the teacher to suspect the emotional disturbance. Teachers should be alert to the following signs and symptoms.

1. A child may translate his fears and anxieties into physical symptoms. He seems frequently to have something wrong with him physically. He may be prone to accidents. He may worry about his health. He malingers. He finds excuses for his inner tensions in some physical difficulty.

2. Another child may attempt to solve the anxiety by going back — or regressing — to earlier forms of behavior. This gives him security because he knows how to deal with problems at an immature level. Such behavior occurs when the child meets frustrating situations in the environment.

3. An emotionally disturbed child may express his fears and anxieties by becoming aggressive toward other people — his teachers, playmates, or parents. In this situation he appears hostile. He tries to overcome his tensions by taking things into his own hands.

4. Instead of becoming aggressive a child may withdraw into fantasy. We call him a daydreamer. He does not relate well to his peer group or to his teachers. He becomes an isolate in the classroom.

5. An emotionally disturbed child may fear failure and criticism. At times he becomes a perfectionist. Everything has to be just right. And when situations or his own behavior are not to his liking he is in a turmoil.

6. He may avoid the real anxieties by developing substitute fears, phobias, or compulsions, to which he attaches his emotional reaction.

Any of these conditions can produce poor social and school adjustment. It does not follow, however, that poor school or social adjustment is always the result of emotional disturbance.

A survey of emotionally disturbed children in California schools has revealed some persistent characteristics of these children.[25] A group of emotionally handicapped and another group of not emotionally handicapped children were identified by teachers in 1955–1956. In 1960 a follow-up of the records of these two groups was made. The significant differences between the groups led the authors to conclude that the emotionally handicapped, as compared to the normal group, were (1) seriously below average in school achievement; (2) sent to the vice-principal more often for disciplinary action; (3) more often dropped from school or left school; (4) more often absent from school without excuses; (5) more frequently sent to the health department for illness, need of rest, or discomfort; (6) more often served by school counselors; (7) more often the subject of home calls by child welfare workers

[25] *The Education of Emotionally Handicapped Children* (Sacramento: California State Department of Education, March, 1961).

and attendance officers; (8) subject to more contacts with police; (9) more likely to be on probation; (10) found more frequently to commit penal and vehicle code violation; (11) more frequently referred to local guidance clinics.

The Prevalence of Emotionally Disturbed Children in School

The large majority of socially and emotionally disturbed children are enrolled in regular classrooms with normal children. A study by Ullmann found that teachers identified 8 per cent of their pupils as maladjusted.[26] Their ratings correlated .86 with the ratings of 22 clinicians. Ullmann also reports that the ratio of boys to girls was four to one. (Interestingly he notes that among adult applicants to psychiatric clinics women outnumber men.) The 8 per cent figure, he comments, compares favorably with the 7 per cent maladjusted reported by Wickman and the 12 per cent reported by Rogers.

Bower, studying the methods of identification of the emotionally handicapped in school, found that 87 per cent of the clinically known emotionally handicapped children were likewise so rated by their classroom teachers. The teachers rated 10.5 per cent of school children as overly aggressive or defiant, or overly withdrawn and timid. Bower summarized his findings on identification as follows:

1. Children's judgments of other children's personality were surprisingly accurate and predictive.
2. Teachers' judgments of emotional disturbance were very much like the judgments of clinicians.
3. Teachers selected about the same number of children as being overly withdrawn or timid as overly aggressive or defiant.
4. At least three children in each average classroom could be regarded as having emotional problems of sufficient strength to warrant the appellation "emotionally handicapped children."
5. The differences between emotionally handicapped children and their classmates increase in each succeeding grade level.[27]

Socially Maladjusted Children

Studies on behavior deviations in school, including the surveys on prevalence cited in the last section, do not usually separate emotionally disturbed and socially maladjusted children. In general, however, so-

[26] Charles E. Ullmann, *Identification of Maladjusted School Children*, Public Health Monograph No. 7 (Washignton: Government Printing Office, 1952).
[27] Eli M. Bower, *Early Identification of Emotionally Handicapped Children in School* (Springfield, Ill.: Charles C. Thomas, 1960), p. 62.

cial maladjustment refers to children who are causing trouble at home or at school, incorrigibles, truants, predelinquents, or delinquents. Ordinarily, a child 8 years of age who steals or who injures another child with a knife or other weapon is considered socially maladjusted or predelinquent. The same behavior by a boy of 15 or 16 might result in arrest and court action, and the child is labeled delinquent.

Background Characteristics

Children classified as socially maladjusted or delinquent are a concern of the school. To adapt programs for them it is necessary to understand some of the factors associated with their behavior deviations:

1. Many come from broken homes, or homes which have not accepted them.

2. Many come from homes of the "lower class" as described by sociologists.

3. Some come from homes which have cultural conflicts; that is, the parents' culture differs from the school or peer culture with which the child must cope.

4. Some are slow learners and become frustrated with the requirements of the school.

5. Some associate with peer groups — gangs — which are attempting to defy authority.

6. Some hate parents, teachers, police, and others in authority.

7. Some come from families who appear always to depend on public aid. They have never had anything.

8. Many are unhappy, discontented, and emotionally disturbed over the conditions of their lives.

9. Many are neglected children.

Delinquency

One of the major subcategories of social maladjustment is delinquency. This type of behavior deviation has been the subject of many studies and much discussion. Kvaraceus and Miller have defined delinquency as "behavior by nonadults which violates specific legal norms or norms of a particular societal institution with sufficient frequency and/or seriousness so as to provide a firm basis for legal action against the behaving individual or group."[28]

Kvaraceus has listed eighteen characteristics which can be observed in school. He calls this compilation a "Delinquency Proneness Check List." Delinquency-prone children would be considered socially maladjusted.

[28] William C. Kvaraceus and Walter B. Miller, *Delinquent Behavior: Culture and the Individual* (Washington: National Education Association, 1959), p. 54.

DELINQUENCY PRONENESS CHECK LIST[29]

	Yes	No	Not Sure
1. Shows marked dislike for school.	....	....	....
2. Resents school routine and restriction.	....	....	....
3. Disinterested in school program.	....	....	....
4. Is failing in a number of subjects.	....	....	....
5. Has repeated one or more grades.	....	....	....
6. Attends special class for retarded pupils.	....	....	....
7. Has attended many different schools.	....	....	....
8. Intends to leave school as soon as the law allows.	....	....	....
9. Has only vague academic or vocational plans.	....	....	....
10. Has limited academic ability.	....	....	....
11. Is a child who seriously or persistently misbehaves.	....	....	....
12. Destroys school materials or property.	....	....	....
13. Is cruel and bullying on the playground.	....	....	....
14. Has temper tantrums in the classroom.	....	....	....
15. Wants to stop schooling at once.	....	....	....
16. Truants from school.	....	....	....
17. Does not participate in organized extra-curricular programs.	....	....	....
18. Feels he does not "belong" in the classroom.	....	....	....

According to Kvaraceus,

Since 1948 the volume and the rate of juvenile delinquency have shown a steady increase in the United States. About a half million children are now being referred to the juvenile courts of the nation each year. A 70-percent increase took place in the number of cases reported between 1948 and 1955. . . . The rate of increase of juvenile delinquency has exceeded by more than four times the rate of population increase. If this trend continues, more than a million youngsters can be anticipated in the juvenile courts in the near future.[30]

Kvaraceus estimates that 2 per cent of children between the ages of 7 and 17 have a court contact in a year. Of these there are five boys to one girl. In addition to these statistics, the delinquency rate in large cities and particularly in slum areas in large cities is high compared to

[29] William C. Kvaraceus, "Juvenile Delinquency," *What Research Says to the Teacher,* No. 15 (Washington: American Educational Research Association of the National Education Association, August, 1958), p. 17; also, "Forecasting Juvenile Delinquency," *Journal of Education, Boston University,* CXXXIV, No. 4 (April, 1956).

[30] Kvaraceus, "Juvenile Delinquency," p. 3.

that in rural districts and small towns and in neighborhoods of higher socioeconomic levels.

Many young people transgress the laws laid down by society but are not termed delinquent because the transgressions are minor or few, or, in some cases, because the youngster has avoided being apprehended. Murphy and his colleagues studied 114 boys who were participating in the Cambridge-Somerville Youth Study and found that 13 of them had no violations, 40 were official delinquents, and 61 were unofficial delinquents.[31] The official delinquents had more frequent and more serious transgressions than the unofficial delinquents. In another study, in which over a thousand high school boys and girls were compared with boys and girls in training schools for delinquents, Short and Nye found that those in training schools committed delinquent acts more frequently and of a more serious nature than did the high school students.[32] The questionnaire revealed that 50 per cent of high school boys admitted they had violated the law but had not been caught. The results of these and other studies indicate that the legal definition of "delinquent" does not represent a particular qualitative personality type but actually behavior on a continuum.

Educational Provisions

Educational programs for socially and emotionally maladjusted children are organized at different levels. Figure 26 presents the graded order of programs currently in existence: (1) the regular school program for mental health for all children, (2) special services for socially and emotionally disturbed children in the regular grades, (3) special classes in regular schools, (4) special day schools, (5) residential schools for emotionally disturbed children and residential schools for truants and delinquents. These different provisions offer a series of facilities for different children. When the program for mental health does not succeed, extra services in the regular grades are initiated. When this program is not sufficient or adequate, special classes are organized. More intensive provisions can be made in regular day schools for those who cannot adjust to a special class. When these facilities are not in existence or are not successful, residential treatment is provided as a last resort. A discussion of these different provisions follows.

[31] Fred J. Murphy, Mary M. Shirley, and Helen L. Witmer, "The Incidence of Hidden Delinquency," *American Journal of Orthopsychiatry,* 16 (1946), 686–696.

[32] J. F. Short and F. I. Nye, "Extent of Unrecorded Juvenile Delinquency: Tentative Conclusions," *Journal of Criminal Law, Criminology and Police Science,* 49 (1958), 296–302.

FIGURE 26

Educational Facilities

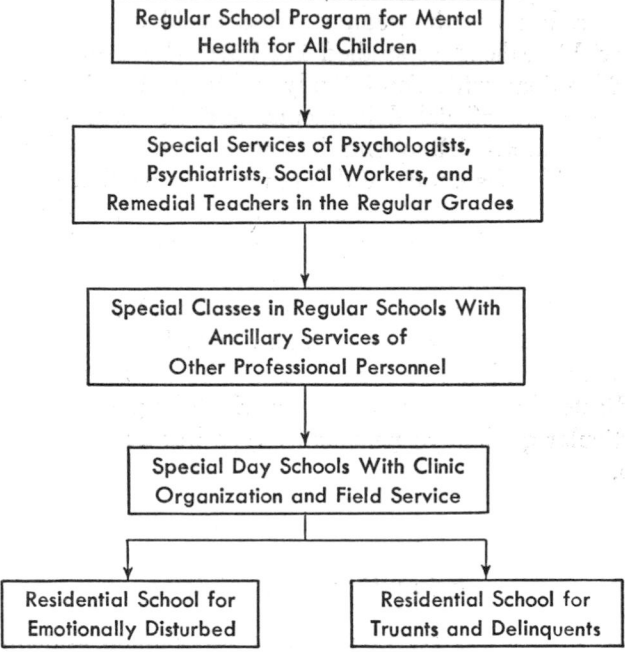

The School's Responsibility for Mental Health

It is well recognized that the professional personnel who deal with disturbed children are usually psychiatrists, psychologists, and social workers. But all of us know that there are not enough of these professionals to actually diagnose and treat all of the emotionally disturbed or socially maladjusted children in our midst. Only the most severely disturbed children or delinquents are referred to them. The people who have daily contacts with growing children are, of course, the *parents* and *teachers*. Since society has very little control over the activities of parents, this leaves us with the teachers as the largest group of professional personnel who deal with all children. It is teachers, then, who have the greatest opportunity to help with the mental hygiene of our youth — not because they have the knowledge and techniques of the psychiatrist, psychologist, or social worker, but because they have daily contact with the great bulk of the children in our society. It appears that the school is recognizing its responsibility as a major mental hygiene agency and that teachers are becoming important mental hygiene personnel. More and more we are employing psychiatrists, psychologists, and social workers as part of the school team to help the teachers achieve their goals in the development of the personality of children.

Teachers are trained to assist children to develop, not only in academic achievement, but also in social adjustment and personality. One role of the school is to develop personality, to prevent maladjustment, and to create situations in which children can grow to be strong individuals without anxieties and tensions. This is an ideal we have not yet achieved.

Counseling Parents. The reasons for emotional disturbances in children are not only varied but complex. In previous sections we have discussed some factors in maladjustment relating to home conditions and child-rearing practices. Studies and ideas in this area have resulted in a barrage of advice to parents. Some of it has appeared to parents to be not only impossible but contradictory. Note the following bits of conflicting advice.

Do not do too much for your child. Let him learn to settle his own problems. Do not overprotect him lest he become frustrated when he enters school and cannot depend on anyone as he has been doing at home.	OR	Do things for your child so that he will know that you love him. Give him plenty of affection so that he will not feel rejected.
Do not be too strict with your children. This produces repressions and inhibitions which may result in emotional disturbance.	OR	Do not be too lenient with your children. This produces a poor superego and lack of inner control.
Be democratic with your children; plan their activities with them.	OR	It is important that you be directive with your children until such time as the children can plan for themselves.

The contradictory advice we give parents reminds us of the well-known fable of the man and the boy taking the donkey to market. If neither rode the donkey someone called them foolish. If the boy rode the donkey he did not respect his father. If the father rode the donkey he was unfair to the boy. If both rode the donkey they were cruel to the animal. In their efforts to satisfy all advisers by carrying the donkey they lost him in the stream.

The advice on overprotection, rejection, discipline, freedom, autocratic and democratic control is actually not contradictory. It appears that there is a delicate balance between overprotection and rejection, discipline and freedom, and autocratic and democratic attitudes which must be maintained to produce a healthy, normal child. This balance is, of course, difficult to define since it depends on the child and the personality of the parents. People do not change their attitudes because they have read something or have been told about overprotection or rejection.

Regardless of how much we attribute all difficulties of children to the home, we still have the children in the school. Some of the criticisms of the home are also applicable to the school, which is just another phase of the child's life. Children are reared by both the home and the school. For these reasons we must look into the adequacy of the school as an agency for fostering mental health and alleviating emotional disturbances.

Studying Children. A study of a child's behavior should lead us to some hypotheses concerning the child's frustration and anxiety. It should indicate to us how his psychological needs for security or adequacy are being thwarted. An understanding of these factors will help us to analyze our school curriculums and school practices to determine how they affect the emotional problems of children, how they promote feelings of security and adequacy, and how they reduce frustrations. There are many situations in school which lead to frustration of children and which accentuate emotional problems.

It should be pointed out that any one school factor alone does not produce an emotionally disturbed child. Some children are not affected by certain school practices; others are. This may mean that a child who has a slight emotional disturbance because of home factors can become quite noticeably disturbed by factors in school which further his feelings of inadequacy and insecurity. During the war many men broke down in the front lines. Many others were not affected. Those who broke down emotionally had apparently been adjusting to civilian life. It was not the situation alone but the situation plus whatever emotional problems they brought with them that caused the breakdown. A similar state of affairs exists in school, for the school can help children to develop stronger personalities or can increase emotional disturbance. Some of the school factors which thwart or help the feelings of security and adequacy and which lead to greater frustration or decrease frustration can be identified.

Curriculum and Classroom Procedures. Most educators can point to factors in the curriculum or in classroom procedures which contribute to insecurity and feelings of inadequacy and so cause frustration and emotional disturbance.

An example may be taken from the primary school. All children seem to be expected to learn to read in the first grade. Educators have known that all children are not ready at this age, yet through the pressure of parents and curriculum standards children are often pushed beyond their abilities. What is this practice doing to the feeling of security, the feeling of adequacy, and the degree of frustration? Every teacher at the primary levels has seen children who were not able to learn to read during the first grade, who became distractible when urged to read, and who showed much evidence of emotional disturbance in these stress situations.

In the secondary field, the curriculum is keyed to a certain proportion of the high school population. Many children become frustrated, fail their studies, and leave the school within a year or two. Others who are unable to leave school because of age have created the necessity for establishing special schools for problem children. How to adjust the curriculum to all the children, thus avoiding failures and frustrations while maintaining standards for those who can achieve, has not yet been solved.

In every lesson we have an opportunity to develop feelings of security and adequacy in children, although with a large group sometimes it is inevitable that the comprehension and interest of the dull will be surpassed and that the bright will be frustrated and bored. In presenting a science unit a fourth-grade teacher found that some children were becoming frustrated. They were inattentive and restless and began teasing the other children. To make the lesson more interesting the teacher showed a movie, following it by discussion and further explanation of the lesson, with much success for most of the children. At that point one of the very bright children, thoroughly bored, rose to ask the teacher if she considered them a bunch of morons. "We got the point," he said. "Let's have something new." The teacher explained to him that not all children did understand and that he could do something else when lessons which he had already mastered were repeated.

Adapting Instruction to Individual Abilities. A basic principle of teaching with which all are familiar is adapting instruction to individual abilities. One boy in a class showed a great number of reversal errors in spelling lessons. The psychologist examined him and found that he made very few errors or reversals in writing when he was alone. Further investigation showed that in a group he was very tense and that under tension he made many reversals in writing. To reduce tension, the teacher asked him to write every *other* word in a spelling lesson and to take all the time he wanted. The tension was eased and the spelling improved.

Failure and Promotion Systems. If we accept the hypothesis that normal mental health depends to a large extent on developing feelings of security and adequacy and the ability to meet frustrations calmly, the topic of failure and promotion is of vital importance.

When a child fails a course in high school, does it mean that he hasn't learned anything? Usually he has. When a child fails to be promoted, is his feeling of security shaken? Does he feel less adequate? Does he experience frustration? Does failure help him to be a stronger person? Our system of social promotion has not solved this problem. Whether we hold students back or advance them, their peers know they are retarded and tell them so. We have been unable to meet this problem adequately while holding courses of study rigid, grade by grade.

Actually, the greatest amount of truancy in a school system is among the failures in school. A high proportion of children who become delinquent are failures in school. The children who hate school are those who are failing and whose security and feeling of adequacy or accomplishment has been threatened. We don't fail them if they don't grow an inch a year. Yet our school system has not devised a way to evaluate growth in all areas according to potentialities, rather than by absolute standards. We have not caught up with the principles of mental health in our grading and promotion practices.

Programs in Regular Grades with Ancillary Services

Just enrolling socially maladjusted and emotionally disturbed children in the regular grades is not considered a program. Additional professional personnel are required to help the teacher, the child, and the parent. These ancillary personnel are psychologists, social workers, remedial teachers, and diagnostic specialists.

The Psychologist. School systems are increasingly employing psychologists, charged with diagnosing children's problems and assisting with remediation in the form of play therapy, supportive or interpretative therapy, and counseling and guidance. In addition, the psychologist can serve as a consultant to the teacher, explaining to her the diagnosis and suggesting ways in which she can manage the child in the classroom.

The Social Worker. Social workers are gradually becoming standard personnel in most school systems. In some states the responsibility for the adjustment of the child to the home and school rests with the school social worker. Her duties are to obtain information about the child's behavior at home, to evaluate the status and attitudes of the parents and siblings, to counsel the parents on the most appropriate ways of managing the child, and often to deal with the child in individual or group sessions. The school social worker becomes, to some extent, the coordinator of therapeutic programs for the child as they involve the home, the school, and the community.

The Remedial Teacher. Many socially and emotionally maladjusted children are educationally retarded. Some have learning disabilities which either cause or contribute to the social maladjustment. A remedial teacher can have an important role in ameliorating the maladjustment. First, she deals with the child individually, giving him much-needed recognition and approval. Second, through remedial work she has him experience success in achievement, thus reinforcing his sense of adequacy and self-esteem. Third, through academic success and his own more satisfactory self-concept, she helps him discover that he can react more normally with others without resorting to compensatory and often deviant behavior. This change does not occur overnight, of course, and he often needs much guidance in "unlearning" previous behavior.

The Community Clinic. In addition to the ancillary personnel employed by the school system, the school has access to community mental health clinics, where medical and psychiatric personnel, psychologists, and social workers are available to give counsel and advice to the regular teacher and to parents. Community clinics are increasing in number but because of the extreme shortage of psychiatrists, and especially child psychiatrists, many of them have not been able to meet the demands for case analysis and treatment.

Kvaraceus and Ulrich have surveyed practices in the schools of the United States with particular reference to socially maladjusted children.[33] They have suggested guidelines and practices in eight areas:

1. *Identifying the youngster needing help in the classroom.*
2. *Providing help within the classroom* by upholding the dignity of every individual and enabling each pupil to achieve at a level commensurate with his ability.
3. *Providing help through curriculum adjustments* including adjustments for those with special emotional and/or cultural needs. School is milieu therapy for delinquent and predelinquent children.
4. *Providing help through integrated special services* including those of psychologists, social workers, counselors, special teachers, doctors, and nurses, as needed.
5. *Providing help through special classes.*
6. *Working with the family,* recognizing that few parents want to be negligent or to raise a delinquent youngster.

[33] W. C. Kvaraceus and W. E. Ulrich, *Delinquent Behavior: Principles and Practices* (Washington: National Education Association, 1959).

7. *Working with law-enforcement and court personnel.*
8. *Working with community agencies,* recognizing the school's leadership role in forming and continuing community-wide efforts.

Special Classes in Elementary Schools

In spite of the preventive measures which are employed in schools and communities and the efforts to retain maladjusted children in the regular grades, some children are so disruptive to the regular classroom that it has been necessary to establish special classes for them in the regular schools, in the smaller cities as well as in the larger urban areas. In large cities various kinds of organizations have evolved for the education of socially maladjusted and emotionally disturbed children. These facilities also provide for truants and delinquent children. Examples from several school systems will illustrate the types of provisions which are used in most large cities.[34]

Chicago maintains social adjustment centers for incorrigible and truant boys under 12 years of age located in six regular elementary schools. These centers enroll the children for special work and also assign them to the regular grades for part of the day. Their major feature is the increased ancillary personnel including psychologists, physicians, psychiatrists, and what they designate as field adjustment teachers. The latter are qualified social workers who coordinate the work of the school, home, courts, and community agencies. Similar programs are in operation in other cities.

In Detroit special classes are organized as home rooms in the various elementary schools. Many of them are for preadolescent boys. The programs offer social work services as well as remedial instruction and education in the practical arts, shops, and recreation.

Some cities and states organize special classes for emotionally disturbed children with major emphasis on a structured classroom situation with defined limits of behavior, especially for the hyperactive and aggressive. Kansas City has small self-contained classrooms for six or eight emotionally disturbed children working at various levels of achievement.

Some of the factors which are usually considered in establishing special classes in the regular schools are (1) size of class, (2) curriculum adjustment, (3) special teachers, and (4) needs and interests of the children.

1. Since most of these youngsters will have academic disabilities and individual problems of behavior and be in need of recognition and personal attention, the group is kept small. The less homogeneous the children in academic ability and special needs, the smaller the class

[34] Jack W. Birch, "Special Classes and Schools for Maladjusted Children," *Journal of Exceptional Children,* 22 (May, 1956), 332–337.

should be. Classes range from six or eight for emotionally disturbed children to ten or fifteen for predelinquents.

2. Curriculum adjustment must be available and flexible. This does not mean that academic subjects should be neglected because the children have been conditioned to dislike school. Their dislike of school usually stems from one of two causes: (a) They may have failed to keep up with their classmates in the past, because of truancy, disabilities, disinterest, or emotional tensions, so that they avoided school because of frustration. In such cases a remedial program beginning at their immediate level of achievement is indicated and often welcomed. (b) They may have rejected school work because it was associated in their minds with "sissy stuff" or "failure." The curriculum, therefore, must be changed to present material closely allied with the pupils' needs but capable of developing the necessary learnings. This requires creativity, understanding, and adaptability on the part of the teacher.

3. Not every teacher is willing or able to work with this type of child. A competent, experienced teacher is required who has a broad understanding of and ability to utilize various principles of learning, curriculum development, and child development. He should be adaptable and flexible. He should understand the background, attitudes, interests, and goals of the children, whether they are emotionally disturbed or norm-violating. Sensitivity to the feelings, needs, and background of the children is of major importance.

4. Needs and interests of these children should be taken into account. Again it should be pointed out that one of their most urgent needs is successful accomplishment. To meet it may call for straying from the usual content and appealing to specific interests and motivations, deriving desired learnings incidentally. This applies to materials, curriculum, and activities. A report from the Detroit schools has expressed this idea aptly:

> The educational goals that have particular worth to middle-class pupils are frequently lightly regarded by the norm-violating group. Textbooks written around middle-class ideals and with illustrations of conforming children are so antagonistic to the concepts of the nonconforming youth that they reject them as tools of instruction. For these reasons, the teacher is required to develop the instruction around the needs of the group and with materials which have been specially constructed or adapted.[35]

Special Day Schools

In many cities special school buildings or wings of regular schools

[35] Quoted by Kvaraceus and Ulrich, *op. cit.*, from Detroit Public Schools, *Ungraded Classes for the Socially Maladjusted* (Detroit: Department of Special Education, 1958), pp. 3–4.

have been used for programs for socially maladjusted, emotionally disturbed, incorrigible, truant, and delinquent children. In Detroit three special schools are provided for boys over 12 years of age. Such programs have been in operation in Detroit since 1883.[36]

In Chicago the Montefiore and Mosley schools are large special day schools for maladjusted boys. Each has a small branch in another building for maladjusted girls. These schools enroll the more severely maladjusted children who cannot remain in the regular grades or in the special centers. The children are transported to the schools from various sections of the city, and the program is for a full day. It includes academic work, remedial education (the majority of the children are retarded educationally), shop courses, speech correction, psychiatric interviews, and social work service. There is a mental health clinic, and field services through social work into the home and community are maintained. The majority of the children are school truants and incorrigible, and have been charged with minor delinquencies. These schools serve an intermediate function between the regular school and the residential school for those requiring twenty-four-hour management and education.

New York City has had special classes since 1940 for boys under 12 who have come in contact with the courts. In 1947 the "600" classes were organized and later the junior "600" classes, which are similar to those established in 1940. There are roughly 3500 children in the senior "600" schools, both boys and girls. Some of these are institutional schools and some are day schools. They enroll both emotionally disturbed (and psychotic) children and disruptive and delinquent children.

The special features of a day school for emotionally disturbed or socially maladjusted children are similar to those described under special classes. The main purpose is to adjust the program to the children's abilities, to establish within the classrooms a milieu therapy program, to offer educational programs in which the children will succeed and thereby establish a more wholesome self-concept, and to utilize a multidisciplinary approach of psychiatry, psychology, social work, remedial education, and a content curriculum suitable to the emotional problems and social-class needs of the children.

Residential Schools for the Socially Maladjusted

Residential schools for socially maladjusted children are designed for those who cannot adjust in day schools and classes, whose behavior is such that it is detrimental to other children, and who require twenty-four-hour-a-day supervision and management. Customarily, residential schools

[36] Birch, *op. cit.*, p. 334.

are managed by departments of social welfare, but in some situations they are under the supervision of the public school system.

There is a wide variety of private and public residential schools for socially maladjusted children. These include:

Schools in Temporary Detention Homes. Children who are in trouble, especially those whose homes cannot manage them, are placed in detention homes, usually under the supervision of the Juvenile Court. Education is offered these children in small groups or individually while they are awaiting examination and court action. Education in such a situation is often on an individualized basis since the children are generally of a wide age range and a wide range of intellectual abilities. Ordinarily, the children are in a detention home for short periods of a week to six or eight weeks. The educational program is utilized in this setting partly for educational but mostly for therapeutic purposes.

Residential Schools for Delinquents. Residential schools have been established for delinquent children or youth who are unable to be at large in society, or whose home is of such a nature that the child cannot live at home and attend a day school. In some of the large cities like New York and Chicago these schools, sometimes known as parental schools, are operated on a twenty-four-hour-a-day basis and are administered by the public school board of education. The schools are for the more severe delinquents who are not profiting from a special class or a day school.

By far the most common type of residential school is the state training school. It accepts court commitments for juveniles and has been variously termed an industrial school, reform school, correctional school, or training school. Usually these residential institutions accept only boys or only girls. Their purpose is to rehabilitate the delinquents under their care and to return them to the community.

Unfortunately, most of our residential institutions for delinquents are custodial and punitive rather than geared to intensive rehabilitation, which requires much more in the way of money and personnel than the public is at present ready to allot. Furthermore, until we have more empirical data on causation and remedial methods, much exploratory work will be necessary.

Research has shown very little change in attitudes or personality following institutional residence. Caditz compared ninety-four boys committed to a state training school with ninety-seven unselected high school sophomores on successive tests of the Minnesota Multiphasic Inventory and the Edwards Personal Preference Schedule.[37] He concluded

[37] A. B. Caditz, "Effect of a Training School Experience on the Personality of Delinquent Boys," *Journal of Consulting Psychology*, 23 (1959), 501–509.

that the training school experience did not show significant changes between the two groups. He did find that delinquent boys from broken homes gained somewhat.

Weeks compared the attitudes of boys sent to a short-term treatment facility with those committed to a correctional institution and concluded that neither group changed their attitudes toward law and order or toward their families or life in general.[38]

In evaluating changes in behavior following group psychotherapy in an institution setting, Gersten found slight gains in emotional security and personality integration but no noticeable gains observable by the staff.[39]

Group-Worker Program. One of the most outstanding techniques in dealing with delinquency has been the use of workers who are assigned by a social agency to go into neighborhoods where certain gangs are operating and "pick-up" relationships with them through some contact whereby they can be of service to the boys. As friendship develops, the workers gradually become advisers and consultants. Such workers have been instrumental in diverting efforts toward gang wars, stealing, malicious acts, and other common delinquent activities into more socially acceptable channels such as athletics, organized dances, and earning money for the maintenance of the group. Team sports have played a big role. Through these activities the gang (usually transformed into an organized club) can gain status and solidarity through competitive sports rather than gang war. They also gain status through holding the best dances, earning money to buy identifying jackets, and so forth.

Tentative statistics from such a program in Boston showed a 107 per cent drop in "average yearly rate of commitment of male juveniles to state Youth Service facilities" during a group-worker program in 1955–1956.[40] During this same period the commitment rate of areas outside the program increased 46 per cent.

Residential Treatment Centers for Emotionally Disturbed Children

Although residential schools for delinquent children have been in existence for many years, residential treatment centers for emotionally disturbed children did not come into being until after World War I.[41]

---

[38] H. A. Weeks, *Youthful Offenders at Highfields* (Ann Arbor: University of Michigan Press, 1958).

[39] Charles Gersten, "An Experimental Evaluation of Group Therapy with Juvenile Delinquency," *International Journal of Group Therapy*, 1 (1951), 311–318.

[40] Walter B. Miller, "The Impact of a Group Work Program on Corner Groups," *Social Service Review*, 31 (December, 1957), 395 n.

[41] *Psychiatric Inpatient Treatment of Children* (Washington: American Psychiatric Association, 1957).

Psychatric units for children have now been established in mental hospitals and in special treatment centers for children.

In general, authorities feel that, if possible, treatment of emotionally disturbed children in the home is preferable to institutionalization. Efforts have been made to provide for these children in schools, at home, and in the community. The irreducible remainder, however, those who cannot be treated in their own homes or in foster homes, require residential care and treatment.

The programs of most of these schools or hospitals center around milieu therapy, a total therapeutic environment. The child-care workers in the dormitories, the nurses, recreational and occupational therapists, the teachers, the cooks, and the remedial specialists surround the children hourly. The psychotherapists, the child psychiatrists, clinical psychologists, and psychiatric social workers see them several hours a week.

The multidisciplinary approach is the basis of the usual program in residential treatment centers. Redl and Wineman have described the philosophy of what they call a "residential setting with a total treatment design." Here treatment, education, or rehabilitation — whatever it may be called — is conducted by all employees of the center who deal with the child.

> We really think that the question of just how the cook acts when Johnny steals a second dessert is as much part of a "treatment process" as what the psychiatrist may have said in an interview, that the question of which arts and crafts materials are picked and how the workshop is being handled can be as much actual "treatment" as the "talk" we had with the children the other day. We go even further than that — we are convinced that the very way the house is laid out, the very policies of housekeeping that are in vogue, in short, everything that happens during a day and night may be made part of the most essential treatment plan. . . .[42]

This statement represents the point of view of psychologists who stress environment, education, and counseling. Many of the treatment centers for children are associated with mental hospitals and psychiatric units. In these centers the emphasis is on psychiatric treatment with therapeutically planned group living. Other personnel became ancillary to an integrated psychiatric approach. This point of view has been presented at a conference on inpatient psychiatric treatment for children as follows:

> The institution or unit provides a therapeutically planned group living situation within which individual psychotherapeutic approaches are

[42] Fritz Redl and Daniel Wineman, *Controls from Within* (Glencoe, Ill.: The Free Press, 1952), p. 41.

integrated. It offers the child support for growth, with individual psychiatric treatment according to individual needs, and provides appropriate facilities for schooling, recreation, and other activities.[43]

The conferees also felt that these residential units should be termed "hospitals" rather than homes or residential schools.

Restatement

It was indicated earlier that most emotionally disturbed and socially maladjusted children are educated in the regular grades, or in special classes, or in special day schools. When these facilities are not adequate for the child, he is placed in a residential school or hospital. Many residential centers have as their purpose the rehabilitation of the child in the shortest possible time so as to return him to his home or a foster home where he can attend the appropriate class or special class best suited to his needs. It is therefore necessary for the residential centers to work with community agencies and schools since they receive children from these facilities and hopefully return them to home and school.

Summary

1. A behavior deviation has been defined as that behavior which has a detrimental effect on the child's development and adjustment and/or that behavior which interferes with the lives of other people.

2. The term "behavior deviation" has been used to include a wide range of overlapping problems in children, including (a) emotional disturbance or inner tensions which create anxiety, frustration, fears, and impulsive behavior, and (b) social maladjustment including incorrigibility, truancy, predelinquency, and delinquency.

3. Some bases of behavior deviations in children have been discussed under the categories of (a) psychological factors which appear to be the outcome of frustration and result from the discrepancy between the child's capacity to behave and the requirements of the environment, (b) psychosocial factors resulting from inadequate child-rearing practices and social and cultural influences, and (c) physiological factors including brain injury and physiological anomalies.

4. Educational provisions include (a) prevention program within the school system, (b) special services in the regular grades, (c) special classes in regular schools, (d) special day schools, (e) residential schools for delinquent children, and (f) residential centers for emotionally disturbed children.

[43] *Psychiatric Inpatient Treatment of Children*, p. 2.

DISCUSSION QUESTIONS

1. In addition to the examples in the text, list some examples from your experience of incidents of "abnormal fixation," "aggression," "regression," and "resignation" in people as a result of frustration.

2. List the factors in a home which might result in behavior deviations in children. How can you explain the relationship of these factors to emotional disturbance or delinquency?

3. What effect might an extensive program of slum clearance have on the rate of delinquency? Explain your answer.

4. How can you differentiate between emotional disturbance and social maladjustment?

5. Some communities have less delinquency than others. What has research identified as the major differences between these communities? Do the same factors apply to emotional disturbance?

6. Someone has stated that there is less emotional disturbance in authoritarian families than in democratic families, and also less mental illness in authoritarian countries than in democratic countries. If this statement is true, how can you explain it?

7. What preventive measures for maladjustment and delinquency can you identify in your home community?

8. Since the school is increasingly serving as the community mental health agency, what can you predict will be added to school systems (besides those provisions listed in the text) to make the school more effective as a mental health agency?

SELECTED REFERENCES

Aichhorn, A. *Wayward Youth.* New York: Meridian Books, 1955. (Reprint)

Alt, Herschel. *Residential Treatment for the Disturbed Child.* New York: International Universities Press, 1960.

Bettelheim, B. *Love Is Not Enough.* Glencoe, Ill.: The Free Press, 1955.

Bloch, Herbert A., and Frank T. Flynn. *Delinquency.* New York: Random House, 1956.

Bowers, Eli. *Early Identification of Emotionally Handicapped Children in School.* Springfield, Ill.: Charles C. Thomas, 1960.

Cloward, Richard A., and Lloyd E. Ohlin. *Delinquency and Opportunity.* Glencoe, Ill.: The Free Press, 1960.

Cohen, Albert K. *Delinquent Boys*. Glencoe, Ill.: The Free Press, 1955.

Kvaraceus, William C., and Walter B. Miller. *Delinquent Behavior,* Vol. I. Washington: National Educational Association, 1959.

Kvaraceus, William C., and William E. Ulrich. *Delinquent Behavior: Principles and Practices*. Washington: National Education Association, 1959.

Mackie, Romaine P., W. C. Kvaraceus, and Harold M. Williams. *Teachers of Children Who Are Socially Maladjusted*. U.S. Office of Education. Washington: Government Printing Office, 1957.

Maier, N. R. F. *Frustration: A Study of Behavior Without a Goal*. New York: McGraw-Hill Book Company, 1949.

Merton, Robert K. *Social Theory and Social Structure*. Glencoe, Ill.: The Free Press, 1957.

Nye, F. Ivan. *Family Relationships and Delinquent Behavior*. New York: John Wiley and Sons, 1958.

Redl, F., and D. Wineman. *Children Who Hate*. Glencoe, Ill.: The Free Press, 1951.

Redl, F., and D. Wineman. *Controls From Within*. Glencoe, Ill.: The Free Press, 1952.

Reid, J. H., and Helen R. Hagen. *Residential Treatment of Emotionally Disturbed Children*. New York: Child Welfare League of America, 1952.

Roucek, Joseph S., ed. *Juvenile Delinquency*. New York: Philosophical Library, 1958.

14

Administrative Services and the Preparation of Teachers

The success of a special education program in administration, supervision, and instruction is in large part dependent upon an adequate organizational structure. But just as necessary is a system of teacher preparation for each of the areas of specialization. This chapter will deal with these two requisites for special education: administrative services and teacher preparation.

Administrative Services

There are numerous public and private organizations which promote many aspects of special education. The American Foundation for the Blind, the National Association for Retarded Children, the Volta Bureau for the Deaf, and the United Cerebral Palsy Associations are examples of organizations devoted to services for one type of exceptional child. This chapter, however, will deal only with governmental organization at three levels — federal, state, and local. Through its various agencies at these three levels, the government attempts to serve all areas of special education, whereas private organizations are generally more specialized.

Administrative Services at the Federal Level

Traditionally, in this country the federal government has not had a direct legal or administrative role in education. Its function has been to promote, stimulate, and improve education by (1) providing funds and resources to aid state educational programs in certain areas; (2) establishing limited educational programs for certain groups, such as the Indian population and military dependents; (3) providing scholarships and fellowships for certain groups of students; (4) establishing advisory, consultative, and research services in education; and (5) disseminating information on education.

The United States Department of Health, Education, and Welfare has a number of constituent agencies which promote and facilitate the care and education of exceptional children. These agencies will be described briefly.

The United States Office of Education. The U.S. Office of Education was established in 1867 and is still the only federal office concerned exclusively with education. Not until 1930 did the Office organize a Section on Exceptional Children and Youth, whose concern is to promote and facilitate adequate programs for exceptional children within the respective state and local school systems.[1]

The primary ways in which the Office of Education serves to further special education in this country are as follows:

1. Information is disseminated through publications to state and local school systems. Important among these are surveys of enrollment of children in special education programs, research reports, and bulletins on programs for exceptional children.

2. The cooperative research program was begun in July, 1956, and by 1960 had given financial assistance to more than 100 research projects in the field of special education. About two-thirds of these have been in the area of mental retardation, and the remaining have included research on blind, deaf, hard-of-hearing, speech-impaired, socially maladjusted, and gifted children. Research has also been promoted by the establishment of the National Defense Act of 1958. In addition to providing funds to support research projects in state departments of education, universities, and local school systems, the Office of Education also conducts research, often of the survey type, as indicated in the preceding section.

3. A third major function of the Office of Education is advisory. Conferences are called by the Office on specific problems relating to excep-

[1] *Annual Report,* U.S. Department of Health, Education, and Welfare (Washington: Government Printing Office, 1960).

tional children in cooperation with state departments, colleges and universities, and local school systems. Consultative services are available to state and local authorities.

4. The function most directly concerned with alleviating the problems arising from a lack of adequately trained personnel is that of providing fellowships for the preparation of leadership personnel. A program has been developed under Public Law 85–926, passed by Congress in 1959. It provides for fellowships to graduate students who desire to become (a) instructors in colleges and universities preparing teachers of the mentally retarded or (b) supervisors and administrators of special education programs. Although the original law was confined to mental retardation, another law, Public Law 87–276, passed in 1961, authorized fellowships for teachers of the deaf. Efforts are being made to extend these laws to supply fellowships to graduate students interested in any category of exceptional children.

The Office of Vocational Rehabilitation. The program of the Office of Vocational Rehabilitation is operated by state agencies under plans federally approved and partially financed from federal funds.

1. The service program of rehabilitation through these agencies provides for mentally and physically disabled adults over the age of 16 and includes necessary physical examinations; medical, surgical, psychiatric, therapeutic, and hospital services; prosthetic services; counseling and guidance; training for employment; tools, equipment, and licenses; and placement and follow-up. The federal Office stimulates and advises the state agencies in rehabilitation practices.

2. In addition to financing service programs, the Office of Vocational Rehabilitation supports research activities. In 1954 Congress enacted Public Law 565, which provides for research grants, extension and improvement of services, and special demonstration projects. In 1960 there were sixty-four such demonstration projects, twenty-one of which involved occupational centers for the mentally retarded. Sixteen dealt with the visually handicapped, and the others included the areas of cerebral palsy, emotional problems, epilepsy, and chronic illness.

3. A third service of the Office of Vocational Rehabilitation is financial support for training professional workers. Fellowships and grants to universities aid in the training of vocational rehabilitation personnel in medicine, counseling, speech pathology, audiology, and prosthetics.[2]

The Children's Bureau. The Children's Bureau, a subagency of the Social Security Administration, deals primarily with maternal and child health services (including juvenile delinquency), crippled children's services, and child welfare services. Its program includes the following:

[2] *Annual Report,* 1960.

1. It administers the program for crippled children's services. All states except Arizona participate in this program, which is designed "to locate children who require care and to provide restoration through diagnosis, medical and surgical treatment, and alleviation of unfavorable social and psychological influences which adversely affect the degree and duration of the disability."[3]

2. It administers a new program of grants for research and demonstration projects in the field of child welfare as authorized by a 1960 amendment to the Social Security Act which also increased the annual appropriation for the three areas of maternal and child health services, crippled children's services, and child welfare services.

3. It publishes pamphlets for parents and distributes technical reports disseminating knowledge in all the areas discussed above. In 1960 the Bureau devoted a large amount of time to juvenile delinquency prevention and control through conference planning, reports, and consultation. The Bureau also held a training workshop for probation personnel and throughout the year cooperated with many other agencies toward the end of reducing the problem of juvenile delinquency.

Public Health Service. The major emphasis of the Public Health Service is on the health of the nation. There are research programs under various divisions. Two of these divisions — the Institutes for Mental Health and the Institute for Neurological Diseases and Blindness — grant funds for research in many areas of exceptionality, including those concerned with the mentally retarded, cerebral palsied, emotionally disturbed, blind, partially sighted, and others.

It will be noted from the preceding sections that the federal government supports and promotes programs for many types of exceptional children, primarily through (1) supplying matching funds for services; (2) granting funds for research in improvement of services offered and in prevention and alleviation of disabling conditions; (3) disseminating information through publications; (4) advising state and local communities and school systems; and (5) granting fellowships to students in the various professions of medicine, social welfare, psychology, education, vocational rehabilitation, and related disciplines.

Special Education at the State Level

Education of all children, including exceptional children, is legally and traditionally the responsibility of the respective states. Each state has within its organizational structure a state department of education,

[3] *Annual Report*, 1960, pp. 65–66.

and the latter usually has a bureau or division of exceptional children. This bureau or division is responsible for the administration, promotion, and supervision of the state program.

Personnel. Personnel of a state division of exceptional children consists of (1) a state director, who is responsible for the overall administration of the program, and (2) state specialists or consultants in each of the areas of exceptionality sponsored by the state department.

The state director, according to a U.S. Office of Education study,[4] is responsible for the following activities.

1. Preparing the state budget for the education of exceptional children.
2. Helping in the passage of sound legislation and discouraging the passage of unsound legislation.
3. Distributing the appropriated state funds to local school districts on an equitable and legal basis.
4. Fostering and improving local programs.
5. Establishing standards for eligibility of children for special classes or services, teacher certification, and quality of education.
6. Recruiting teachers and cooperating in teacher education.
7. Encouraging in-service growth of teachers by providing for state workshops, conferences, and other in-service training programs.
8. Supervising educational programs in residential schools for the mentally retarded, deaf, and blind.
9. Maintaining interagency relationships.
10. Preparing publications in a wide variety of areas for the guidance of local school systems.
11. Selecting and directing a corps of specialized assistants for the various programs of exceptional children.
12. Encouraging and sponsoring research on problems in the education of exceptional children.

This list of duties and responsibilities may appear overwhelming for one individual. And indeed it is, for few states rely on only one person in a state department for all of these duties. Ordinarily, the director has a corps of assistants, termed specialists, supervisors, or consultants, who assume many of the responsibilities of the director in one or two areas of exceptionality. They are specialists, such as speech correctionists, former teachers of the mentally retarded, or former teachers of one of the other types of exceptional children. Generally they have had advanced training and experience in their field of specialization and are qualified to

[4] Romaine P. Mackie and Walter Snyder, *Special Education Personnel in State Departments of Education,* U.S. Office of Education, Bulletin 1956, No. 6 (Washington: Government Printing Office, 1957).

evaluate programs and to help teachers and local directors in improving their programs. State directors rely heavily on these state consultants for the administration of the state program.

The similarities in duties of directors and consultants is indicated in Figure 27, which shows the percentage of time spent by directors and specialists in the various functions. While the director spends 55 per cent of his time in administrative duties in the state department, the specialist spends 37 per cent. The specialist puts more time into the local communities and into direct services to children.

Financial Support. It has been found that educating exceptional children, which requires added services and smaller classes, is more expensive to school systems than educating an average child by mass techniques. For this and other reasons, the education of exceptional children in the public schools has progressed less rapidly than many have wished.

To encourage school systems to organize provisions for the various kinds of exceptional children, a plan has evolved whereby interested local

FIGURE 27

Percentage of Time Spent in Various Functions by Special Education Personnel

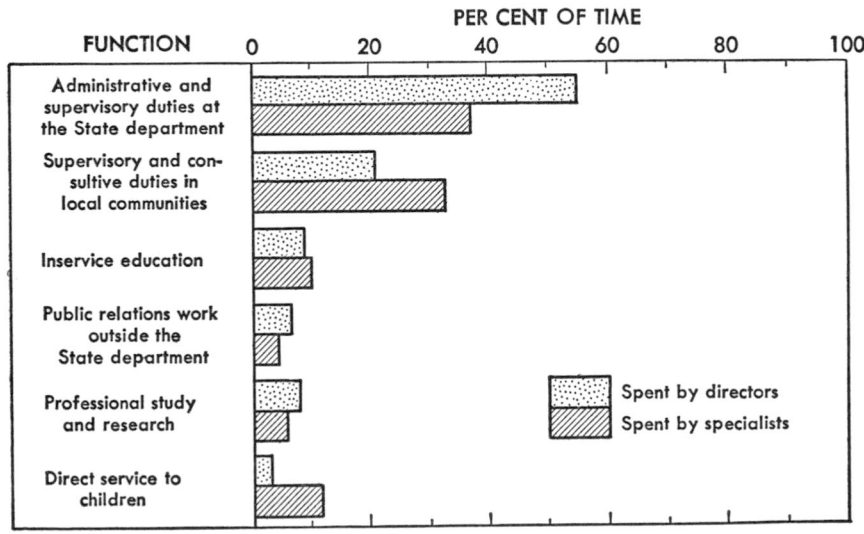

Source: Romaine P. Mackie and Walter Snyder, *Special Education Personnel in State Departments of Education,* U.S. Office of Education, Bulletin 1956, No. 6 (Washington: Government Printing Office, 1957), p. 28.

school systems can obtain financial help from state sources to reimburse them for the difference between the cost of educating an average child and the cost of educating an exceptional child. This is what is sometimes known as "the excess cost principle." In other words, the local school district is responsible for educating all children, but the state will help with the excess cost over and above the cost of regular programs. States vary in their ways of reimbursing school districts, some reimbursing according to the number of children enrolled, others by a classroom unit, and still others by the professional personnel employed.

State legislators have encouraged this movement in order to decrease costs to welfare departments. It has been estimated, for example, that keeping a mentally retarded child in a state institution for life costs the state approximately $50,000. Keeping some handicapped children at home and providing the extras they need in a school system is not only the best procedure for the children and their families but markedly less expensive to the state. For these reasons the various states have passed laws and have appropriated funds to help support special classes or services for exceptional children who can profit from remaining in the community.

Although this movement has been expanding since the beginning of this century, it has been accelerated since World War II. The most recent compilation of state laws pertaining to exceptional children indicated that by 1956 all forty-eight states had established provisions for exceptional children through legislative action, and forty-six of them had appropriated funds for reimbursement to school districts for one or more types of exceptional children.[5] This report showed that forty-four of the states provided reimbursement for both the physically and the mentally handicapped. It is anticipated that eventually all state departments of education will be providing subsidies to local school systems for all types of exceptional children, the gifted as well as the handicapped.

Special Education in Local School Districts

The type of organization of special education programs at the local level naturally varies with the size of the program, the kinds of exceptional children included, and the community attitudes toward the existence and expansion of the program.

In some small school systems the director of special education may have full responsibility for establishing, administering, supervising, and implementing the special education program. Sometimes an elementary supervisor or assistant superintendent assumes the duties of special education director on a part-time basis.

[5] "A Report on State School Laws, Special Education of Exceptional Children," *School Life*, 39 (November, 1956), 9.

In larger systems, or those in which the special education programs have expanded, a trained professional specialist is required as a full-time director of special education. Often his duties consist in large part in supervising the special teachers and classes within the program. The director may in turn employ full-time supervisors in the various areas of exceptionality. These supervisors work closely with the special education teachers and are responsible to the director.

In 1956 the U.S. Office of Education published a report on the competencies needed by special education directors and supervisors, and on their backgrounds, personalities, and duties.[6] Information was obtained from 103 directors of special education in local school systems who assumed full-time overall direction of several areas of exceptionality and from 50 supervisors who assumed full-time responsibility for one or more areas. A brief description of the functions performed by these directors and supervisors will illustrate the nature and scope of a local special education program. All of the functions mentioned are exclusive of those of the special teachers within the classroom itself.

1. About a third of the local directors' time (37 per cent) was spent in preparing and reviewing reports and budgets; interviewing applicants for special education positions; setting criteria for membership in special classes and for special services; determining the correct placement of youngsters in suitable facilities; general consultations with state and federal personnel, other school administrators, parents, and community agency representatives.

2. About a fourth of the directors' time (28 per cent) was spent working directly with teachers of exceptional children and in curriculum planning. Some consultation time was also spent with physicians, school nurses, curriculum supervisors, and regular teachers and supervisors.

3. Direct services to children (13 per cent) included individual and group testing, counseling, case study, teaching of exceptional children, making home calls, arranging clinic appointments, job placement, and follow-up.

4. The remainder of the time was given to public relations, in-service training of teachers, study, and research.

The supervisor or specialist in a local school district assumes responsibility for, and assists with, many functions of the local director. The major difference, similar to that at the state level, is in the greater specialization of the supervisor in one or two areas of exceptionality and in his ability to directly help teachers to be more effective in the classroom.

[6] Romaine P. Mackie and Anna M. Engel, *Directors and Supervisors of Special Education in Local School Systems*, U.S. Office of Education, Bulletin 1955, No. 13 (Washington: Government Printing Office, 1956).

The Preparation of Teachers of Exceptional Children

Professional training of teachers of exceptional children developed after, and in response to, the establishment of special classes and programs for exceptional children. Originally, teachers entering the field had been trained in the areas of elementary and secondary education or clinical psychology. The development and expansion of teacher training in special education at the college level is relatively new. In 1929, 43 colleges and universities in this country offered some courses for the preparation of teachers of exceptional children.[7] This number rose to 71 in 1931, 101 in 1936, and 175 in 1948. However, of the 175 colleges listing courses in 1948, only 77 reported an integrated sequence of courses in one or more areas of exceptionality (including courses given only in summer sessions), and of these 77 colleges, 66 had a sequence of courses in speech correction. There were 26 centers for the deaf and 22 for the mentally retarded. By 1954, 122 colleges reported a course sequence regularly offered, not including summer sessions.[8] Although this number appears large, it should be pointed out that 67 of these colleges were offering a sequence only in speech correction or in speech and hearing. Of the 55 colleges having other sequences, 40 gave a sequence of courses on the mentally retarded, 22 on the deaf, 13 on the crippled, and 10 on the socially maladjusted. Only 3 colleges offered a sequence in the preparation of teachers of the blind. By 1962 the number of colleges offering sequences had increased substantially, but current statistics were not yet available.

The expansion of teacher training is also reflected in the increasing activities of the states in establishing certification requirements for teachers. In 1931 only eleven states had certification requirements in one or more areas of exceptionality; by 1954, thirty-two states and the District of Columbia had established such standards.[9]

Development of Teacher Preparation in Special Education

It is apparent that the success of programs for exceptional children is primarily dependent upon the personnel who have daily contact with the children themselves — the teachers. Regardless of what the federal gov-

[7] Elise H. Martens, *Opportunities for the Preparation of Teachers of Exceptional Children* (Chicago: National Society for Crippled Children and Adults, 1949), p. 1.

[8] Romaine P. Mackie and Lloyd M. Dunn, *College and University Programs for the Preparation of Teachers of Exceptional Children,* U.S. Office of Education, Bulletin 1954, No. 13 (Washington: Government Printing Office, 1954), p. 12.

[9] Romaine P. Mackie and Lloyd M. Dunn, *State Certification Requirements for Teachers of Exceptional Children.* U.S. Office of Education, Bulletin 1954, No. 1 (Washington: Government Printing Office, 1954), p. 5.

ernment, the state, or the local school system does at the administrative level, these provisions can only facilitate, not accomplish, the work of the teacher. The following section deals with the qualification of special education teachers and their preparation in various areas of service to exceptional children.

The development of programs for the preparation of teachers of exceptional children in the United States has taken place for the most part in this century. The early patterns of training focused primarily on preparing teachers for work in residential schools. Teachers of the blind, deaf, and mentally retarded who were planning to teach in residential schools often went to these institutions and served as apprentices to teachers under a program called cadet training. Cadet training, which took up approximately one year and included observation, practice teaching, and formal instruction by the staff members, was widely used during the early 1900's.

The Perkins School for the Blind at Watertown, Massachusetts, was one of the first institutions to use a cadet training program.[10] Perkins affiliated with Harvard University in 1921 and has continued to offer teacher training programs for college credit since that time. Many teachers of the blind in both the United States and other countries received their training at the Perkins School.

In 1904 the Vineland Training School at Vineland, New Jersey, initiated cadet training of teachers for the mentally deficient, operating summer schools for teachers from other parts of the country.[11] Didactic instruction, observation, and practice teaching were offered. The course consisted of three weeks of study of "feeble-mindedness" and three weeks given to training and discipline. This course became one of the most popular in the United States at that time and was later approved for college credit by Lehigh University and Rutgers University. During 1918, a class of fifty-eight teachers received certificates at the conclusion of the summer session. Many of the early leaders in the education of retarded children originally received their training at Vineland. The training course was discontinued in 1932 when colleges and universities began to provide training programs.

Other institutions, such as the Clarke School for the Deaf in Northampton, Massachusetts, the Central Institute for the Deaf in St. Louis, and the Lexington School for the Deaf in New York, also began by offering cadet training programs, but each later affiliated with collegiate institutions and became a part of a college training program.

[10] Gabriel Farrell, "The Harvard-Perkins Course for Instructors of the Blind," *Journal of Exceptional Children*, 10 (April, 1944), 170–172, 179.

[11] Helen Franklin Hill, "Vineland Summer School for Teachers of Backward and Mentally Deficient Children," *Journal of Exceptional Children*, 11 (April, 1945), 203–209.

Colleges and universities generally began to organize programs for the preparation of teachers of various types of exceptional children in the 1920's. The Milwaukee State Teachers College (now University of Wisconsin in Milwaukee), Detroit Teachers College (now Wayne University), Michigan State Normal (now Eastern Michigan College), and Teachers College, Columbia University, initiated curriculums within the college program.

At first many of the courses offered at the college level were summer courses for experienced teachers. It was believed necessary to have had preparation and two to five years of experience in teaching normal children before going into the field of exceptional children. The teacher training programs for exceptional children had to be superimposed on the regular education programs.

Another pattern for the preparation of teachers, and the one now preferred by most authorities, is based on a four- or five-year college program. Instead of being required to have teaching experience with normal children as a prerequisite to entering the field, students are required to include courses in elementary or secondary education and to do practice teaching with normal children as a part of their preparation for teaching in their area of specialization. Added to this program are the specialized courses in the various exceptionalities and practice teaching in the field of specialization.

General Personal Qualifications

A number of studies have investigated the personal traits believed to be necessary for teachers of exceptional children. In a summary report of an extensive study conducted by the U.S. Office of Education on the qualifications and preparation of special education teachers, Mackie, Dunn, and Cain state that, according to over three-fourths of the teachers queried, special education teachers need personal characteristics different in kind or degree from those of regular teachers.[12] Included were the need for extra patience, mental alertness, flexibility, resourcefulness, enthusiasm, emotional stability, personal warmth, friendliness, understanding, and sympathy, together with objectivity and sensitivity.

Teachers in certain areas of exceptionality emphasized other traits; for example, teachers of the blind mentioned the need for a pleasant voice, while teachers of the gifted mentioned humility, and teachers of the maladjusted felt that a sense of humor was more important than it is for regular teachers.

[12] Romaine P. Mackie, Lloyd M. Dunn, and Leo F. Cain, *Professional Preparation for Teachers of Exceptional Children: An Overview*, U.S. Office of Education, Bulletin 1959, No. 6 (Washington: Government Printing Office, 1960), p. 16.

Lord and Kirk suggest some of the major characteristics which are of importance for a teacher of exceptional children:[13]

1. *Capacity for self-direction* is necessary since special teachers are often assigned to schools in which they are required to organize their own programs and outline procedures without any technical assistance from other teachers, principals, or supervisors.

2. *Patience and perseverence* are especially required, since many exceptional children have learning disabilities necessitating extra work, persistence, and patience on the teacher's part. Teachers of these children must be optimistic and satisfied with less gain on the students' part than is seen with nonhandicapped children.

3. Teachers of exceptional children must be *experimentally minded,* since they have fewer published materials and fewer ready-made instructional devices at their disposal than do regular teachers. They must, therefore, be able and willing to experiment with methods, materials, and procedures on their own.

4. Certain *physical characteristics* are important in some areas. While a teacher who is herself orthopedically impaired could well serve as a speech correctionist, it might be difficult for her to teach crippled children, as she would be unable to move or carry them as is often required. A deaf teacher could not teach deaf or hard-of-hearing children by the oral method for it would not be possible for her to meet the demands of auditory training and voice control. In general, any physical limitation of the teacher must not be allowed to restrict her service to the children she teaches.

5. *Personal adjustment* is essential. The teacher often deals with both children and parents who are intimately involved with personal problems, and she must not become unduly emotional or oversentimental.

General Teacher Preparation

The preparation of teachers of exceptional children covers four general areas of education, as illustrated in Figure 28.

Area 1. *General cultural education.* All teachers of exceptional children are required to obtain a general cultural education through their college program. The bachelor's degree requires that their program include studies in liberal arts, including natural and biological science, mathematics, humanities, and social science.

Area 2. *Preparation in elementary or secondary teacher education.* Every teacher of exceptional children should have a background in gen-

---

[13] Francis E. Lord and Samuel A. Kirk, "The Education of Teachers of Special Classes," *Forty-ninth Yearbook of the National Society for the Study of Education,* Part II (Chicago: University of Chicago Press, 1950), pp. 103–116.

FIGURE 28

Areas of Study Required for Teachers of Exceptional Children

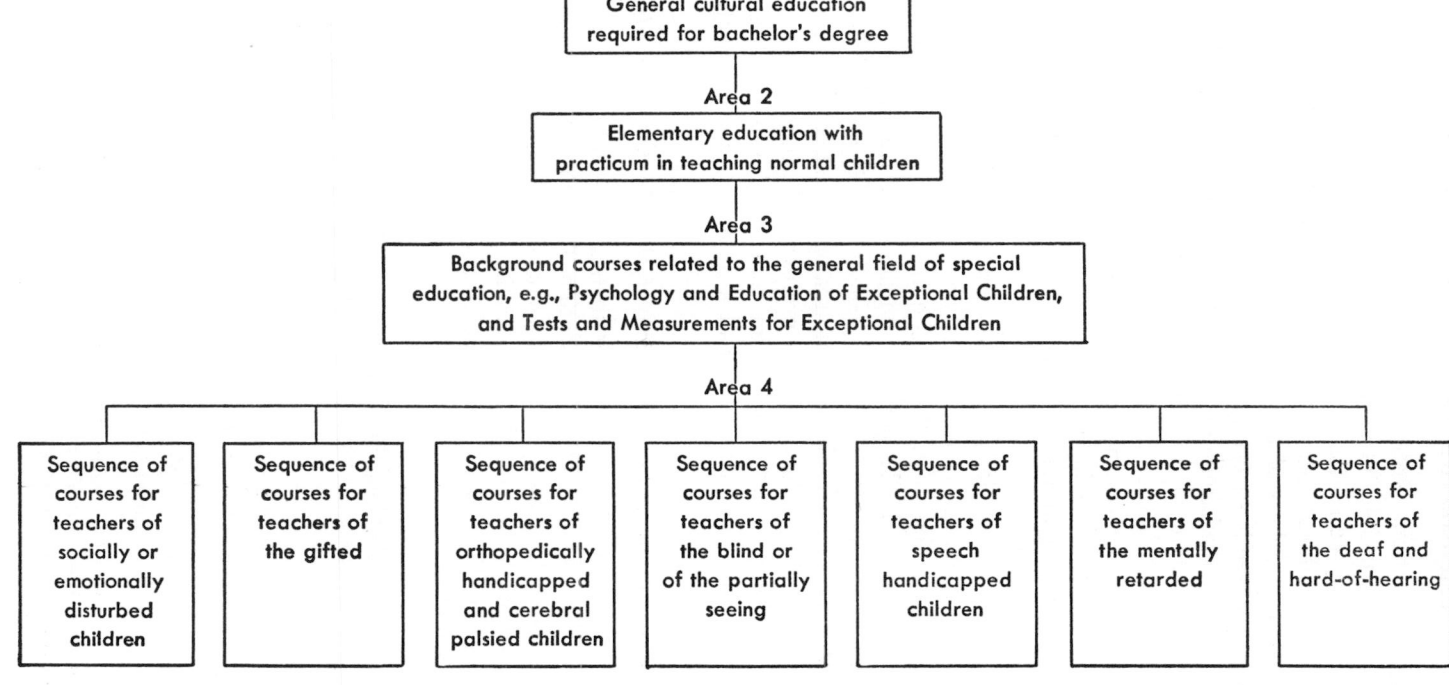

eral education. Ordinarily the requirements for this phase of the work include principles of elementary and secondary education, techniques of elementary education, arts and crafts, music, and student teaching with normal children. Many teachers of exceptional children can also be certified as teachers of elementary children upon completion of the bachelor's degree in special education.

Area 3. *Background courses related to the general field of special education.* Before specializing in any area of exceptionality, all teachers of exceptional children are required to take certain additional courses not required of elementary teachers. These include courses dealing with the psychology and education of all groups of exceptional children, behavior problems of children, and educational tests and measurements for exceptional children.

Area 4. *Professional preparation in a specialized area.* When a teacher is preparing to teach exceptional children, whether the mentally retarded, the gifted, the deaf, the speech handicapped, or any other type, she must have the background of education and training indicated in the first three stages before intensive specialization is undertaken. Beyond these first three stages, each different area of special education requires a specific curriculum. The minimum professional programs for the preparation of teachers are listed below for some of the areas of exceptionality in which these programs have had a degree of standardization throughout the country.

Specialization in the Education of the Mentally Retarded

A student who is preparing to teach mentally retarded children first completes his liberal arts education, the sequence of courses in elementary education, and background courses relating to exceptional children. In addition, he completes specialized courses which cover four broad areas of distinctive competencies needed by teachers of the mentally retarded:

1. Understanding the characteristics of the mentally retarded child and his place in society.
2. Developing a functional curriculum through relating the broad personal and social needs of the mentally retarded.
3. Understanding and applying pedagogical procedures based on an understanding of the known learning characteristics of the mentally retarded.
4. Selecting, developing, and using appropriate instructional materials and equipment in teaching mentally retarded children.[14]

[14] Romaine P. Mackie, Lloyd M. Dunn, and Harold M. Williams, *Teachers of Children Who Are Mentally Retarded,* U.S. Office of Education, Bulletin 1957, No. 3 (Washington: Government Printing Office, 1957), p. 6.

The sequence of specialized courses offered by most colleges which provide programs for the preparation of teachers of the mentally retarded covers the following:

Characteristics of the mentally retarded are taken up in courses conveying general knowledge about the field of mental retardation and biological, psychological, social, and educational characteristics of educable and trainable mentally retarded children.

Courses in theories and methods of teaching mentally retarded children often include one or two semesters of work in which the general problems of classroom organization, curriculum, the preparation of materials, the techniques of teaching reading, writing, spelling, and social studies, and the content of the curriculum for the mentally retarded are presented to students.

Most teachers of retarded children are required to facilitate the work of a speech correctionist or to do some work in speech and language with retarded children in the classroom. For this reason they must take a beginning course in *speech correction.*

Candidates for a certificate or degree in the field of teaching the mentally retarded are required to do *student teaching with mentally retarded children.* Good programs in this area give students an opportunity to observe and practice at two or three levels as in a primary and an intermediate class for the mentally retarded. When the student has completed his sequence of courses and practice teaching with both normal and mentally retarded children he is then prepared to organize, administer, and teach a class for the mentally retarded.

Specialization in the Education of the Deaf

Teachers of deaf and severely hard-of-hearing children usually include in their program of preparation the three areas of general cultural education, general elementary education, and background courses relating to exceptional children. In addition, they take a sequence of courses in speech development and speech correction as well as specialized courses in the education of the deaf. A group of experts outlined the necessary competencies of a teacher of the deaf as follows:[15]

1. *Communication.* The teacher of the deaf must be well informed about the process of communication, including hearing, speech, language, lip reading, and vision. These have been discussed in Chapter 7.

2. *Curricular adaptions.* Teachers of the deaf are required to adapt the curriculums for the hearing to the needs and abilities of deaf children. Both general adaptations, and adaptations in reading and other subject-matter areas are included.

[15] Romaine P. Mackie, *Teachers of Children Who Are Deaf*, U.S. Office of Education, Bulletin 1955, No. 6 (Washington: Government Printing Office, 1956).

3. *Psychological tests and measurements.* Teachers of the deaf should have an understanding of tests and measurements, especially as they relate to deaf children.

4. *Social adjustment.* Teachers should understand the social limitations imposed by deafness and the techniques and resources for facilitating adjustment.

5. *Home-school relations.* The teacher should be well versed in the methods of facilitating parent efforts to augment the program of the school.

The Conference of Executives of the American Schools for the Deaf has recommended the following courses which should be included in a training program over and above work in elementary education:[16]

	Semester Hours	
	Minimum	*Maximum*
1. The teaching of speech to the deaf.	4	6
2. The teaching of language to the deaf.	4	6
3. Methods of teaching elementary school subjects	4	6
4. Methods of teaching speech reading (lip reading) to the deaf and hard-of-hearing.	2	3
5. History, education, and guidance of the deaf.	2	3
6. Auditory and speech mechanisms.	2	3
7. Hearing tests and auditory training.	2	3
8. Observation and student teaching.	6	10
Total semester hours	26	40

Specialization in the Education of Crippled Children

The curriculum for training teachers of crippled children (exclusive of the cerebral palsied) is not as highly specialized as are curriculums for the preparation of teachers in other areas. With the increase in the enrollment of cerebral-palsied children in classes for the orthopedically handicapped, some programs of teacher preparation have added courses which facilitate the understanding and handling of problems of children with cerebral dysfunctions. The ordinary college program for teachers of crippled children includes the following:

A survey of orthopedic defects explores crippling conditions, their causes and treatment. Knowledge of the contributions of medical specialists and the work of the physiotherapist, the occupational therapist, and the specialist in health education is usually covered in this course.

[16] The Conference of Executives of the American Schools for the Deaf, "Minimum Course Requirements," *American Annals of the Deaf,* 104 (September, 1959), 312.

Adaptation of the classroom environment includes a knowledge of equipment, materials, and physical aids used with crippled children, as well as of the organization and administration of classes for crippled children.

Practice teaching with crippled children of various types is a requirement for prospective teachers of crippled children.

The above program provides minimum requirements for teachers of non-cerebral-palsied crippled children. However, the recent influx of the cerebral palsied into classes for crippled children and the development of classes strictly for the cerebral palsied have made it advisable to include further training of teachers of the crippled. This should include:

1. Some specialized training in *speech correction,* since teachers of the cerebral palsied come into daily contact with language and speech problems.

2. At least an introductory course covering *mental retardation,* since many cerebral-palsied children are mentally retarded.

3. A *diagnostic and remedial teaching* program, since teachers in this area must be much more qualified than the ordinary remedial reading teacher to deal with learning disabilities.

4. *Practice teaching specifically with cerebral-palsied children.*

Specialization in Speech Correction

Teachers of speech-handicapped children are usually itinerant, traveling from school to school and giving speech correction lessons to individual children or small groups of children in each school. It is not necessary for them to have as much classroom experience with normal children as do other teachers of exceptional children. However, they should have some working knowledge of elementary classes in order to know the speech problems encountered by the elementary classroom teacher and to be able to suggest to her the things she could use in the classroom situation for the correction and prevention of speech defects. Training centers for the preparation of speech correctionists generally follow the requirements for membership in the American Speech and Hearing Association.[17] The minimum requirements for clinical certification for speech and hearing therapists in the American Speech and Hearing Association include the courses and professional experiences listed on page 382.

Specialization in Education of Partially Seeing Children

The U.S. Office of Education study of the competencies of teachers of partially seeing children found that the competency committee and 130

[17] American Speech and Hearing Association, *American Speech and Hearing Association Directory* (Danville, Ill.: Interstate Printers and Publishers, 1961).

Requirements for Membership in
American Speech and Hearing Association

	Semester Hours	
	Basic	Advanced
1. Basic areas, including anatomy and physiology of the ear and vocal mechanisms, phonetics, etc.	6	9–12
2. Specialized, professional course content in speech correction and speech pathology	12	21–24
3. Specialized, professional course content in audiology	3	6–9
4. Other areas, including child development and psychology	9	15–18
Total semester hours	30	60
5. Clinical practicum	200 clock hrs.	355 clock hrs.
6. Professional experience after training	One year	Four years

superior teachers of the partially sighted agreed on the following areas of competency:[18]

1. *Knowledge of medical conditions.* This includes (a) anatomy, physiology, pathology, and hygiene of the eye; (b) knowledge of functions of ophthalmologists and optometrists; (c) recognition of eye fatigue and other conditions indicating need for medical referral.

2. *Pupil adjustment.* The ability to counsel the partially seeing child on his personal attitudes toward his physical handicap, his social problems, and his life goals was rated as very important.

3. *Evaluation of the child.* Skill in using various types of tests and records and in interpreting medical and social reports is important, but the need for it depends to a large extent upon the resources avaliable in the school and community. A knowledge of tests available in large type and of vision screening tests and procedures was also emphasized.

4. *Curriculum, teaching techniques, and materials.* It is crucial, since many, and increasingly more, partially seeing children are being educated in the regular classroom, that the special teacher be able to integrate the curriculum, methods, and materials with those of the regular classroom.

5. *Professional literature.* A knowledge and understanding of the significant literature relating to partially seeing children is important.

[18] Romaine P. Mackie and Edith Cohoe, *Teachers of Children Who Are Partially Seeing,* U.S. Office of Education, Bulletin 1956, No. 4 (Washington: Government Printing Office, 1956).

6. *Interpersonal relationships.* Ability to work well with parents, regular teachers, and other professional people was especially stressed, particularly since the teachers of partially seeing children function on a consultant basis.

The National Society for the Prevention of Blindness recommends that teachers of partially seeing children have (1) a minimum of three years of successful experience teaching normal children; (2) two semester hours in organization and administration of school programs for the partially sighted; (3) two semester hours in special class methods and materials; (4) two semester hours in student teaching and observation with the partially sighted; and (5) two semester hours in the anatomy, physiology, and hygiene of the eye.[19]

Specialization in Education of the Blind

The competencies which have been found necessary for teachers of the blind include the following:[20]

1. *Successful teaching experience with sighted children.*
2. *An extensive orientation to the psychological concomitants of blindness.* It is important that teachers of the blind develop skills in identifying the causes of social and emotional problems in blind children and be able to counsel with them.
3. *A knowledge of special procedures to acquaint the blind child with his environment.* This includes an ability to teach the use of residual vision and energy conservation.
4. *Ability in teaching travel skills.* Often the teacher of blind children is the person in the best position to teach the highly specialized techniques utilized by the blind in travel.
5. *Abilities to teach the reading and writing of braille.*

The American Foundation for the Blind recommends a knowledge of conditions and hygiene of the eye, student teaching and clinical observation, regular teaching experience, and a knowledge of all types of atypical children, in addition to the obvious requisites of a mastery of braille reading, writing, and teaching.[21] A typical training program for teachers of the blind requires (1) two semester hours in diseases and hygiene of the eye; (2) four semester hours of special methods of teaching the blind; (3) two to four semester hours in techniques of braille; and (4)

[19] Marjorie Young, "Certification of Teachers of Partially Seeing Children," *Journal of Exceptional Children,* 19 (April, 1952), 207–215.

[20] Romaine P. Mackie and Lloyd M. Dunn, *Teachers of Children Who Are Blind,* U.S. Office of Education, Bulletin 1955, No. 10 (Washington: Government Printing Office, 1955).

[21] American Foundation for the Blind, *Training Facilities for the Preparation of Teachers of Blind Children in the United States,* Education Series No. 4 (New York: The Foundation, 1953).

two to four semester hours of clinical observation and practice teaching of the blind.

Other courses frequently offered or suggested cover such areas as the history and psychology of blindness, professional literature, and resources available to teachers.

Specialization in Education of the Emotionally and Socially Maladjusted

Since much of the specialized work with maladjusted children is done by guidance personnel, counselors, school psychologists, and others whose primary training has been outside of education, relatively few programs are available specifically for teachers in this area. In 1954 only ten colleges and universities in the nation reported a sequence of courses and only nine states certified teachers in this area.[22]

Stullken's recommendations for personnel working with maladjusted children may be highlighted as follows:[23]

Personality is of the utmost importance. The teacher of maladjusted children should not be irritable, fussy, or infantile; she should have respect for self and others and a good sense of humor; she should be flexible and adaptable.

Special training should include a good background in (1) mental hygiene; (2) abnormal, child, and adolescent psychology; (3) educational, vocational, and personal guidance; (4) emotional aspects of personal handicaps and educational disabilities; (5) testing; (6) social psychology; (7) case-work procedures; and (8) crafts, hobbies, and recreational use of leisure time.

Experience in clinical and group-work procedures is essential for the teacher. Although the value of teaching experience with normal children is disputed, it is recommended by some.

Standard sequences of courses for teachers of socially and emotionally maladjusted children have not yet developed fully because of (1) the tenuous and theoretical nature of our knowledge of causative factors and remedial processes, and (2) the fact that until recently teacher-training institutions have steered clear of involvement in this area, relying, rather, on psychiatrists, psychologists, and social workers to handle the problem.

Developing an adequate teacher preparation program will include:

1. Selection of well-trained, experienced teachers whose personality and interests are suitable for the teaching of children with behavior deviations.

[22] Mackie and Dunn, Bulletin 1954, No. 13.
[23] Edward H. Stullken, "Special Schools and Classes for the Socially Maladjusted," *Forty-ninth Yearbook of the National Society for the Study of Education,* Part II (Chicago: University of Chicago Press, 1950), 281–301.

2. A two-year graduate sequence of courses in (a) theories of personality and their application to children with behavior disorders; (b) the theory and application of individual and group processes with these children; (c) the diagnosis and remediation of learning disabilities (including disabilities found in learning speech and language, as well as those in reading and other school subjects); and (d) an understanding of the community agencies available for children with behavior deviations.

3. Internship in an educational program for socially and emotionally maladjusted children.

Specialization in the Education of the Gifted

In the light of the emphasis now placed on the education of the gifted, it is perhaps surprising that in 1954 only one state certified teachers of the gifted and only two colleges offered preparation in this area.[24] In 1960, Gallagher tabulated courses in teaching the gifted offered in seven colleges and universities.[25] The courses were on (1) education of the gifted, (2) methods of teaching the gifted, (3) psychology of the gifted, (4) identification and guidance of the gifted, (5) research in problems of the gifted. No school offered more than two of these courses.

Wilson gives the six competencies suggested by preliminary data from the U.S. Office of Education study as follows:[26]

1. The ability to foster in gifted pupils social responsibility, a desire to serve society, and a recognition of the worth of others.
2. The ability to create an environment in which the gifted participate efficiently in group discussions and in wholesome social relations.
3. The ability to develop a classroom atmosphere for gifted pupils that is conducive to good mental health.
4. The ability to teach the gifted to use the problem-solving approach to learning, to apply this to independent study and research, and to evaluate their own progress.
5. A knowledge and understanding of the social and emotional problems that may be created for a gifted pupil by his accelerated mental development.
6. The ability to develop a flexible, individualized enriching curriculum which is suited to the individual gifted pupil's needs and which avoids identical, stereotyped demands.

[24] Mackie and Dunn, Bulletin 1954, No. 1, p. 49.

[25] James J. Gallagher, *Analysis of Research on the Education of Gifted Children* (Springfield, Ill.: Office of the Superintendent of Public Instruction, 1960), p. 120.

[26] Frank T. Wilson, "The Preparation of Teachers for the Education of Gifted Children," in *Education for the Gifted, Fifty-seventh Yearbook of the National Society for the Study of Education,* Part II (Chicago: University of Chicago Press, 1958), p. 364.

Summary

1. Administration of special education programs is facilitated through governmental agencies at the federal, state, and local levels. The federal government supports research and training, and disseminates information through publications, conferences, and consultations. The state government reimburses local school districts for special services, establishes standards, certifies teachers and programs, and offers consultative service to local school districts. The local school administration is responsible for the actual operation of the program. In addition to governmental agencies, many private groups and associations have been responsible for the initiation of many of the services in behalf of exceptional children.

2. The preparation of specialized teachers for the various groups of exceptional children has become the responsibility of colleges and universities. At present most states have colleges which offer a sequence of specialized courses in one or more areas of exceptionality. Curriculums are offered for the preparation of teachers of the gifted, mentally retarded, partially seeing, blind, speech handicapped, orthopedically handicapped and cerebral palsied, socially maladjusted and emotionally disturbed, and deaf and hard-of-hearing.

DISCUSSION QUESTIONS

1. In reading about the functions of the various federal bureaus, do you feel that these are overlapping functions, or do the various functions complement one another?

2. Suppose that you have the ambition to be a state director of special education. List the training and experience you will need to prepare yourself for this position.

3. From the most to the least extensive, rank in order the areas of exceptional children that require the greatest degree of specialization in terms of the number of semester hours of courses needed in Area 4 of Figure 28.

4. Select two areas of exceptional children in which you might wish to teach and outline your four-year course of study. Are there any discrepancies between the program in the text and your state certification requirements? Between the program in the text and your college requirements for specialization in these areas?

Selected References

College and University Programs for the Preparation of Teachers of Exceptional Children. U.S. Office of Education, Bulletin 1954, No. 13. Washington: Government Printing Office, 1954.

Directors and Supervisors of Special Education in Local School Systems. U.S. Office of Education, Bulletin 1955, No. 13. Washington: Government Printing Office, 1956.

Opportunities for the Preparation of Teachers of Exceptional Children. U.S. Office of Education, Bulletin 1937, No. 17. Washington: Government Printing Office, 1938.

Opportunities for the Preparation of Teachers of Exceptional Children. Chicago: National Society for Crippled Children and Adults, 1949.

Professional Preparation for Teachers of Exceptional Children: An Overview. U.S. Office of Education, Bulletin 1959, No. 6. Washington: Government Printing Office, 1960.

Speech Correctionists: The Competencies They Need for the Work They Do. U.S. Office of Education, Bulletin 1957, No. 19. Washington: Government Printing Office, 1958.

State Certification Requirements for Teachers of Exceptional Children. U.S. Office of Education, Bulletin 1954, No. 1. Washington: Government Printing Office, 1954.

Teachers of Children Who Are Blind. U.S. Office of Education, Bulletin 1955, No. 10. Washington: Government Printing Office, 1955.

Teachers of Children Who Are Deaf. U.S. Office of Education, Bulletin 1955, No. 6. Washington: Government Printing Office, 1956.

Teachers of Children Who are Mentally Retarded. U.S. Office of Education, Bulletin 1957, No. 3. Washington: Government Printing Office, 1957.

Teachers of Children Who Are Partially Seeing. U.S. Office of Education, Bulletin 1956, No. 4. Washington: Government Printing Office, 1956.

Teachers of Children Who Are Socially and Emotionally Maladjusted. U.S. Office of Education, Bulletin 1957, No. 11. Washington: Government Printing Office, 1957.

Index of Names

Foote, F. M., 211
Force, Dewey G., Jr., 33, 205, 290, 291
Forlano, G., 205
Fouracre, Maurice H., 241, 257, 275
Fowler, E. P., 160, 161, 162
Frampton, Merle E., 6, 33, 241
Francis, R. J., 128
Freedheim, Donald K., 251, 252
French, Edward L., 149
French, Joseph L., 41, 83
French, Richard S., 241
Freud, Sigmund, 338
Frisina, D. R., 177
Furbee, Catherine, 296
Fusfeld, Irving, 190

Galisdorfer, Lorraine, 211
Gall, Elena D., 6, 33
Gallagher, James J., 37, 41, 42, 45, 59, 64, 72, 83, 108, 385
Gallaudet, Edward Minor, 174
Gallaudet, Thomas Hopkins, 173
Garrett, James F., 292
Garrison, I. K., 131
Garrison, Karl C., 33
Gates, Arthur I., 166
Gates, R. R., 95
Gens, G., 315
Gersten, Charles, 360
Gesell, Arnold, 158, 221
Getzels, J. W., 39, 59
Gibbons, Helen, 211
Gillan, Lela O., 84
Ginglend, David R., 149
Gladwin, T., 89, 90, 94, 104
Goddard, H. H., 97, 103, 130
Goetsch, Helen B., 36, 37
Goldberg, I. Ignacy, 137, 138
Goldstein, Herbert, 112, 113, 130, 135
Gonick, Mollie R., 33, 286, 292
Goodenough, Florence L., 33
Goodhill, Victor, 161
Gore, Beatrice S., 275
Gowan, John Curtis, 71
Greene, M., 328
Groht, Mildred, 186, 194
Guilford, J. P., 38, 59, 79
Guilliford, R., 131
Gunzburg, Herbert C., 149

Hagen, Helen R., 364
Hahn, E. F., 328, 329
Halverson, H. M., 222
Hannigan, Helen, 316
Hargis, D. E., 329
Harmon, N. Bishop, 206
Hathaway, Winifred, 196, 197, 209, 211
Haüy, Valentin, 228
Havighurst, Robert J., 39, 40, 67, 73, 74, 83
Hayes, Samuel P., 222, 223, 224, 225, 241
Healy, W., 340
Heck, A. O., 34
Hedgecock, LeRoy D., 151, 166, 195
Hegge, T. G., 120, 268
Heider, Fritz and Grace, 194, 195
Heinicke, Samuel, 173
Heltman, H. J., 329
Henderson, Florence, 212
Henderson, Robert, 135
Hewitt, L. E., 338, 339
Hildreth, Gertrude, 83
Hilgard, Ernest R., 333
Hill, Arthur S., 149
Hill, Helen Franklin, 374
Hitler, 3
Hobson, James R., 61
Hofsteater, Howard T., 185
Hohman, Leslie B., 251, 252
Holdsworth, W. G., 318, 329
Hollingworth, Leta, 41, 73, 74, 83
Hood, Oreste E., 130, 149
Hopkins, T. W., 248, 249, 252, 253, 254, 255, 275
Horn, J. L., 34
Hottel, J. V., 147
Howe, Samuel Gridley, 6, 229

Ilg, F. L., 221
Illingworth, R. S., 249, 250, 275
Ingram, Christine P., 130
Inskeep, Annie, 130
Irwin, J. V., 317, 329
Irwin, Robert B., 6, 229, 241
Itard, Jean Marc Gaspard, 99, 103
Izard, C. E., 286

Index of Subjects

Deaf children — *Continued*
early home training of, 188–89
early indications of deafness, 158–59
education of, 167, 172–92
language development of, 184–86
occupational adjustment of, as adults, 191–92
reading achievement of, 187
speech development of, 181–83
teachers of, 178, 187, 190, 376, 379–80
Deafened child, 153, 192
Delayed speech, 303, 314–16, 324
Delinquency, 28, 330, 331, 332, 339–42, 347–49, 354, 356
in the gifted, 57
and mental retardation, 110, 135
residential schools dealing with, 359–60
unofficial, 349
Delinquency Proneness Check List, 347, 348
Democracy and education, 3
Demonstrations, for the blind, 233
Denasal speech, 308
Denmark, cleft palate data in, 319
Dental *s*, 305
Depression, 135, 191
Desks, adjustable, 208
Detention homes, 359
Detroit, attention to behavior deviants in, 356, 357, 358
classes for crippled in, 278
Detroit Teachers College, 375
Developmental anomalies of the eye, 198, 200
Diabetes, 200, 281
Diagnosis, of hearing loss, 164, 168
of learning disabilities, 272
of mental retardation, 118, 119
of psycholinguistic disorders, 268–72
of speech difficulty, 300–301
of visual defects, 202
"Diagnosogenic" theory of stuttering, 312
Dictaphones, 208
Diphtheria, 160, 250
Discipline, erratic, in home, 340

Discrepancy, concept of, 336–37
in growth, 8, 12, 14, 21, 29, 51, 63, 64, 74, 76
Distortions, sound, 305
Divergent thinking, 79, 80
Divorce, 57
Dramatization, 144
Drill, excessive, 77
Drug therapy, 261, 280
Drugs, toxic, 161
Durrell-Sullivan Reading Achievement Test, 187
Dysarthria, 254, 301, 322
Dyscalculia, 264
Dysgraphia, 264
Dyslalia, 301
Dyslexia, 264, 265–68
Dyslogia, 302
Dysphasia, 302
Dysphonia, 302
Dysrhythmia, 302

Ear, infections of, 160–61
structure and functioning of, 162–64
training of, in speech correction, 309
See also Auditory defects *and* Listening
Early admission to school and college, 61, 62–63, 76
Eastern Michigan College, 375
Economic usefulness, 143, 146–47
Edinburgh, first school for deaf in, 173
Educable mentally retarded children, 86, 87, 88, 90, 92, 98, 100, 101
case study of, 105–7
characteristics of, 109–11
in the community, 113–15
education of, 111–13, 115–28
growth pattern of, 107–9
Education, administrative services in, 365–72
aims of, 111, 112, 142–43, 231
of the blind, 226–38
categories in, 85–86
of the cerebral-palsied, 255–62
of crippled children and those with health problems, 281–85
of the deaf, 167, 172–92
equal opportunity for, 3, 36

Idiopathic speech, 298

Illinois, deaf children in, 156
mentally retarded children in, 133, 135, 146
University of, 260

Illumination, 207, 208

Imagery, mental, 225, 238

Imbeciles and idiots, 135

Imitation period in speech development, 297

Incidental learning, 121

Independence, for the blind, 236
for the cerebral-palsied, 260, 262
for the crippled, 284, 288, 291

Individual differences, 7–8

Individualized instruction, 70, 76, 121, 207, 232, 233, 285, 353, 359

Inductive method of teaching language to the deaf, 186

Infantile paralysis. *See* Poliomyelitis

Influenza, 94, 159, 160, 250

Information, broad, of gifted children, 78

Inhibitions, 121, 339

Inner ear, 162

Institutions for exceptional children, 28
for the blind, 228
for the crippled, 282
for the mentally retarded, 113, 134–35, 139, 145–46, 257
See also Residential schools

Integrated plan for teaching the blind and partially seeing, 206–7, 209, 210, 230

Integration of handicapped into society, 6

Intelligence, in the blind, 222
in the cerebral-palsied, 251, 252, 253
in the deaf, 177–78
distribution of, 85, 90, 91, 92
low; *see* Mentally retarded children
of partially seeing children, 203
superior; *see* Gifted children

Intelligence tests, 4, 7, 39, 40, 44–45, 55, 56, 58, 59, 90, 91, 109, 128, 140, 177, 203, 204, 222, 251–52, 253, 271

Intensity of sound, 158
vocal, 309

Interest, centers of, 123
of gifted children, 56, 78–79

Internal strabismus, 199

Interpersonal relations, 7n., 125; *see also* Personal adjustment

Intracranial tumor, 161

Introverted behavior, 330; *see also* Withdrawal behavior

Iowa Silent Reading Test, 187

IQ, of cerebral-palsied children, 251, 252, 253, 271
of children of the mentally retarded, 115
of deaf children, 178
distribution of, 8, 9
of the educable mentally retarded, 100, 106, 107, 109, 115, 126
of the gifted, 8, 9, 22, 38, 39, 41–42, 46, 50, 55, 57, 58, 59, 66, 67, 73
of the partially seeing, 204
of the trainable mentally retarded, 133, 140, 146

Isolates, 79, 126, 330, 332, 345

Italians, giftedness among, 58

Itinerant teachers, 26, 117, 169, 170, 171, 190, 207, 230–31, 257, 381

Jacksonian epilepsy, 280

Jena method of teaching lip reading, 171

Jews, giftedness among, 58

John Tracy Clinic, 188–89

Junior high school, 124

Juvenile Court, 359

Kansas City, classes for the emotionally disturbed in, 356

Keratitis, 200

Keystone Telebinocular, 202

Kindergarten, age of admission to, 61
cerebral-palsied children in, 258
for the deaf, 189
mentally retarded children in, 122
speech correction in, 306–7

Kinesthetic cues, 183, 188, 236

Kinesthetic sensitivity in the blind, 225

Kuhlmann Tests of Mental Development, 140